The Digital Nexus

Cultural Dialectics
Series editor: Raphael Foshay

The difference between subject and object slices through
subject as well as through object.
— Theodor W. Adorno

Cultural Dialectics provides an open arena in which to debate questions
of culture and dialectic—their practices, their theoretical forms, and
their relations to one another and to other spheres and modes of inquiry.
Approaches that draw on any of the following are especially encouraged:
continental philosophy, psychoanalysis, the Frankfurt and Birmingham
schools of cultural theory, deconstruction, gender theory, postcoloniality, and
interdisciplinarity.

Series Titles

Northern Love: An Exploration of Canadian Masculinity
Paul Nonnekes

Making Game: An Essay on Hunting, Familiar Things, and the Strangeness
of Being Who One Is
Peter L. Atkinson

Valences of Interdisciplinarity: Theory, Practice, Pedagogy
Edited by Raphael Foshay

Imperfection
Patrick Grant

The Undiscovered Country: Essays in Canadian Intellectual Culture
Ian Angus

The Letters of Vincent van Gogh: A Critical Study
Patrick Grant

"My Own Portrait in Writing": Self-Fashioning in the Letters of
Vincent van Gogh
Patrick Grant

Speaking Power to Truth: Digital Discourse and the Public Intellectual
Edited by Michael Keren and Richard Hawkins

The Digital Nexus: Identity, Agency, and Political Engagement
Edited by Raphael Foshay

The Digital Nexus

Identity, Agency,
and Political Engagement

edited by RAFAEL FOSHAY

AU PRESS

Published by AU Press, Athabasca University
1200, 10011 – 109 Street, Edmonton, AB T5J 3S8

ISBN 978-1-77199-129-2 (print)   978-1-77199-130-8 (PDF)
978-1-77199-131-5 (epub)   doi: 10.15215/aupress/9781771991292.01

A volume in Cultural Dialectics series:
ISSN 1915-836X (print)   1915-8378 (digital)

Cover design by Marvin Harder
Interior design by Sergiy Kozakov
Printed and bound in Canada by Friesens

The appendix, "Do Machines Have Rights? Ethics in the Age of Artificial
Intelligence," is a reprint of Paul Kellogg's interview of David J. Gunkel, which was
first published in *Aurora*, issue 2014.

Library and Archives Canada Cataloguing in Publication
    The digital nexus: identity, agency, and political engagement / edited by
Raphael Foshay.

(Cultural dialectics)
Includes bibliographical references.
Issued in print and electronic formats.

    1. Digital media—Social aspects. 2. Digital media—Political aspects. 3. World
Wide Web—Social aspects. 4. World Wide Web—Political aspects. I. Foshay,
Raphael, 1950-, editor II. Series: Cultural dialectics

HM851.D58 2016   302.23'4   C2015-908545-4
                                                               C2015-908546-2

We acknowledge the financial support of the Government of Canada through the
Canada Book Fund (CBF) for our publishing activities.

 Canadian   Patrimoine
Heritage   canadien

Assistance provided by the Government of Alberta, Alberta Media Fund.
Government
of Alberta ■

Contents

Acknowledgements

This book began as an international symposium of invited speakers, with the present volume of thematically related essays as its goal. The symposium met under the title "Identity, Agency, and the Digital Nexus" on April 5–7, 2013, in Edmonton, Alberta, Canada. The symposium was generously funded by a Connection grant from the Social Sciences and Humanities Research Council of Canada (SSHRCC), and by timely financial and administrative support by the Research Office of Athabasca University. I would like to thank Acting Associate Dean of Research Dr. Donna Romyn, the research office manager, Rebecca Heartt, and the financial administrator, Crystal Brown, for their help throughout the planning of the symposium and the editing of the volume.

I would also like to thank Athabasca University's M.A. Program in Integrated Studies for administrative help and for the donation in kind of my time and energy as program director to the organization of the symposium and the editing of the present volume. I thank Corinna Lewis, administrative officer in the MA-IS Office, for her help with many tasks. An equally warm thank you goes to the Organizing Committee, made up of faculty members of the Faculty of Humanities and Social Sciences at AU: Derek Briton, Jay Smith, Evelyn Ellerman, Paul Kellogg, and Wendell Kisner, and, from Computing Services, Daryl Campbell (Jay, Paul, and Daryl are contributors to the present volume). I would also like to extend especially warm thanks to organizing committee member and MA-IS Program colleague Dr. Paul Kellogg, who gave generously of his time at both the planning and the symposium-organizing stages.

The Digital Nexus: Identity, Agency, and Political Engagement is the second symposium/book project mounted under the auspices of Athabasca University's M.A. Program in Integrated Studies. The first took place in 2008, resulting in *Valences of Interdisciplinarity: Theory, Practice, Pedagogy*, published by Athabasca

University Press in 2011. I would like to acknowledge AU Press for its support of this project from the symposium, through the peer review and editorial stages, to publication in its open access format. AU Press is the first university press in North America to be founded as an open access press. Its enlightened embrace of digital dissemination of the fruits of research clearly attests the importance of digital technology to the future of scholarship and of the centrality of digital computerization and the Internet to the Academy. Special thanks to Kathy Killoh and Pamela Holway at Athabasca University Press, and to the internal and external peer reviewers of the volume for their support, guidance, and many constructive recommendations.

Introduction

The Computational Turn and the Digital Network

Raphael Foshay

The realm of the "digital" is a variegated, rapidly unfolding, and experientially encompassing phenomenon, directly and indirectly reshaping many aspects of our global, national, and individual lifeworlds. The media of communication that are informed by digital code are multifarious, extending well beyond the reach and limitations of traditional analog reproduction: digital code enables new kinds and levels of communication across media platforms, from television to computers and mobile devices, combining text and audiovisual content with the interactivity made possible by the fusion of computerization with the Internet, the World Wide Web. While being enabled and engendered by the electronic platform of the computer, computerization itself synergizes with the Internet to create a totalizing virtual environment of connectivity—a domain that at an early stage of its emergence was termed cyberspace—within which we all now conduct daily life, whether as nations or corporations, institutions or interest groups, communities or private citizens. So habituated have we now become to this sphere of interactive connectivity that the term "cyberspace" itself has become quaint and disused. In its current iteration as Web 2.0 it surpasses an earlier, content-delivery model of the web now seen as transitional between television and the Internet's highly interactive and multimedia environment: what "cyberspace" denoted has so thoroughly become the air we breathe that it would now be impossible, not only on a practical level, to return to an existence deprived of the web and cellular networks, it would be unimaginable on almost any grounds that one could consider: social, political, economic, scientific, educational, communicational, military … the list goes on. Further, the communicational domains of the digital network are not only public but also private, increasingly woven into both our livelihoods and personal lives, ubiquitously present or proximate, and engaging us in all aspects of our daily interactions with one another, with institutions, and, indeed, in concert with the Global Positioning System (GPS), with our physical and social environs. Our lifeworld has become digital, networked, and connected, and yet it has been a mere twenty-five years since Tim Berners-Lee invented the World Wide Web.

Writing in 1964, and observing the meteoric rise of television in particular, Marshall McLuhan anticipated the encompassing nature of media change:

> In a culture like ours, long accustomed to splitting and dividing all things as a means of control, it is sometimes a bit of a shock to be reminded that, in operational and practical fact, *the medium is the message*. This is merely to say that the personal and social consequences of any medium—that is, of any extension of ourselves—result from the new scale that is introduced into our affairs by each extension of ourselves, or by any new technology. (1964: 9; my emphasis)

As an intellectual historian, McLuhan investigated the historical context of analog electronic media and its impact on twentieth-century society. He first situated electronic media in relation to the regime of print, and before that of alphabetic writing itself. In the concluding pages of *The Gutenberg Galaxy: The Making of Typographic Man* (1962), McLuhan points to the profound impact of any major change in media regimes, like the printing press and, in his own lifetime, electronic media platforms such as radio, telephone, and television.

> But it has been the business of *The Gutenberg Galaxy* to examine only the mechanical technology emergent from our alphabet and the printing press. What will be the new configurations of mechanisms and of literacy as these older forms of perception and judgement are interpenetrated by the new electric age? The new electric galaxy of events has already moved deeply into the Gutenberg galaxy. Even without collision, such co-existence of technologies and awareness brings trauma and tension to every living person. Our most ordinary and conventional attitudes seem suddenly twisted into gargoyles and grotesques. Familiar institutions and associations seem at times menacing and malignant.

These multiple transformations, which are the normal consequence of intro-
ducing new media into any society whatever, need special study. (278–79;
my emphasis)

It is such special study that the present volume brings to the current stage of
the advance of digital media. The totalizing scope of the combined effects of
computerization and the worldwide digital network have gathered us all up in
what the philosopher and media theorist Bernard Stiegler has described as the
tsunami-like quality of the digital revolution, an inundation that carries with
it the traumas, or at the very least the tensions, that McLuhan acknowledges,
threatening to sweep away the moorings of cultural forms and practices that
have shaped the very institutions that enabled—were the conditions of possibility for—the sea-change of digitalization, and disrupting the sense of context and
continuity that compose the very ingredients of the notion of lifeworld (Husserl,
1970: 127–29). As Bernard Stiegler observes:

> The growth of digitalisation since 1992 has brought with it a genuine
> chain reaction that has transformed social life at its most public level,
> and the life of the psychic individual at its most intimate level. [Nicholas
> Carr's 2012 book *The Shallows: What the Internet Is Doing to Our Brains*]
> bears witness to the immense distress that has accompanied this
> meteoric rise—which increasingly seems to resemble a tsunami—and
> that has, by his own account, significantly disrupted the mental capaci-
> ties of Nicholas Carr himself. And this tsunami threatens to wipe out all
> the inherited structures of civilisation on every continent, which may
> in turn produce immense disillusionment and tremendous disaffection.
> (2012a: 30)

Despite such an ominous warning, however, Stiegler is far from a digital dystopian. Rather, he rings for digital technology the kind of cautionary but affirmative bell that McLuhan rang in the previous generation in relation to analog
electronic media technology. In a recent (2012) strongly argued position paper,
citing Kant's clarion essay "An Answer to the Question: What Is Enlightenment?"
(1784), Stiegler calls for a reconstitution of the Enlightenment project for the
digital age, attending to the blind spots and contradictions that have haunted
the project of modernity, the dark sides of modernity explored, for instance,
in Horkheimer and Adorno's *Dialectic of Enlightenment* (conceived as it was in
1944 by two exiled Jewish thinkers in the shadow of Nazism). Endorsing recent
efforts by Tim Berners-Lee and Harry Halpin under the rubric of philosophical

engineering (see the interview with Berners-Lee in Halpin and Monnin, 2014), Stiegler argues for new efforts toward foundational enquiry into the implications of digitalization:

> The new philosophy that must arise from the worldwide experience of the web, and more generally of the digital, across all cultures, an experience that is in this sense universal—this new philosophy, these new Enlightenments, cannot merely be that of digital lights: it must be a philosophy . . . of the shadows that inevitably accompany all light. (2012a: 31)

Indeed, Stiegler sees digital culture as the only route out of the neoliberal economism and consumerism that have increasingly subsumed, with such disturbing social and political consequences, the Enlightenment values of universal equality and dignity at the heart of the revolutionary project of modernity. As Stiegler emphasizes:

> There are many ways in which digitalisation clearly holds promise, and socialising digitalisation in a reasoned and resolute way is (I am convinced of this) absolutely imperative if the world is to escape from the impasse in which the obsolete consumerist industrial model finds itself. But if this is the case, then this socialisation in turn requires the creation and negotiation of a new legal framework that itself presupposes the formation of new "Enlightenments." (2012a: 30)

It is of compelling importance that as students and subjects of digitalization we bring to the social, institutional, and environmental challenges of technological change an understanding of the scope and structural character of the transformations we are undergoing. The essays in this volume respond to the demands of theoretical understanding, cultural change, and political analysis as we enter on the third decade of the convergence of digital technologies in multimedia computing and the World Wide Web. The "nexus" of converging technologies, along with the cascading changes caused by networked connectivity in every sphere of civic, commercial, and private life, call for concerted analysis. In this introduction to the articles that follow, I will point to the thematic concerns that have shaped the approach taken in this volume to questions of identity, agency, and the digital nexus. The title of the volume refers to concerns both subjective and objective: questions of identity, with regard both to the converging nature of digital technologies and to their impact on personal experience and social life; questions relating to the (often perplexingly novel kinds of) agency of the already ubiquitous and rapidly evolving digital realm. Questions are also entailed concerning our abilities to actively engage with, use, and direct the power of the digital network for good and its potential destructiveness for core institutions and traditions. There are questions as well surrounding an accurate grasp of the World Wide Web, and the challenges that ubiquitous connectivity undoubtedly delivers to public and private life.

—⚉—

Before introducing the essays themselves, under their three general categories of theory, culture, and politics, I will provide some context for why "identity" and "agency" were chosen as predominant concerns in relation to digitalization. First, however, I will begin with an overview of the theoretical mapping of digitalization achieved in the work of the already quoted Bernard Stiegler, arguably the most comprehensive philosopher of media technology currently writing (see Stiegler 1994, 1996, 2001, and 2013). Stiegler locates digitalization within the overall historical evolution of language as the process of "grammatization." Grammatization Stiegler defines, after the historical linguist Sylvain Auroux (1992), as "the history of the exteriorization of memory in all its forms: nervous and cerebral memory, first linguistic, then auditory and visual, bodily and muscular memory, biogenetic memory" (2010: 71). Alphabetic writing is the principal example of such a strategic parsing of experience. As John Tinnell explains: "Alphabetic writing, for example, breaks down the flux of speech into a finite system of recognizable characters that are, on the one hand, iterable and modular, and on the other hand, capable of orthographic stability" (Tinnell, 2012). For Stiegler, human beings are from the beginning identified by their systematic and evolving invention and use of tools; in Stiegler's lapidary formulation, "anthropogenesis is a technogenesis" (2012b: 15). It is the range and extent of their technical inventiveness that allow humans to emerge as a distinctive species, and it is grammatization and language in particular that are the key vehicles of human self-invention and construction of the complex apparatus of physical, ideational, and imaginal culture. Stiegler explains: "In sum, each epoch of psychosocial individuation configures itself by means of its own form of discretization [or grammatization]. This process of self-configuration is borne out by the epochs we have considered: those of the lithic tool, the transition to ideogrammatic writing, the alphabet, and digitization" (2010: 70). In other words,

Stiegler positions digitization not merely as successive to the era of mechanical print, but as a chapter of writing within the overall evolutionary structure of human grammatization. Digitization is an epochal shift in the technical self-configuration of human beings because it is a major transformation in the regime of grammatization as writing:

> The digital technical system constitutes a global and contributory pub-
> lication and editorialization system that radically transforms the "public
> thing," given that the res publica, presupposes a form of publicness,
> of "publicity"—what the Aufklärung called the Öffentlichkeit [public
> sphere]—sustained by publication processes. (2012a: 32)

Digital writing, especially in the stage of Web 2.0 and the advent of social media interactivity, is fundamentally distinct from the audiovisual technologies that directly precede it, since, in concert with print-era writing, it restores agency to users, enabling active and interactive capacities, in contrast to what with radio, television, and film was a one-way disposition of passive consumption.

Central to the function of technics in human evolution, for Stiegler, is their role as a means to support, record, retain, and extend memory, both individual and collective. In other words, the most important role of technical inventions for human evolution has been as hypomnemata, external means to record experience as aids to memory and means to inscribe, undertake reflection, discover narrative patterns, and accumulate organized thought, understanding, and bodies of law and knowledge. As Mark B. N. Hansen explains, Stiegler sees digital multimedia as "a new ecology of associated hypomnesic milieus" that will inaugurate "a new conjugation of technics and memory":

> By renewing the possibility for self-expression, and hence for self-exter-
> iorization, today's digital hypomnemata restore the positive dimension
> to our coevolution with technics . . . furnishing artificial supports for
> individual (and collective) memories that exist within and are nourished
> by a larger memnotechnological milieu—the system of the Internet.
> (2010: 65)

Such a utopian and epochal valuation of the importance of digitization contrasts with the darkly prophetic warnings cited earlier regarding the trauma associated with structural changes in media environments. Stiegler is strongly aware of the contrast of light and shadow in the undertaking of human civilization. Since the inception of the philosophical tradition, writing, as a technical hypomnema, has been viewed as at worst a dangerous and at best an ambiguous phenomenon. In the *Phaedrus*, in particular, Plato has Socrates contrast hypomnesis, an external recording, with anamnesis, an internal primordial remembering that is the preferred goal of disciplined philosophical inquiry. Writing, as with other forms of representation or *mimēsis*, is twice removed for Plato's Socrates from the sources of true knowledge, residing, unlike those unchangeable sources, within the variable coordinates of everyday space-time experience and human craft. In contrast to the Socratic method of the *elenchus*, of dialogical inquiry, writing, as a mere technique, is unable in Socrates' view to interact with its reader:

> When it has once been written down, every discourse roams about everywhere, reaching indiscriminately those with understanding no less than those who have no business with it, and it doesn't know to whom it should speak and to whom it should not. And when it is faulted and attacked unfairly, it always needs its father's support; alone it can neither defend itself nor come to its own support. (Plato, *Phaedrus*: 275d-e)

For Plato's Socrates, then, writing is a dangerous tool, functioning with the potentially dangerous healing or poisoning effects of a medicinal *pharmakon* (medicine, drug, remedy), substances that must be used with knowledge and understanding because of their power both to heal and to poison. As Derrida argues in "Plato's Pharmacy" (1981: 103), writing is essentially anarchic, ambivalent, and uncircumscribed by the restraining oppositions and hierarchies of logocentric reason.

Likewise, Stiegler is actively concerned about the darker side of the digital milieu. In its exteriorizing of memory and knowledge retention, it has a capacity to shortcircuit deliberative consciousness and collapse the learning process that has been developed over centuries of print culture. He grounds what he explicitly categorizes as these "pharmacological" concerns, both in recent work in the neurophysiology of reading and in the phenomenological tradition of Edmund Husserl. Husserl articulated three stages by which we interact with and retain experience in memory. Primary experience or perception is a form of retention in that we consciously register this experience in the midst of undergoing and internalizing what is happening around us, to us, and within our responses to those occurrences. Secondary retention is our recollection of the primary experience after the fact; it is retention in the form of memory. Tertiary retention is the phase of exteriorization of memory through grammatization, a turning of the temporal memory (with its manifold of sensory, emotional, and intentional responses) into a spatialized expression through language and/or some other material medium of expression:

> This mental reality [the secondary retention of memory] can thus be projected onto a support that is neither cerebral nor psychic but rather technical. The web grants access to such a space, through which shared, digital tertiary retentions are projected and introjected, constituting as such a new public, global, and contributory space, functioning at the speed of light. What light and what shadow, what Enlightenment and what Darkness, can and must this bring us? (2012a: 34)

At this stage of his argument, Stiegler invokes several categories of the recently rediscovered philosopher of technology, Gilbert Simondon (1924–1989), in particular those of individuation and transindividuation. These terms differentiate the stages of individual and social tertiary retention, the discrete phases in which individual self-understanding is formed through reflection on the secondary retentions of memory (and sometimes the tertiary retentions of writing or other exteriorizing expressions of that reflective process). Transindividuation is the phase in which social groups, communities, and institutions are formed on the bases of shared needs for cooperation, organization, and action around secondary reflection on experience, a stage that depends increasingly—as complexity in larger social units necessarily multiplies—on tertiary retentions, with their many "pharmacological" capacities of healing and poison.

With the advent of systematic practices of tertiary retention, however, serious changes occur in the way human beings perceive and conceive the secondary retentions of memory. Invoking recent progress in the neurophysiology of reading, for instance, in the work of Maryanne Wolf, Stiegler observes that "the brain is literally written by the socio-technical organs, and where our own brains, which she calls 'reading brains,' were once written by alphabetical writing, but are now written by digital writing" (2012a: 35). Quoting Wolf directly, to the effect that human beings "were never born to read" (Wolf, 2007: 3), Stiegler emphasizes that writing, an invention after all only a few thousand years in application, has restructured our brains, changing the way we are able to think, and so altering our intellectual evolution. In light of the further move to reading in digital environments, Wolf remarks: "We make the transition from a reading brain to an increasingly digital one" (2007: 12). Stiegler emphasizes that rewriting the brain can involve overwriting or outright replacement of patterns that have taken centuries to refine and which constitute major achievements in our evolution and adaptation. As Walter Ong emphasizes, regarding the interaction of our levels of attention, once human beings have become literate they think differently than they did within the former context of oral culture. With their practices of exterior representations of thought and memory, tertiary levels of attention act on the way we construct our experience, how we perceive the world (primary retention), and how we work with our recollection and memory of experience (secondary retention):

> A deeper understanding of pristine primary orality enables us better to understand the new world of writing, what it truly is, and what functionally literate human beings really are: beings whose thought processes do not grow out of simply natural powers but out of these powers as structured, directly or indirectly, by the technology of writing. Without writing the literate mind would not and could not think as it does . . . even when it is composing its thoughts in oral form. (1982: 77; quoted in Stiegler, 2012a: 37)

The implications of the reformulation of secondary by tertiary forms of retention is that major changes in tertiary retention change our ways of think-ing (secondary retention) and even, in certain respects, our ways of perceiving (primary retention). If ways of thinking in secondary retentive memory involv-ing recollection and structures of thought (narrative, schematic, analytic, and so on) are disrupted in the habituation to digital environments, key stages and elements of identity formation on which fundamental institutions of society rely may unravel, become short-circuited, leading to serious consequences. Both the fabrics of our social institutions as well as the psyches and personalities of the citizens on whom those institutions rely may be affected. For instance, with respect to Simondon's aptly named function of individuation, in which persons differentiate themselves from their environments and articulate their experi-ences in communication with other human beings within increasingly complex social and material traditions, the longstanding medium of that process of indi-viduation has been until recently that of print, with its characteristic patterns of expression and reception. The advent of global digital connectivity introduces substantively new patterns of sociality, of written expression. Consequently, tertiary influences on secondary patterns of individuation may change, and may alter how one works with primary perceptions of one's environment. To some degree the shape and forms of primary perception itself may change (as, for instance, we spend more and more of our waking hours engaged with various kinds of screens and less in interacting with persons, objects, and actual, rather than virtual, environments). The transindividual nature of social groups of all kinds assumes and in some cases imposes certain levels of individuation on the part of members, contributors, leaders, or simple participants. The act of reading in a mechanical print environment is an inherently individuating experience. In its typical form, it involves the focus of readers on the printed page in a manner that disengages them from social interaction, enabling solitary interaction with the text. This is a formative experience of everyone who comes of age and undergoes an education toward adult citizenship in a literate culture. To fundamentally change this mode of individuation, and to restructure the relationship between individuation and transindividual social formations, on the global scale that is enabled (and increasingly imposed) by the web and social networking, is to administer a pharmakon of unknown healing and/or baneful effects, of an entirely new and still-to-be understood type. Digitization is a human experiment, unprecedented in its globalized scope, in social and evolutionary transformation, and its results we can only anticipate as a substantive change in the configuration of personal and collective experience and of social, economic, and political practice.

Thus far, we have considered interior vectors of the impact of digitization and the increasingly ubiquitous connectivity of the web. Following the revelations of Edward Snowden in June of 2013, however, we know that as users of digital media and the Internet we are objects of official surveillance, subject to scrutiny of a hitherto unimaginable scale and degree of invasiveness. Snowden, a contract employee of the U.S. National Security Agency, in a series of stunning media disclosures in 2013, revealed that the NSA, in partnership with the so-called Five Eyes partners (the NSA-equivalent agencies in Australia, Canada, New Zealand, and Great Britain), had been conducting global surveillance of all Internet and phone activity, demanding and receiving direct access to private user accounts and phone records in Google, Yahoo, and Verizon, spying on both citizens and heads of state of friendly and unfriendly nations alike (including, for example, German Chancellor Angela Merkel). An NSA mission statement titled "Sigint Strategy 2012–2016" reveals that the NSA plans for continued expansion of surveillance activities, with the "stated goal to 'dramatically increase mastery of the global network' and 'acquire the capabilities to gather intelligence on anyone, anytime, anywhere'" ("Edward Snowden" 2014). While there is widespread public outrage in the media, the U.S. courts are currently divided on the legality and constitutionality of these NSA activities, with the likelihood that the matter will need to be decided in the Supreme Court. Snowden has become a fugitive, his U.S. passport revoked, currently in temporary asylum in Russia, a hero to those concerned at the unprecedented intrusion on personal autonomy and privacy he exposed, while he is pursued for prosecution and vilified by the security-minded public alarmed at the implications of the post-9/11 environment. That security agencies of leading developed nations would consider it within their rights to spy indiscriminately on citizens without restraint and in the absence of accountability goes counter to all reasonable expectations of privacy, threatening fundamental democratic rights, as well as the established understandings of the bounds of government oversight of citizen rights.

Science writer George Dyson draws the link between foreign military intelligence and domestic security: the United States now has the satellite-enabled ability, and policy, to execute drone strikes against potential foreign enemies. Dyson voices the disturbing question that follows from the Snowden revelations regarding the blanket surveillance of a country's own citizens: "Why kill possibly dangerous individuals (and the inevitable innocent bystanders) when it will soon become technically irresistible to exterminate the dangerous ideas themselves?" (2013). With the level of detail and coverage of current data trails for every user of digital media, a new level of intrusion and predictive ability comes into play:

> The ultimate goal of signals intelligence and analysis is to learn not only what is being said, and what is being done, but what is being thought. With the proliferation of search engines that directly track the links between individual human minds and the words, images, and ideas that both characterize and increasingly constitute their thoughts, this goal appears within reach at last. "But, how can the machine know what I think?" you ask. It does not need to know what you think—no more than one person ever really knows what another person thinks. A reasonable guess at what you are thinking is good enough. (Dyson, 2013)

Dyson identifies the problem with such kinds of statistically determined prediction. Citing mathematician David Hilbert's 1936 elucidation of the Decision Problem, in which he demonstrates the impossibility of proving veracity in even simple arithmetic propositions, Dyson draws the logical connection to the ability of firewalls to accurately filter security risks: "For any system complicated enough to include even simple arithmetic, no firewall that admits anything new can ever keep everything dangerous out." The problem, he argues, is that panoptical scrutiny of this kind filters out and dampens positive as well as negative thought and potential action:

> It will never be entirely possible to systematically distinguish truly dangerous ideas from good ones that appear suspicious, without trying them out. Any formal system that is granted (or assumes) the absolute power to protect itself against dangerous ideas will of necessity also be defensive against original and creative thoughts. And, for both human beings individually and for human society collectively, that will be our loss. This is the fatal flaw in the ideal of a security state. (Dyson, 2013)

In the sphere of everyday life and participation in the marketplace, the degree and kind of surveillance of our activities as online consumers is of an encompassing scale and uncanny granularity. Google and Facebook are financed by both the ad placement on their webpages and by the sale of the information they glean from their users. For instance, Google's recent acquisition of "the startup company Behavio will soon give it the power to track your location 24 hours a day, as well as to predict where you will be and who will meet you there—hours, days, or even weeks into the future" (Epstein, 10, May 2013). Google has invested heavily in development of its online mapping function:

> Today, Google's map includes the streets of every nation on earth, and Street View has so far collected imagery in a quarter of those countries. The total number of regular users: A billion people, or about half of the Internet-connected population worldwide. Google Maps underlies a million different websites, making its map A.P.I. among the most-used such interfaces on the Internet. At this point Google Maps is essentially what Tim O'Reilly predicted the map would become: part of the information infrastructure, a resource more complete and in many respects more accurate than what governments have. (Fisher, 11 Dec. 2013)

Fully 20 percent of Google searches involve where-related questions, resulting in the appearance of its mapping function as part of the results. In an article entitled "Google's Plan for Global Domination," Adam Fisher observes: "The Internet land grab, . . . can be reduced to three key battles over three key conceptual territories.

What came first, conquered by Google's superior search algorithms. *Who* was next, and Facebook was the victor. But *where*, arguably the biggest prize of all, has yet to be completely won" (2013). With mobile devices now on the person of an increasing proportion of the global population, and with wearable computing in active development, GPS positioning will soon make the physical whereabouts and movements of everyone on the grid readily and thoroughly trackable.

In *Code: Version 2.0* (the second, much-revised edition of his *Code and Other Laws of Cyberspace* [1999]), Lawrence Lessig recalls the utopian and libertarian optimism of the early promoters of the World Wide Web in the 1990s:

> The space [i.e., cyberspace] seemed to promise a kind of society that real space would never allow—freedom without anarchy, control without government, consensus without power. . . . The claim for cyberspace was not just that government would not regulate cyberspace—it was that government could not regulate cyberspace. Cyberspace was, by nature, unavoidably free. Governments could threaten, but behavior could not be controlled; laws could be passed, but they would have no real effect. There was no choice about what kind of government to install—none could reign. (2006: 2–3)

By 2005, the picture emerging regarding the relation of the Internet to regulatory agencies looked fundamentally different. As Siva Vaidhyanathan observes, "While once it seemed obvious and easy to declare the rise of a 'network society' in which individuals would realign themselves, empower themselves, and undermine traditional methods of social and cultural control, it seems clear that networked digital communication need not serve such liberating ends" (quoted in Lessig, 2006: 5).

By the time of current writing (early 2014), it is obvious that, given the security, regulatory, and commercial interests described above, we are looking at a significantly changed landscape of cyberspace in 2014 and the years to follow. Lessig's argument in 1999 and again, with emphasis, in 2006 was that the Internet was not only regulable, it was subject to a control that, from its original, inherently flat, multinodal and distributed architecture (see Hui, 2010: 5–7), seemed not only unthinkable but inherently impossible. The march of bureaucratization in modernity, with its marvels and horrors of social rationalization, might have taught us otherwise (think healthcare systems and prolongation of average lifespans on the one hand, and implacable genocides on the other). Lessig's arguments now call for organized resistance and pushback on the part of all those who want to see realized the powerful potential for creative and constructive good of a free, open, and responsible Internet:

> Liberty in cyberspace will not come from the absence of the state. Liberty there, as anywhere, will come from a state of a certain kind. We build a world where freedom can flourish not by removing from society any self-conscious control, but by setting it in a place where a particular kind of self-conscious control survives. We build liberty as our founders did, by setting society upon a certain constitution. (4)

—◊—

Before turning to the essays themselves, the promised word of explanation regarding the thematics of "identity" and "agency" in relation to what we have termed the "nexus" of digital culture. Bernard Stiegler's call for a renewal of the project of Enlightenment in the context of the closely linked phenomena of globalization and digitization is a salutary reminder both of the unfinished project of modernity, of the darker sides of its nineteenth- and twentieth-century technological and bureaucratic history, and of the closely imbricated challenges and opportunities that accompany the pervasive impact of the newly emerging digital epoch. The phrase "unfinished project of modernity" invokes a representative work of analysis performed by Jürgen Habermas in his *Philosophical Discourse of Modernity* (1987). In continuity with Horkheimer and Adorno's already mentioned *Dialectic of Enlightenment* (first published in 1947), Habermas brings his Frankfurt School origins and what he terms his "late modern" (rather than postmodern) intersubjective theoretical model of communicative action to bear on analysis of late twentieth century debates surrounding postmodernity. He argues that the announcement of "postmodernity" is premature; that the project of modernity, rather, remains "unfinished." Habermas takes as definitive the understanding of Enlightenment values and principles articulated by Kant. For instance, in his in manifesto-like essay of 1784, "An Answer to the Question: What Is Enlightenment?" Kant declares the centrality of individual freedom, dignity, and responsibility at the core of the project of modernity:

> *Enlightenment is mankind's exit from its self-incurred immaturity.*
> Immaturity is the inability to make use of one's own understanding without the guidance of another. *Self-incurred* is this inability if its cause lies not in the lack of understanding but rather in the lack of the resolution and the courage to use it without the guidance of another. *Sapere*

aude! Have the courage to use your *own* understanding! is thus the
motto of the enlightenment. (Kant, 1784: 58)

Kant understands the principle of the free and individual exercise of the autonomy of the will to be grounded apodictically in the *a priori* of a categorical
imperative. The dignity and, indeed, sublime identity of the enlightened individual resides in its self-authorizing agency, itself choosing the law to which the
individual is to become subject. As Kant argues in *Groundwork of the Metaphysics
of Morals*: "Autonomy of the will is the property of the will by which it is a law
to itself (independently of any property of the objects of volition)" (Kant, 1785:
4:440).

   Along with such an elevation of the individual to freedom from the authority of the traditions and institutions of the past, Habermas argues, comes also
an uprooting of free individuality from the social and cultural soil of inherited
worldviews, whether theological or metaphysical. Along with Hegel and much
subsequent reception of Kant, Habermas observes that, while so emphatically
asserting the role of freedom, Kant deepens and aggravates the characteristic
dualism of modern thought explicit in the Cartesian opposition of subject and
object (*res cogitans* and *res extensa*). Kant's critical epistemology inures the knowing subject from the objective world of things-in-themselves. In his three great
critiques he differentiates the knowledge realms of science, morality, and art—
thought, action, and judgement—in ways that present difficulties for any understanding of identity and moral action in modernity, at both the personal and
the social levels. Defining his own position with reference to Hegel's critique
of Kantian dualism and separation of realms of knowledge, action, and judgement, and in keeping with elements of Hegel's own theory of recognition (which
Habermas claims remain unexploited by Hegel), Habermas argues for the intersubjective and social, rather than the individual and *a priori*, construction of
identity. Introducing a volume of essays addressing the reception of Habermas's
The Philosophical Discourse of Modernity, Maurizio Passerin D'Entrèves situates
Habermas's analysis of the postmodern critique of modernity:

> Against the depiction of modernity as a spent epoch, as having
> exhausted the promises and projects of its philosophical mentors in
> the Enlightenment, Habermas set out to defend [in *The Philosophical
> Discourse of Modernity*] the unrealized normative potential of modern-
> ity. This defence is based on Habermas's theory of modernity and
> communicative rationality presented in his earlier two-volume work,

The Theory of Communicative Action. In that work Habermas offered a systematic theory of societal and cultural modernization capable of explaining both the achievements and the pathologies of modernity. Crucial to that effort was the paradigm shift from the philosophy of consciousness to the philosophy of language, and from a subject-centred to a communicative conception of reason and rationality. (Passerin D'Entrèves, 1997: 1)

In his shift to an intersubjective model of communicative rationality, then, Habermas takes up a position, D'Entrèves argues, midway between Kantian and Hegelian philosophy of consciousness, rooted in the autonomy of individual self-determination, and postmodern argument for identity as mere social construction. Habermas understood the latter as a rhetorical rather than fully rational model of identity, as distinct from his own model of communicative action, governed by communicative reason rather than rhetorical persuasion.

One can argue, after revisionary modernists such as Habermas, for a differently grounded conception of intersubjective identity and agency. Or, after postmodernists such as Lyotard, Foucault, Derrida, and Žižek, one can seek consistency within modes of critical analysis of the inherent aporias in all attempts to objectively ground autonomous subjectivity and social practices. In either case the newly evolving digital virtualization and mediatization of twenty-first century social environments intensify the ongoing issues inherent in Enlightenment traditions of social self-understanding. Stiegler's call for a reinvigoration of Enlightenment values attuned to the ambiguous pharmacological effects of digitalization recognizes the deepening challenges of modernity, along with its inextricable, intensifying involvement with technological transformation of the natural, social, and psychic environments of globalizing contemporary society.

As a result, the pharmacological bivalency of digitization is accompanied by polarities within questions of identity and agency inherent to the project of modernity, polarities that pre-exist digital technology, but which are deepened by its aggravation of the inherent subject/object dualism that haunts modern philosophical and scientific worldviews. On the one hand, as creators of digital technology, we actively shape our collective and personal identities through the creative and destructive powers of exponential technological transformation. On the other, the increasingly ubiquitous scope of our incursions into our natural and social environments is transforming human identity and relationships, within society and also between society and the manifestly disrupted natural environment. In other words, *The Digital Nexus: Identity, Agency, and Political Engagement* refers both to questions of human identity and self-determination and also to the increasing force, energy, intelligence, and ingenuity of our technologically saturated human environment. Where in this book we have used the term "digital nexus" for the convergence of technologies and the technical infrastructures of media and Internet, technology writer Kevin Kelly has seen the necessity of creating a new term in order to signify the transformative nature of the technological sphere. In *What Technology Wants*, Kelly explains:

> I dislike inventing words that no one else uses, but in this case all known alternatives fail to convey the required scope. So I've somewhat reluctantly coined a word to designate the greater, global, massively interconnected system of technology vibrating around us. I call it the technium. The technium extends beyond shiny hardware to include culture, art, social institutions, and intellectual creations of all types. It includes intangibles like software, law, and philosophical concepts. And most important, it includes the generative impulses of our inventions to encourage more tool making, more technology invention, and more self-enhancing connections. (2010: 11–12)

It is with the "computational turn" from industrial to information technology that Kelly sees a significant change in the scope and nature of our involvement with technology:

> As we refined this stuff through generations of technological evolution, it lost much of its hardness. We began to see through technology's disguise as material and began to see it primarily as action. While it inhabited a body, its heart was something softer. In 1949, John von Neumann, the brainy genius behind the first useful computer, realized what computers were teaching us about technology: "Technology will in the near and in the farther future increasingly turn from problems of intensity, substance, and energy, to problems of structure, organization, information, and control." No longer a noun, technology was becoming a force—a vital spirit that throws us forward or pushes against us. Not a thing but a verb. (41)

The technological environment that we have created is thus increasingly creating us, gaining a momentum and a kind of agency that Kelly argues poses new questions. What Kelly calls the technium and, in this volume, we have referred to as the digital nexus is thus a new form of human action and identity, one that redraws the boundaries between society and natural world and between human beings and their social environments. The "unfinished project of modernity" has been delivered—and delivers—an unanticipated turn of the screw of modernity.

—⚬⚬—

The essays in this volume are presented according to their dominant concerns, under the categories of theory, culture, and politics. Dominant concerns are by no means exclusive ones: these organizing categories are useful when understood to be consciously implicative and interactive with one another. Given the strong emphasis in cultural theory in recent decades on political implications and arising problems, there are overt political concerns, for example, among the essays in Section Two, "Digital Culture," though they focus primarily on cultural commentary and analysis. The areas of concern stated in the title of the collection, *The Digital Nexus: Identity, Agency, and Political Engagement*, speak to the convergence of digital media in the way digitization, in its multimedia nature, transforms the overall environment within which identity expresses itself and action is undertaken. Such transformational effects of digitization have intellectual and theoretical implications. Elizabeth Eisenstein, in her classic study of the enabling effects of the invention of the printing press on the emergence of modernity, articulates the way a vital technology enacts the convergence of social, political, and intellectual forces:

> One cannot treat printing as just one among many elements in a complex causal nexus for the communications shift transformed the nature of the causal nexus itself. It is of special historical significance because it produced fundamental alterations in prevailing patterns of continuity and change. . . . Intellectual and spiritual life, far from remaining unaffected, were profoundly transformed by the multiplication of new tools for duplicating books in fifteenth-century Europe. . . . The printing press laid the basis for both literal fundamentalism and for modern science. It remains indispensable for humanistic scholarship. It is still responsible for our museum-without-walls. (1979: 703–4)

As Eisenstein articulates, "the communications shift transformed the nature of the causal nexus itself." This is the premise the present volume of essays seeks to underline. Foundational changes in media of publication have transformative effects on social milieux, since they create new conditions and means of

expression for thought and communication, social congregation and interaction, and political argument and engagement.

In Section One, "Theory," the noted philosopher of technology Andrew
Feenberg, in "The Internet in Question," opens the volume with a balanced
canvassing of the overall implications of the web. Feenberg has been a pion-
eer in research with and into the Internet, and his long reflection on the relation between technology and society provides the reader with an even-handed
adjudication of the extremes of web utopia and dystopia. In Chapter Two,
"Emergent Meaning in the Information Age," Ian Angus brings his longstanding
engagement with the nature of communication to bear on a Husserlian phenomenological reading of the ways in which digital media change our understanding of language as the fundamental condition of community. In Chapter
Three, "Responsible Machines: The Opportunities and Challenges of Artificial
Autonomous Agents," philosopher of technology David J. Gunkel engages the
ethical implications of digitally enabled software and hardware. A distinguishing
factor of digital encoding is its capacity for a new layer of cognitive technological
complexity: the ability to learn from its own processes and to make adjustments
on the basis of the data generated. What are the implications of machines that
are able to act as "autonomous agents"? If they are responsive to themselves
and their environments, able to make adjustments on the basis of feedback, is
such responsiveness a form of responsibility, and if so do they also enjoy the
rights associated with responsible roles in the human community? Gunkel raises
some necessary and provocative questions about the ethical nature of rights and
responsibilities in the light of digital agency. In Chapter Four, computer systems expert Daryl Campbell asks about the philosophical implications of the
open-source software movement. His essay is a specific instance of the question
addressed by the volume as a whole: what order of effect does digitization have
on communication and forms of coordinated action such as the invention and
elaboration of software programming? Campbell brings the thought of French
philosopher Alain Badiou to bear on the nature of "event" in evaluating leading
characteristics of this movement.

Section Two takes up representative issues in digital culture. In Chapter
Five, "Hacktivist (Pre)Occupations: Self-Surveillance, Participation and Public
Space," Carolyn Guertin, a pioneering specialist in digital narrative, provides
an illuminating overview of recent crossover reflexive art projects that perform
critical commentary on the pervasive surveillance that has become an inte-
gral feature of digitally monitored public, commercial, and corporate spaces.

In Chapter Six, "Institutions and Interpellations of the Dubject, the Doubled and Spaced Self," Mark McCutcheon explores the ways in which digital media interpellate their users, calling on postcolonial theory to articulate the hybrid forms of ambivalent subjectivity, or dubjection, that arise from colonization of subjectivity by the pervasive presence of and involvement with digital media. In Chapter Seven, "The Network University in Transition," in a case study of York University (Canada), Bob Hanke studies the impact of digital networks on the university, and the institutional tensions that arise in academic life with digitalization. One of the remarkable features of the web as a publication medium is the intensification of writing it has fostered, as a result of the immediate publication and debate it enables. In Chapter Eight, "Spinning the Web: Critical Discourse Analysis and its Online Space," Leslie Lindballe explores the relevance of critical discourse analysis to the ways in which written language is affected, both overtly and in subtle ways, by its reframing of language in the multimedia networked environment of the Internet termed the blogosphere. In Chapter Nine, in the suggestive "Paramortals, or Dancing with the Interactive Digital Dead," the late Roman Onufrijchuk sees in the current popular culture preoccupation with the half-life of the undead a symptom of the ambiguous virtual transcendence offered by the rich multimedia data streams each of us is creating and which we will leave behind us, as it were, in our "wake" (as Professor Onufrijchuk himself poignantly does at his recent passing, Memory Eternal).

The interactive, multimedia, and immediate character of the Internet enables new forms of social congregation, knowledge diffusion, and political engagement. From the Arab Spring to Wikileaks to the Edward Snowden revelations, it has become starkly evident that the digital environment changes the dynamics of political identity and agency in ways both empowering and disempowering. In Section Three, "Digital Politics," Peter J. Smith (Chapter Ten, "The Rise of the National Surveillance State in Comparative Perspective") and Karen Wall and Lorna Stefanick (Chapter Eleven, "Democracy and Identity in the Digital Age") address the unprecedented kinds and levels of surveillance at work both in the political and the general public sphere. The scope of digitally enabled surveillance, whether political, commercial, or military, entirely redefines the former boundaries between the public and private spheres, raising profound legal and political challenges and complexities. Josipa G. Petrunić (Chapter Twelve, "The Digital Democratic Deficit: Analysis of Digital Voting in a Canadian Party Leadership Race") provides a close-grained case study of the complexities and dilemmas of digital voting technology, while Maria Bakardjieva (Chapter

Thirteen, "Navigating the 'Mediapolis': Digital Media and Emerging Practices of Democratic Participation") and Sharone Daniel (Chapter Fourteen, "The Construction of Collective Action Frames in Facebook Groups") investigate the new forms of social and political action and cooperation enabled by social media.

REFERENCES

Carr, Nicholas. 2011. *The Shallows: What the Internet Is Doing to Our Brains*. New York and London: W.W. Norton.

Clarke, Paul. "Sir Tim Berners Lee." http://www.webfoundation.org/about/sir-tim-berners-lee/.

Dyson, George. 2013. "NSA: The Decision Problem," *Edge*. 27 July. http://www.edge.org/conversation/nsa-the-decision-problem.

"Edward Snowden." *Wikipedia*, accessed January 11, 2014. http://en.wikipedia.org/wiki/Edward_Snowden.

Eisenstein, Elizabeth. 1979. *The Printing Press as an Agent of Change: Communications and Cultural Transformations in Early-Modern Europe*. Cambridge: Cambridge University Press.

Epstein, Robert. 2013. "Google's Gotcha," *US News and World Report*, 10 May. Accessed January 11, 2014. http://www.usnews.com/opinion/articles/2013/05/10/15-ways-google-monitors-you?page=3.

Fisher, Adam. 2013. "Google's Road Map to Global Domination," *New York Times*, 11 December. Accessed January 12, 2014. http://www.nytimes.com/2013/12/15/magazine/googles-plan-for-global-domination-dont-ask-why-ask-where.html?pagewanted=all&_r=1&.

Habermas, Jürgen. 1987. *The Philosophical Discourse of Modernity: Twelve Lectures*. Cambridge: MIT Press.

Halpin, Harry and Alexandre Monnin. 2014. *Philosophical Engineering: Toward a Philosophy of the Web*. Oxford: Wiley Blackwell.

Hansen, Mark N.B. 2010. "Introduction to Bernard Stiegler, 'Memory.'" In *Critical Terms for Media Studies*, eds. W. J. T. Mitchell and Mark N. B. Hansen, 64–66. Chicago: University of Chicago Press.

Horkheimer, Max, and Theodor W. Adorno. 1944. *The Dialectic of Enlightenment: Philosophical Fragments*. Ed. Gunzelin S. Noerr. Trans. Edmund Jephcott. Stanford, CA: Stanford University Press, 2002.

Hui, Yuk. 2010. "The Computational Turn, Or, a New Weltbild." *Junctures: The Journal for Thematic Dialogue* 13, 41–51. http://www.junctures.org/index.php/junctures/article/view/6/4.

Husserl, Edmund. 1970. *The Crisis of European Sciences and Transcendental Phenomenology*. Trans. David Carr. Evanston: Northwestern University Press.

Kant, Immanuel. 1784. "An Answer to the Question: What Is Enlightenment?" In *What Is Enlightenment: Eighteenth Century Answers and Twentieth Century Questions*, ed. James Schmidt, 58–64. Berkeley: University of California Press, 1996.

———. 1785. *Groundwork of the Metaphysic of Morals*. Ed. and trans. Mary Gregor. Cambridge: Cambridge University Press, 1997.

Kelly, Kevin. 2010. *What Technology Wants*. New York: Viking.

Lessig, Lawrence. 2006. *Code: Version 2.0*. New York: Basic.

McLuhan, Marshall. 1962. *The Gutenberg Galaxy: The Making of Typographic Man*. Toronto: University of Toronto Press.

Ong, Walter. 1982. *Orality and Literacy: The Technologization of the Word*. London and New York: Routledge.

Passerin d'Entrèves, Maurizio. 1997. "Introduction." In *Habermas and the Unfinished Project of Modernity: Critical Essays on The Philosophical Discourse of Modernity*, eds. Maurizio Passerin d'Entrèves and Seyla Benhabib, 1–37. Cambridge: MIT Press.

Stiegler, Bernard. 1998. *Technics and Time, 1: The Fault of Epithemeus*. Stanford, CA: Stanford University Press.

———. 2009. *Technics and Time, 2: Disorientation*. Stanford, CA: Stanford University Press.

———. 2011. *Technics and Time, 3: Cinematic Time and the Question of Malaise*. Stanford, CA: Stanford University Press.

———. 2010. "Memory." In *Critical Terms For Media Studies*, eds. W. J. T. Mitchell and Mark N. B. Hansen, 66–87. Chicago: University of Chicago Press.

———. 2012a. "Die Aufklärung in the Age of Philosophical Engineering," *Digital Enlightenment Yearbook 2013*. 29–39. M. Hildebrandt et al. Leiden: IOS Press.

———. 2012b. "Relational Ecology and the Digital *Pharmakon*." *Culture Machine* 13. http://www.culturemachine.net/index.php/cm/issue/view/24.

Tinnell, John. 2012. "Originary Technicity and Grammatization: Twin Pillars of Stiegler's Project." 8 June. Accessed January 12, 2014. http://jtinnell.blogspot.ca/2012/06/originary-technicity-and-grammatization.html.

Wolf, Maryanne. 2007. *Proust and the Squid: The Story and the Science of the Reading Brain*. New York: Harpers.

Part One

Digital

Theory

1 The Internet in Question

Andrew Feenberg

The purpose of this chapter is to affirm the democratic potential of the Internet. Affirmation is called for by the context of contemporary critical theory, in which the Internet figures increasingly as the problem rather than the solution to the crisis of democracy. This marks a change from early optimistic assessments that still inspire a diminishing band of commentators. But mainstream academic opinion has turned against what is now considered "hype," the exaggerated expectation that the Internet would contribute to the democratization of society.

I take the criticisms of the Internet seriously; however, I also note a certain exaggeration that makes me wonder about the motives behind the vehemence with which they are sometimes offered.

The critiques do bring important aspects of the Internet to light. We have had enough experience with it by now to realize that it is a mixed phenomenon unlikely to fulfil the promise of democratic transformation it inspired in the early years. The critics have hit on some of the reasons for its limited and contradictory impacts. I will argue, however, that their evaluation is one-sided. They focus exclusively on the Internet's most problematic aspects and underestimate important accomplishments. An analysis of the Internet as a technology in its formative stage, before it has achieved a standard configuration, offers a more comprehensive view. I will show that the political and social contradictions of the Internet are reflected in its technological features, which do not resolve into a coherent whole.

The first half of this chapter discusses two important critiques of the Internet and argues that they mistake aspects of the technology for the whole. The latter half introduces methodological considerations and applies the method to the Internet.

TWO CRITIQUES

Critiques of the Internet from the standpoint of political economy and cultural theory have merit, and I have chosen to respond here to Christian Fuchs and Jodi Dean, articulate champions of counter-hype who skillfully deflate the myth of the Internet as a revolutionary technology.

Fuchs has written an innovative Marxist analysis of the Internet, combining the theories of free immaterial labour and the "multitude" with audience commodity theory (Fuchs 2010). He argues that advanced capitalism is an information society in which the production of knowledge has become essential to the reproduction of capital. Marx claimed that the productive power of knowledge increases with the development of society. As a collective product knowledge is essentially social, but under capitalism it is privately appropriated. Like the common lands divided up and expropriated at the origins of capitalism, knowledge belongs to an ideal commons divided up and exploited by advanced capital. In Hegelian terms, Fuchs writes, the existence of knowledge (under capitalism) contradicts its essence (as social.) Fuchs concludes, "With the rise of informational capitalism, the exploitation of the commons has become a central process of capital accumulation" (Fuchs, 2010: 190).

If capitalism is an information society, the knowledge producers constitute an exploited class. They include many workers in industry and government, students and researchers in universities, and also those whose "immaterial labour" contributes to social reproduction, such as house workers and many types of service workers. Fuchs follows Michael Hardt and Antonio Negri in emphasizing the significance of immaterial goods. These include communicative and affective goods as well as knowledge (in the usual sense of formally constituted bodies of information). Since all these goods are produced in the commons through communication and sharing, their appropriation by capital represents a "colonization" of an increasingly important sector of society. And since knowledge flows from these multiple sources, the industrial proletariat is no longer the only or indeed the principal exploited class. Fuchs adopts Hardt and Negri's term "multitude" to refer to this complex new underclass.

This brings us to the crux of Fuchs's argument about new media. The commons now includes those Internet sites where individuals communicate and thereby contribute to the sum of knowledge. The production of user-generated content becomes the occasion for profit-making activity on the part of the companies that provide the popular web platforms, but the users are paid nothing for their efforts. The unique structure of the Internet enables this new form of knowledge production and also supports the exploitation of the free labour of the producers. Since exploitation is measured as a ratio between wages and the value of the products produced, the rate of this new form of exploitation is virtually infinite!

Fuchs draws on Dallas Smythe's audience commodity theory to explain how companies realize profits from free labour on the Internet. Smythe argued that in selling advertising time, media companies were in effect marketing commodified audiences. Smythe's argument was based on his analysis of television, the dominant medium at the time he wrote. Fuchs claims that social networking platforms such as Facebook operate in a similar way, accumulating users and selling them as an audience to advertisers. But now the exploitation has intensified, since the audience no longer attends to a content produced by the corporations that exploit it, but produces its own content and freely offers it up to attract the audience the corporations commodify and sell. Thus the activity of Internet users "does not signify a democratization of the media toward a participatory or democratic system, but the total commodification of human creativity" (Fuchs, 2010: 192).

The broadening of the notion of exploited class suggested by Hardt and Negri and its application to users of the Internet responds to the actual fragmentation of struggles in advanced capitalism. Fuchs wants to construct a counter-hegemony based on a theme unifying these struggles. They can potentially converge around resistance to the colonization of the commons and the exploitation of the knowledge produced by the multitude. Whatever the nature of the exploited group, it contributes to the production of alien wealth. Together, they can resist capitalism as did the proletariat at an earlier stage. The theory cannot unite them, of course, but it can indicate the lines along which unity might be possible under the right conditions. Fuchs makes a powerful case for this strategy.

Although Fuchs has identified important aspects of the Internet, his argument has weaknesses. The Internet is truly the site of new forms of production and exploitation, as he shows. But his evaluation is surprisingly reductive. He appears to define the Internet by the exploitation of free labour and the commodification of its products. Whatever the content of the communications, the simple fact that corporations profit from it determines its essence. He writes, "the contemporary Internet is a class-structured space that is dominated by corporations that use this medium for capital accumulation and advertising" (2011: 310). It is obvious that user activity is profitable for corporations, but it is less obvious that this is the most important thing one can say about it.

Indeed, Fuchs himself appears to recognize this in later articles and books that argue for what he calls a "dialectical" understanding of the Internet as a class-conflicted and not merely a class-structured space (2014a). He argues that he intends this dialectical view in his writings on the political economy of the Internet, but focuses there on only its corporate aspect. He then opposes an alternative nonprofit Internet to the existing one in which corporations play a large role. Thus he writes that "commercial social media do not constitute a public sphere and a participatory web. . . . Social media are mainly commercial and mundane spaces—politics are the exception to the rule" (2014b: 60–61). As a result he seems to leave an opening for the widely influential reductive interpretation of the Internet he appears to hold in his writings on political economy. In any case, Fuchs's dialectical interpretation is useful, and I will later underpin it with an analysis of the technological basis of the dialectic.

In the writings under consideration here, Fuchs overlooks a significant difference between capitalist production and production on the Internet. This has to do with the relation of capitalist form and content in the two cases. When capitalists appropriated the original commons by fencing it in and expelling the peasants, they transformed the land itself, submitting it to entirely new usages. The essence of capitalism here is thus not just commodification but the transformations that resources undergo as they are commodified. At a later stage labour was submitted to a similar transformation. Capitalism reorganized the labour process to generate abstract labour: labour that can be quantified and controlled to produce profit. Marx calls this "real subsumption." The content, in the sense of what workers do at work, was penetrated by the commodity form.

As applied to television, the audience commodity theory of mass media resonates with Marx's theory of commodification at two levels because audience attention can be packaged and sold, and also because the content toward which that attention is directed is rationalized and controlled. Only the first happens on Facebook or Google. It is true that corporations find ways to commodify the knowledge commons. But the commons is not reduced to a productive resource for capital, as was the land appropriated by capital at an earlier stage. The economic aspect of the new commons is parasitic on an independent content, a wide range of meanings and activities that persist even after the imposition of the commodity form. The content that users produce for their mutual entertainment and enlightenment is commodified in the same way that telephone conversations are commodified by telephone companies operating as common carriers. The users' conversations are not controlled in a labour process managed by the telephone companies or by social networking sites. The metaphoric link between factory labour and Internet "labour" breaks down.

Capitalism profits from many activities that are not labour, and communication on the Internet is just one of them. A sunny beach invites tourists who spend money in hotels and restaurants, but the tourists cannot be said to work for capital when they sunbathe on the beach. The university creates business opportunities for sandwich shops in the neighbourhood of the campus, but classrooms are not sites of free labour for the shopkeepers. Babies offer a business opportunity for diaper makers without performing free labour for the diaper company. The incidental character of the profitable activity associated with each of these situations prevents reduction to their economic function. Similarly, information provided by users is not work producing surplus value.

Another problem with Fuchs's political economy of the Internet is that he takes off from earlier media theories of television, as in his reference to audience commodity theory. He is right that audiences on the Internet self-assemble and are commodified and sold to advertisers. But the analogy between television and the Internet ignores an important difference between them: the audience commodity theory was proposed once television had achieved its standard form, but the Internet is still in flux.

Television, as a technical achievement, had the potential to serve a multitude of functions. It could have had wide applications for local broadcasting and could have incorporated interaction in combination with the telephone. Perhaps a generation of technical work on such systems would have produced a sophisticated and effective medium for education, culture, and political enlightenment. But the sad history of television charts its reduction to the narrow entertainment and news functions presupposed by the audience commodity theory (Williams, 1974). There is no corresponding history of the Internet, at least not yet. Explaining the Internet with a combination of the television analogy and the theory of free labour forecloses the future of the technology.

At this point in its development, the analogy that seems most relevant to the Internet is not television but a public space such as the sidewalk. Social interaction on the Internet is not primarily labour but exactly what it seems, that is, social interaction. Although production undoubtedly goes on, the economics are not those of labour under capitalism. Capitalists take advantage of the Internet, as do the owners of buildings who rent space along a busy street where people chat with each other and shop. Advertisers are like store owners who pay rent for a good location. Data-mining user contributions enhances the value of the rental property by enabling targeted advertising. What is commodified thereby is what is effectively rented: space on web pages and, through it, audience attention. The users and their contributions are exploited to be sure, but only in the usual common-sense meaning of the term, not in accordance with Marxist value theory.

Fuchs often appears to dismiss the democratic implications of the Internet because of its economic function, but the human significance of online interaction persists despite its place in the capitalist economy. The contributions of Internet users cannot be reduced to their economic function any more than can conversations on the sidewalk. Whether those contributions have a democratic value requires further analysis of their actual content in their context.

This is what Jodi Dean attempts in her cultural critique of the Internet (Dean, 2005; 2010). Let's consider her argument against Guy Debord's claim that reciprocal communication has an emancipatory potential that mass communication lacks (2010: 108–13). Debord was the founder and leader of the Situationist International and the author of a critical classic of the 1960s, *The Society of the Spectacle*. He had a dystopian view of advanced capitalism very similar to the position of such Frankfurt School theorists as Theodor Adorno and Herbert Marcuse. Roughly summarized, they argued that a technocratic-capitalist elite dominates a subordinated population held in thrall by the mass media and consumerism. The introjection of system requirements makes coercive suppression unnecessary for the most part because the manipulated individuals reproduce the system spontaneously. This relation of voluntary subservience differs from traditional forms in that it is based not on moral conscience but on a libidinal attachment to the rewards of conformity.

According to Debord, breaking out of this syndrome requires dramatic exemplary acts by a small minority of dissenters able to deconstruct the virtual chains binding the mass. He hoped that provocation from the margins would become a catalyst for the breakdown of the system. The French May Events of 1968 could be interpreted as a confirmation of this approach, and in fact the Situationist critique of mass society did play an inspirational role in the movement. Similar actions by the New Left in the United States were less effective but succeeded in breaking the iron grip of 1950s conformism. We still benefit from that breakthrough today.

Dean complains that in emphasizing the top-down nature of advanced capitalism, exemplified in the mass media, Debord idealizes the potential of bottom-up activity to disrupt the system. But in fact, she argues, we now have the bottom-up alternative to the mass media Debord dreamed of. It is called the Internet and, far from disrupting advanced capitalism, it reproduces it ever more effectively. Free communication on the Internet has not had the emancipatory effects foreseen by those like Debord who criticized the centralized, one-way communicative structure of the mass media. She argues that we have entered a new stage of "communicative capitalism" that renders older theories such as Debord's obsolete.

Dean argues that far from defeating the dystopian vision of a totally administered society, most communication on the Internet reinforces it. The Internet erases the all-important gap between meaning and reality. The distinction between symbol and thing, fantasy and fact, is essential to the possibility of both truth and resistance. On the Internet the distinction disappears and with it the authority of any particular meaning collapses. The disruptive feature of the Internet is the ease with which users externalize their own discourse and multiply alternative sources of information. No longer committed to anything, the user is unreal to him- or herself. No longer persuaded by anything, the user cannot leave the cocoon of the derealized self. Reflexivity, which the Enlightenment identified with the autonomous individual, here renders the individuals helpless before the power of the system. This is in fact the hysteria of reflexivity, a bottomless pit of second thoughts, which destroys the "symbolic efficiency" essential to belief and action.

Dean relates these aspects of life in cyberspace to a strange phenomenon unforeseen by the early prophets of a society liberated by communication on computer networks. This is the enormous flood of useless contributions sent out by Internet users who neither expect nor receive any meaningful response from the imaginary public they address. This is indeed puzzling. At first one posts messages on Facebook in the expectation of a reply, but gradually it becomes clear that no reply is forthcoming—and eventually, that none is necessary. The systematic lack of serious content and responsiveness undermines the emancipatory implications of communicative freedom. Sending trivial messages out into the void of cyberspace is not the true reciprocal communication about matters of substance imagined by those like Debord or Habermas who identified participation with democracy. Under these new conditions participation has no emancipatory effects.

To explain this phenomenon, Dean deploys the categories of Slavoj Žižek's interpretation of Lacanian psychoanalysis. The explanation turns on the difference between desiring what one lacks, and desiring the lack itself. This latter form of desire involves obsessive repetition in the pursuit of something elusive, which is attained so far as possible in the very pursuit of it. The pursuit itself becomes its own object and yields a kind of enjoyment that draws the individual in again and again. Anyone who has played a video game on the Internet will recognize the syndrome. In sum, Dean describes communication on the Internet on the model of obsessive-compulsive neurosis.

But the effects are not merely individual. Participation in the network shapes a subjectivity that is unable to contend with the political realities of capitalist society. This is a subject that is caught in a web of communication without content, a subject that substitutes debate for action, that mistakes participation for power. The individuals have the illusion of acting politically whenever they express an opinion or sign an online petition, but in reality they are victims of technological fetishism. The Internet does not automatically amplify their opinions into significance but simply registers them as empty placeholders for real political action. She writes, "Our participation does not subvert communicative capitalism. It drives it" (Dean, 2010: 114). The circulation of messages on the Internet thus depoliticizes the population and integrates it into communicative capitalism. Dean admits that there can be effective political uses of the Internet, but she considers these to be relatively insignificant compared to the overall depoliticizing effect of the technology in democratic societies like ours.

I find Dean's analysis of the failure of communication on the Internet persuasive up to the point where she draws these political conclusions. On what grounds does she consider the type of activity on which she focuses to be the Internet's most significant effect, able to actually reshape users' subjectivity? This is reductive. She assumes that with her explanation of Facebook, she has grasped the Internet's essence and the mechanism of political control. But she ignores many other types of online interactions. There are many sites that host serious discussions, sometimes concerning issues of political significance. Slashdot is an example. It is a meeting place for "techies." After the recent suicide of Aaron Swartz, they engaged seriously with issues of copyright and intellectual property law. Medical patients have used the Internet to inform themselves, for mutual aid and to influence health policy. In 1995 I studied the two discussion forums for ALS patients on the Prodigy computing network (Feenberg, 1996). Today I see more than 100 listed in a Google search. Examples such as these are easy to multiply, yet they play no role in Dean's explanation of the Internet.

The notion that the Internet replaces real political action inspires Malcolm Gladwell as well as Dean. In an article in *The New Yorker* he contrasts the courage of the black activists who sat in at lunch counters in the South with the trivial engagement of those who sign online petitions (Gladwell, 2010). His argument can serve as a reductio of Dean's. Gladwell confuses a means of communication that assists political action with the action it assists, and also claims that users of the Internet generally make such a confusion. But where is the evidence that the people who sign Internet petitions would have gone out into the streets in the absence of an easy alibi for staying home? I am unconvinced both by the inappropriate contrast of online communication with "real" action, and by the notion that anyone is actually dumb enough to confuse the two.

I propose an alternative hypothesis. Dean and Gladwell are not wrong to argue that on the Internet individuals are able to express political opinions before an imaginary public effortlessly and at no personal risk. This does change things, but not in the way they claim. The difference is in the testimonial value of the expression, which is much reduced when it involves no effort or risk. I think it unlikely that those who sign online petitions believe they have done something comparable to sitting in at a segregated lunch counter. They are perfectly aware that their views expressed online will not have as much impact as the same views expressed in a context that shows the full extent of their commitment. Hence they can hardly expect radical change in response to online petitions as they might from demonstrations in the street. But by the same token there is also no reason to suspect a substitution of the one for the other. If anything, the ability of dissenting views to reach a public, however imaginary, may encourage others to come forward. What is involved there is play with isolation and popularity rather than illusions about political action. The loneliness of the dissenter is reduced in a society that has the Internet.

Dean's critique depends on the notion that we have moved on from the type of capitalist society criticized by Debord and the Frankfurt School to a new stage that is based not on top-down hierarchical control and psychological introjection but, paradoxically, on free communication and participation structured in such a way as to reproduce the system. Her approach is the culmination of a trend that begins with Foucault's rejection of Marxist explanations of capitalism in terms of class power, for which he substituted his own notion of power as a play of discipline and resistance. He argued that capitalism depends less on political control than on the shaping in a wide variety of institutions of a type of subjectivity adjusted to the institutional requirements of capitalism. Today his approach seems more relevant than ever to explaining the perpetuation of capitalism in a society that offers ever more possibilities of free self-expression.

The transition to this new paradigm has inspired a great deal of recent discussion, such as Gilles Deleuze's concept of the "control society" (1992) and more recently Luc Boltanski and Eve Chiapello's (2007) concept of the "new spirit" of capitalism. Whereas the antidystopian theories of earlier critics focused on technocracy and the seductive power of consumer goods, these new critics argue that we are now faced with the self-subjugation of the population through communicative interaction and participation.

Such theories, like Dean's, are based on transformations taking place in the advanced sectors of the economy where flexible career paths, personal branding, post-Fordist participatory production methods, and now also blogging and social networking, play important roles. But the older theories of technocratic control and consumerism are still convincing. Most of the population still lives in the world they describe, ruled not by obscure protocols but by visible hierarchical superiors legitimated by claims of technical competence. The masses are attached to the system through material rewards more than through the structures of the network. Perhaps today some of those rewards take the form of enjoyment of communication as such, without hope of significance or reciprocation, as Dean explains. But this hardly replaces automobiles and home appliances, houses and sports, as basic integrative mechanisms. Furthermore, despite the cognitive chaos of the Internet, most people still accept the claims of doctors and scientists, teachers and preachers, and many people still follow political leaders and shapers of opinion in the mass media.

The discovery that communication can be absorbed into the rituals of consumer society is an important insight, but it is still the case that in this society truly free, reciprocal bottom-up communication has emancipatory potential and such communication does occur on the Internet. Indeed, every radical movement today builds on it. I therefore disagree with Dean's quasi-quantitative evaluation of the relative significance of politics versus integrative activity on the Internet. Politically significant communication may be less common than the sort of thing Dean criticizes, but it nevertheless plays an important role.

Dean's critique depends on an illusion specific to the technology of the Internet, its ability to record everything that happens on the screen. I can best explain why this is important through the metaphor of the sidewalk I introduced in the discussion of Fuchs's theory. On the sidewalk many things go on. Since we don't have transcripts of the communications that take place there, as we do for the Internet, we cannot compare the various activities on the basis of their radical political or integrative effects. Everything is discussed on the sidewalk, but surely most of it is as boring and pointless as the chatter Dean analyzes. Because it is ephemeral, no one criticizes the sidewalk for this reason. The democratic significance of free speech on the sidewalk cannot be reduced to a question of proportions.

Despite the exorbitant influence of a small number of popular web sites, there is still a great deal of variety, and room for nonconformity. Even the passive expression of dissenting opinion is an advance over the near-universal consensus in which those my age grew up. Debord's hope that an alternative to the mass media would make a difference is not wholly disappointed. We live in a far more contentious social world than the happy days of yore. It is true, to be sure, that there is little effective political resistance, but I see no evidence that the Internet is responsible for that. It cannot simply be dismissed because it has not solved the difficult conundrum of getting Americans to join radical political organizations. The cultural incapacity of Americans to create a durable Left requires a better explanation than the supposed depoliticizing effects of MoveOn.

In sum, I do not agree with Dean that the Internet as a whole is usefully characterized by the type of interaction taking place in sites such as Facebook, or that it is responsible for the weakness of Left activism today. Which brings me back to my starting point: What explains the vehemence with which the Internet is criticized by so many intellectuals today?

I believe critics like Fuchs and Dean are caught up in an internecine struggle within the contemporary intelligentsia that distracts them from important aspects of the Internet. The Internet was hailed at first in such expansive terms that a critical reaction was inevitable. It has not had the revolutionary impact that was promised, but the expectation that it would was always unrealistic. A critique based on disappointment with such an unrealistic expectation is distorted by its dependence on its object.

The collapse of the New Left created a demand for an alternative to political organization. Given the idealization of science and technology in American culture, it is not surprising that many American radicals sought a technical fix. An erroneous self-interpretation among participants in open-source programming and other types of online "commons" promised just such a fix. But clearly the Internet is not able to bear the weight of these utopian hopes. It is useful to criticize exaggerated claims, but at this point in time we should have gotten beyond the exclusive focus on them. The Internet as we know it is under attack from serious enemies; its important, if limited, contribution to democratic politics may well be extinguished in the coming years by changes in regulation and technology.

THE LAYERS OF THE INTERNET

Fuchs and Dean offer critiques of the Internet based on political economy and a cultural theory informed by psychoanalysis. They pay little attention to the technology of the Internet itself. To the extent that technology figures in their accounts at all, it appears as finished and complete, with a single dominant social impact.

The Internet is a technical system first and foremost. Its social meaning is inextricably intertwined with its technical character. By the same token, our social life is now inseparable from the technology. Much social theory fails to make this connection. We are accustomed to think about society in abstraction from the technologies that make it possible. Even Marxists tend to abstract the economic aspects of capitalism from the underlying technology.

In arguing for attention to technology I am not returning to an outmoded technological determinism. We need a method that recognizes the essentially technical character of society and the social character of technology. Just as there are divisions in society, so this method must uncover the conflictual character of the technical sphere, reflected in the ambivalence of technical systems, the potentials they contain that are foreclosed by the dominant social powers and the resistance to those powers. I call such a method "critical theory of technology," or "critical constructivism" (Feenberg, 2010: Chap. 4). It is based on ideas drawn from Frankfurt School critical theory, from Marx, and from constructivist technology studies.

From Marx and the Frankfurt School I derive the notion that important technologies in capitalist society are adapted to the requirements of the capitalist system but also contested from below. I borrow from the constructivist approach the emphasis on the role of interpretation and networks in technical development. The constructivist contribution introduces contingency into the analysis of technical development, while the Marxist contribution ties the contingent social influences on technology to hegemonic forces and counter-hegemonic struggles. Design is the terrain on which social groups increasingly attempt to advance their interests through technology.

There is a basis for this approach in one of Marx's important texts on method, the "Introduction to the Critique of Political Economy." Marx writes, "The concrete is concrete, because it is a combination of many objects with different destinations, i.e. a unity of diverse elements. In our thought, it therefore appears as a process of synthesis, as a result, and not as a starting point, although it is the real starting point and, therefore, also the starting point of observation and conception" (Marx 1904, 293).

This passage anticipates the genealogical method Foucault derives from Nietzsche. Social objects such as artifacts and institutions are assemblages of various components joined by their functional role in society rather than through an intrinsic essence. The parts may disaggregate and recombine in a different social context. Marx's example is money, which has a different form and meaning at different stages in social development. The history of an artifact or institution cannot rely on an a priori definition of a fixed substance that undergoes the impact of external accidents, but must trace transformations in its construction out of "diverse elements."

This genealogical approach can be applied to technology. An artifact's line of development appears to reveal the implications of a pre-existing essence, but in fact its elements and usages change in ways that favor some possible branches of development and foreclose others. Looking back from the standpoint of the successful branch, we project the criteria of development it fulfills back onto the origin, which then appears to initiate a teleological process. But this is an illusory teleology. A proper social history would uncover transformations rather than assuming stabilities.

In such cases the history of the object is the history of the social forces contending for control of its technical code. Technologies are complicated by the diverse interests they serve. These interests impose more or less coherent assemblages of structures and functions. Technologies may appear to depend simply on the coherence of the causal mechanisms they enlist in human purposes, but a deeper level of analysis reveals ambiguities due to the many social influences they represent.

Technologies are concrete in Marx's sense because they realize in technical form various layers of function and meaning corresponding to the actors who shape them. The transformations technologies undergo as their technical codes are contested in the public sphere take different forms. Some technical controversies are zero-sum games in which the winner takes all, but the inherent flexibility of technology often makes compromise possible. Conflicting interests may find a modus vivendi or be reconciled in the final design. In such cases each relevant social group contributes a layer to the final result. Layering is thus a useful concept for understanding the design process and competition between designs.

Design proceeds through bringing together layers of function corresponding to the various meanings actors attribute to the artifact. The study of technology must identify the layers and explain their relations. Technological closure, the standardization around a unique technical code, may involve trade-offs, compromises resulting in a less than perfect design for all parties to the controversy. But sometimes innovations satisfy all the contending parties without loss of efficiency, making alliances between actors possible where formerly there was conflict. Critical constructivism employs the concept of layering to explain these unique characteristics of technical politics.

Can we apply this approach to the Internet? From the standpoint of technology studies it seems clear that the Internet is at an early stage in its development, when many contending forces act on its design for sometimes conflicting, sometimes complementary purposes. Because Fuchs and Dean define the Internet in terms of economics and the mainstream culture of social networking, its political usages appear as anomalies. Their analyses are confined to a single layer of functionality. Another critic, Darin Barney, presents a similar view, writing that "these alternative and resistant practices still represent a tear in a salty sea of hegemonic encounters with the broad scope of digital technology and its culture. To take the measure of the present conjuncture we need careful work that documents and even promotes tactical political uses of these technologies, but we also need to place these uses in the broader context of what remains a very powerful set of technologies configured to advance and secure what Jacques Rancière has described as the 'unlimited power of wealth'" (2011). In sum, the Internet for these writers is essentially a corporate instrument, whatever other functions it may exceptionally serve.

Judgments such as this assume that business has been far more successful in corralling the Internet for its purposes than is plausible, given the enormous variety of content and initiatives that the Internet serves. But the counter-argument can go deeper than such quantitative comparisons. A serious study of the Internet must take into account its technological evolution, which is still incomplete. This refocuses the discussion. Dean cites Galloway and Thacker (2007), who criticize "the uncanny, unhuman intentionality of the network as an abstract whole" (quoted in Dean, 2010: 114). This is what she tries to explain, but the assumption that the Internet forms a "whole" is questionable. A more comprehensive understanding of the Internet would find a place for its political aspect within a complex matrix of functions. The constructivist approach allows for such complexity (Feenberg and Friesen, 2012).

Since many actors objectify their demands in the features of the technology, no simple definition can explain it. The Internet is not unified but is intrinsically divided and conflicted. The analytic problem consists in disentangling this complexity and assigning each aspect of the technology to the social forces underlying it. I will focus here on two of these forces, the business interests that are attempting to transform the Internet in accordance with their needs, and those public actors that employ features of the Internet to participate in the life of the society. They both draw on resources available on the Internet in its current multistable condition, but they emphasize different features in different combinations.

The future of the Internet depends on which actors prevail in determining its technical code. Business interests support what I will call a "consumption model" of the Internet that corresponds to a technical code incompatible with some of the requirements of what I will call the "community model." The two models coexist today in a system without clear definition. The consumption model privileges features that support commercial transactions and advertising, while the community model relies on other features that support online community and public life. The two models each vie for control of the future of the Internet, its ultimate technical code, but so far neither has been able to prevail (Feenberg and Bakardjieva, 2004).

The Internet is thus a terrain of struggle rather than a definite "thing" with a singular essence. Fuchs's argument highlights important features of the consumption model while ignoring the competing community model, which does not fit his schema. But incoherence is characteristic of a technology that is still in its early stages of development, before it reaches closure around a univocal definition of purpose. The critique of the Internet should focus on the struggle rather than assuming it is already over and done with to the exclusive advantage of business. In what follows I will attempt to unravel the complexity into the two distinct strands that describe the Internet today.

From the critical constructivist standpoint, the Internet is an ambiguous phenomenon. The struggle over its technical code is an attempt by the actors to resolve the ambiguity by privileging the layers of the technology that favor their interests. Closure around one or another technical code can occur in two different ways: through a radical simplification of the features of the Internet, or a new configuration that recombines and reconfigures those features to the satisfaction or at least the passive acceptance of all influential actors. I contend that we do not and indeed cannot know how the ambiguity will be resolved at this time. The best we can do as theorists is to chart the conflicting layers and identify the actors behind them.

The Internet has five layers appropriated by these actors for their different purposes. These layers are: nonhierarchical structure, anonymity, broadcasting, data storage, and many-to-many communication. In some cases, actors share layers, making a different use of the same resource. But in other cases, pressures to change or combine layers in new ways to accommodate special interests threaten to alter the character of the Internet. This is the scene of struggle that must be analyzed in detail to understand the state of the technology.

THE LAYERS OF THE INTERNET DEFINED

Nonhierarchical Structure

The nonhierarchical structure of the Internet complicates business applications while favouring public usages. The Internet protocol creates a disseminated network rather than a centralized system like a broadcasting network. There is no one at the helm, no Rupert Murdoch who can kill a story he does not like, no ABC or NBC that can dominate the news, no company that can dictate taste and trends. This is not to deny that advertisers get their message out, or that certain voices on the Internet are more influential than others. But that is a far cry from the kind of predictable, well-managed, central control business prefers. Neither advertising nor the politics of influence give corporations control over content comparable to their television and radio networks.

But does business want control? The picture is complicated by the huge revenues earned by Facebook and Google. These sites dedicated to communication and information sell advertising rather than entertainment. The entertainment is provided by the users themselves. What is called Web 2.0 seems to be a new model of capitalist enterprise based not on control of users but on their agency. Those who generalize from these examples claim that we have entered a new stage of capitalism which Jodi Dean calls "communicative capitalism." Successful as they are, however, they represent a small percentage of the U.S. economy. I doubt that they inaugurate a fundamental change in capitalism. Furthermore, the distribution of entertainment will dramatically increase the wealth to be extracted from the Internet. This is what everyone is waiting for, but progress has been slow.

The problem is clear from a consideration of the alternatives. A business-controlled medium such as television protects intellectual property and focuses users' attention on a restricted set of offerings and advertising. The Internet in its present form cannot come close to this model. The French Teletel system, a successful early computer network based on a different protocol, explored a promising alternative business model (Feenberg, 2010: Chap. 5). It tracked the usage of services and charged users by the minute on their phone bills. This sort of intimate detail about user activity and control of billing is simply not possible with the Internet protocol. It was not conceived with business in mind and is not adapted to its needs. The military created the Internet protocol for a system of trusted computing centers. It is still marked by this origin today. Advertising as a revenue source came rather late to the Internet and is a work-around. It is by no means clear that the advantages of targeting, made possible by data-mining social networks, compensate for the limitations imposed by the proto-col. Subscription services offer another business model, but so far they have not been very successful. This may change as more entertainment is delivered over the Internet.

Ideally, a consumption-oriented technical code would impose greater secur-ity to insure good service and better control over distribution to protect intel-lectual property. Business interests have called for an end to network neutrality to insure that commercial services such as entertainment get greater bandwidth at the expense of public usages and communication. They are making progress on this front but the struggle is by no means over. So far no technical fix such as "watermarking" has succeeded in preventing theft of intellectual property. It is difficult to say what modifications of the Internet protocol would help. Instead, business has turned to legal suppression and more recently to offering conven-ient services that attract purchasers for goods that can be accessed elsewhere at no cost. Nevertheless, the Internet has had a massive impact on the entertain-ment industry, which will continue to grow unless radical technical solutions are implemented. If such solutions prevail, the Internet would be transformed into something resembling television, a system controlled by a few networks and cable companies rather than the decentralized, nonhierarchical configuration we currently enjoy.

Anonymity

Apart from these business-related inconveniences of the nonhierarchical structure, it supports anonymity, which has favored political activity on the Internet. Anonymity protects any form of stigmatized or antisocial activity. Much of this activity has a commercial character, for example, the paid distribution of pornography. But anonymity also serves community. Individuals who would otherwise be fearful of the consequences of expressing unpopular views are free to do so in forums where they debate the issues of the day or gather with others to clarify their ideas and act. Although it is possible at some expense to break through the veil of anonymity, it has been used effectively to build political opposition. In countries under dictatorial rule anonymity has had explosive consequences. Since both commercial actors and online activists benefit from anonymity, neither has lobbied for obligatory real-name identities. That is primarily a concern of governments, a third relevant social group. But so far, at least in democratic societies, government has mainly offered legal and regulatory support for the demands of the other two actors. The surveillance and control functions of the Internet have only affected its meaning in countries such as China.

Broadcasting

Broadcasting on the Internet has the potential to reach millions. It marks an astonishing advance over earlier ways of reaching a public. The feature is free and instantaneous, which makes it attractive for many different kinds of actors. Entertainment can be delivered to mass audiences with this feature. In the consumption model the Internet functions as a replacement for television, CDs, and DVDs. Since we are only at the beginning of this development it is impossible to say how drastically it will reshape the Internet, as media companies struggle to protect their intellectual property and ensure the best possible delivery of their products. The community model also relies on broadcasting for public interventions, protests, fundraising, and other political tasks. Combined with anonymity, broadcasting is a powerful political tool. It has been used to mobilize citizens on a large scale for demonstrations and elections. Of course political movements managed earlier with technologies such as the telephone, the mimeograph machine, and the cassette tape. As Fuchs and Dean would surely agree, it is silly to call the Arab Spring a "Facebook revolution," but the Internet does offer much improved tools for rapid mass mobilization. So long as communication on the Internet is free and anonymous, broadcasting will serve both commerce and community.

Data storage

Stored data on the Internet has a variety of functions. The consumption model privileges storing the data for commercial purposes. Data is collected by the owners of social networking sites, analyzed, and sold to improve the performance of advertising. Users search the Internet for goods, which has created huge new markets linking buyers and sellers globally. Stored data is also available to governments for surveillance. Occasionally the dissenters get hold of data embarrassing to governments and corporations and publish it on the Internet for all to see. In the community model data storage need not be privately owned, although currently most online community activity takes place on proprietary networks. Even within that context, certain kinds of data access are restricted to protect privacy. Companies such as Facebook and Google promise to restrict their intrusions to data mining and not examination of individual accounts. The data is only fully available to members of each online community (and in rare cases the police). It can then be used by individuals to reconstruct their past statements and commitments, much like a diary or agenda. It is especially useful to online communities as a record of their history.

Data storage would be confined to community usages if online communities moved away from proprietary platforms or if privacy rights were interpreted to prohibit data mining. By the same token, proprietary networks threaten online community when they go too far in breaking down privacy to improve advertising. So far a rough equilibrium has been achieved in which data storage is useful to both business and ordinary users.

Many-to-many communication

The Internet supports online community, gatherings of like-minded individuals, through a unique feature, the ability of users to share a common file. Access to the file is access to all those with similar access. Messages sent to the file are seen by all, in contrast with mail and email, which are addressed to individuals rather than to a group. Online community is an important innovation. It offers the first electronic mediation of small group activity.

Most social life goes on in small groups, as well as education and political discussion. Since online communities assemble groups without regard for geographic distance, scattered individuals can come together around a theme of discussion or struggle that would otherwise be unrepresented in public life. In the early days of commercial computer networking and the Internet, many-to-many communication supported the invention of exciting new forms of sociability. This is the background to the expectation that computer networking would bring about revolutionary social change. No doubt the prophets of networking exaggerated the transformative power of technology, especially the computer. But what Dean has shown is that this expectation was disappointed not simply because of the limited impact of the technology, but because the evolution of many-to-many communication did not amplify the original pattern on which the expectation was based. Instead, a new pattern emerged in which most many-to-many communication failed to produce true community. The failed communities that characterize this stage have integrative effects.

It may well be true, as Dean contends, that most activity in online communities such as Facebook is empty of meaning. And the exploitation of the data produced by these communities is indisputable, as Fuchs argues. Indeed, there are even groups created by corporations to place products or to identify changing tastes. But the same is true in one way or another of every public venue. And there are still a great many online communities in which authentic reciprocal communication takes place. It is no surprise that capitalism seeks and finds opportunity everywhere. The critics do not explain why this should uniquely qualify the Internet when so many different kinds of groups exist engaged in so many different activities.

Online communities engage not only in conventional politics but in an expanded notion of politics in every area of common life. Medical patients form groups to share ideas about their illnesses and to influence care and research. Parents use the Internet to organize protests over school policy. Users of public resources such as parks mobilize through the Internet when the resource is threatened with budget cuts. All sorts of civic problems and frustrations become the occasion for community action. In each case the participant interests of members of a sociotechnical network are articulated politically. This "subactivism" is an extension of politics into daily life; it shifts the boundaries of the personal and the political (Bakardjieva 2012).

The ambiguity of these features explains how they can serve in very different strategies of very different actors. The dissemination of popular films, pornography, and calls to revolution all employ broadcasting. Anonymity protects criminals as well as dissenters. Online communities gather rock fans as well as revolutionaries. And so on. Different combinations of these layers favor consumption or community. In its present form the Internet is compatible with both but it will only remain hospitable to online community and the political activities it supports so long as something approaching the free flow of information and network neutrality are preserved. These conditions, which are accidental consequences of the Internet's military origins, are incompatible with the most ambitious plans of the business users of the network, but they must be protected for the Internet as we know it to survive.

CONCLUSION: A NEW DIALECTIC

The fracture in the meaning of the Internet, the multifunctionality of its features, and the struggle over its future are not unique to this technology, although they may be more visible here than elsewhere. All technologies establish networks in the sense that they bring people and things together in combinations determined by a mix of symbolic and causal relations. And many of these technological networks are traversed by contradictory programs representing different and conflicting interests. The tendency to define the network by the program of the dominant group enrolled in it must be resisted. All programs are equal in principle. Each has a claim to appropriate the network's resources and to attempt to organize the network around the interests it represents (Feenberg, 1999: 114–19).

Consider the case of a factory belonging to owners who organize it to make a profit, its workers who attempt to defend or enlarge their share in the wealth it produces, and its community that imposes limitations on its activities in response to externalities such as pollution. Legally considered, the owners' program defines the only legitimate purpose of the factory, but in reality no one party has a monopoly of its resources. Each actor views it from a different perspective, which reveals different aspects and privileges different modes of action. All three must coexist, and therefore must make concessions to each other. Their programs and compromises may alter the technologies that bring them together.

This is the pattern we observe in the case of the Internet, with frequent overlapping of functions and occasional conflicts. Most users of the Internet are at ease in its complexity and don't try to sum it up in a single concept. They shift from one program (in both senses) to another as the need arises. But the critics have selected one aspect of the whole and conceptualized the entire network on the terms of a single program. I have attempted here to restore the ambiguity and the complexity of the network by analyzing it as a contested technology.

In this respect technology is an instance of a much larger problem, the ambiguity of rationality itself. The critics of the Internet propose a radical revision of the Frankfurt School's dialectic of Enlightenment. The original dialectic in Theodor Adorno and Max Horkheimer showed that progress in rationality has not had the liberating effects the Enlightenment expected. Dean proposes a structurally similar theory. We expected participation and communication to be liberating but in fact they have had the opposite effect. Dean has developed a version of the concept of integration through protocol, through the structure of interaction, which was pioneered by Michel Foucault and Gilles Deleuze. Presumably, we have entered a new stage in the development of capitalism in which people self-integrate through their interactions, without the need for the legitimation strategies and consumer rewards that integrated the society at an earlier stage.

Dean's analysis of the Internet is comparable to Herbert Marcuse's theory of repressive desublimation. Marcuse showed that lifting the repression of sexuality did not have the emancipatory consequences one might have expected but instead strengthened the grip of the system. Like Marcuse deflating the politics of sexual liberation, Dean deflates the politics of cyberspace. But like Marcuse, Adorno and Horkheimer were careful to propose a rational critique of reason (Horkheimer and Adorno, 2002: xvi). They were aware that there is a risk in criticizing coopted emancipatory advances. The risk is that one will lose sight of the advance itself in the critique of its cooptation by the system. Underestimating what has been gained in criticizing the cooptation of emancipatory advances results in political paralysis.

In fact, there is far more critical thought and radical political action today as compared with the high point of the mass media in the 1950s and the early 1960s. Dean's theory is one-sided. It leaves out the uncoopted uses of the technology that still have liberating implications. We need to study the Internet in much more careful empirical terms in order to understand this ambiguity as it applies to communication and participation. This is what I propose in arguing that the Internet is a contested technology.

This approach shows that condemnation of the Internet is premature. There are more pressing problems today than refuting Internet hype. What about the corporate forces attempting to take over the content of the Internet for the distribution of entertainment? And the intensification of government surveillance?

How can such challenges be defeated when we focus our critical energies on precisely the aspect of the Internet that is threatened by these hegemonic forces, namely, its communicative role? It is time to move on from counterhype to a serious confrontation with these threats to the Internet, imperfect though it be. It is still an evolving technology at an early stage in its evolution. We do not know what final form it will take. Keeping an open mind about the Internet's future is not a naïve, uncritical stance but, on the contrary, makes political engagement with that future possible.

REFERENCES

Bakardjieva, Maria. 2012. "Subactivism: Lifeworld and Politics in the Age of the Internet." In (Re)Inventing the Internet, eds. Andrew Feenberg and Norm Friesen, 85–108. Rotterdam: Sense Publishers.

Barney, Darin. 2011. Interviewed by Laureano Ralon for Figure/Ground Communication, April 12. Accessed November 15, 2012. http://figureground.ca/interviews/darin-barney/.

Boltanski, Luc, and Eve Chiapello. 2007. The New Spirit of Capitalism. Trans. Gregory Elliot. London: Verso.

Dean, Jodi. 2005. "Communicative Capitalism: Circulation and the Foreclosure of Politics." Cultural Politics 1: 51–74.

———. 2010. Blog Theory: Feedback and Capture in the Circuits of Drive. Cambridge: Polity Press.

Debord, Guy. 1994. The Society of the Spectacle. Trans. Donald Nicholson-Smith. New York: Zone.

Deleuze, Gilles. 1992. "Postscript on the Societies of Control." October 59: 3–7.

Feenberg, Andrew. 1996. "The On-Line Patient Meeting," principal author with CNS staff. Journal of Neurological Sciences 139: 129–31.

———. 1999. Questioning Technology. New York: Routledge.

———. 2010. Between Reason and Experience: Essays in Technology and Modernity. Cambridge, MA: MIT Press.

Feenberg, Andrew, and Maria Bakardjieva. 2004. "Consumers or Citizens? The Online Community Debate." In Community in the Digital Age, eds. Andrew Feenberg and Darin Barney. Lanham: Rowman and Littlefield.

Feenberg, Andrew, and Norm Friesen, eds. 2012. (Re)Inventing the Internet. Rotterdam: Sense Publishers.

Fuchs, Christian. 2010. "Labor in Informational Capitalism and on the Internet." The Information Society: An International Journal 26(3): 179–96.

———. 2011. *Foundations of Critical Media and Information Studies*. London and New York: Routledge.

———. 2014a. *Occupy Media! The Occupy Movement and Social Media in Crisis Capitalism*. Winchester, U.K., and Washington, D.C.: Zero Books.

———. 2014b. "Critique of the Political Economy of Informational Capitalism and Social Media." In *Critique, Social Media and the Information Society*, eds. Christian Fuchs and Marisol Sandoval. New York and London: Routledge.

Galloway, Alexander R., and Richard Thacker. 2007. *The Exploit: A Theory of Networks*. Minneapolis: University of Minnesota Press, 2007.

Gladwell, Malcolm. 2010. "Small Change: Why the Revolution Will Not Be Tweeted." *The New Yorker*, 10 October. http://www.newyorker.com/reporting/2010/10/04/101004fa_fact_gladwell.

Horkheimer, Max, and Theodor W. Adorno. 1944. *The Dialectic of Enlightenment: Philosophical Fragments*. Ed. Gunzelin S. Noerr. Trans. Edmund Jephcott. Stanford, CA: Stanford University Press, 2002.

Marx, Karl. 1904. *A Contribution to the Critique of Political Economy*. Trans. N. I. Stone. Chicago: Charles H. Kerr.

Williams, Raymond. 1974. *Television: Technology and Cultural Form*. London: Fontana.

2 Emergent Meaning in the Information Age

Ian Angus

IS THERE A CRISIS OF MEANING PRODUCED BY THE DIGITIZATION OF CULTURE?

In his path-breaking work of the 1930s, *The Crisis of European Sciences and Transcendental Phenomenology*, Edmund Husserl argued that European culture had *necessarily* fallen into a crisis of meaning due to the hegemony of Galilean science with its mathematization of nature over the modern concept of knowledge (Husserl, 1970: 5–7). Since meaning and value were not a part of the objectivistic model of Galilean science, this hegemony reduced issues of meaning and value to subjective-relative prejudices outside the sphere of reason. Only a new form of science that would incorporate a conception of subjectivity within itself could restore meaning and value to the centre of the concept of reason and thereby overcome the crisis.

The necessary loss and restoration of meaning was embedded in the mathematization of nature, whereby nature was understood as fundamentally a mathematical structure underneath qualitative and subjective appearance. The relation between number and experience as a world-historical theme is investigated by other philosophers beside Husserl, of course. Martin Heidegger described information as

> the appraisal that as quickly, comprehensively, unequivocally, and profitably as possible acquaints contemporary humanity with the securing of its necessities, its requirements, and their satisfaction. . . . For the determination of language first of all creates the sufficient grounds for the construction of thinking machines and the building of frameworks for large calculations. . . . As an appraisal, information is also the arrangement that places all objects and stuffs in a form for humans that suffices to securely establish human domination over the whole earth and even over what lies beyond this planet. (Heidegger. 1996: 124)

While this formulation states what is at issue in information as a world-historical form, it states it as a matter of the rule of number over experience, such that the implication can only be (in a manner characteristic of Heidegger's philosophy) the setting-aside of number for experience, which is stated as an ontology. Thus, his meditation ends by asking, "Are we obliged to find paths upon which thinking is capable of responding to what is worthy of thought instead of, enchanted by calculative thinking, mindlessly passing over what is worthy of thought?" (Heidegger, 1996: 129). While thought indeed needs to pass beyond entrapment within number-thinking, this way of formulating the issue leaves out the possibility that it is number-thinking itself that needs to be thought. Ontology is assumed as a "simply beneath" that can be rediscovered by setting aside the world of abstraction from which number is generated.

Alain Badiou similarly characterizes the rule of number in world-historical form, though in reverse image to the Heideggerian priority of ontology over number. He claims in similar terms to both Heidegger and Husserl that "the reign of number . . . imposes the fallacious idea of a bond between numericality and value, or truth" (2008: 213), but in order to assert that "number is a form of being, and that, far from being subtended by the function of the subject, it is on the contrary the basis of number . . . that the function of the subject receives its small share of being" (2008: 25). Ontology is thus reduced to the presentation of the bare "x" of number theory.

> The first presented multiplicity without concept has to be a multiple of nothing. . . . Ontology commences, ineluctably, once the legislative Ideas of the multiple are unfolded, by the pure utterance of the arbitrariness of a proper name. This name, indexed to the void, is, in a sense

that will always remain enigmatic, the proper name of being. (Badiou, 2007: 57–59)

By reducing ontology to number, in mirror-image to Heidegger's reduction of number to ontology, Badiou can assert that the primary ontological being is the "x" grounded in set theory—that is to say, a being of no particular sort whose being is only such as to be one of a certain multiplicity.

Only Husserl formulates the issue precisely as one of tracing back the sedimented meanings of formal abstractions to their ground in the lifeworld such that they can be *reactivated* through phenomenological intuition. It is not only a question of *both* number and ontology but of *the precise connection between* number and ontology. This is what is at issue in the Husserlian problematic of "grounding," or the tracing of abstractions back to their origin in immediate intuition. But I do not want to simply apply a Husserlian account of intuition to the contemporary problem of the cultural meaning of number. Instead, I want to use this contemporary problem to motivate an inquiry into meaning that will require revision of Husserlian phenomenology to complete. While taking its cue from Husserl's investigation, the current issue is whether contemporary digitization of culture poses a crisis for knowledge comparable to the crisis of the sciences: does the digitization of knowledge undermine the experience and concept of subjectivity that could ground an integration of reason with meaning and value?

WHAT IS THE DIGITIZATION OF CULTURE?

In beginning to define the phenomenon of the digitization of culture, we can take a clue from the structure of the word "digitization" itself, in which the suffix "-ization" means "putting into the form of," where the form in question is "digit," or, more commonly, "digital." Digitization is an active process of putting into digital form that which is not initially in such a form. It is of course the case that contemporary cultural products may be inscribed directly into digital form, but cultural products as a whole have not been in a digital form. Digitization of culture refers both to the direct inscription of cultural products into digital form and the putting of cultural products not in that form into digital form. It is thus both a primary and a secondary cultural process: primary in the sense that it affects the form of some contemporary cultural products in their process of production and secondary in the sense that those that are not so affected in the process of production are secondarily affected by being subsequently translated into that form. Digitization not only says something about the leading edge of the contemporary cultural process but also something about how the contemporary cultural process incorporates and transforms cultural production and heritage that does not occur at this leading edge.

Digitization is most often defined through the sign system in which it is expressed. As is well known, the digital form is a series of ones and zeros in a binary code. A complex code, a code with many possibilities for inscription of a signifier, conveys a great deal of information with a very few signs. For example, since the English alphabet contains twenty-six signifiers, the mere inscription of a single signifier excludes twenty-five possibilities. A code of several hundred signifiers would exclude several hundred minus one possibility at each inscription. A binary code, by contrast, excludes only one other sign and thus conveys very little information with each inscription. If, however, a very large number of inscriptions are made, a very simple code can convey a large amount of information. A cultural product in digital form is a number, that is to say, an abstract formal sign that, like any sign, is understood as such within a certain code. The simplicity of the binary code requires that the number be exceptionally long. It is this combination of a minimal code and very large capacity for storage that defines digitalization in a technical sense. Texts, photographs, and so on in digital form are expressed as extremely long binary numbers and it is the difference between these numbers that expresses the difference between the cultural products.

Number is a basic and pervasive aspect of human experience. More exactly, the fundamental human experience of speaking can be investigated by formal disciplines that abstract certain features of speech for scientific determination. The formal discipline that studies number concerns itself with the relation between different contents such that they can be collectively connected together. Such collective connection is the essence of counting with numbers. Jacob Klein noted that reflection on speaking leads to the formal disciplines of grammar and logic, but that also

> the act of speaking presupposes the distinguishing of one word from
> another and the relating of one word to another. It presupposes, that is,
> counting. For counting is distinguishing and at the same time relating
> one thing to another. At all times, therefore, speaking and the thinking
> involved in it have been understood as a sort of computing. This does

not mean that in speaking we have an explicit knowledge of numbers. But reflecting and pursuing our exploratory questioning, we arrive at the formal discipline of arithmetic, that is, the science of numbers and their relations on which all our computing is based. (Klein, 1985: 164)

Number is in this sense a formal knowledge of a fundamental aspect of human speech. Digitization relies on this formal discipline to express cultural products as numbers.

Application of the theory of number to digitization yields only a *technical definition*, however: that is to say, a definition of its internal structure. It does not extend to the use of number in human making or doing, nor, more specifically, to the role of digitization in human culture. While cultural products are expressed digitally as numbers, they function to give *a certain form* to culture in its role within human experience. We may call this a *cultural definition* of digitization that would pertain to its primary and secondary roles in culture and the formation of such culture from human experience. For the institution of digital culture, it is not the form of number that matters primarily, but the function of the form of number in human experience and the inserting of this form as the basic process of cultural formation and transmission.

A cultural definition of the digitization of culture is inseparable from the question about the institution of digital culture and the question of whether it provokes a crisis by undermining the integration of reason with meaning and value.

The form of culture constituted by digitization of culture is constituted by the primary and secondary processes of translating culture into numerical form but also making it available within human experience. Clearly, in the secondary process, where a preexisting cultural form is translated into digital form—such as the scanning of a text or photograph and insertion of that scan within a downloadable document—the digital form is a *representation* of another cultural form (a cultural form that is itself a representation, for example, a text or image) in the sense that it both refers back to that prior form and contains the content of that prior form within itself. Furthermore, it refers back in such a way that the content of that form is made available through the digital form, so that it is not only a representation of a prior form but also an *experiential form* which is experienced itself as a cultural content. At least in the case of the secondary process, digitization is both the representation of a cultural form and a cultural form itself. In the case of the primary process of digitization of culture, where a cultural content is inscribed directly into digital form—such as the writing of a text on a computer or taking a photograph on a digital camera and its insertion within a downloadable document—it is clearly a cultural content as an experiential form. Because of the digital form of inscription, however, the cultural content is already "copiable," or, more exactly, *producible without restriction* (since there is no original) and communicable and therefore *represented* so that—even though there is no *prior* cultural form to which it refers—the digital form refers to the cultural content that it itself is.

Thus, the digital form of culture, whether as a primary or secondary process, is both a cultural content and the representation of that same cultural content. The numerical form of digitization, its internal form as captured by a technical definition, when applied to cultural content expressing human experience, enables an identity of that cultural content with its representation. Digital culture is this making-identical of content and representation through the numerical form described in the technical definition of digitization.

Since the content of a cultural expression contains cultural knowledge, and the representation of cultural content makes that knowledge available in a shared framework, digitization of culture is both knowledge and communication. Because of the identity of content and representation in digitization, knowledge and the communication of this same knowledge become identical. The form of digitization collapses the distinction between knowledge and communication—between what is known and persuasion to utilize what is known, or, in the widest possible optic, between science and rhetoric (Angus, 2005). The digitization of culture inaugurates the collapse of this classical distinction because the relation that it establishes between numerical form and cultural content establishes the representation and thus *repeatability* of this cultural content identically with the inscription of the cultural content itself. The digitization of culture institutes *information* as identically the content and representation of culture. In order to understand the concept of information as the central institution of digital culture, we must understand how it collapses knowledge into the form of information and communication into the form of information, such that information is both knowledge and its communication. Information is thus the cultural definition of the digitization of culture that raises the question of whether information provokes a crisis for culture by undermining the integration of reason—which now takes the form of information—with meaning and value. The ground for a retrospective investigation of the institution of digital culture is the contemporary *convergence of knowledge and its communication based upon an inscription that is simultaneously the representation of itself.*

INFORMATION AS FORM OF KNOWLEDGE

Information is a form of knowledge that consequently refers to an aspect of the world about which it is knowledge. It formulates, or gives a certain form, to that knowledge. That form is distinct from other forms of knowledge about the world—say, in speaking, or writing, or drawing—even though these other forms can retrospectively be characterized as containing information. Knowledge in the form of information is a historical latecomer that nevertheless can be used to describe some common content of other forms of knowledge.

Information as Cybernetic Circuit
The form of knowledge in information conveys two fundamental aspects of knowledge: its quantitative aspect and its relational aspect. Information is knowledge of which one may have "more" or "less," "enough" or "too much." It is knowledge understood primarily from the side of its quantity, even though to characterize this quantity it requires a reference to "context," we usually say very generally, but more exactly to the relational aspect of that information. One has enough or too much information in relation to other information with a greater or lesser proximity, or relevance, to the information in question. The quantity of information is defined through its relational aspect and the relational aspect is defined through an information system. An information system is an organized array of mutually pertinent information.

We may recall here that a cybernetic system—such as a house with a heating regulator inside itself—functions as an internally organized, self-steering, self-correcting, system in relation to its environment such that, while the organization of the internal system responds to the external environment, it is its internal organization that defines the nature of this response.

> Feedback is a method of controlling a system by reinserting into it the results of its past performance. If these results are merely used as numerical data for the criticism of the system and its regulation, we have the simple feedback of the control engineers. If, however, the information which proceeds backward from the performance is able to change the general method and pattern of performance, we have a process which may well be called learning. (Wiener, 1954: 61)

Internal self-regulation distances each internal component from its environment by routing this relation through the totality of internal organization. Each internal component of the system reacts to environmental influence through the structuring of the whole system and not individually. This internal organization, which thereby achieves a high degree of self-monitoring and self-correction, is constituted by each internal component of the system functioning as *information* for the other components.

A person inside a house with an internal heating regulator benefits from the maintenance of the temperature of the house at an approximately even level—say between 18 and 20 degrees centigrade—and does not normally need to pay attention to when the heater is functioning and when it is off. However, should the person feel too cold, then it is possible for that person to raise the temperature of the self-regulating sensor a couple of degrees. Ideally, this resetting of the regulator achieves a new equilibrium at which the person feels more comfortable. Note here two things: that changing the regulating level of a self-regulating system, in this simple case, requires an actor who resets the sensor. If the sensor could reset itself, except on a preset model such as a recording device that regularly resets daytime and nighttime sensor temperatures, it arguably becomes a living system because the sensor becomes an actor.

> This circular organization constitutes a homeostatic system whose function is to produce and maintain this very same circular system by determining that the *components* that specify it be those whose synthesis or maintenance it secures. Furthermore, this circular organization defines a living system as a unit of interactions and is essential for its maintenance as a unit; that which is not in it is external to it or does not exist. The circular organization in which the *components* that specify it are those whose synthesis or maintenance it secures in a manner such that the product of their functioning is the same functioning organization that produces them, is the living organization. (Maturana and Varela, 1980: 9)

In responding as a self-organized system to environmental prodding, such that the sensor resets itself differently to monitor the functioning of the system as a whole, the sensor acts as the overseer of the whole information system—the part that regulates the whole in response to environmental prodding. This would be the bottom line of a biological, living system as opposed to the physical, first-order cybernetic one.

The second thing to note is that the person who feels cold *feels cold*. From the viewpoint of the system, the feeling cold functions as information for the resetting of the regulator. Feeling cold becomes information by being set within the relational context of other information such that it functions as information. But one can feel cold without it becoming such information. I may simply remain cold because it is not my house to alter or because I can't afford more oil or gas. Information contains a reference to what I called previously a "cultural content," or in this case a physiocultural state of feeling cold, but *it is not this aspect of material cultural content itself.* This is precisely what is achieved by the intensification of internal organization such that reference to the environment is routed through the totality of the system rather than each component individually so responding. *The form of information is quantitative relation to other information within an organized system, not directly to states of affairs outside those relations.* The development of the concept of information from that of a self-regulating, cybernetic system means that information is simultaneously both the movement of information within a system and the self-monitoring and self-regulation of that system. Practice and the theory of that practice collapse in cybernetic information. Knowledge has become information in a form that converges with its communication.

FROM INFORMATION TO EMERGENT MEANING

This preliminary characterization of information as a quantitative and relational form of knowledge allows a more detailed schematization of levels of complexity of information. This schematization elaborates a cultural definition of digitization, which refers to the way number in its digital systematization functions within human experience by inserting this form into the basic process of cultural formation and transmission.

The smallest amount of information is the piece.[a] A *piece of information* can only be defined as the smallest amount with reference to the topic or theme in relation to which it functions as information—that is to say, the relational totality of relevant information. This determination is impossible without a

---

a In *Love the Questions: University Education and Enlightenment* I used the term "bit" but distinguished it from its technical meaning. It now seems clearer to adopt a different terminology entirely for the cultural definition and classification of information (Angus, 2009: 113–6).

much greater and more complex arrangement of information than the piece itself. There is always more than one piece of information but the *relevance* of a piece depends upon a totality of information, not its reference to an element of the experienced world, and can in that sense only be defined retrospectively, as it were, as a piece of a totality. This totality of information can appear in two forms: as an indeterminate multitude of other pieces of information or as a totality organized by a theme. Here we have, *in nuce*, the cultural problem of information: there is a great deal of it and it isn't necessarily organized into a meaningful whole. The problem of the meaning and value of the digitization of culture is in large part contained in the issue of how a plethora of pieces of information might be selected and organized to become a meaningful whole. And the cultural failure to be able to institutionalize this process of selection and organization may indeed be called a "crisis of culture."

We may distinguish three higher-level collectivities of pieces of information that are built upon this primitive piece. There is a *pile* of information, which is an unorganized larger collection with indefinite magnitude made up of individual pieces of information. Such a pile exhibits the cultural crisis: we have piles of information without a sense of the relevance of piece to pile or overlap of piles. We are awash in such a plurality of piles, so much so that the coherence that a culture requires to organize its sense of meaning and value is essentially lacking. We don't know when we have enough information, when we have too much, or whether the information being gathered is of any real relevance.

Out of several piles of information, a *bunch* of information might, under certain conditions, be constituted—and here we would have the first step out of the crisis. I use the term "bunch" here thinking of a bunch of grapes or flowers, or fingers bunched into a fist. It signifies in the first place a significant number—at least a pile, and maybe several piles—but, more important, a pile with a certain sort of discernible, though perhaps weak, organization within itself. Flowers are bunched by florists according to their shape and colour; grapes are bunched by the logic of growth in their stems; a fist is bunched by its fingers and cannot contain a toe. The transformation of a pile, or several piles, into a bunch involves the problem of *emergent organization* that can, if sufficiently followed through, lead to the organization of knowledge in the form of information into cultural knowledge pertinent to the organization and persistence of a culture in time and space. If we can determine, in micro-logical fashion, what happens to turn a pile into a bunch, then we begin to address the construction of cultural meaning in the age of information.

Bunches of information can be collected into a *discourse*. By a discourse I mean an organized presentation of bunches of information that elaborates a coherent perspective on a theme. The term "discourse" breaks from the primarily quantitative terminology that precedes it to emphasize the internal qualitative organization that it achieves, such that cultural meaning is expressed and the discourse itself can enter into a wider relation between discourses that address cultural value.

Now, all I have done here is to propose a terminology that aims to aid the definition of the problem of the crisis of culture in the age of information. The terminology can neither solve the problem nor even assert that the problem can be, in principle, resolved. It does, however, pinpoint where such a resolution is to be sought and what would constitute the possibility of such a resolution. How, out of the combination of higher collectivities of pieces of information, can a meaningful whole emerge that would be comparable to earlier discourses of cultural meaning and value that did not begin from the quantitative and relational form of information?

The fundamental difference that distinguishes this proposed form of *emergent meaning* from information from earlier meaningful cultural wholes is that such wholes were articulated in the first place as wholes with parts whose place within the whole was thereby determined. Their relative natural worldview, to use Max Scheler's terminology (Scheler, 1980: 74), was given as a whole whose wholeness expressed meaning and value. Their problem, therefore, was to ask how a given situation that implicated a distinct part of the cultural whole could be understood and evaluated in relation to that cultural whole. Questions were oriented, first, to how this situation should be characterized in relation to distinct parts of the cultural whole and, second, to how the cultural whole determined the meaning and value of the part. Our problem is the inverse, though not the extant inverse. In any situation there is a plethora of information. Any piece of information coexists with an indefinite, but very large, plurality of other pieces of information. Every piece of information thus appears within an indefinite horizon represented by the Internet as the source of multitudes of more information. Our problem is how individual pieces of information within this indefinite horizon can become sufficiently organized to express cultural meaning and not fall back into the persistent background buzz of accumulating information.

Out of this organization, through the process of emergent meaning—if there can indeed be such a process—would be constructed a *subject* of discourse that could engage in the constitution of cultural meaning and value. The many discourses today that lament the decline of the subject, and the crisis of meaning, basically assume that such a process of emergent meaning is impossible, so that contemporary digitized culture cannot be a culture in anything like the sense in which we used to talk about cultural meaning. A contemporary subject of cultural meaning would be an emergent property of higher-level collectivities of information.

Overcoming the crisis of meaning and value produced by the digitization of culture would have to show that such emergent structure that could confer subjectivity and meaning is indeed possible under certain conditions even in the age of information. But before addressing this fundamental issue, let us address the second aspect of information brought forward by the collapse of knowledge and its communication: information as a medium of translation between media of communication.

INFORMATION AS MEDIUM OF TRANSLATION

Prior to the convergence of knowledge and its communication in information, one could distinguish between knowledge as a cultural content and its communication, or, in classical terms, philosophy and rhetoric (Angus, 2005). Communication can be studied from the viewpoint of its cultural content and its influence on the sociocultural formation or it can be studied from the viewpoint of the *medium of communication* that conveys the cultural content from place to place, or subject to subject, to exert an influence. If one focuses on the cultural content of communication, the specificity of the medium of communication recedes, whereas if one focuses on the medium of communication, the cultural content recedes in favour of the material relations constituted by the medium. Since the phenomenon of the digitization of culture includes within itself the possibility of the communication of cultural content—that is to say, the dispersal through the internet and related channels—focus on the medium of communication is essential to pose the question of the implications for meaning and value.

Theory of Media of Communication

A medium of communication sets up a relationship between a point of origin and a point of termination of the communication that is inscribed within a given medium; for example, a relationship between a speaker, author, or sender and an auditor, reader, or receiver. The nature of this relationship is defined by the specific character of the medium in each case. So that the relationship between speaker and auditor, in the case of the medium of speech, sets up a face-to-face relation that, consequently, includes aspects of appearance, gesture, and timbre. Author and reader are separated by an indefinite distance and therefore do not meet face to face, but through a text that is written on paper, papyrus, scroll, or computer screen. Appearance, gesture, and timbre are absent but finished, repeatable, and portable text allows for an individual distanced from surrounding social relations to be absorbed in the meaning of the text, to reflect upon it, to return to check it, and to later communicate with other readers of the same text (who read it at widely separated times and places). The study of various media of communication and their inherent features, including the way in which they affect social relationships and the circulation of meaning in a culture, is now an established field of study that is nowadays called "media ecology" (Angus, 2000: 37–38).[1]

In the context of the digitization of culture, however, the main concern is not the shifting relationships among media of communication, the media ecology, but rather the status of digitized communications within the media ecology. It is often unclear whether the digital medium should be treated as a new medium of communication, in principle comparable to other media such as speech, scroll, book, radio, television, and so on, or whether it is an influence—perhaps an external influence based in electric or computer technology—that acts on all media. The latter captures something of the truth, insofar as any content of any medium can be given a digital form. This is why digitization poses a crisis for cultural meaning and value and is not just a shift within the media ecology. But a closer look will allow a more exact definition.

If we look at a computer screen as a contemporary user experiences it, we experience in succession written text, recorded speech, diagrams and illustrations, photographs, music, musical notation, and more. Each of these might previously have been considered a separate medium. But nowhere do we experience "the digital" as the content of the screen. The computer screen that connects with other computer screens does set up a determinate lateral relation between users. Much has been made of the "network" relation that computer communication constitutes. Enthusiasts often claim that such non-hierarchical networks prefigure a new form of democracy, whereas conservatives wonder whether the speed and immediacy of contact eliminates the space required for reflective thought.

The social relationship that inheres in computer communication is indeed of the network kind and this is undoubtedly of great significance, but neither can it be overlooked that the different media of communication that appear on the screen suggest that digital communication is not a medium in the same sense as the other media that it often uses and portrays.

Let us note a couple of aspects of this situation: First, while different media and their contents are portrayed, or *represented*, on the screen as a content, this is done in a manner that re-embeds them within the network social relations of digital communication. As Marshall McLuhan often reminded us (McLuhan, 1964: 60), media are not simply separate; in the media ecology, the content of a new medium is often an old medium. The huckster, the town crier, and the play appear on television, for example. In so doing, the previous media become content (in the sense that they are what is represented) while the social relations that were *constituted* by the old medium disappear in the new. It seems clear that this also happens with digital communication: books downloaded to be read appear *alongside* other digital possibilities and *within* the network of social relations that they constitute. In this sense, digitization is a medium resembling previous media, in that its constitutive social relations resituate those of other media as its manifest content.

We should note also, however, that the fact that these materials appear alongside each other allows for them to be edited and assembled in new ways. Again, we may see an analogy in the way that television allowed selling, announcing, and entertaining to enter into new relationships. But there is something more going on with digitization: all of these media forms—including the computer form, if we wish—can be translated into and out of each other through digitization, such that *digitization is a universal medium of translation of cultural contents*. It translates the contents of any medium into itself and thus can, with great speed, edit and reassemble them, and then re-embed the new content in another medium—either itself or in printed form as a book, a photo, and more. The aspects of representation and constitution are in principle collapsed through a universal medium of translation, even though the final content becomes re-embedded in a specific medium where the constitutive social relations of that medium apply. This distinction is not often clear because we tend to assume—living, as we do, within the predominance of the digital medium— that the re-embedding will always be of digital form. This, even though we often print up written texts and use them as if they were written manuscripts at academic conferences in a manner no different than many years ago.

Digitization functions as both a universal medium of translation and also as a specific medium comparable to others, in that its specific network social relations prevail when re-embedding is within the digital form.[2] Digitization is both a specific medium of communication and a medium of translation between media of communication. While previous media translated prior media when appropriate and possible, digitization is distinguished by its possibility of universal translation and also by the fact that, since it obviously coexists with itself, re-embedding of the translated contents is likely to be within the digital medium. Perhaps we should reserve this latter possibility for consideration of the digitization of culture: not only the translating of all prior cultural content into digital form but the re-embedding of the products of such translation within the digital medium.

Digitization and Cultural Meaning

We need, then, to isolate what aspects of this full digital medium of both translation and communication pose issues for cultural meaning and value. It is no secret that the key aspect of digital translation and communication is speed. Conversely, we may say that every form of limited translation between media prior to digitization required an essential *delay* characteristic of the medium in question. A culture, which may be defined as a media ecology in temporary equilibrium, is defined formally by the speed, or delay, in translation between media. It is defined substantially by the cultural content transmitted through the media ecology—which is to say, equally by those silences constituted by what is untranslatable between media of communication in the media ecology. Delay in translation sets the formal boundaries of cultural content and innovation, whereas the cultural content that is itself communicated is simultaneously haunted by the impossible translations of content that construct the cultural *unconscious*—that which is not sayable within the media ecology and/or pushed to its margins by the dominant media. Thus, one structuring feature of digital culture is nearly simultaneous translation/communication such that the boundaries of previously separate cultures are routinely transgressed. Such transgression means that products of digital culture are necessarily interpreted within different cultural meanings than those that dominated during their production. Digital culture in this sense subverts any established context of interpretation and replaces such previously stable contexts with the necessity for an interpreter to *establish* a context of interpretation.[3] Cultural interpretation becomes *transversal* and abandons the problem of *depth*. To summarize, while previous cultural productions were produced and interpreted within relatively stable contexts of meaning, so that it was the search for an adequate interpretation that dominated cultural meaning, contemporary digital culture produces the search for a relevant context of interpretation and tends to regard any proffered interpretation as simply one possible interpretation among others (Poster, 2006).

If we understand culture at least provisionally in this fashion, as defined by the media ecology, then two characteristics of digitization stand out: First, speed of translation and communication means that delay in translation between media is increasingly reduced to zero. Second, digitization as a universal medium of translation means that the silences produced by impossible translations are increasingly reduced to zero. This is the basis of the common observation that information is accelerating beyond all capacity to follow it while the meaning of such information is increasingly hard to fathom. Digitization of culture does indeed pose a crisis for culture because, without delay and silence, culture approximates a pure transparency without stabilized meaning. This transparency is often the subject of either utopian praise or dystopian blame because it undermines any stable context of meaning, but it is more significant at this point to ask what such transparency does to contemporary possibilities for the interpretation of cultural meaning—for "crisis" understood as both loss and recovery, in Husserl's sense.

The form of communication as information through universal translation between media means that communication converges with knowledge. A meta-medium of translation is the basis for defining the specific form of knowledge inherent in each medium. Communication in this form converges with knowledge as self-monitoring to become the form of information.

DOES DIGITIZATION PROVOKE A CRISIS OF MEANING AND VALUE?

The difficulty of a diagnosis of crisis is that one has to show how a grave issue arises *necessarily*, and not merely contingently, within the current situation and, simultaneously, through this same diagnosis, how this grave issue can be overcome. Crisis is neither decline nor ascent. It is a moment of decision in which the necessity of decline and the possibility of ascent are grounded in the phenomenon itself such that diagnosis points the way to a possible solution even though it cannot guarantee an outcome. Cultural crisis encapsulates our own struggles with meaning and value. Out of the cultural definition of information we need to clarify the necessity of decline and the possibility of ascent. This is the substance of our conclusion.

Information becomes the central institution of digital culture by collapsing knowledge into the form of information and communication into the form of information, such that information is both knowledge and its communication. Digitization of culture is instituted as both knowledge and communication that is identically the content and representation of culture, its *doing* as well as its *monitoring*, in the form of information. This convergence, or collapse, of classical distinctions between content/representation, practice/theory, and knowledge/communication clarifies the ground of the institution of digital culture. The above sections investigated information-as-knowledge and information-as-communication *separately*, in order to clarify the nature of this convergence.

The question animating this analysis is the significance for meaning and value of the digitization of culture. In investigating information as knowledge earlier in this chapter, we have seen that information as knowledge poses the issue of how emergent meaning can appear in successively more complex collectivities of information built up out of its simple pieces. The core of this question—how quantity of information can turn into a structuring quality—was posed above, though not yet addressed directly. In investigating information as communication in that section of this chapter, we have seen that information as a medium of translation poses the issue of a culture increasingly tending toward transparency. Since information collapses the distinction between knowledge and the communication of this same knowledge, it is time, in conclusion, for us to address how both of these aspects of information stand with the crisis of meaning and value in digitized culture.

Let us state in summary form the characteristics of information that allow us to understand it as the institution of digital culture: information is both knowledge and its communication, content and representation; it operates within a self-monitoring and self-regulating network; it is a universal medium of translation of cultural contents which can define the knowledge-boundaries of different media of communication.

Our two parallel inquiries lead us to the two convergent aspects of the fundamental situation of the digitization of culture: Since every piece of information occurs within a horizon that includes an indefinite and very large number of pieces of information, how can an emergent structure appear within a pile of information? Since the speed of digital translation and communication reduces the delay traditionally attached to cultural translation and communication to

approximately zero, which means that the silences that constitute the unconscious of a cultural form also reduce to relatively zero, how can meaning and
value congeal within the context of such a transparency of cultural meaning?
Putting both of these formulations together: how can meaning and value emerge
from the structuring of piles of information within the infinite horizon of a cultural form of pure presence, with neither silence nor unconscious, constituted
by immediate transmission? From where can structuring come if not from the
silence and delay that has determined subject-positions within a culture?

The characteristics of information show that digitization does indeed
provoke a crisis of culture: without delay and silence, culture approximates a
pure transparency; even though information contains the possibility of emergent meaning, such meaning does not emerge directly or automatically from
the accumulation of information. The danger of pure transparency is lack of
meaning or value. Restoration of meaning and value through emergent meaning implies that—unlike the subsumption and organization of individual meaning by an overweening "relative natural worldview" in traditional meaning
systems—emergent meanings contain the possibility of bottom-up meaning
construction.

The clue here is in the observation that in the construction of a circuit of
information, "feeling cold" motivates the sensor to re-establish a renewed equilibrium between regulator and environment. "Feeling cold" in this context functions as information for the whole information system, even while the "feeling
cold" itself is left outside by that system, since the perceiving itself is not information but perception. Information is quantitative and relational, whereas, even
for a node within the system, the feeling of the "feeling cold" is a state of affairs,
or a perception. In other words, the rendering as quantitative and relational
renders the specificity of the registering of the state of affairs as irrelevant to
quantitative relationality. Note that this "feeling cold" does not refer to a subject
outside the information system, but to a node of perception within it. Similarly,
I will not appeal to a subject external to the epoch of information but to per-
ceptual nodes within it. Nevertheless, I am arguing, the difference between a
registering perceptive state of affairs and its quantitative-relational reckoning
within a total information system still applies.

It is this *registering node* within the information system that, when cancelled
or ignored, produces the crisis of digital culture. Similarly, it is the generation
of a different attitude from this registering node that can overcome the crisis.
As delay and silence approach zero, the node is cancelled as a registering site,

to become almost entirely absorbed into the information system as a whole. But this absorption can never be complete. It is in the small and continuous difference between complete absorption and the singularity of the registering site that the crisis and healing of digital culture occur. How does this difference appear and how can it be widened into cultural meaning?

If the registering at the registering site is accepted as itself a phenomenon of interest, the speed of absorption is slowed and from this delay originates the emergence of structuring of piles of information. This phenomenon may be called *intensity*. I have spoken up until now of "meaning and value" as one phrase, but whereas "meaning" traditionally would be considered prior to a higher-level valuation, I want to suggest that this relation has reversed because of the epochal form of information. The root experience of *value* is the significance of the singularity of the registering site as a site for interest and investigation, to which the term "intensity" refers. Such intensity can be characterized as a remnant of Husserl's demand that sign-systems, such as numbers, be rooted in immediate intuition: it no longer has the self-evidence and universality required by Husserl but does contain the "experiential" moment on which these were based—even though "experience" here is no longer a presupposed foundation but a lack found within sign-systems that points to an outside always operative in every actual operation of a sign-system. To be information, a sign-system must matter, and in mattering it encounters a singularity of a certain intensity. The intensity of the registering is the delay of absorption into the information circuit, which provides the motive for structuring piles of information that constitutes value and thereby the meaning of such piles as they become bunches and discourses.

Such an embrace of the singularity of the registering site focuses on the intensity of the registering as that which in the registering is not taken up into the circuit. It is a localizing move (Angus, 2008: 13–36). This intensity becomes *structuring* as a value that grounds the emergent meaning of bunches of information. It is a risk taken at the registering site, and even by the registering site, which is co-extensive with philosophy itself.[4] Once the node becomes a site or location, and not merely a node in a circuit, as a result of the intensive singularity of its registering, value and meaning emerge to structure information. Such value and meaning institute delays and silences that form the horizon of a culture. A culture is instituted that is not digital culture but an emergent culture within digitization.

ACKNOWLEDGEMENTS

I would like to thank the Shadbolt Fellowship (2012) in the Faculty of Arts and Social Sciences at Simon Fraser University and the Social Sciences and Humanities Research Council (grant #435-2012-0209) for support in writing the manuscript on which this chapter is based.

NOTES

1 Media ecology has also been called the "Toronto School of Communication" due to the fact that Eric Havelock, Harold Innis, and Marshall McLuhan each worked, at least for a while, in Toronto. In my previous work (Angus, 2000), I have used the term "comparative media theory" to underline that the characteristics of a given medium only become clear when one is "outside" that medium, that is to say, within another medium. I have discussed the relative validity of the various terms and the contemporary near-consensus on "media ecology" in an interview (Ralon).

2 The recognition of this universality of translation that is becoming ubiquitous in contemporary civilization is the key factor that takes media analysis from being a mere catalogue of different forms toward a general theory of culture. "Now that we have extended not just our physical organs but the nervous system, itself, in electric technology, the principle of specialism and division as a factor of speed no longer applies. When information moves at the speed of signs in the central nervous system, man is confronted with the obsolescence of all earlier forms of acceleration, such as road and rail. What emerges is a total field of inclusive awareness" (McLuhan, 1964: 103). "The general digitalization of channels and information erases the differences among individual media" (Kittler, 1999: 1).

3 This is a universalization of the changed situation of the classical practice of quotation that I have previously analyzed. "There is a reversal here of the relationships of (in)completion as they occur in traditional quotation. In quotation, the single quotation is incomplete in the sense that its complete meaning depends on the whole text—the original text, the new text, and the relation between the two. Incompletion is on the side of the quotation whereas completion is on the side of the whole text. In contrast, a bit of information is complete since it is single and closed upon itself, whereas its proximity to other bits through the infinite addition made possible by the Internet renders it incomplete. The larger structure is now incomplete; the smaller structure is complete. Is it any wonder that knowledge has come to mean bits of information?" (Angus, 2009: 116).

4 "The beginning of philosophy is in a decisive act whereby the situation of the thinker is interrogated as a way of understanding the human condition. . . . One is forced to risk a decisive act that institutes, brings into being, a philosophy" (Angus, 1997: 105).

REFERENCES

Angus, Ian. 1997. *A Border Within: National Identity, Cultural Plurality, and Wilderness*. Kingston and Montréal: McGill–Queen's University Press.

———. 2000. *Primal Scenes of Communication: Communication, Consumerism, and Social Movements*. Albany: SUNY Press.

———. 2005. "Media, Expression and a New Politics: Eight Theses." *Media and Cultural Politics* 1(1): 89–92.

———. 2008. *Identity and Justice*. Toronto: University of Toronto Press.

———. 2009. *Love the Questions: University Education and Enlightenment*. Winnipeg: Arbeiter Ring.

Badiou, Alain. 2007. *Being and Event*. Trans. Oliver Feltham. London: Continuum.

———. 2008. *Number and Numbers*. Trans. Robin MacKay. Cambridge: Polity.

Heidegger, Martin. 1996. "The Principle of Reason." In *The Principle of Reason*, trans. Reginald Lilly. Bloomington: Indiana University Press.

Husserl, Edmund. 1970. *The Crisis of the European Sciences and Transcendental Phenomenology*. Trans. David Carr. Evanston, IL: Northwestern University Press.

Kittler, Friedrich. 1999. *Gramophone, Film, Typewriter*. Trans. Geoffrey Winthrop-Young and Michael Wutz. Stanford, CA: Stanford University Press.

Klein, Jacob. 1985. "The Idea of Liberal Education." In *Lectures and Essays*, eds. Robert. B. Williamson and Elliott Zuckerman. Annapolis, MD: St. John's College Press.

Maturana, Humberto R., and Francisco J. Varela. 1980. *Autopoiesis and Cognition: The Realization of the Living*. Dordrecht: D. Reidel.

McLuhan, Marshall. 1964. *Understanding Media: The Extensions of Man*. New York: The New American Library.

Poster, Mark. 2006. *Information Please: Culture and Politics in the Age of Digital Machines*. Durham, NC: Duke University Press.

Ralon, Laureano. "Interview with Ian Angus." Available at *Figure/Ground Communication* website at http://figureground.ca/interviews/ian-angus/.

Scheler, Max. 1980. *Problems of a Sociology of Knowledge*. Trans. Manfred S. Frings. London: Routledge and Kegan Paul.

Wiener, Norbert. 1954. *The Human Use of Human Beings*. Garden City, NY: Doubleday

Responsible
Machines

The Opportunities and Challenges
of Artificial Autonomous Agents

David J. Gunkel

During the first conference on cyberspace convened at the University of Texas in 1990 (ancient times as far as the Internet is concerned), Sandy Stone provided articulation of what can now, in retrospect, be identified as one of the guiding principles of life on the Internet. "No matter how virtual the subject becomes, there is always a body attached" (Stone, 1991: 111). What Stone sought to point out with this brief but insightful comment is the fact that despite what appears online, users of computer networks and digital information systems should remember that behind the scenes or the screen there is always another user— another person who is essentially like us. This other may appear in the guise of different virtual characters, screen names, profiles, or avatars, but there is always somebody behind it all.

This Internet folk wisdom has served us well. It has helped users navigate the increasingly complicated social relationships made possible by computer-mediated communication. It has assisted law enforcement agencies in hunting down con men, scam artists, and online predators. And, perhaps most importantly, it has helped us sort out difficult ethical questions concerning individual responsibility and the rights of others in the digital nexus. But all of that is over. And it is over, precisely because we can no longer be entirely certain that "there is always a body attached." In fact, the majority of online activity is no longer (and perhaps never really was) communication with other human users but interactions with machines. Current statistics concerning web traffic already give the machines a slight edge, with 51 percent of all activity being other than human (Foremski, 2012), and this statistic is expected to increase at an accelerated rate (Cisco Systems, 2012). Even if one doubts the possibility of ever achieving what has traditionally been called "strong AI," the fact is our world is already populated by semi-intelligent artifacts, social robots, autonomous algorithms, and other smart devices that occupy the place of the Other in social relationships and communicative interaction.

The following investigates the opportunities and challenges made available by these increasingly responsible machines—machines that are designed for and are able to respond to us as another autonomous agent and in so doing may have a legitimate claim to some level of rights, responsibilities, or both. The examination of this will proceed in three steps or movements: the first will review the way we typically deal with technology and moral responsibility. It will, therefore, target and reconsider the instrumental theory of technology, which defines the machine as nothing more than a tool or contrivance serving human interests. The second will consider the opportunities and challenges that autonomous technologies pose to this default setting. Recent developments in robotics, learning algorithms, and decision-making systems exceed the conceptual boundaries of the instrumental theory and ask us to reassess who or what is a moral subject. Finally, and by way of conclusion, the third part will draw out the consequences of this material, explicating what this machine incursion means for us, our world, and the other entities we encounter here.

DEFAULT SETTING

Initially, the very notion of "responsible machines" probably sounds absurd. Who in their right mind would pitch an argument for this? Who would dare suggest that a technological artifact could or should be considered an autonomous agent? Don't we already have enough trouble with human beings? So why muddy the water? This line of reasoning sounds intuitively correct. In fact, it seems there is little to talk about. Machines, even sophisticated information processing devices such as computers, smart phones, software algorithms, robots, and so on, are technologies, and technologies are mere tools created and used by human beings. A mechanism or technological object means nothing and does nothing by itself; it is the way it is employed by a human user that ultimately matters.

This common-sense evaluation is structured and informed by the answer that is typically provided for the question concerning technology.

We ask the question concerning technology when we ask what it is. Everyone knows the two statements that answer our question. One says: Technology is a means to an end. The other says: Technology is a human activity. The two definitions of technology belong together, for to posit ends and procure and utilize the means to them is a human activity. The manufacture and utilization of equipment, tools, and machines, the manufactured and used things themselves, and the needs and ends that they serve, all belong to what technology is (Heidegger, 1977: 4–5).

According to Heidegger's insightful analysis, the presumed role and function of any kind of technology, whether it be the product of handicraft or industrialized manufacture, is that it is a means employed by human users for specific ends. Heidegger terms this particular characterization of technology "the instrumental definition" and indicates that it forms what is considered to be the "correct" understanding of any kind of technological contrivance (1977: 5).

As Andrew Feenberg (1991: 5) characterizes it in the introduction to his *Critical Theory of Technology*, "the instrumentalist theory offers the most widely accepted view of technology. It is based on the common sense idea that technologies are 'tools' standing ready to serve the purposes of users." And because an instrument "is deemed 'neutral,' without valuative content of its own" (Feenberg, 1991: 5), a technological artifact is evaluated not in and of itself, but on the basis of the particular employments that have been decided by its human designer or user. The consequences of this are succinctly articulated by Jean-François Lyotard in *The Postmodern Condition*:

> Technical devices originated as prosthetic aids for the human organs or as physiological systems whose function it is to receive data or condition the context. They follow a principle, and it is the principle of optimal performance: maximizing output (the information or modification obtained) and minimizing input (the energy expended in the process). Technology is therefore a game pertaining not to the true, the just, or the beautiful, etc., but to efficiency: a technical "move" is "good" when it does better and/or expends less energy than another. (Lyotard, 1984: 44)

Lyotard begins by affirming the traditional understanding of technology as an instrument or extension of human activity. Given this "fact," which is stated as if it were something beyond question, he proceeds to provide an explanation of the proper place of the technological apparatus in epistemology, ethics, and aesthetics. According to his analysis, a technological device, whether it be a simple corkscrew, a mechanical clock, or a digital computer, does not in and of itself participate in the big questions of truth, justice, or beauty. Technology is simply and indisputably about efficiency. A particular technological "move" or innovation is considered "good," if, and only if, it proves to be a more effective means to accomplishing a user-specified objective.

But the instrumental theory is not merely a matter of philosophical reflection; it also informs and serves as the conceptual backdrop for work in artificial intelligence (AI) and robotics, even if it is often not identified as such. "Legal and moral responsibility for a robot's actions," Joanna Bryson (2010: 69) asserts, "should be no different than they are for any other AI system, and these are the same as for any other tool. Ordinarily, damage caused by a tool is the fault of the operator, and benefit from it is to the operator's credit. . . . We should never be talking about machines taking ethical decisions, but rather machines operated correctly within the limits we set for them." For Bryson, robots, software algorithms, and other sophisticated AI systems are no different from any other technical artifact. They are tools of human manufacture, employed by human users for particular purposes, and as such are merely "an extension of the user" (Bryson, 2010: 72). Bryson, therefore, would be in agreement with Marshall McLuhan, who famously characterized all technology as media—literally the means of effecting or conveying—and all media as "the extensions of man" (McLuhan, 1995).

Characterized as an extension or enhancement of human faculties, sophisticated technical devices like robots, AIs, and other computer systems are not considered the responsible agent of actions that are performed with or through them. "Morality," as J. Storrs Hall (2001: 2) points out, "rests on human shoulders, and if machines changed the ease with which things were done, they did not change responsibility for doing them. People have always been the only 'moral agents.'" This formulation not only sounds level-headed and reasonable, it is one of the standard operating presumptions of computer ethics. Although different definitions of "computer ethics" have circulated since Walter Maner first introduced the term in 1976, they all share an instrumentalist perspective that assigns moral agency to human designers and users. According to Deborah

Johnson, who is credited with writing the field's agenda-setting textbook, "computer ethics turns out to be the study of human beings and society—our goals and values, our norms of behaviour, the way we organize ourselves and assign rights and responsibilities, and so on" (Johnson, 1985: 6). Computers, she recognizes, often "instrumentalize" these human values and behaviours in innovative and challenging ways, but the bottom line is and remains the way human agents design and use (or misuse) such technology.

And Johnson has stuck to this viewpoint even in the face of what appears to be increasingly sophisticated technological developments. "Computer systems," she writes in a more recent article, "are produced, distributed, and used by people engaged in social practices and meaningful pursuits. This is as true of current computer systems as it will be of future computer systems. No matter how independently, automatic, and interactive computer systems of the future behave, they will be the products (direct or indirect) of human behaviour, human social institutions, and human decision" (Johnson, 2006: 197). Understood in this way, computer systems, no matter how automatic, independent, or seemingly intelligent they may become, "are not and can never be (autonomous, independent) moral agents" (Johnson, 2006: 203). They will, like all other technological artifacts, always be instruments of human value, decision-making, and action.

According to the instrumental theory, therefore, any action undertaken via a machine is ultimately the responsibility of some human agent—the designer of the system, the manufacturer of the equipment, or the end-user of the product. If something goes wrong with or someone is harmed by the mechanism, "some human is to blame for setting the program up to do such a thing" (Goertzel, 2002: 1). Following this line of argument, it can be concluded that all machine action is to be credited to or blamed on a human programmer, manufacturer, or operator. Holding the machine culpable would, on this account, not only be absurd but also irresponsible. Ascribing agency to machines, Mikko Siponen (2004: 286) argues, allows one to "start blaming computers for our mistakes. In other words, we can claim that 'I didn't do it – it was a computer error,' while ignoring the fact that the software has been programmed by people to 'behave in certain ways', and thus people may have caused this error either incidentally or intentionally (or users have otherwise contributed to the cause of this error)."

This insight is codified by the popular adage, "It's a poor carpenter who blames his tools." In other words, when something goes wrong or a mistake is made in situations involving the application of technology, it is the human designer, manufacturer, or operator of the tool and not the tool itself that should be blamed. Blaming the tool is not only logically incorrect, insofar as a tool is just an extension of human action, but also ethically suspect and even "dangerous" (Johnson and Miller, 2008: 124), because it is one of the ways that human agents often try to deflect or avoid taking full responsibility for their actions. "By endowing technology with the attributes of autonomous agency," Abbe Mowshowitz (2008: 271) argues, "human beings are ethically sidelined. Individuals are relieved of responsibility. The suggestion of being in the grip of irresistible forces provides an excuse of rejecting responsibility for oneself and others." Consequently, blaming the computer (or any other technology) is to make at least two fundamental mistakes. First, it wrongly attributes agency to something that is a mere instrument or inanimate object. This logical error mistakenly turns a passive object into an active subject. It confuses means and ends, to put it in Kantian language. Second, it permits human users to deflect moral responsibility by putting the blame on something else. In other words, it allows human users to scapegoat the computer (Nissenbaum, 1996: 35) and deflect responsibility for their own actions.

THE NEW NORMAL

The instrumental theory not only sounds reasonable, it is obviously useful. It is, one might say, instrumental for parsing questions of responsibility in the age of increasingly complex technological systems. And it has a distinct advantage in that it locates accountability in a widely accepted and seemingly intuitive subject position, in human decision-making and action, and it resists any and all efforts to defer responsibility to some inanimate object by blaming or scapegoating what are mere instruments, contrivances, or tools. At the same time, however, this particular formulation also has significant theoretical and practical limitations, especially as it applies (or not) to recent technological innovations.

First, the instrumental theory reduces all technology, irrespective of design, construction, or operation, to a tool—an instrument, prosthesis, or medium of human agency. "Tool," however, does not necessarily encompass everything technological and does not exhaust all possibilities. There are also machines. Although "experts in mechanics," as Karl Marx (1977: 493) pointed out, often confuse these two concepts calling "tools simple machines and machines complex tools," there is an important and crucial difference between the two and that difference ultimately has to do with the location and assignment of agency. Indication of this essential difference can be found in a brief parenthetical remark offered by Heidegger in the 1954 essay "The Question Concerning Technology." "Here it would be appropriate," Heidegger writes in reference to his use of the word "machine" to characterize a jet airliner, "to discuss Hegel's definition of the machine as autonomous tool [selbständigen Werkzeug]" (1977: 17). What Heidegger references, without supplying the full citation, are Hegel's 1805–7 Jena Lectures, in which "machine" had been defined as a tool that is self-sufficient, self-reliant, or independent. Although Heidegger immediately dismisses this alternative as something that is not appropriate to his way of questioning technology, it is taken up and given sustained consideration by Langdon Winner in *Autonomous Technology*,

> To be autonomous is to be self-governing, independent, not ruled by an external law of force. In the metaphysics of Immanuel Kant, autonomy refers to the fundamental condition of free will—the capacity of the will to follow moral laws that it gives to itself. Kant opposes this idea to "heteronomy," the rule of the will by external laws, namely, the deterministic laws of nature. In this light the very mention of autonomous technology raises an unsettling irony, for the expected relationship of subject and object is exactly reversed. We are now reading all of the propositions backwards. To say that technology is autonomous is to say that it is nonheteronomous, not governed by an external law. And what is the external law that is appropriate to technology? Human will, it would seem." (Winner 1977: 16)

"Autonomous technology" refers to technical devices that directly contravene the instrumental theory by deliberately contesting and relocating the assignment of agency. Such mechanisms are not heteronomous tools to be directed and used by human agents according to their will but occupy, in one way or another, the place of an autonomous agent. As Marx (1977: 495) succinctly described it, "the machine, therefore, is a mechanism that, after being set in motion, performs with its tools the same operations as the worker formerly did with similar tools." Understood in this way, the machine occupies not the place of the hand tool of the worker but the worker him/herself, the active and autonomous agent who had wielded the tool.

Second, autonomous machines are not only a perennial favorite of science fiction (from the monster of Mary Shelley's *Frankenstein* to the HAL 9000 computer and beyond) but are rapidly becoming science fact, if not already part of social reality. According to Ray Kurzweil's estimations, the tipping point—what he calls the "singularity"—is near: "Within several decades information-based technologies will encompass all human knowledge and proficiency, ultimately including the pattern recognition powers, problem solving skills, and emotional and moral intelligence of the human brain itself" (Kurzweil, 2005: 8). Similarly, Hans Moravec forecasts not only the achievement of human-level intelligence in a relatively short period of time but an eventual surpassing of it that will render human beings effectively obsolete and a casualty of our own evolutionary success.

We are very near to the time when virtually no essential human function, physical or mental, will lack an artificial counterpart. The embodiment of this convergence of cultural developments will be the intelligent robot, a machine that can think and act as a human, however inhuman it may be in physical or mental detail. Such machines could carry on our cultural evolution, including their own construction and increasingly rapid self-improvement, without us, and without the genes that built us. When that happens, our DNA will find itself out of a job, having lost the evolutionary race to a new kind of competition (Moravec, 1988: 2).

Even seemingly grounded and level-headed engineers such as Rodney Brooks, who famously challenged Moravec and the AI establishment with his "mindless" robots, predicts the achievement of machine intelligence on par with human capabilities in just a few decades. "Our fantasy machines," Brooks writes, referencing the popular robots of science fiction (i.e. HAL, 3CPO, Lt. Commander Data, etc.), "have syntax and technology. They also have emotions, desires, fears, loves, and pride. Our real machines do not. Or so it seems at the dawn of the third millennium. But how will it look a hundred years from now? My thesis is that in just twenty years the boundary between fantasy and reality will be rent asunder" (Brooks, 2002: 5).

Predictions of human-level (or better) machine intelligence, although fueling imaginative and entertaining forms of fiction, are, for the most part, still futuristic. That is, they address possible achievements in the fields of AI and robotics that might occur with technologies or techniques that have yet to be fully developed, prototyped, or empirically demonstrated. Consequently, strict instrumentalists are often able to dismiss these prognostications as nothing more than wishful thinking or speculation. And if the history of AI is any indication, there is every reason to be skeptical. We have, in fact, heard these kinds of fantastic hypotheses before, only to be disappointed time and again. As Terry Winograd (1990, 167) wrote in an honest assessment of progress (or lack thereof) in the discipline, "artificial intelligence has not achieved creativity, insight, and judgment. But its shortcomings are far more mundane: we have not yet been able to construct a machine with even a modicum of common sense or one that can converse on everyday topics in ordinary language."

Despite these shortcomings, there are current implementations and working prototypes that appear to possess some significant degree of autonomy and that complicate the identification and assignment of agency. There are, for instance, learning systems, mechanisms designed not only to make decisions and take real world actions with little or no human direction or oversight but also programmed to be able to modify their own rules of behaviour based on results from such operations. These machines, which are now rather common in commodities trading, transportation, health care, manufacturing, and even culture appear to be more than mere tools. Consider, for example, what has happened in the financial and commodities exchange markets in the last fifteen years. At one time, trades on the New York Stock Exchange or the Chicago Board Options Exchange were initiated and controlled by human traders in "the pit." Beginning in the late 1990s, financial services organizations began developing algorithms to take over much of this effort (Steiner, 2010). These algorithms were faster, more efficient, more consistent, and could, as a result of all this, turn incredible profits by exploiting momentary differences in market prices. These algorithms analyzed the market, made decisions, and initiated actions faster than human comprehension and were designed with learning subroutines that could alter their initial programming in order to be able to respond to new and unanticipated opportunities. And these things worked; they generated incredible revenues for the financial services industry. As a result, over 70 percent of all trades are now machine-generated and controlled (Scott, 2012: 8). This means that our financial situation—not only our mortgages and retirement savings but also a significant part of the national and global economy—is now directed and managed by machines that are designed to operate with a considerable degree of autonomy.

The social consequences of this can be seen in a remarkable event called the Flash Crash. At about 2:45 pm on 6 May 2010, the Dow Jones Industrial Average lost over 1,000 points in a matter of seconds and then rebounded just as quickly. The drop, which amounted to about 9 percent of the market's total value or 1 trillion U.S. dollars, was caused by a couple of trading algorithms interacting with and responding to each other. In other words, no human being initiated the action, was in control of the event, or could be considered responsible for its outcome. It was something undertaken and overseen by the algorithms, and the human brokers could only passively watch things unfold on their monitor screens, not knowing what had happened, who had instituted it, or why. To this day, no one is quite sure what actually occurred (Slavin, 2010). No one, in other words, knows exactly who or even what was responsible for this brief financial crisis.

A less nefarious illustration of machine autonomy can be found in situations involving the consumption and production of culture. Currently recommendation algorithms at Netflix, Amazon, and elsewhere increasingly decide what cultural objects we access and experience. It is estimated that 75 percent of all content obtained through Netflix is the result of a machine-generated recommendation (Amatriain and Basilico, 2012). Consequently, these algorithms are, in effect, taking over the work of film, book, and music critics and influencing—to a significant degree—what films are seen, what books are read, and what music is heard. But machines are not just involved in the distribution and exhibition aspects of the culture industry; they are also actively engaged on the creative side. In the field of journalism, for example, algorithms now write original content. Beyond the simple news aggregators that currently populate the web, these programs, like Northwestern University's Stats Monkey, automatically compose publishable stories from machine-readable statistical data. Organizations such as the Big Ten Network currently use these programs to develop content for web distribution (Slavin, 2010: 218). These applications, although clearly in the early stages of development, recently led Kurt Cagle, managing editor of XMLToday.org, to provocatively ask whether an AI might compete for and win a Pulitzer Prize by 2030 (Kerwin, 2009: 1).

Similar transformations are occurring in music, where algorithms and robots actively participate in the creative process. In classical music, for instance, there is David Cope's Experiments in Musical Intelligence or EMI (pronounced "Emmy"), an algorithmic composer capable of analyzing existing compositions and creating new, original scores that are virtually indistinguishable from the canonical works of Bach, Chopin, and Beethoven (Cope 2005). And then there is Shimon, a marimba-playing jazz-bot from Georgia Tech that not only improvises with human musicians in real time but "is designed to create meaningful and inspiring musical interactions with humans, leading to novel musical experiences and outcomes" (Georgia Tech, 2013; Hoffman and Weinberg, 2011).

Although the extent to which one might assign "agency" and "responsibility" to these mechanisms remains a contested issue, what is not debated is the fact that the rules of the game have changed significantly. As Andreas Matthias points out, summarizing his survey of learning automata:

> Presently there are machines in development or already in use which are able to decide on a course of action and to act without human intervention. The rules by which they act are not fixed during the production process, but can be changed during the operation of the machine, by the machine itself. This is what we call machine learning. Traditionally we hold either the operator/manufacturer of the machine responsible for the consequences of its operation or "nobody" (in cases, where no personal fault can be identified). Now it can be shown that there is an increasing class of machine actions, where the traditional ways of responsibility ascription are not compatible with our sense of justice and the moral framework of society because nobody has enough control over the machine's actions to be able to assume responsibility for them. (Matthias, 2004: 177)

In other words, the instrumental definition of technology, which had effectively tethered machine action to human agency, no longer adequately applies to mechanisms that have been deliberately designed to operate and exhibit some form, no matter how rudimentary, of independent action or autonomous decision-making. This does not mean, it is important to emphasize, that the instrumental definition is on this account refuted tout court. There are and will continue to be mechanisms understood and utilized as tools to be manipulated by human users (that is, lawn mowers, corkscrews, telephones, digital cameras, and so on). The point is that the instrumentalist definition, no matter how useful and seemingly correct in some circumstances for explaining some technological devices, does not exhaust all possibilities for all kinds of devices.

Finally, in addition to sophisticated learning automata and robots, there are also mundane objects such online chatterbots and nonplayer characters that, if not proving otherwise, at least significant complicate the instrumentalist assumptions. Miranda Mowbray, for instance, has investigated the complications of moral agency in online communities and massively multiplayer online role-playing games (MMORPGS).

> The rise of online communities has led to a phenomenon of real-time, multi-person interaction via online personas. Some online community technologies allow the creation of bots (personas that act according to a software programme rather than being directly controlled by a human

user) in such a way that it is not always easy to tell a bot from a human within an online social space. It is also possible for a persona to be partly controlled by a software programme and partly directly by a human. . . . This leads to theoretical and practical problems for ethical arguments (not to mention policing) in these spaces, since the usual one-to-one correspondence between actors and moral agents can be lost. (Mowbray, 2002: 2)

Software bots, therefore, not only complicate the one-to-one correspondence between actor and moral agent but make it increasingly difficult to decide who or what is responsible for actions in the virtual space of an online community. Although these bots are by no means close to achieving anything that looks remotely like intelligence or even basic machine learning, they can still be mistaken for and pass as other human users. This is, Mowbray points out, not "a feature of the sophistication of bot design, but of the low bandwidth communication of the online social space" where it is "much easier to convincingly simulate a human agent" (2002: 2).

Despite this knowledge, these software implementations cannot be written off as mere instruments or tools. "The examples in this paper," Mowbray concludes, "show that a bot may cause harm to other users or to the community as a whole by the will of its programmers or other users, but that it also may cause harm through nobody's fault because of the combination of circumstances involving some combination of its programming, the actions and mental or emotional states of human users who interact with it, behaviour of other bots and of the environment, and the social economy of the community" (2002: 4). Unlike artificial intelligence, which would occupy a position that would, at least, be reasonably close to that of a human agent and therefore not be able to be dismissed as a mere tool, bots simply muddy the water (which is probably worse) by leaving undecided the question whether they are or are not tools. And in the process, they leave the question of moral agency both unsettled and unsettling.

THE RISE OF THE MACHINES

In November of 2012, General Electric launched a television advertisement called "Robots on the Move." The sixty-second video, created by Jonathan Dayton and Valerie Faris (the husband/wife team behind the 2006 feature film *Little Miss Sunshine*), depicts many of the iconic robots of science fiction travelling across great distances to assemble before some brightly lit airplane hangar for what we are told is the unveiling of some new kind of machines—"brilliant machines," as GE's tagline describes it. And as we observe Robby the Robot from *Forbidden Planet*, KITT the robotic automobile from *Knight Rider*, and Lt. Commander Data of *Star Trek: The Next Generation* making their way to this meeting of artificial minds, we are told, in an ominous voiceover, that "the machines are on the move."

Although this might not look like your typical robot apocalypse (vividly illustrated in science fiction films and television programs such as *Terminator*, *The Matrix Trilogy*, and *Battlestar Galactica*), we are, in fact, in the midst of an invasion. The machines are on the move. They are everywhere and doing everything. They may have begun by displacing workers on the factory floor, but they now actively participate in all aspects of intellectual, social, and cultural life. This invasion is not some future possibility coming from a distant alien world. It is here; it is now. And resistance is futile. As these increasingly autonomous machines come to occupy influential positions in contemporary culture—positions where they are not just tools or instruments of human action but actors in their own right—we will need to ask ourselves important but rather difficult questions: At what point might a robot, an algorithm, or other autonomous system be held responsible for the decisions it makes or the actions it deploys? When, in other words, would it make sense to say "It's the computer's fault"? Likewise, at what point might we have to consider seriously extending rights—civil, moral, and legal standing—to these socially aware and interactive devices? When, in other words, would it no longer be considered nonsense to suggest something like "the rights of machines"?

In response to these questions, there appear to be at least three options, none of which are entirely comfortable or satisfactory. On the one hand, we can respond as we typically have, treating these mechanisms as mere instruments or tools. Bryson makes a case for this approach in her provocatively titled essay "Robots Should Be Slaves": "My thesis is that robots should be built, marketed and considered legally as slaves, not companion peers" (Bryson, 2010: 63). Although this might sound harsh, this argument is persuasive, precisely because it draws on and is underwritten by the instrumental theory of technology—a theory that has considerable history and success behind it and that functions as the assumed default position for any and all considerations of technology. This decision—and it is a decision, even if it is the default—has both advantages and disadvantages. On the positive side, it reaffirms human exceptionalism, making it absolutely clear that it is only the human being who possesses rights and responsibilities. Technologies, no matter how sophisticated, intelligent, and influential, are and will continue to be mere tools of human action, nothing more. But this approach, for all its usefulness, has a not-so-pleasant downside. It willfully and deliberately produces a new class of instrumental servants or slaves (what we might call "slavery 2.0") and rationalizes this decision as morally appropriate and justified. In other words, applying the instrumental theory to these new kinds of machines, although seemingly reasonable and useful, might have devastating consequences for us and others.

On the other hand, we can decide to entertain the possibility of rights and responsibilities for machines just as we had previously done for other non-human entities such as animals (Singer, 1975) and the environment (Birch, 1993). And there is both moral and legal precedent for this outcome. In fact, we already live in a world populated by artificial entities who are considered legal persons having rights and responsibilities recognized and protected by both national and international law—the limited liability corporation (French, 1979). Once again, this decision sounds reasonable and justified. It extends moral standing to these other socially active entities and recognizes, following the predictions of Norbert Wiener (1988: 16), that the social situation of the future will involve not just human-to-human interactions but relationships between humans and machines. But this decision also has significant costs. It requires that we rethink everything we thought we knew about ourselves, technology, and ethics. It requires that we learn to think beyond human exceptionalism, technological instrumentalism, and all the other -isms that have helped us make sense of our world and our place in it. In effect, it calls for a thorough reconceptualization of who or what should be considered a moral subject.

Finally, we can try to balance these two extreme positions by taking an inter-mediate hybrid approach, distributing agency and responsibility across a net-work of interacting human and machine components. This particular version of "actor network theory" is precisely the solution advanced by Johnson in her essay, "Computer Systems: Moral Entities but not Moral Agents" (2006: 202): "When computer systems behave there is a triad of intentionality at work, the intentionality of the computer system designer, the intentionality of the system, and the intentionality of the user." This proposal also has its advantages and disadvantages. In particular, it appears to be attentive to the exigencies of life in the digital nexus. None of us, in fact, make decisions or act in a vacuum; we are always and already tangled up in networks of interactive elements that com-plicate the assignment of intentionality, agency, and responsibility. And these networks have always included others—not only other human beings but institutions, organizations, and even machinic elements.

This combined approach, however, still requires that one decide what aspects of agency and responsibility belong to the machine and what should be attributed to the human being. In other words, the hybrid approach, although attempting to strike a balance between strict "instrumentalism" and "machine morality," will still need to decide between who counts as a moral subject and what can be considered a mere object. In fact, everything, as Jacques Derrida points out, depends on decisions between these two seemingly simple words (2005: 80). Johnson, for instance, still comes down on the side of human exceptionalism: "Note also that while human beings can act with or without artifacts, computer systems cannot act without human designers and users. Even when their proximate behaviour is independent, computer systems act with humans in the sense that they have been designed by humans to behave in certain ways and humans have set them in particular places, at particular times, to perform particular tasks for users" (Johnson, 2006: 202). But this is not the only possible or even the best formulation, and other theorists and practitioners (Wallach and Allen, 2009, Anderson and Anderson, 2011, Lin et al., 2011) have advanced different versions of shared agency and responsibility, some of which tip the scale in the direction of increasing machine autonomy.

In any event, how we decide to respond to the opportunities and challenges of this machine question will have a profound effect on the way we conceptualize our place in the world, who we decide to include in the community of moral subjects, and what we exclude from such consideration and why. But no matter how it is decided, it is a decision—quite literally a cut that institutes difference and makes a difference. We are, therefore, responsible both for deciding who or even what is a moral subject and, in the process, for determining the very configuration and proper limits of moral responsibility in the digital nexus.

REFERENCES

Amatriain, Xavier, and Justin Basilico. 2012. "Netflix Recommendations: Beyond the 5 Stars." *The Netflix Tech Blog*. http://techblog.netflix.com/2012/04/netflix-recommendations-beyond-5-stars.html.

Anderson, Michael, and S. Leigh Anderson. 2011. *Machine Ethics*. Cambridge: Cambridge University Press.

Birch, Thomas. 1993. "Moral Considerability and Universal Consideration." *Environmental Ethics* 15: 313–32.

Brooks, Rodney A. 2002. *Flesh and Machines: How Robots will Change Us.* New York: Pantheon Books.

Bryson, Joanna. 2010. "Robots Should Be Slaves." In *Close Engagements with Artificial Companions: Key Social, Psychological, Ethical and Design Issues,* ed. Yorick Wilks, 63–74. Amsterdam: John Benjamins.

Cisco Systems. 2012. Cisco Visual Networking Index: Global Mobile Data Traffic Forecast Update, 2011–2016. San Jose, CA: Cisco Systems. http://www.cisco. com/en/US/ solutions/ collateral/ns341/ns525/ns537/ns705/ns827/white_paper_ c11-520862.pdf.

Cope, David. 2005. *Computer Models of Musical Creativity.* Cambridge, MA: MIT Press.

Derrida, Jacques. 2005. *Paper Machine.* Trans. Rachel Bowlby. Stanford, CA: Stanford University Press.

Feenberg, Andrew. 1991. *Critical Theory of Technology.* Oxford: Oxford University Press.

Foremski, Tom. 2010. "Report: 51% of Website Traffic is 'Non-human' and Mostly Malicious." *ZDNet.* http://www.zdnet.com/blog/foremski/report-51-of-website-traffic-is-non-human-and-mostly-malicious/2201.

French, Peter. 1979. "The Corporation as a Moral Person." *American Philosophical Quarterly* 16(3): 207–15.

Georgia Tech Center for Music Technology. 2013. "Shimon." http://gtcmt.gatech. edu/projects/shimon.

Goertzel, Ben. 2002. "Thoughts on AI Morality." *Dynamical Psychology: An International, Interdisciplinary Journal of Complex Mental Processes.* http://www. goertzel.org/ dynapsyc/2002/AIMorality.htm.

Hall, J. Storrs. 2001. "Ethics for Machines." KurzweilAI.net. http://www.kurzweilai. net/ethics-for-machines.

Heidegger, Martin 1977. *The Question Concerning Technology and Other Essays.* Trans. William Lovitt. New York: Harper and Row.

Hoffman, Guy, and Gil Weinberg. 2011. "Interactive Improvisation with a Robotic Marimba Player." *Autonomous Robots* 31(2–3): 133–53.

Johnson, Deborah G. 1985. *Computer Ethics.* Upper Saddle River, NJ: Prentice Hall.

———. 2006. "Computer Systems: Moral Entities but Not Moral Agents." *Ethics and Information Technology* 8:195–204.

Johnson, Deborah G., and Keith W. Miller. 2008. "Un-Making Artificial Moral Agents." *Ethics and Information Technology* 10:123–33.

Kerwin, Peter. 2009. "The Rise of Machine-Written Journalism." *Wired.co.uk*. http://www.wired.co.uk/news/archive/2009-12/16/the-rise-of-machine-written-journalism.aspx.

Kurzweil, Ray. 2005. *The Singularity Is Near: When Humans Transcend Biology*. New York: Viking.

Lin, Patrick, Keith Abney, and George A. Bekey. 2012. *Robot Ethics: The Ethical and Social Implications of Robotics*. Cambridge, MA: MIT Press.

Lyotard, Jean-François. 1993. *The Postmodern Condition: A Report on Knowledge*. Trans. Geoff Bennington and Brian Massumi. Minneapolis: University of Minnesota Press.

Marx, Karl. 1977. *Capital: A Critique of Political Economy*. Trans. Ben Fowkes. New York: Vintage Books.

Matthias, Andrew. 2004. "The Responsibility Gap: Ascribing Responsibility for the Actions of Learning Automata." *Ethics and Information Technology* 6: 175–83.

McLuhan, Marshall. 1995. *Understanding Media: The Extensions of Man*. Cambridge, MA: MIT Press.

Moravec, Hans. 1988. *Mind Children: The Future of Robot and Human Intelligence*. Cambridge, MA: Harvard University Press.

Mowbray, Miranda. 2002. "Ethics for Bots." Paper presented at the 14th International Conference on System Research, Informatics and Cybernetics. Baden-Baden, Germany. 29 July–3 August. http://www.hpl.hp.com/techreports/2002/HPL-2002-48R1.pdf

Mowshowitz, Abbe. 2008. "Technology as Excuse for Questionable Ethics." *AI and Society* 22: 271–82.

Nissenbaum, Helen. 1996. "Accountability in a Computerized Society." *Science and Engineering Ethics* 2: 25–42.

Patterson, Scott. 2012. *Dark Pools: The Rise of the Machine Traders and the Rigging of the U.S. Stock Market*. New York: Crown Business.

Singer, Peter. 1975. *Animal Liberation: A New Ethics for Our Treatment of Animals*. New York: New York Review of Books.

Siponen, Mikko. 2004. "A Pragmatic Evaluation of the Theory of Information Ethics." *Ethics and Information Technology* 6: 279–90.

Slavin, Kevin. 2011. How Algorithms Shape Our World. *TED Talks*. http://www.ted.com/talks/kevin_slavin_how_algorithms_shape_our_world.html

Steiner, Christopher. 2012. *Automate This: How Algorithms Came to Rule the World*. New York: Penguin Group.

Stone, A. R. 1991. "Will the Real Body Please Stand Up? Boundary Stories About Virtual Culture." In *Cyberspace: First Steps*, ed. Michael Benedikt, 81–118. Cambridge, MA: MIT Press.

Wallach, Wendell, and Colin Allen. 2009. *Moral Machines: Teaching Robots Right from Wrong*. Oxford: Oxford University Press.

Wiener, Norbert. 1988. *The Human Use of Human Beings: Cybernetics and Society*. Boston, MA: Da Capo Press.

Winner, Langdon. 1977. *Autonomous Technology: Technics-out-of-Control as a Theme in Political Thought*. Cambridge, MA: MIT Press.

Winograd, Terry. 1990. "Thinking Machines: Can There Be? Are We?" In *The Foundations of Artificial Intelligence: A Sourcebook*, eds. Derek Partridge and Yorick Wilks, 167–89. Cambridge, MA: Cambridge University Press.

4   Open Source Transparency

The Making of an Altered Identity

Daryl Campbell

The Free/Libre Open Source Software (FLOSS) movement may be considered the progenitor of an entire family of movements that have emerged as possible variants of this model: crowdsourcing, wikinomics, citizen engineering, social networking, end-user development, collective intelligence (Zhai et al., 2012: 61; Tapscott and Williams, 2008). FLOSS has remained relevant as a movement focused on creators and developers — "produsers," not just users — of leading-edge technological advances. The continued growth of FLOSS makes it significant for gaining further insight into the maturing logic that sustains this revolutionary movement (Deshpande and Riehle, 2008). To gain insight into this logic, we isolate one dimension of the movement to measure it against proprietary software development.

There are multiple levels on which the term "open" operates within the FLOSS movement. Openness, in this paper, is explored with particular reference to transparency in the sense of showing the self. The Internet and digital technologies create conditions where networked activity and communication may be captured and stored for, unconstrained access and replay. The resulting unlocked potentiality in this transparent record of users' activity may be seen as an active agent in the development of a transformed mode of production.

This raises a question: Is the transparency fostered by the technologies structuring the FLOSS movement evidence of an eventual disturbance that is inducing a new collective identity and agency? Alain Badiou's phenomenological studies can help us analyze this question.[1]

For Badiou, a group identity, operating at a collective or community level, is one stripped of any pathos of subjectivity (Badiou, 1991: 24–32). If we give technology an equal footing with other constituent members, we can proceed by first defining a group identity, then outlining how the FLOSS movement's group identity demonstrates a non-identity with the established commercial software development model. What results is a new post-event group identity, a regional dis-placement within the domain of software development. We can use Badiou's thinking to assist the analysis, but FLOSS introduces some complications for the restricted parameters Badiou sets out for relations.

A PHENOMENAL ACCOUNT OF GROUP IDENTITY

In *Logics of Worlds*, Badiou's phenomenological account of what appears—or comes to exist—in a world, the identity of a world at a structural level is calculated through a mapping of the objects, and elements composing those objects, projected onto a base space. This mapped space, not unlike a roadmap of a geographical territory, is named the "transcendental index." The mapping, or function, operates to measure the degrees of difference or identity between the objects, including an identity function for each object (2009: 358–59). The resulting space transcribes the descriptive phenomenal world into an identity. This is not the transcendental subject of Kant but instead an account of subject-less objects, an a-subjective transcendental materially generated from the given phenomenal account of the world. "The transcendental is not subjective, nor is it as such universal (there are multiple worlds, multiple transcendentals)" (301).

Inside the cover jacket of *Second Manifesto for Philosophy*, Badiou, with artist Monique Stobienia, diagrams a topological space. The objects and elements of that space are mapped onto an external space forming a transcendental index, evoking images of a Platonic allegory. In Figure 4.1, we recreate the diagram in a prefigured construction similar to Goldblatt's illustration of a bundle from topos theory (Goldblatt, 1984: 89). Each object in the bundle representing the given world has a mapping, referred to as a stalk, with an end point in the base space. These end points, as outputs of the functional mapping, record into this space a valuation of the relational degree of appearance of the objects and elements of the given world.

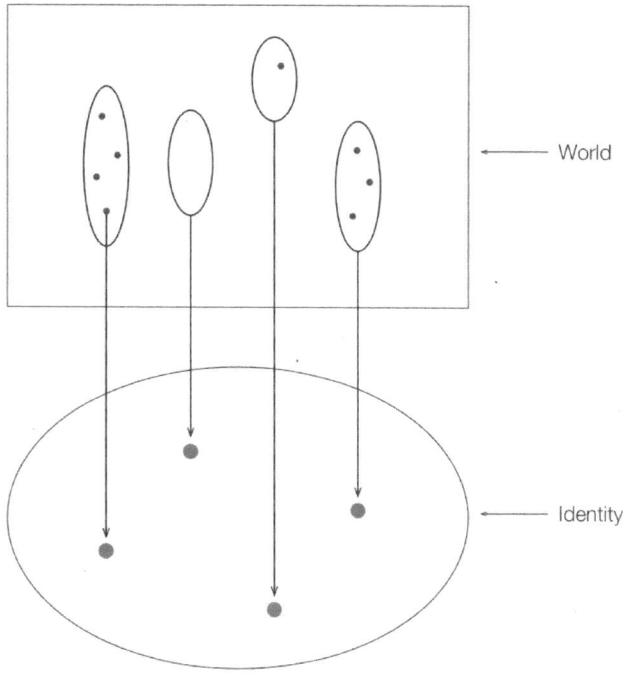

Figure 4.1. Transcendental index as identity of a world

Using logical operators, an object and the elements composing it range from appearing minimally to the maximum degree of exposure. Two elements of an object or two objects will differ to a certain degree. These elements will be related based on some ordering of their degree of difference, which could range from zero degree of difference to the maximal measurable difference. The transcendental index now houses the identity congealing the calculated results of that world's entire play of differences and identities. Working from within the envelope of an existing world, an underlying identity is revealed from what is bundled together in this world.[2] This highly abstract conception of a group or world identity we draw from fragments of Badiou's phenomenological studies, borrowing, as Badiou does, from category theory.[3]

The generalized space, or world, of our analysis is any organization, commercial or community-based, formed for the purposes of software development. In this study, we focus on a couple of mappings for the attributes that exist as elements of objects that uniquely contribute to the identity of this world. In this treatment objects can be either individuals, groups of individuals, or software performing a function. The particular function that maps our measured end points takes into account the input elements for that object that would indicate the level of authority within organization, and a second element indicating the visibility exposure of the object and its work or involvement in the organization. We posit that the generally recognized identity of this world prior to FLOSS would be an ordinal ranking of the objects with increasing authority correlated inversely with a decreasing level of visibility exposure to the inner workings for members of this object. As you rise through the ranks of authority there is more concealment of critical aspects of the organization's operations. This would be consistent with Foucault's analysis of the panopticon effect of the visibilities in modern societies. Prior to FLOSS, managers operate with more lines of visibility open to them to their direct reports than the lines of sight open in the reverse direction.

This identity—the bundled aggregation of subcomponent identities and their relational ordering inscribed into this world through the transcendental index—is what we'll view as an identity beyond individual identity; we will call it the group identity of a world or community. The objects and relations that appear maximally go furthest in uniquely defining group identity. The objects that are most intensely visible and with the highest degree of self-identification take on a primordial statement about a world's identity (Badiou, 2011: 84–85). At the other end of the spectrum are those objects that appear minimally. That an object can appear minimally, barely distinguishable, leads to the thought that it could also not appear. The delta between the brightest-appearing to the dimmest can be now be thought as going one degree further past what doesn't appear. Given that appearing is now equated with existence, from the thought of what doesn't appear we have that which is in-existent in a situation. The structured group identity of a world has within it the possibility of an in-existent making an appearance.

Anyone oriented to Badiou through his earlier work *Being and Event* will be aware of the absence in this discussion of the ontological level. Given that Being is multiplicity for Badiou, the objects composing a given world are the path into understanding the multiples—the sets and their elements—which constitute this world. Relations and their mappings overlay the underlying multiples in his atomistic model. The relations captured between the objects contribute to the configuration of the world, but Badiou doesn't see a change in relations as capable of changing a world (Badiou, 2011: 310–12). What we interject into Badiou's account is this: when examined at the global level, the relations between objects may take on object-like status; or what appears as an object may just be a relation (an account held by many category theorists).

An event in a world of appearing, in this account, is when an object or some element that composes it, which was thought to not exist, comes to appear maximally in the post-evental world order. This in-existence is not the appearance of an object from another world but that which, while still structured within a world's composition, had gone unnoticed as a possibility in that existing world. Brought on by an event, there is the emergence of a new identity with the coming into existence of an altered transcendental index. The event is a window into how we might read this future world where objects and relations now fall under a different transcendental ordering, an altered group identity.

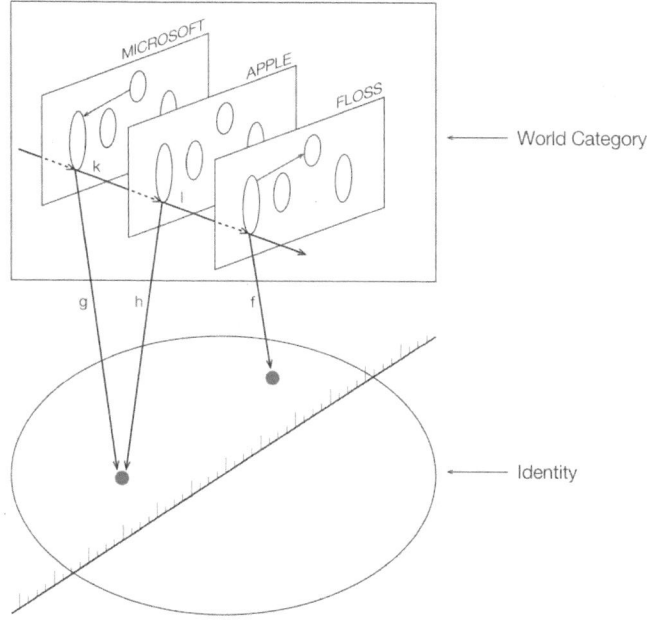

Figure 4.2. World with altered transcendental index

Figure 4.2 is a diagramming of the world affected by an event. When compared as an entire world-category, the various software organizations as one enveloped world, the mappings into the transcendental index between each organization should commute. That is, if the mapping holds between comparable objects found in both the Microsoft and Apple organizations, and the similar objects map to the same location in the identity index, then we are assured of an identity that can be reached via some isomorphism. If the arrow from h following arrow k commutes with arrow g, then there is structural consistency. Our analysis of the direction of transparency in FLOSS will attempt to show that a mapping to a similar authority level, arrow l, will lead to a differing degree of transparency, arrow f, when FLOSS is included in the global envelope of software development organizations. Our focus is on the structure and impact of visibilities undergoing a discontinuous break brought on by FLOSS from the normal relation under which visibilities previously operated.

Foucault, with his analysis of the panopticon effect, provides the definitive reference point for how visibilities function (Foucault, 1995: 195–228). Foucault's analysis of visibility provides a normative account of how technologies have assisted the masters of the capital-parliamentarian world order. "The exercise of discipline presupposes a mechanism that coerces by means of observation" (170). In this account, the microphysical level of power distributions, where visibilities operate, pervasively produces the automatic application of power. In places where authority is concentrated, the gaze penetrates maximally through to all levels. Where authority is held tenuously, there is only a dim gaze. In the corporate model of software development we presume to follow the identity of the established capital-parliamentarian order, which supports a full spectrum of exercised visibilities where authority operates from the side of the gaze, even when via technology no one is immediately present.

Even when this microphysics of power, thought of as political technology, doesn't emanate as determined solely by a sovereign state, as an apparatus it contributes an essential structural support for current historical formations. This visibility does not mean that transparency flows in all directions. Capitalist society in general can't elude the imbrication of the impropriety of full disclosure. Foucault provides us with the logic of visibilities in the existing order, but FLOSS thinks visibilities with a twist which takes us from an account of visibilities to that of transparency under an altered configuration. Previously, this transparency was a one-way visibility, with the masters gazing out from the towers of power, "eyes that must see without being seen" (Foucault, 1995: 171).

Following Badiou further, we can detect in his work two different senses of identity: static and active. "All identity is the dialectical play of a movement of creation (active) and a movement of purification (static)" (Badiou, 2008: 66). Static, or inert, identity is the form of self relating to self (Badiou, 2006a: 148–52). Static identity is that brush with difference where a self determines how it is "different from the rest" (Badiou, 2008: 64). The transcendental indexing includes this measure of self-relating for each object from which the world is composed. "Static," here, is not an isolation in time, since "the phenomenon integrates into its phenomenality the variations that constitute it over time" (Badiou, 2009: 359). Working from all that is known about a given world, the transcendental indexing functions as the static identity of the associated world.

Any given world will undergo modifications. In an active identity mode, a plurality of differences are embraced, "an expansion of identity" (Badiou, 2008: 65). In any process of identity expansion, an active identity is operative. Active identity expansions are explorations of further development of the various stalks that compose the bundle constituting an identity. This active identity expansion can lead in two directions. In the process of the expansion of a given world, it could expand in complexity and variation, yet all the while retain its identity. Under this condition the transcendental remains the unaltered. When the modifications remain isomorphic to the original state, the transcendental can account fully for the change.[a] Is FLOSS yet another development to be subsumed by the existing world, an active identity expansion that leaves the static identity of the corporate software development world under the smooth operation of the status quo? Alternatively, an active identity expansion could disturb the structure of the transcendental indexing, the global identity. In this case there is no inverse mapping, no subsumption, leaving the new state in a non-isomorphic transformation. Something has happened. With FLOSS, is there an identity expansion that brings an in-existent to the surface and exposes another order?

TRANSPARENCY IN FLOSS DEVELOPMENT

The revolution that this analysis describes has its inception at the site of Richard Stallman's Gnu Public License (GPL), which was designed to invert the normal intent of copyright (to restrict access), instead protecting the right of a license holder to refrain from restricting access (McGowan, 2005: 363). "The terms free and 'libre' (free in the sense of liberated in French and Spanish) are employed to signal a second of the important features of this innovation, the covenants guarding software from commercial expropriation. The intention of these covenants is to create a 'liberated zone' of software available for inspection and

---

a Following group theory, a group maintains its identity when for every transformation there is a corresponding inverse mapping (Badiou, 2006a: 148–52).

modification subject to the requirement that it will remain open in any subsequent distribution" (Dalle, David, den Bensten, and Steinmueller, 2008: 301, n. 1). Already we recognize an alteration in the previous lines of sight through inspection of source code that property rights obscure when they block access to source code.

Inseparable from the GPL in the FLOSS revolution is the intent of Linus Torvalds in making, over the Internet, a redoubled universal appeal for assistance with his fledging Linux operating system licensed under the GPL. The unrestricted access to source code, additionally reflected in the low cost or free access to the products, warrants the signifier "open" that this movement goes by. "Open source code development is defined in large part by its transparent process of collaborative development and the intellectual property regime and license that underpins it" (Cornford, Shaikh, and Ciborra, 2010: 811). Rather than dwelling on the GPL's significance in structuring this movement through guaranteed transparent access to the software, we will instead investigate the transparency at the core of the FLOSS software development processes, which we posit as one of the maximally appearing structural supports of the FLOSS configuration.

In the pioneering days of open source, Eric Raymond coined a mantra of the movement, "Given enough eyeballs, all bugs are shallow," which he declared as "Linus's Law" (Mateos-Garcia and Steinmueller, 2008: 334). Research has tried to validate whether FLOSS outperforms proprietary software when visibility of the source code produces a larger audience that in turn improves the testing and maintenance cycle of software development (Crowston, Wei, Howison, and Wiggens, 2012: 24). While identifying the improved reliability of code with Linus's Law is significant in explaining the unique nature of FLOSS, it overlooks the full impact of the microphysics of transparency.

There exists a technological dimension to the transparency encountered through the tools employed, the way they are employed, and the culture of practice behind this alternative development of software. Without the Internet and the overcoming of constraints of time and distance, the possibilities for a voluntary, highly distributed development effort don't exist. Software's humanly readable form of source code is not typically distributed when the software is purchased from proprietary software development firms; in FLOSS communities, however, the software code is freely accessible and with, for example, a GPL license it remains exposed in the public domain in perpetuity. This is a sympathetic relation of unconstrained access to the finished product held in harmony with the transparency the contributors operate with in the development process of this altered mode of production.

Specifically, the technological tools that the FLOSS community deploys for promoting the climate of transparency in their development process include chats, online project documentation, wikis, repository logs, issue/bug tracking, newsgroups, mailing lists, and version-control systems that provide access to the source code (Gutwin, Penner, and Schneider, 2004: 73–74, 78; Cornford, Shaikh, and Ciborra, 2010: 812). At the level where FLOSS is a community of open-source communities, there are repositories such as SourceForge, Savannah, and Freshmeat, which host a vast collection of projects with open access to the software and project artifacts. Inscribed in these tools, along with the GPL license and access to source code, is alignment with a culture of transparency. The constitution of a FLOSS community is inseparable from the built-in practice of exposing information. "In particular, there is a strong culture of 'making it public' where developers are willing to answer questions, discuss their plans, report on their actions, and argue design details, all on the mailing list" (Gutwin, Penner, and Schneider, 2004: 73).

Mailing lists play a critical part in the discussion of design decisions for source code development. FLOSS communities spend more time arguing the pros and cons of design and coding strategies than is traditionally spent in firms (Mateos-Garcia and Steinmueller, 2008: 335–36). "Almost *all* communication is done via the mailing lists. In the words of one of our developers . . . , 'If it doesn't happen on list, it doesn't happen'" (Gutwin, Penner, and Schneider, 2004: 76). The mailing lists, stored in searchable archives, maintain a complete historical record—a memory preserved in digital code. Strictly speaking, these tools could be configured to restrict access, but the experiment of FLOSS is to leave access open for the community and the general public. "They [the email and chat messages] are public, and so allow all the developers on the list to become peripheral participants in each others' conversations" (72). What identifies FLOSS maximally is that the default and enforced position is open. In-camera is anathema to this community practice. It is abnormal for one to encounter insufficient read permissions. This is not to say that there aren't boundaries to graduated access, since we acknowledge the existence of hierarchies within FLOSS practices, but the visibility of the communication exchanges or project artifacts remains unobscured across all boundaries.

Software development in this community construction, not unlike the case with proprietary software, is managed using a version control system (VCS).

Software stored in a VCS contains metadata that keeps track of every contribution submitted to the repository. Typically the commit logs of these contributions, which include the name of the person submitting the change, short comments about the change, and the content of the change, are automatically sent to mailing lists. The content of each change is preserved in the repository along with a record of code deletions. The VCS metadata makes it possible to compare differences in code content between any two points in time. It also makes it possible to reconstruct all the steps in the progress of the code contributions between these points in time (Cornford, Shaikh, and Ciborra, 2010: 812). Anyone not familiar with software development may recognize this concept of historical change recording in the track-change capability of word processors or as mirrored in the "revert to previous version" capability of wikis. Previously, a copy of the open-sourced code could be picked up from a repository; now the community approach is to permit read access to the VCS so that the entire sequenced history of the development of the code is recorded, visible, and replayable. Foucault had analyzed how the birth of the clinic brought with it the gaze of master and pupil, physician and student, focused on the surface effects of the disease (Foucault, 1994: 107–111). Here the gaze, even if without the feedback from interrogation, is focused both on the surface and on the effects below the surface to fully expose the complete inner workings of the FLOSS body of work.

This particular openness to the world creates a view from anywhere. A progression into a FLOSS community would typically begin with a prospective community member becoming acquainted with some aspect of a FLOSS project. This could begin with freely accessing the code and test-driving it, reading project documentation to comprehend project intent, reviewing bug-tracking to overcome a difficulty, or searching the mailing list discussions to understand the future direction of the project. "Interested parties may lurk and pick up information without being very visible" (Gutwin, Penner, and Schneider, 2004: 76). At this stage, legitimacy of membership in the community begins even if one is lurking in the shadows. The embryonic phase of identity construction absorbs through a gaze all the exposed body parts and organs of the FLOSS community. Participation begins from the periphery or the margins. From here contributors looking to participate in a project are free to self-select where to direct their efforts based on an affinity with a community where there is maximum exposure to the group's identity. Identity formation coincides with each level of access promotion across concentric boundaries, advancing toward core developer status or falling back through reduced interest in the project.

At a second stage of identity construction, participants can progress by asking questions on mailing lists, "reporting bugs, collecting feature requests, offering patches, or providing usage feedback" (Fang and Neufeld, 2009: 15). In the Debian[4] community one particular promotion is the granting of Non-Maintainer Upload (NMU) status, which grants broader permission for uploading critical bug fixes that recognized maintainers may not get to (Coleman, 2005: 10). "As one developer on IRC told me half-jokingly, an NMU reveals 'our laundry for public inspection'" (11). Even when confronted with the risk of unprofessional participation, the default setting to "open" remains a trait of this alternative order. These values have been sewn right into the fabric of Debian's Social Contract as part of the governing directives:

> 3. We will not hide problems: We will keep our entire bug report data-base open for public view at all times. Reports that people file online will promptly become visible to others. (Debian, 2004)

What are the effects when transparency is maximized? The general effect of the inverted direction of the gaze is heightened group awareness (Gutwin, Penner, and Schneider, 2004). How do individual identities in communities of practice form under such conditions of community awareness? We can examine how this transparency contributes to identity formation for individuals who begin the participation process from the outside peering in and progress, on their own accord, to increased involvement. In the course of this examination we are uncovering the group or collective identity of FLOSS and, simultaneously, how transparency assists individual identity development.

Fang and Neufeld's research directed at explaining sustained participation using legitimate peripheral participation (LPP) theory confirms this behaviour of FLOSS communities (Fang and Neufeld, 2009). Combining participation and situated learning, FLOSS, as a community of practice, provides the conditions for individual identity construction. Identity construction in this model is a process of identity-work and identity-regulation. "Identity-work refers to identity changes perceived by the focal individual as a result of access to understanding of the community artifacts" (22). Transparency comes into play through providing a maximum exposure to community artifacts against which a participant can build identity-work. "Identity-regulation refers to identity changes regulated in the local social context and is enacted as access to control in the OSS community" (22). Visibility of the participant's engagement in the community permits maximum exposure across code contributions, design suggestions, and troubleshooting support that lead to access or promotion. Transparency opens entry to these communities through the tools that can permit unrestricted access to the digitally preserved historical record, thus maximizing the ability to fully contextualize one's participation. LPP explains the identity-work that this participation generates, as participants initiate and then manage their participation. Full exposure of this participation contributes to the community's identification of the competence of participants and their subsequent progression through increasing access to community artifacts. The inverted play in the direction of gaze leading to transparency contributes to the newly formed group identity of FLOSS. The founding of a new dimension of visibility in turn produces an altered mode of production, with an appeal to enhanced means of active individual identity expansion.

Independent of participants' motivation, as they step out of the shadows and demonstrate they've been observing, they in turn have their identities recognized. In the original theoretical development of legitimate peripheral participation, the transition into a community was accompanied by a mentor. In the FLOSS model, technology contributes a persistent helping hand. "The novice is 'guided' by what is embedded in the code, mailing lists and forum postings that the novice reads, adapts and contributes rather than being guided by an individual serving in the mentor role, a role ordinarily thought to require human interaction" (Mateos-Garcia and Steinmueller, 2008: 335). Those on the periphery are legitimated. The legitimacy is possible because of what can be gleaned from external visibilities. Progressing forward, contributors can align their participation, building from an unobstructed view of the project's knowledge base. The increased recognition by the community contributes to the LPP notion of identity-regulation. FLOSS is a radicalization of a community of practice where the unique dimension is unbarred transparency, and where one of the things under observation is individual identity construction.

CONCLUSION

The identified examples of active identity expansion from within the FLOSS movement demonstrate that modifications have occurred. If the expansion is premised on the deployment of an inverted direction of visibility, previously seen as nonviable, the change driven by this event has the potential to be transformative. The world that FLOSS departs from operates under microphysical layers of visibilities that support the dominant power positions. In this traditional, hierarchical context, authority's field of vision always surpasses any reciprocal visibility. With the FLOSS movement, there is still the pervasive effect of visibilities. Now, however, the gaze is willfully inverted and directed at those exercising the most authority or holding the most power in the community. Visibilities are not curtailed, but rather expand to a maximum degree. The gaze being willingly inverted from those holding the most power to those choosing to forego a power hierarchy was previously unimaginable;[b] it remains the in-existent, within the logic of visibilities under its normative functioning within the world of software development.

A derivative effect is that FLOSS becomes more than a straight reversal between the viewer class and those subjected to the panoptical gaze. A presence on the Internet combined with a commitment to open access means there is no restriction on who can now peer in and choose whether or not to participate. Transparency and accessibility are multipliers of change effects over the previous world of visibilities, though initiated with an inversion merely in one relation. When the in-existent element is made an operative and indeed determining principle, then a recalibration of all relations has to be worked into the new transcendental of this fresh order. The beginnings of an unanticipated collective identity can be detected.

Having borrowed devices from Badiou for thinking structural identity and change, we contend, contra Badiou, that a change in relation has precipitated the altered mapping between objects. From Figure 4.2, there has been a reversing of direction for the internal relation between objects in the FLOSS frame. A change in relation results in the need for a recalibrated transcendental index. Badiou resists attributing to relations the power to transform a transcendental and the identity of a world order (Badiou, 2009: 310–12). We have shown that exposure to visibility can be treated as an element of an object, but it is a change in relations that has produced the change in the charge of the element. We hold that the inversion in the direction of the gaze is an alteration in relations, and one self-selected by the principal agents behind FLOSS projects. We argue that relations, arrows and morphisms in category theory terms, can also take on the form of an object when viewed from the level of the identity of a world.[5]

---

b Where accounts previously described the inversion of the panopticon as the synopticon (Stefanick 2011, 127-128), the FLOSS account may differ because the context is a mode of production where the principal agents self-select the positioning of the gaze on themselves.

Badiou has been critiqued for not paying attention to the underlying relation between capitalists and workers that structures the capital-parliamentarian order (Sotiris, 2011: 37–43). With the inversion of gaze that FLOSS produces, we have a new component to account for, one that also threatens to undermine one of the defining relations of the capital order itself. This altered relation shows all the signs of producing a new identity. Either way, this is an in-existent component rising up to maximally appear in a reconfigured order.

It is immaterial in theory if the ones being gazed at take form as a corporate entity. However, can a commercial software development company sustain an inverted gaze that leaves no bastion of authority exempt from exposure of all its goings-on? There would be no more "taking things internal," if that meant out of sight, in the face of a difficulty. Transparency in a proprietary world would have to progress past the carefully managed screening and redaction of what is released to the public to reach the level of transparency found in the FLOSS world, where there is visibility through to all aspects of the production process, with no regressing from this practice. These would be testable points where any regression that was confirmed would cancel out the claims of an altered identity, leaving the entities from the previous state returned to their isomorphic beginning. We speculate that this previously in-existent, altered relation functions as an impediment in the former regime's logic. We could then support that FLOSS is an evental disruption introducing fundamental change capable of producing high-quality software and demonstrating an alternative world with a reordered transcendental.

Technological advancements have created the conditions for furthering the pervasive panopticon effect. The transparency of FLOSS remains an instance of this effect. FLOSS operates with the logic of panopticon, but reverses the positions of observer and observed. The one-way mirror has been installed backwards. The blind spot in Foucault's analysis was the possibility that visibility could be inverted to a transparency turned on those in power, even while they are complicit in invoking this reversed effect. This reversal of the direction of transparency is not unlike the GPL reversing the effects of the normal operations of copyright. The panopticon enacted an effect:

> Because, in these conditions, its strength is that it never intervenes, it is
> exercised spontaneously and without noise, it constitutes a mechanism
> whose effects follow from one another. Because, without any physical
> instrument other than architecture and geometry, it acts directly on
> individuals; it gives "power of mind over mind." (Foucault, 1995: 206)

The agency derived through structured visibility now acts upon those lead-ing. Those on the periphery are granted full disclosure, in addition to the com-munity benefitting from transparency operating along all sightlines. Power is infused throughout the community. Just as anyone can step in behind the glass in the panopticon tower and put the discipline effect into operation, equally so can anyone in the FLOSS architecture of transparency. The new possibilities cre-ated with the technologies deployed in managing the source and communica-tions in FLOSS communities, when combined with willingness to invert the gaze, have made a difference.

With the event of Free/Libre Open Source Software structured as it is on at least two prominent pillars—the GPL and transparency-openness—an altered collective identity appears on the scene. If the FLOSS movement has proven to possess an alternative identity, then the capital-parliamentarian order might be considered its path of etiological descent. The event begins materially situated within an existing world order. From this existing order, with its operation of visibilities, we have confirmed a disruption of evental proportion. The ensuing result is the exposure of a new group identity, with the full impact of its struc-tural agency yet to be determined.

Badiou doesn't leave us much to work with if the goal is to explain the agency that brought about this event. Disappointingly, he attributes the arrival of an event more to chance than any agency (Badiou, 2011: 110–11). The possibility of this account of evental reshaping leaves technological determinism still in play. However, Badiou does reintroduce the theory of subject as the agency involved in the struggle, exploring through enquiries to fully develop the identity of this new world order brought on by an encounter with an event. Nietzsche's warn-ing about the void staring back has been ignored, and instead the benefits to be gained from increased exposure to the void's gaze are welcomed. The truth behind FLOSS supports the truth behind Badiou's conception of the event. The void, in the form of the open, a lurking participant in every situation, can peer into a situation and become manifest.

NOTES

1 Badiou's phenomenological studies, considered here, include *Logics of Worlds* (2009), *Briefings on Existence* (2006a), and *Second Manifesto for Philosophy* (2011).
2 This account is not far removed from the thought of quantum field theorists. "You can regard properties as having an existence, independently of objects that

possess them. Properties may be what philosophers call "particulars"—concrete, individual entities. What we commonly call a thing may be just a bundle of properties: color, shape, consistency, and so on . . . Out there in the world, things are nothing but bundles of properties" (Kuhlman, 2013: 47).

3 Badiou outlines his formal dependency on category theory in *Logics of Worlds* (2009: 537–39) and in *Briefings on Existence* (2006: chap. 13).

4 Debian is one of the genuine FLOSS communities that produces a distribution of Linux. A distribution contains the Linux operating system packaged with additional software and supporting developments packages to enhance the computing environment.

5 Quantum field theorists also propose that the fundamental ontology appears to actually be relations. "In other words, objects do not have intrinsic properties, only properties that come from their relations with other objects . . . The only interesting and new position would be that everything emerges purely on the basis of relations" (Kuhlmann, 2013: 46).

REFERENCES

Badiou, Alain. 1991. "On a Finally Objectless Subject." In *Who Comes After the Subject?*, ed. Eduardo Cadava, Peter Connor, and Jean-Luc Nancy, 21–32. New York: Routledge.

———. 1992. *Manifesto for Philosophy*. Trans. Norman Madarasz. Albany: SUNY Press.

———. 2006a. *Briefings on Existence: A Short Treatise on Transitory Ontology*. Trans. Norman Madarasz. Albany: SUNY Press.

———. 2006b. *Metapolitics*. Trans. Jason Barker. London: Verso.

———. 2008. *The Meaning of Sarkozy*. Trans. David Fernbach. London: Verso.

———. 2009. *Logics of Worlds: Being and Event, 2*. Trans. Alberto Toscano. London: Continuum.

———. 2011. *Second Manifesto for Philosophy*. Trans. Louise Burchill. Cambridge: Polity Press.

Coleman, E. Gabriella. 2005. "Three Ethical Moments in Debian." *Social Science Research Network*. Accessed February 8, 2013. doi:10.2139/ssrn.805287.

Cornford, Tony, Maha Shaikh, and Claudio Ciborra. 2010. "Hierarchy, Laboratory and Collective: Unveiling Linux as Innovation, Machination and Constitution." *Journal of the Association for Information Systems* 11: 809–37.

Crowston, Kevin, Kangning Wei, James Howison, and Andrea Wiggins. 2012. "Free/ Libre Open Source Software Development: What We Know and What We Do

Not Know." *ACM Computing Surveys* 44.2.7: 1–35. Accessed March 28, 2012. doi:10.1145/2089125.2089127.

Dalle, Jean Michel, Paul A. David, Matthijs den Besten, and W. Edward Steinmueller. 2008. "Empirical Issues in Open Source Software." *Information Economics and Policy* 20: 301–4. doi:10.1016/j.infoecopol.2008.09.001.

Debian. 2004. "Debian Social Contract." Ratified 26 April. http://www.debian.org/social-contract.

———. 2011. "Non-Maintainer Upload." Last modified 30 June. http://wiki.debian.org/NonMaintainerUpload.

Deshpande, Amit, and Dirk Riehle. 2008. "The Total Growth of Open Source." In *IFIP Advances in Information and Communication Technology* 275, pt. 1, *Open Source Development, Communities and Quality*, eds. Barbar Russo, Ernesto Damiani, Scott Hissam, Björn Lundell, and Giancarlo Succi, 197–209. Boston: Springer. doi:10.1007/978-0-387-09684-1_16.

Fang, Yulin, and Derrick Neufeld. 2009. "Understanding Sustained Participation in Open Source Software Projects." *Journal of Management Information Systems* 25(4): 9–50. doi:10.2753/MIS0742-1222250401.

Foucault, Michel. 1994. *The Birth of the Clinic: An Archaeology of Medical Perception.* Trans. A. M. Sheridan Smith. New York: Vintage.

———. 1995. *Discipline and Punish: The Birth of the Prison.* Trans. Alan Sheridan. New York: Vintage.

Goldblatt, Robert. 1984. *Topoi: The Categorial Analysis of Logic.* Amsterdam: Elsevier Science Publishers.

Gutwin, Carl, Reagan Penner, and Kevin Schneider. 2004. "Group Awareness in Distributed Software Development." In *Proceedings of the ACM Conference on Computer-Supported Cooperative Work.* 72–81. New York: ACM Press. doi: 10.1145/1031607.1031621.

Kuhlmann, Meinard. 2013. "What Is Real?" *Scientific American* 309(2): 40–47.

Mateos-Garcia, Juan, and W. Edward Steinmueller. 2008. "The Institutions of Open Source Software: Examining the Debian Community." *Information Economics and Policy* 20: 333–44. doi:10.1016/j.infoecopol.2008.06.001.

McGowan, David. 2005. "Legal Aspects of Free and Open Source Software." In *Perspectives on Free and Open Source Software*, ed. Joseph Feller, Brian Fitzgerald, Scott A. Hissam, and Karim R. Lakhani, 361–91. Cambridge: MIT Press.

Sotiris, Panagiotis. 2011. "Beyond Simple Fidelity to the Event: The Limits of Alain Badiou's Ontology." *Historical Materialism* 19(2): 35–59. doi:10.1163/156920611X573789.

Stefanick, Lorna. 2011. *Controlling Knowledge: Freedom of Information and Privacy Protection in a Networked World.* Edmonton: Athabasca University Press.

Tapscott, Don, and Anthony D. Williams. 2008. *Wikinomics: How Mass Collaboration Changes Everything*. New York: Portfolio.

Zhai, Zhi, Tracy Kijewski-Correa, Ashan Kareem, David Hachen, and Gregory Madey. 2012. "Citizen Engineering: Evolving OSS Practices to Engineering Design and Analysis." In *IFIP Advances in Information and Communication Technology* 378, pt. 1, *Open Source Systems: Long-Term Sustainability*, ed. Imed Hammouda, Björn Lundell, Tommi Mikkonen, and Walt Scacchi, 61–77. Boston: Springer-Verlag. doi:10.1007/978-3-642-33442-9_5.

Part Two

Digital
Culture

5 Hacktivist (Pre)Occupations
Self-Surveillance, Participation, and Public Space

Carolyn Guertin

Surveillance technologies are everywhere. We are now almost constantly photographed, tracked, monitored, recorded, and stored. Often this surveillance is so insidious and surreptitious that we neither realize it is occurring nor attribute any harm to it. George Orwell would shudder at what we submit to. Google Glass and other commercial products with their always-on surveillance cinema potential just deepen this threat. Always shifting between the two rhetorical poles of security and safety, this tracking happens everywhere, in spaces both real and virtual. Surveillance artist Peter J. Cornwell says, "The involuntary traces ... we leave everywhere on the Internet are ... more difficult to recognize" than those in the real world, "and almost impossible to recall."

Many Internet sites that we visit, especially those of technology companies, secretly interrogate our computers: analyzing our habits, reporting the serial numbers of products that we have loaded, and leaving information for later exploitation. One's information fingerprint is now a persistent and monotonically expanding trace, distributed among countless computers across the globe and in space and independent of any specific surveillance agenda (Cornwell, 2002: 597).

Who knows what about us is impossible to determine. Who they might share it with or how long they might keep it is untraceable. As the potential for the integration of automated, networked, intelligent technologies that span multiple systems increases, a rhetoric of safety feeds these ever-greater encroachments on our rights to privacy (Cornwell, 2002: 597). There is a revolution coming in information privacy, and ubiquitous intelligent cameras mark the end of privacy as we have known it. Witness, for instance, the Mood Meter created by the MIT Media Lab in 2012. Using real-time facial recognition software to create live displays of how the inhabitants of a room or a building are feeling, Fast Company Design Magazine likens it to how we catch a vibe about a gathering, or how we read the emotional temperature of a room. Javier Hernandez Rivera and M. Ehsan Hoque log smiles with their camera and software. That information is then live-fed back into the room with emoticons in the place of their faces. Dubbed a "mood barometer," the purpose of this interaction is to gauge whether, in fact, happiness—or at least a smile—is contagious. The software is very effective at prodding people who are unhappy or in a neutral mood to act happier. Simply acting happy is infectious. As many studies have proved, pretending to be happy, or smiling when you are not, does have a real impact on your actual mood. This interactive installation software seeks feedback from participants, unlike many of the new dataveillance techniques: the systematic monitoring of a person's finances, communications, and digital interactions ask for no feedback, and in fact are nearly invisible to their subjects.

Prior to former NSA contractor Edward Snowden's whistle-blowing revelations about the activities of the U.S. National Security Agency, we did not know whether or when we were being tracked, or how long the info would be stored, or with whom it might be shared. In a post-Snowden era, we now know that American telephone companies routinely hand metadata over to government offices and that user-friendly digital surveillance systems such as Prism and XKeystroke (XKS) snare vast amounts of unencrypted data. Increasingly smart technologies, especially photographic ones, sift, store, and analyze our data, keeping it (in theory at least) in perpetuity. Viruses hijack our browsers, capturing our search data and preferences. From overt CCTV filming to the seemingly innocuous tracking of our grocery store or online purchases, to the extraction of data from our Web surfing, to the monitoring of Facebook photos, we are rich veins of data to be mined by the networked systems from many different sources. These techniques make the Stasi, the relentless police of the German Democratic Republic's Ministry for State Security, look like amateurs. The GDR employed a fleet of officers and informants—more than half a million at its peak—and 10,000 of those were employed solely in the business of monitoring and transcribing conversations (Levin, 2002: 579). Primarily employing auditory technologies, the Stasi's methods predate the digital information explosion of personal computers and were in decline in the 1980s up until they were disbanded after the fall of the Berlin Wall. Now we have moved into a post-panoptic system, into the realm of automated dataveillance.

ECHELON is the industrialized West's answer to the Stasi. It is the surveillance system of the U.S. and the U.K., Canada, Australia, and New Zealand. It was formed in 1947 in a secret agreement between the United States and Britain. Later, other countries, including Denmark, Norway, Germany, and Turkey, became "third party" participants. ECHELON's existence only became public knowledge in 1988 when it essentially moved to a 2.0 phase with all-new mainframes. It is a system that tags key words and "sniffs" all data traffic between civilians and the military, routinely tagging any of its so-called dictionary terms, names, and phrases (Levin, 2002: 579). Something that enabled greater access for ECHELON systems was the conversion of the ISDN (short for the Integrated Services Digital Network protocol) to an all-digital global format in the 1990s. This change was fueled by the arrival of the World Wide Web, and these upgrades in turn transformed the dial-up market and made high-speed Internet access possible. The ISDN protocol, established by the United Nations, ensures that global telecommunications systems can handshake. This system is why it is possible to make a phone call to India or Nigeria, for instance, despite radically different phone companies and systems. ISDN systems are now on the wane, and soon to be eclipsed by broadband. What is unique about ISDN systems, though, is what has enabled the NSA's vast spy network—they provide easy access for dataveillance: "ISDN protocol are not only optimized to deliver data to ECHELON like sniffer systems, but also allow one to take any phone 'off the hook' without it ringing in order to listen in to any domestic or office space" (Levin, 2002: 580). It is known that these ECHELON-like systems had astronomical capacities for storing data back in the 1990s; we can only speculate as to how much of our personal data they hold now. The *Guardian* reports, "In 2012, there were at least 41 billion total records collected and stored in XKeyscore for a single 30-day period" (Greenwald, 2013).

In the two decades since, other technologies have come thick and fast. The Danish stroboscopic camera, Jai, was released in 2011. It is said to be able to detect any conversation behind a closed window within visual range, which is about a kilometer away. A laser version by PK Electronick can take hundreds of pictures in a matter of seconds and individually photograph all the participants in a crowd (Levin, 2002: 579). The Q-Tel molecular scans that are being released in 2013 for airport security are even scarier: "the machine can sniff out a lot more than just explosives, chemicals and bioweapons" (NAC, 2012). The manufacturer, Genia Phototonics, says it can "penetrate clothing and many other organic materials and offers spectroscopic information especially for materials that impact safety such as explosives and pharmacological substances" (NAC, 2012). In other words, it will know what you had for breakfast and what molecular tags you have, such as whether you are predisposed for a particular type of cancer. It is small, portable, and can be operated anywhere within fifty meters of subjects without anyone ever knowing (NAC, 2012). It gives governments the means to sample populations, record their molecular data, and move "well beyond eavesdropping" (NAC, 2012).

Within consumer culture, data is gold too. Self-surveillance—the act of submitting your own data to corporate interests such as Amazon, TiVo, or Facebook—becomes a revolutionary gesture of participation (Andrejevic, 2007: 15) ... or so corporations would have us believe. With the advent of social media, we now log our own data in the service of multinationals as we seemingly embrace the arrival of a technological Big Brother as participatory surveillors (Batchler, 2012: 92–99; Turner, 2012: 8). A number of digital media artists and groups, however, have turned the tables—or, more exactly, the camera—on themselves by using digital media and self-surveillance as a means of writing their own digital narratives outside of the parameters of social media control. Exploring the ubiquitous potential of surveillance technologies as a medium of self-expression, guerrilla methods by artists are producing site-specific works that use these tactics to repossess all-seeing cameras for aesthetic ends. Social activists also use the potentialities of self-surveillance to reveal and to disguise, to network and to disconnect as a way of both communicating and avoiding detection.

The Occupy Movement uses a blend of social media, self-surveillance, and both official and unofficial media footage to keep their politics in the public consciousness, while also keeping themselves out of the public eye. To succeed, the Occupy Movement must be present and situated, but anonymous and dynamic. Embracing the philosophy that the revolution will not be televised (because once it is, it is subsumed within what Guy Debord called the "Society of the Spectacle"), #OCCUPY offers new nonvisual data-based strategies for networked organizing, collaborative creation, and collective aesthetic acts. Leading thinkers in the situationist movement, Guy Debord (in *The Society of the Spectacle*) and Raoul Vaneigem (in *The Revolution of Everyday Life*) advocated against the transactional nature of capitalism in favour of living every moment consciously as a way of constantly reinventing life, reality, and society. Through transforming one's self, they argued, one altered one's relation to power structures and to the world. Using rhetorical strategies (including the *dérive*, *détournement*, and psychogeographic exploration) as an anti-aesthetic that has been very influential to the #OCCUPY Movement, the situationists called for local acts to replace both mediated spectacle and highbrow art in order to create "a new genre of creation" (Situationists International Texts). #OCCUPY is certainly a genre of that ilk. Self-surveillance rethinks aesthetic approaches to creative practice in provocative ways.

Participation in public space has the potential to challenge the installed public cameras and formal systems of control precisely by using the politics of location to speak against official discourses. Returning collective action and public narrative to town squares, these groups and artists are reinventing narrative for a digital culture generation. The spontaneous uprising of collective, multilinear narratives in global public space has rendered the Square the new center of participatory art, and these actions are a roadmap to where future technologies might take us.

Guerrilla use of public technologies is one version of what German artist Joseph Beuys called social sculpture. Beuys defined social sculpture as a cultural reflection on and an active intervention into a community or environment for the purpose of creating a space for unexpected interactions and situational participation. Social sculpture, by design, explores the relationship between aesthetics, social processes, and ecosystems through performance, environmentalism, and political engagement. In the early days of the Web, when networked computer technology was still fairly primitive by our current standards, Mexican-American performance artist Guillermo Gomez-Peña and collaborator Roberto Sifuentes launched a high-tech event called "Naftaztec: Pirate Cyber-TV for AD 2000." As Latinos, he and Sifuentes had been stung by the libertarian rhetoric that maintained cyberspace was a politically neutral space of equal access, a space allegedly free from the barriers of race, gender, and class. For Gomez-Peña, this was a cop-out that denied the crises of social and racial inequality that engulfed and continues to engulf the United States (Gomez-Peña, 2000: 295–308).

The pair actively played with the stereotypes of Mexicans as techno-illiterates and illegal aliens, and hijacked cable television in 1994. These Pirates, critiquing American culture, interrupted evening news broadcasting in 3.5 million American homes. This was not a hack. It was an experimental satellite broadcast in multi-lingual television; they purchased the airtime and transmitted this alleged pirate intervention to hundreds of community cable outlets. In total they were on air for ninety minutes. They were promoting an altered view of reality. Part of the broadcast included The Chicano Virtual Reality Machine, which could videotape personal and collective memories, and a Virtual Reality Bandanna, which would allow Americans "to experience first hand the psychological sensation of racism" (Gomez-Peña, 2000: 39). They renamed the Internet the Chicano Interneta and surfers were allowed to post written and visual comments at their website. The broadcast won the prize as best experimental video at the San Antonio Cine Festival in 1994.

Another performance troupe that seized the eyes of the law to repurpose these official cameras for their own ends was the Surveillance Camera Players. From 1996 until 2006, the Players set out to remake what they called the "tools of social control," that are used both to enslave them within consumer culture and police them against shoplifting, stealing from employers, sabotaging, or vandalizing goods or property that belong to others. Making explicit the connection between the eye of the lens and the hand of the law through their pro-privacy acts, the Surveillance Camera Players set out to make use of these cameras that they claimed had lowered crime rates so profoundly that, they said, they left security guards without anything to watch. Seen as a kind of programming, the troupe used the surveillance cameras as an audience of their own productions, which could happen at a surprise location at the same time (Tuesdays at 8:30, for instance) as a sort of regular guerrilla programming with performances that started out as one-time productions of plays, like the staging of a silent version of *Waiting for Godot*. Some cameras they used were monitored live and others recorded to tape, so productions were tailored specifically to the venue. They say,

> as guerrillas, we must ensure that we do not relish the camera.
> Surveillance is not passive and it is not our friend. We must not mistake
> the subversive possibilities offered by the abundance of equipment
> meant to curtail, monitor, and control our desires with a neat new
> device provided for us by the spectacle. We don't need this garbage to
> have a good time, any more than we need TV, but if the enemy is going
> to clutter our landscape with watchful eyes, we should look into those
> eyes and let them know how silly we think they are. Guerrilla program-
> ming is production of an action, not consumption of a product. It may
> be that the surveillance camera can give us a focus point on the street

(or the mall, or the cafe, or the bathroom) in which to utilize the few salvageable aspects of performance art or "happenings" without the elitism and reliance on the media inherent in such fluff. (Surveillance Camera Players)

Fast-forward to the days of the Occupy Movement, and the notion of entertaining, amusing, and morally edifying "the surveilling members of the law enforcement community" no longer seems so amusing (Surveillance Camera Players). One group, the Institute for Applied Autonomy, has created an app that repurposes the data collected by the Surveillance Camera Players. The troupe had produced a map of all of the cctv locations in public space in New York City. The Institute took this data and created a "path of least surveillance" (Institute for Applied Autonomy): a web-based app called iSee that helps individuals plan a route that avoids detection. Events in Tiananmen Square had demonstrated in a gruesomely dramatic fashion how easily the ubiquitous surveillance camera could be repurposed by hostile police and army should the occasion arise. In the wake of the September 11th attacks on New York, the Institute wanted to be sure that protesters were safe. By clicking on the iSee "map, a user indicates points of origin and destination" (Institute for Applied Autonomy) and can then safely navigate through unsurveilled urban space.

When interactive media artist Hasan M. Elahi's name was mistakenly added to the watch list by the cia, he turned the camera on himself to practice protective self-surveillance in *Tracking Transience: The Orwell Project*. A case of mistaken identity for the Bangladeshi-American artist led to six months of interrogation and investigation. It was ultimately Elahi's use of social media that saved him from a stint in Guantanamo because he was able to call up Google calendar and demonstrate that he could not have done what he was being accused of. As a response to those months of trauma, Elahi preempted any further incidents by wiring himself with a gps and relentlessly documenting his own movements, his meals, and his activities. This means that he is always trackable in real time by the fbi or anyone else. His website documents all of these activities, often to the tune of more than 100 photos per day. Others, too, practice this kind of art, as lifecamming and live blogging become more and more popular for twenty-first century Proustians.

According to digital media theorist Christiane Paul, streamed experience is the closest thing to live experience in our mediated age (Paul, 2008: 18). Live experience in a mediated age is elusive. Capture or streaming is becoming the default mode for life-like experiences. Capture can be simple, like Noah Kalina Everyday (see Kalina). This was a six-year experiment in which the artist photographed himself every day and then compressed these images into a time-lapsed film that he posted on YouTube. Or capture can be complex. Witness Manu Luksch's fifty-five-minute feature film *Faceless* (Luksch, 2007), for instance, which stars Tilda Swinton and was created through capture with CCTV cameras over many months.

Using the British Data Protection Act of 1998 and other privacy legislation to reclaim data records and surveillance footage for her own ends, Luksch gains access to her publicly viewed data and images. The use of CCTVs is strictly controlled in some countries, such as Denmark and Germany. In the U.K., however, they are extremely densely deployed. Penning a "Manifesto for CCTV Filmmakers," Luksch declares a set of rules, establishes effective procedures, and identifies further issues for filmmakers using pre-existing CCTV (surveillance) systems as a medium in the U.K. The filmmaker's standard equipment is thus redundant; indeed, its use is prohibited. The manifesto, according to Luksch, can easily be adapted for different jurisdictions (Luksch, 2006).

Calling her works ambientTV, Luksch advocates not introducing any new cameras or lighting into the scenes. The data subject (or protagonist) must be featured in all key scenes, with the documented activity counting as sensitive or personal data. In addition, all third parties must be rendered unidentifiable; since surveillance cameras don't record sound, filmmakers must determine their own parameters for sounds; and finally, since the footage is subject to such complex copyright and privacy issues, any filmmaker should employ a lawyer before trying to show their finished work (Luksch, 2006).

Faceless explores a futuristic era of calendar reform in which the past and the future have been eliminated from people's lives. We could call Luksch's approach Postcinematic Surveillance—a whole new genre. Following the protocol of her own "Manifesto," Luksch uses these captured images, which anyone can request of themselves, to construct a surreal, choreographed world where everyone's face is obliterated (as required by the privacy law). Luksch posits the guerrilla filmmaker as a viral agent and a "symbiont." She says that the most prolific documentarists are no longer to be found in film schools and TV stations. In some European and American cities, every streetcorner is under constant surveillance using recording closed-circuit TV (CCTV) cameras. Such cameras are typically operated by local government, police, private security firms, large corporations and small businesses, and private individuals, and may be automatic or controlled (zoomed and panned) from a remote control room. Filmmakers, and in particular documentarists of all flavours, should reflect on this constant gaze, she says. Why bring in additional cameras, when much private and public urban space is already covered from numerous angles? (Luksch, 2006). In the act of hijacking these technologies, lighting and cameras become not just unnecessary but forbidden. The hack is complete once Big Brother's eye is used for aesthetic effect.

Media theorist Marshall McLuhan said, "technologies begin to perform the function of art in making us aware of the psychic and social consequences of technology" (McLuhan, 1964: 14). These artistic endeavors invert internalized psychic and social events to make them visible as art. As our technology more and more stands as an interface and a boundary object between us and a world where everything is mediated, these surveillance art efforts have been, until now, largely hardware-driven. With the rise of the smart phone and mobile technologies, self-surveillance, participation, and public space are transformed.

We live in dangerous times. Merely by placing a phone call to the phone company, police departments can "clone" a mobile and download text messages even while it is turned off (Lichtblau, 2012). This is not legal in the U.S., but, regardless, phone companies comply in the interest of public safety. During the Arab Spring many protesters and activists worked with "media-savvy video journalists" to devise new methods of organizing outside of the all-seeing eye of the police, while the latter, in turn, would use similar methods to monitor communication. These journalists are "dubbed vee-jays" and they implement a variety of "dissemination strategies": "Photos and videos are shared across multiple platforms, alongside additional text, context, or transcripts, and often have metadata such as time, date, and location stamps" (Ulbricht, 2012). Content is uploaded live or at regular intervals through an assortment of social media sites and livestream portals, including Bambuser, by satellite connection. When Internet or cellular access gets shut down or disrupted, "footage is collected and distributed via agile alternatives such as runners—[known as] the old-fashioned 'sneaker net'" (Ulbricht, 2012).

During the student protests in London in January 2011, police started corralling students who had taken to the streets. The police used a tactic called "kettling," which traps protesters between their frontline and a cordoned-off area. Protesters are then either herded by police out of the area or are trapped within the enclosure. In many instances, the protesters are then denied access to food, water, and bathroom facilities for long periods of time. In response to this, a group of students and volunteers banded together to create Sukey. This is an app designed to inform protesters of police movements, giving the users directions to avoid being trapped within a cordon. The info travels in real time via any social media platform to and from mobile phones. The source is people monitoring the news and other protesters and observers in the area. "Since many people rely on the authenticity of this information, identification of sources is crucial" (Malevé, 2012: 15).

Sukey searches for messages on Facebook, Twitter, Tumblr, and other social networks using the hashtag #Sukey. The results are then filtered using what one of the programmers calls "a kind of algorithmic reputation management." The use of Sukey has proved very useful for "escap[ing] kettling. But it has also raised many questions regarding [its reliance] on external platforms to establish the reliability and trustworthiness of its sources, in a context where trust is essential" (Malevé, 2012, 15–16).

Sukey taps into the power of social networks "to aggregate and spread information and map out relationships, and used this power to distribute strategic information to protesters. But in doing so, it also fed the data hungry machines of social networks with sensitive information about protesters and their circles of friends" (Malevé, 2012: 15–16). In other words, using Sukey could just as easily trap you as save you. It is designed to work in real space, but it makes apparent how easy it will be for the police to start using digital cordons (Malevé, 2012: 16). And it is equally clear that it is just a matter of time before they will. Social media service providers have been no friends to protesters under NSA and other regulations, and they have the right "to not only 'contribute to prevent' but also to 'terminate' infringements" of usage (Malevé, 2012: 17). We already have seen how easily the dotcom boom wiped out independent providers and "put large, well financed, corporations back in the driving seat" with Web 2.0 (Malevé, 2012: 17–18). While we do the work of social media, "the mission of 2.0," Nicolas Malevé says, "is to destroy the P2P aspect of the Internet: To make you, your computer, and your Internet connection dependent on connecting to a centralized service that controls your ability to communicate" (Malevé, 2012: 18).

Because social media users inevitably use the large providers like Facebook and Twitter, the providers make deals and move further and further from net neutrality. "The infrastructure built for surveillance can thus be recycled in order to develop a commercial model of bandwidth discrimination" (Malevé, 2012: 19). The Occupy Movement and other protesters have created some alternatives that enable you to once again control, monitor, and even alter your social data and location. Open Street Map project (OSM) is one such option. It deals more intelligently with user data and demonstrates how a community designs, maintains, and interprets its own data within a unique framework. OSM is essentially "a Wikipedia for maps," but it reinvents Web 2.0 in some specific ways: it is open about data, metadata, and logged behaviour: rather than merely using the data, users are encouraged to think critically about it (Malevé, 2012: 21). You can also decide what to do with your own logs once you have used them—archive, edit, or delete them?—because it gives you the ability to modify your data. Users formalize their participation through OSM, in order to safeguard the fundamental motives behind their participation and to ensure that no uninvited eyeballs are watching their movements.

Cell phone providers are another weak link in the communication chain and render the DIY cell phones impractical for leading the protest charge; Occupy. here is a better system. An open-source local area network or personal Internet, it establishes "a peer-to-peer network of virtual spaces (autonomous from the Internet) for open political discussions. Anyone within range of an Occupy. here WiFi router with a web-capable smartphone or laptop can join the network 'OCCUPY.HERE,' load the locally hosted website http://occupy.here/ and use the message board to connect with other users nearby." Another app, Serval Rhizome Retriever, "allows news, information, software updates, files, maps etc to be disseminated without any supporting Internet access"; similarly Geolocha, enables geolocation-based chatrooms for protesters on the move because "public" is a space and a group constantly subject to renegotiation.

The camera and camera-enabled technologies have been a major source of resistance and information dissemination for the Occupy Movement. Cop Recorder masks your location and Vibe inhibits access to your location. Cop Recorder is "a network-enabled authority recorder" (occupy-here) that allows for secret audio recording when you have an encounter with an enforcer. It then facilitates an easy anonymous upload to its own OpenWatch.net server. Vibe is a major social media innovation in the #occupywallstreet protest (Nouveau 2011). A microblogging software similar to Twitter, it is anonymous, temporal, and location-based. Created by Hazem Sayed, the Vibe app is revolutionary because it creates a temporal tether for the dissemination of a message. Time frames can be as short as fifteen minutes or as long as thirty days. Similarly, the distance of transmission can be as small as 160 feet and as expansive as the whole world. As a protest tool, it enables mobility. It fosters a fluid ability to hide, dodge, and circumvent real-time police monitoring of social media networks. It is also local, and at its best targets a particular need in a particular place at a particular time.

The first massive decentralized social network in the history of the Internet is called TheGlobalSquare (Roos, 2011). Designed as a tool against censorship and oppression, it works on the Libertarian premise that information should be free. Repurposing peer-to-peer approaches, the creator, FNF, and others "are revisiting older tech such as HAM or CB radio based packet radio systems as stand-alone systems or as nodes in a newly emerging alternative internet" (Nocturnals-Anonymous). The Free Network Foundation (FNF), Project Mesh Net, and Open-mesh.org use Freedom Towers and unregistered routers to create their own independent networks. These three groups are "developing a 'mesh' approach to the internet which, theoretically, would be free, ubiquitous and anonymous" (Nocturnals-Anonymous) and as peer-to-peer networks would eliminate all intermediaries. Their goal, according to Brian Anderson, director of the documentary *Free the Network: Hackers Take Back the Internet*, is to create an uncensorable internet—a network free from government or corporate manipulation and regulation. Together all of these many alternative approaches are starting to coalesce into real opposition to outside control. Since they are not operating in secret, it will be a challenge to defeat official opposition. The FNF speculates:

> If such a "meshnet" does come into existence, we can expect a vigorous reaction by governments the world over. However, where there is no "there" there to regulate, where the transactions are anonymous and essentially untraceable, it remains unclear what steps will be available to a government to assert control over such a system, but we can certainly expect them to try. (Nocturnals-Anonymous)

As Professor Xavier says in *The X-Men*, "anonymity is the first line of defense" (Gürses, 2012: 54). To continue to enable protest and reform, it is crucial that protesters need to be able to do so as anonymous subjects and with anonymous data. "Always a means, never an end in itself" (55), Seda Gürses says that anonymity is generally perceived as a crime, but in fact it is a necessary strategy under oppressive regimes where people's movements are closely controlled. Anonymity as a strategy enables us to strip messages of any useable or traceable information. This is particularly important in the United States and Canada where data is increasingly inaccessible. Under the European Data Protection Directive, anonymous data is free. Anyone can access it, mine it, use it, or even repurpose it. In North America, the reverse is true: we are locked out of access even to anonymous data, and the big brother of social media mercilessly catalogues our own data. Instead, we might well imagine a world such as Karen Mancel and Herman Maat's interactive wearable work, Tele_Trust. Maat says that all communication is "based on trust" (Mancel and Maat, 2009). We can read religious significance into the veil-like wearable technology, but it could also be a high-tech suit that plugs the user into a mode of transmission. Proximity creates a network of bodies and enables communication, as touch triggers snippets of conversation about trust issues. The transmissions that are received are excerpts from interviews with people around the issues of safety, and the dichotomy of public/private space. These messages are transmitted to interactors who touch the wearer, to plug in to that person's personal network. Karen Mancel asks: "Is it necessary to touch somebody to be able to trust him?" (Mancel and Maat, 2009)

In conclusion, I would ask: Where lies the future of public space? If our rights to our personal data, our rights to assemble, and our rights to our molecular autonomy are being stolen from us, then are we forced to adopt an Orwellian kind of doublethink in order to survive? Or is it possible, as the Occupy Movement and a variety of media artists maintain, for us to preserve a space for autonomy? Dataveillance threatens to suck up not just our data, but to anticipate our needs and desires as well. In fact, a study conducted in 2013 by Cambridge University Press (and funded by Microsoft and Boeing), says just that—confirming what Facebook knew all along: given enough data, you can start to make predictions about people's lifestyle and likes and dislikes. Some of the headlines about their report read:

- Your Facebook Likes can predict your sexual orientation with 88 percent accuracy.
- Liking Harley Davidson . . . is predictive of low intelligence, whereas Liking Curly Fries is predictive of high intelligence.
- If you've Liked Hello Kitty, you're more likely to be creative, but not very conscientious. (Marsden, 2013)

The report, called "Private traits and attributes are predictable from digital records of human behavior," has spawned a free online personality test called youarewhatyoulike.com, and clearly the lifestyle choices that it predicts with such accuracy have immediate applications for corporations with products to sell. However, to read that as the whole truth about the study is to miss the most interesting part. As Paul Marsden says in his assessment of the report, Facebook does have a cunning accuracy when it comes to predicting issues with binary or dichotomous structures. What he does not say is that Facebook is modeling dichotomies. It is the opinions, actions, complexities, and contradictions that fall outside of those simple yes/no choices that do not find their way into the study.

Similarly, Jill Magid, a Dutch artist who uses CCTV as a performance medium, says:

> Surveillance cameras create stages, or fixed, monitored platforms. Under their gaze there is a potential for me to act, and a potential to save this act as a recorded event. By watching an area rather than an individual, the camera in its static position seems to favor its context over the pedestrians passing through it. It seems to say: The city is permanent, the civilian ephemeral. In a positive sense, this technology offers me a way to place myself, to become visible (and potentially permanent) within the city, through a medium bigger than myself. It is thus a creative field in which I choose to play. In terms of its political position (as maintaining security or, conversely, invading privacy) I see these positions as qualities of the technology itself—criteria of the tool that simply makes its use, in my way, more loaded. (Lovink, 2004)

So, perhaps, it is ultimately not the body-as-subject, but rather the site-as-subject, where the gaze of surveillance falls, that matters. For, as so many of these artists and programmers have demonstrated, it is the restrictions themselves that fuel innovation. Perhaps it is the struggle against oppression that matters most. As long as we continue to struggle for the right to be anonymous, then we may well find a way to preserve our freedoms and to regain so many of the rights to privacy that we have lost.

REFERENCES

Andrejevic, Mark. 2007. *iSpy: Surveillance and Power in the Interactive Era*. Lawrence: University Press of Kansas.

Batchler, Birgit. 2012. "A Cosy Place for Invisible Friends." In *Sniff, Scrape, Crawl . . . {On Privacy, Surveillance and our Shadowy Data-double}*, ed. Renée Turner, 92–99. Rotterdam: Piet Zwart Institute.

Campbell, Duncan. 2000. "Inside ECHELON." *Telepolis*. 25 July. Accessed March 20, 2013. http://www.heise.de/tp/artikel/6/6929/1.html

Cornwell, Peter J. 2002. "Surveillance of Assailants and Face[value]." In *CTRL [SPACE]: Rhetorics of Surveillance from Bentham to Big Brother*, ed. Thomas Y.

Levin, Ursula Frohne, and Peter Weibel, 594–99. Karlsruhe, Germany: ZKM Center for Art and Media).

Elahi, Hasan M. *Tracking Transience: V2.0*. Accessed March 20, 2012. http://elahi. umd.edu/track/

Free Network Foundation (FNF). Accessed March 28, 2013. http://thefnf.org/

"Free the Network: Hackers Take Back the Web." 2012. YouTube video. Dir. Brian Anderson. Accessed March 20, 2013. https://www.youtube.com/ watch?feature=player_embedded&v=Fx93WJPCCGs#at=91.

Gomez-Pena, Guillermo. 2000. "The Virtual Barrio @ The Other Frontier (or the Chicano Interneta)." In *Electronic Media and Technoculture*, ed. John Thornton Caldwell, 295–308. New Brunswick, NJ: Rutgers University Press.

Greenwald, Glenn. 2013. "XKeyscore: NSA Tool Collects 'Nearly Everything a User Does on the Internet.'" *The Guardian Online*, 31 July. http://www.theguardian. com/world/2013/jul/31/nsa-top-secret-program-online-data.

Gürses, Seda. 2012. "The Spectre of Anonymity." In *Sniff, Scrape, Crawl . . . (On Privacy, Surveillance and our Shadowy Data-double)*, ed. Renée Turner, 52–61. Rotterdam: Piet Zwart Institute.

Institute for Applied Autonomy. 2002. "iSee." In *CTRL [SPACE]: Rhetorics of Surveillance from Bentham to Big Brother*, eds. Thomas Y. Levin, Ursula Frohne, and Peter Weibel, 606–7. Karlsruhe, Germany: ZKM Center for Art and Media.

Kalina, Noah. "Noah Kalina Everyday." YouTube video. http://www.youtube.com/ watch?v=6B26asyGKD0.

Landry, Lauren. 2012. "Is MIT's Media Lab Creating the World's Happiness Barometer?" *BostInno*, 29 May. Accessed March 17, 2013. http://bostinno.com/ all-series/is-mits-media-lab-creating-the-worlds-happiness-barometer-video/

Levin, Thomas Y. 2002. "Rhetoric of the Temporal Index: Surveillant Narration and the Cinema of 'Real Time.'" In *CTRL [SPACE]: Rhetorics of Surveillance from Bentham to Big Brother*, ed. Thomas Y. Levin, Ursula Frohne, and Peter Weibel, 578–93. Karlsruhe, Germany: ZKM Center for Art and Media.

Lichtblau, Eric. 2012. "Police are Using Phone Tracking as a Routine Tool," *New York Times Online*, 31 March. Accessed March 19, 2013. http://www.nytimes. com/2012/04/01/us/police-tracking-of-cellphones-raises-privacy-fears. html?r=0&_r=0

Lovink, Geert. 2004. "Surveillance, Performance, Self-Surveillance: Interview with Jill Magid." Accessed March 27, 2013. http://www.evidencelocker.net/img/ artistTalk.pdf.

Luksch, Manu. 2007. *Faceless*. London and Austria: Amour Fou and Ambient Information Systems.

Luksch, Manu. 2006. "A Manifesto for CCTV Filmmakers," Node-London Reader. Accessed March 20, 2012. http://www.ambienttv.net/content/?q=dpamanifesto

McLuhan, Marshall. 1964. *Understanding Media: The Extensions of Man*. New York: Signet.

Malevé, Nicolas. 2012. "My Meta Is Your Data." In *Sniff, Scrape, Crawl: {On Privacy, Surveillance and our Shadowy Data-double}*, ed. Renée Turner, 10–23. Rotterdam: Piet Zwart Institute.

Mancel, Karen, and Hermen Maat. 2009. "Tele_Trust: Art Installation Documentation." Accessed June 19, 2012. http://teletrust.projects.v2.nl/index.php

Marsden, Paul. 2013. "Your Facebook Likes Predict if you're Gay (But Can They Predict What You'll Buy?) [Download]." *Social Commerce Today*, 12 March. Accessed March 12, 2013. http://socialcommercetoday.com/facebook-likes-predict-if-youre-gay-but-can-they-predict-what-youll-buy-download/

NAC. 2012. "Hidden Government Scanners Will Instantly Know Everything about you from 164 Feet Away." *Gizmodo*, 10 July. Accessed July 10, 2012. http://gizmodo.com/5923980/the-secret-government-laser-that-instantly-knows-everything-about-you

Nocturnals-Anonymous. "The Dark Net Rises: A Private, Secure and Anonymous Meshnet is Emerging." *Tumblr*. Accessed March 20, 2012. http://nocturnals-anonymous.tumblr.com/post/15394717863/the-dark-net-rises-a-private-secure-and-anonymous

Nouveau, Trent. 2011. "How to OccupyWallStreet Anonymously with Vibe." *TGDaily*, 3 October. Accessed March 20, 2012. http://www.tgdaily.com/mobility-features/58830-how-to-occupywallstreet-anonymously-with-vibe occupy-here: http://occupyhere.org/

Paul, Christiane. 2008. *Digital Art*. 2nd ed. New York and London: Thames and Hudson.

Pavlus, John. 2012. "Computers Scan a Crowd, Gauging its Mood." *Fastcodesign.com*, 29 June. Accessed March 18, 2013. http://www.fastcodesign.com/1670113/computers-scan-a-crowd-gauging-its-mood

Project Mesh Net. Accessed March 29, 2013. https://projectmeshnet.org/index.php

Roos, Jerome. 2011. "TheGlobalSquare: An Online Platform for our Movement." *RoarMag.org*, 2 November. Accessed June 20, 2012. http://roarmag.org/2011/11/the-global-square-an-online-platform-for-our-movement/

Roush, Paula. 2010. "From Webcamming to Social Life-logging: Intimate Performance in Surveillant-Sousveillant Space." In *Conspiracy Dwellings: Surveillance in Contemporary Art*, eds. Pam Skelton and Outi Remes, 113–28. Cambridge, MA: Cambridge Scholars Publishing.

Schenker, Dylan. 2013. "Google Glass and the Birth of Surveillance Cinema." *The Creators Project*, 5 March. Accessed March 5, 2013. http://www. thecreatorsproject.com/blog/google-glass-and-the-birth-of-surveillance-cinema

Situationist International. "Détournement as Negation and Prelude." Trans. Ken Knabb. *Internationale Situationniste #3* (December 1959). Accessed August 13, 2014. http://www.cddc.vt.edu/sionline/si/detournement.html.

Surveillance Camera Players. 1995. "Guerilla Programming of Surveillance Camera Equipment." Accessed June 22, 2012. http://www.notbored.org/gpvse.html

———. 2006. We Know You Are Watching: Surveillance Camera Players. New York: Factory School.

The Free Network Foundation: http://thefnf.org

Turner, Renée. 2012. "Sniff, Scrape, Crawl . . . {On Privacy, Surveillance and our Shadowy Data-double}." In *Sniff, Scrape, Crawl . . . {On Privacy, Surveillance and our Shadowy Data-double}*, ed. Renée Turner, 4–9. Rotterdam: Piet Zwart Institute.

Ulbricht, Melissa. 2012. "Activist Media from the Frontlines: Mobile, Strategic, and Much More than just 'Being in the Right Place at the Right Time.'" *Mobile Media Toolkit*. 02 May. Accessed March 12, 2013. http://melissaulbricht. com/2012/05/02/activist-media-from-the-frontlines-mobile-strategic-and-much-more-than-just-being-in-the-right-place-at-the-right-time/.

Institutions and Interpellations of the Dubject, the Doubled and Spaced Self

Mark A. McCutcheon

L'âme est un instrument sur lequel on peut faire entendre indéfiniment des airs nouveaux, mais qui redit de lui-même et chante toujours en sourdine et sans confusion ceux qu'il a joués autrefois. C'est un cahier des feuilles phonographiques.
    Joseph Delboeuf, *Le sommeil et les rêves* (1885)

To those who are still claiming that telecommunications are the latest form of colonization, I would like to suggest that the colonizers are always the first victims of the colonizing technology, usually because they remain resolutely unaware of the psychological impact of the technology they are using to colonize.
    Derrick de Kerckhove, *The Skin of Culture* (1995)

This essay develops the idea of the dubject as a model of remediated[a] subjectivity. It will discuss some theoretical and institutional contexts of the dubject, and then will consider digital manifestations of the dubject with reference to how popular digital applications *interpellate* the user (see Althusser 1971)—that is, how they impose specific ideological and institutional conditions and limitations on applications and on users' possibilities for self-representation. This work is an attempt to think digital identity and agency in the context of postcoloniality, as a complement to the more prevalent approach to mediated identity in terms of postmodernity. This work thus builds my larger research project of applying postcolonialist critique to popular culture, particularly that of Canada's majority white settler society.

At the outset, I want to note the resonance of the keyword of this collection to which an early version of this chapter contributed: the word *nexus*. The *Oxford English Dictionary* defines "nexus" as the state of being connected or linked, with related meanings as network, as node, and as link. A word with such closely related but wide-reaching structural and relational meanings has found widespread uses in popular culture, some of which are noteworthy here. Nexus is the brand name for a line of Cisco data systems; the brand name for a Canada-U.S. border crossing program; and the brand name for a line of Google mobile devices that run the Android operating system. This last example of Nexus as brand is a science-fiction joke: in the canonical film *Blade Runner*, "Nexus 6" is the brand name of a line of corporate-manufactured androids, several of whom are the plot's antagonists. "Nexus 6. [...] Incept date 2016. Combat model. Optimum self-sufficiency. [...] The standard item for military clubs in the outer colonies. They were designed to copy human beings in every way except their emotions" (1982). These androids, or replicants, are distinguishable from humans through biometric indicators of empathy only detectable by a specialized test—they are at once *doppelgängers* and simulacra, superficially identical to humans, defined by their inability to relate.

These connotations—of science-fiction impostors, mobile technology, and border crossing; of doubles, devices, and jurisdictions—converge, a nexus unto themselves, in the specific site of encounter between customs official and traveller. The "impostor" or *doppelgänger* dimension here involves the popular sense

---

a "Remediation" is Bolter and Grusin's (1999) term for the double movement whereby new and old media each strive for both self-effacing immediacy and "hypermediation," a self-reflexive signalling of mediation.

of Canadians as virtually indistinguishable from Americans, a sense that is both widespread and conducive to subversive expressions of national difference (see McCutcheon, 2009a). In a 2006 case concerning a U.S. customs office's search of a traveller's digital devices, U.S. district court judge Dean Pregeson issued a ruling that describes electronic storage devices (in McLuhanesque terms) as "an extension of our own memory . . . capable of storing our thoughts" (2006). This decision provided the impetus for the "border search exception," an expansion of U.S. customs officers' powers that was conferred in 2008, and that gave officers carte blanche authority to search the digital devices of any and every traveller entering the U.S.A., without warrant, in the name of national security. A real-world policy with dystopian implications, the border search exception has just been overturned; in March 2013, a U.S. federal appeals court ruled against the exception, writing that "a person's digital life ought not be hijacked simply by crossing a border" (quoted in Kravets, 2013). A legal expert commentator notes how the ruling pivots on "the idea that you can hold your entire life in your laptop" (Price quoted in Kravets, 2013).

Extending minds, storing memories, holding lives in laptops: comments like these conjure the lived experience of subjectivity under neoliberal global capitalism as a redistribution of identity, a cathexis of prostheses, a certain kind of cyborg subjectivity between performance and recording, an experience that will be explored here under the name of the *dubject*. In prior articles (2009a, 2011, 2012, 2014), I have begun to formulate a theory of the dubject, where I posit it as

> a self committed to its own recording; a subject translated from the site of the individual body to the mediated spaces of representation; a self dubbed and doubled—a *doppelgänger* self whose "live," corporeal presence becomes radically supplemented . . . by its different and distributed embodiments in recordings and representations. . . . In some cases, the trajectory of this displacement becomes a strategy of survival, a tactical retreat: from the real into simulation, from the flesh into the word.
> (2012: 236–37)

So the dubject is an attempt to name the kind of experience George Siemens (2013) has described as "seeing bits and pieces of yourself all over the Internet"; however, this dubject theory also encompasses other media. My initial work on this has situated the dubject not only in its postmodern contexts but also in postcolonial contexts. These contexts include the "black electronic" (Davis, 2004) practices of dub and other sonic fictions (Eshun, 1998), and, more specifically, contexts of cultural and media imperialism, which position the dubject as a victim or fugitive, echoing Marshall McLuhan's ideas of electronic subjectivity as colonized victimhood: "The violence that all electric media inflict on their users is that they are instantly invaded and deprived of their physical bodies and are merged in a network of extensions of their own nervous systems" (1996: 82). My initial work has identified Canadian popular culture as an illustrative site for theorizing the dubject, with reference to its fictional dramatizations in works like David Cronenberg's *Videodrome*, its theoretical iterations in writings by McLuhan, and—more strangely, perhaps, but more to the point—its historical manifestations by cultural practitioners such as Glenn Gould. In Cronenberg's *Videodrome*, the character Brian O'Blivion—a parody of McLuhan—exists only, and uncannily, on television, like Max Headroom. Gould famously forsook live performance for the recording studio; his recording of Bach now approaches interstellar space aboard Voyager 2.[1] On the basis of these contexts and practices, I have argued that "articulating Canada's political economy of comprom-ised sovereignty and its history of colonization by various cultural and media empires, the incarnations and iterations of dubjectivity position the individual citizen as a commodity produced by competing intellectual property claims, the consumer of media as what media themselves consume, the organic self reorganized and reproduced by its technological others" (2011: 261).

But I have realized that positing the dubject as a victim of or fugitive from cultural and media imperialism means misrepresenting Canadian colonialism, by positioning white settler majority persons and productions among the *colonized*, when they more accurately represent the *colonizer*, in the political economy of Canada, as an immigration-based resource extraction colony, established through a systemic segregation and dispossession of Canada's First Nations that provided the model for South African apartheid. Canadian popular culture *is* dominated by the neo-imperialism of mainly U.S.-imported cultural productions and technolo-gies, but Canadian political economy is characterized by its own neo-imperial projects of capital (see Kellogg, 2013). So the Canadian nation-state *does* provide an exemplary postcolonial context for theorizing the dubject—but this is because Canada represents *both* a target of cultural and media imperialism *and* a rapa-cious agent of neo-imperialist capital. In the context of media imperialism, the immigrant and largely European-derived settler population of Canada occupies the position of the colonized with respect to the neo-imperial cultural industries of the U.S.A. and the U.K. But in the context of Canada's historical formation as an invading colonial arm of European state-based imperialism, a formation that continues to structure its relationship to Canada's indigenous peoples in a manner analogous to apartheid, we must of course recognize the massive inequality that remains between the relatively privileged population colonized by media imperialism and the hugely disadvantaged population colonized by settler-invader imperialism.

As I have specified elsewhere (2012), while the focus on Canadian sites and practices of cultural production, scholarship, and social reproduction first gave rise to theorizing the dubject, that focus does not imply that *only* Canadian sites and practices can or should be theorized as sites and practices of the dubject; rather, these sites and practices "signal some potentially wider—and weirder—implications for everyday life in the overdeveloped, technologically overdriven, and hypermediated Western world today" (2012: 238). Accordingly, what follows will sustain a focus on Canadian sites and practices, but will also broaden in scope to consider related sites and practices across the Anglophone overdeveloped world. After all, the neo-imperial incursions, annexations, and exploitations of capitalism and its cultural industries today—including the companies and services discussed here—are not restricted to any specific nation-states, but rather take (and take for granted) the whole world as their market, their laboratory, and their labour pool.

If the dubject represents the colonized under media imperialism, then, it also represents the colonizer, not only in Canada's postcolonial popular culture, but also in broader theoretical and institutional contexts of digital media as a neoliberal, private-public sphere that reproduces and naturalizes dominant forms of subjectivity—those of "imperialist white supremacist capitalist patriarchy" (hooks, 2000: 46). These reproductions and naturalizations of dominant identity formation become clear according to how, and by whom, and *for* whom digital identity and agency have been theorized.

If the remediation and redistribution of the self suggest a kind of survival, then to whom, specifically, is this kind of survival available? The examples I have discussed in prior work on the dubject illustrate the predominance of imperialist white-supremacist capitalist patriarchal normativity and thus a rather privileged demographic (notwithstanding the diverse and sometimes countercultural politics of their productions): Cronenberg's O'Blivion, and his real-world source, McLuhan; the eccentric virtuoso Gould, another icon of mainstream Canadian culture; and examples in Canadian fiction by white male writers William Gibson, Cory Doctorow, Peter Watts, and Tony Burgess. So examples of the dubject I have found thus far constitute a parade of white, male, and relatively affluent exemplars. In contrast, a great deal of the scholarship and theory on which my theorization of the dubject draws has been produced by women and feminist scholars (and not specifically Canadian ones, either). As an attempt to theorize the doubling and spacing of subjectivity in media forms, as well as their possibilities for supplementing the somatically centred liberal-humanist subject with an uncanny "second life," the dubject relates to influential studies of digital identity, such as Turkle's theory of the "second self" (1995), Haraway's cyborg as a model of networked agency and resistance (1991), and N. Katherine Hayles's posthumanism (1999), as well as to more recent work such as Angela Thomas's work on virtual self-authorship (2007) and Emily Apter's theory of the avatar as a coordinator of conflicted and competing psychic drives (2008). While the dubject has commonalities with and conceptual debts to these prior theories of digital identity and "the subject in technics," it differs more broadly from them in emphasizing not the postmodern conditions or poststructuralist models of late capitalist subjectivity (which it does recognize and build on), but, instead, its postcolonial contexts. To Anna Poletti and Julie Rak's recent call for combining auto/biography studies and new media studies to examine digital identity (2014), I would add that a postcolonialist lens can help make intersectional sense of digital identity practices. In this light, the assemblage theory of Jasbir Puar becomes useful for historicizing the "epistemic violence" of hegemonic subject formations, and for deterritorializing identity as provisional agency, as "an encounter, an event, an accident."

Apter and Haraway are worth some discussion here, since my theory of the remediated, doubled, and spaced subject is informed by subject theory: the corpus of poststructuralist theories of the subject, and, more specifically, theories of what Apter calls "the subject in technics" (2008). Poststructuralism develops and destabilizes the subject's grounding in psychoanalysis and phenomenology, theorizing the subject not as primary and self-determining but as "secondary, constructed . . . volatile, standing in its own shadow, and self-divided" (Hawthorn, 1992: 181). What Apter calls the "subject in technics," then, routes this theory through postmodern media theory. Avital Ronnell, for instance, argues that telephony reconfigures the modern liberal subject in more poststructuralist terms: "the call transfers you to the Other. . . . Telephonics imposes the recognition of a certain irreducible precedence of the Other with respect to the self" (1991: 82). The work of Friedrich Kittler (1986/1999) exemplifies "subject in technics" theory: he historicizes the subject as a "discourse network" structured by media technologies—which Kittler shows historically to be products of warfare. For Kittler, modern subjectivity is a kind of simulation program, both sustained and subverted by recording media, and increasingly vestigial to a nascent, globalizing regime of cybernetic, artificial intelligence: "After the storage capacities for optics, acoustics, and writing had been separated, mechanized, and extensively utilized, the central nervous system was resurrected, but as a Golem made of Golems" (170). Building on work like Kittler's, Apter then develops "subject in technics" theory by reading the digital self-imaging practice of creating an "avatar" as a remediated coordinator of the drives that comprise the subject—the avatar as a driver of the drives.

An influential source for the subject in technics is Haraway's theory of the cyborg: a model of radically remediated and trenchantly feminist identity and agency under globalized capitalism. Unfortunately, the canonical status of Haraway's cyborg in critical theory has subjected it to reductive misreadings, like that of the *Cyborgology* blog editors, two Maryland doctoral students, Nathan Jurgenson and P. J. Rey, who have leveraged theory such as Haraway's and tools such as social media and print periodicals to advance their own model of digital subjectivity, which might be called the Augmented Reality argument. In a 2012 refereed article, *Cyborgology* co-editor Jurgenson claims that "the Facebook user is the paradigmatic example of the Harawaysian 'cyborg'" (2012b: 86). Such a claim *seriously* misunderstands Haraway's cyborg, which makes critical use of technologies and networks to mount a queer, feminist resistance to imperialist white supremacist capitalist patriarchy—not a blithe complicity with it, as implied by Jurgenson's reference to the billion-dollar advertising and surveillance business that is Facebook.

Jurgenson and Rey appropriate the term "augmented reality" (first coined around 1990) to critique what they see as a pervasive but flawed premise in writing and research on the digital mediascape, a premise they call "digital dualism": a polarized representation of digital activity that pits "real life" against the internet (and tends to champion the former over the latter). Citing examples in recent work like Nicholas Carr's *The Shallows* (2010) and Sherry Turkle's *Alone Together* (2012), the *Cyborgology* editors are far from alone in criticizing the reductionism of arguments that new media, as new media, are rotting brains, destroying society, or hindering youth literacy. A shrewd and short riposte to such arguments is made by Kathleen Fitzpatrick: "media theorists, confronted with a narrative about the deleterious effects of new modes of communication, have long pointed to Plato ... new technologies are perennially imagined to be not simply the enemy of established systems but in fact a direct threat to the essence of what it is to be human. For this reason, declarations of cultural decline always bear complexly submerged ideological motivations" (2012: 42).

In contrast to Fitzpatrick's view of the *longue durée*, the *Cyborgology* editors ground their argument much more specifically, both in more narrowly socio-logical theory and in more contemporary, twenty-first-century social media and mobile devices. Jurgenson writes:

> Our reality is both technological and organic, both digital and physical, all at once. We are not crossing in and out of separate digital and physical realities, a la *The Matrix*, but instead live in one reality, one that is augmented by atoms and bits. And our selves are not separated across these two spheres as some dualistic "first" and "second" self, but is instead an augmented self. A *Haraway-like cyborg self comprised of a physical body as well as our digital Profile*, acting in constant dialogue. (2011: emphases added)

Interrogating the reductive division of digital and unmediated experience has critical value, but the augmented reality argument is both problematic in its premises and symptomatic of the aforementioned reproduction of the nor-mative subjectivity of imperialist capitalist patriarchy.[2] First, aside from its misprisions of Haraway, this argument nowhere addresses psychoanalytic or poststructuralist subject theory, which is directly relevant to it. Second, the argument often reads like a generation-bound manifesto, too quick to dismiss the nuances of influential authorities' insights on the subject. Most important, this argument ignores the neoliberal political economy of the read-write web as a communications platform produced and structured by neo-imperial capital to facilitate and accelerate profit maximization, market creation, and service priva-tization, as well as state surveillance for the governments that now act mostly as capitalism's hired goons (Annesley, 2001; Hedges, 2012; Schneier, 2013; van Veen, 2011). The augmented reality argument's neglect of digital political economy makes a claim like "Facebook is real life" (Jurgenson, 2012a) problematic, even disturbing, notwithstanding its use for challenging the ideological opposition between human and technology.

Cyborgology appears to be informed by Marc Prensky's model of "digital natives" versus "digital immigrants": formulated in 2001, Prensky's model distin-guishes between older Internet users who have to learn the Internet like a second language and younger users, those who became teenagers after 2000, who are in effect "born digital" and speak fluent Internet. One *Cyborgology* article cites

Prensky, whose influence is also seen in *Cyborgology*'s "About" blurb: "We live in a cyborg society. Technology has infiltrated the most fundamental aspects of our lives: social organization, the body, even our self-concepts. This blog chronicles our new, augmented reality." The undefined but vaguely generation-bound "we," together with the blurb's focus on the "new," suggest Prensky's model as a premise for the augmented reality argument.

Prensky's "natives versus immigrants" model has itself been extensively critiqued, though not enough from postcolonial perspectives (see Bayne and Ross). One brilliant exception is Wayne Barry, who writes that "The whole lexicon of 'digital native', 'digital immigrant', 'digital savage', 'technological migrant', 'digital colonist', and 'digital refugee' is imperialistic in nature and racist by inclination."[3] Prensky's model privileges digital natives over immigrants, reproduces nationalist discourses of atavistic xenophobia, and appropriates the term "native" to describe Internet users who are predominantly *not* natives but settlers and their descendants, and who enjoy widespread broadband access. In contrast, approximately half of all First Nations households and schools have Internet access (Chiefs Assembly on Education 2012), and only 17 percent of First Nations communities have broadband (Canadian Council on Learning 2010).

An analysis of "Canada's digital divide" made in 2001 remains all too relevant: "Geographic or social isolation, high costs, and lack of infrastructure contribute to a 'digital divide' between First Nations peoples and other Canadians. Designed for profitable urban markets, digital networks and content that might address Native needs for education and information have not yet been fully extended to remote communities" (Bredin, 2001: 191). For Canada's native communities, the extreme poverty sustained by systemic federal underfunding (Fontaine, 2013) keeps more basic health and environmental needs more pressing: problems like cold, mould, overcrowding, and sewage fume exposure are not the exception but the norm in reservation schools—as are empty library shelves (Opikokew, 2013). These facts of postcolonial Canada make the "digital natives and immigrants" model as galling as the recent "upsettler" reaction to #IdleNoMore is plainly racist. The glaring omission of political economic critique in the augmented reality argument, in this context, becomes legible as a symptom of its basis in imperialist white-supremacist capitalist patriarchal subjectivity. In step with what Derrida calls "white mythology" (1974: 5), the augmented reality argument universalizes and naturalizes this specific, privileged subjectivity as the ideological norm—the "average" user—not only in its proponents' own identity formations (white, male, and otherwise "WEIRD" in Henrich et al.'s 2009 formulation)[b] but also in its rhetoric, in the consistent and unexamined use of the plural first-person, the presumed, undefined, collective "we" who live real life online.

Hayles has satirized precisely this rhetoric in *How We Became Posthuman* (1999); explaining her book's title, Hayles writes: "'We,' like 'became,' is meant ironically, positioning itself in opposition to the techno-ecstasies found in various magazines, such as *Mondo 2000*, which customarily speak of the transformation into the posthuman as if it were a universal human condition when in fact it affects only a small fraction of the world's population" (6). This "we" that Hayles explicates recurs in the rhetoric of numerous digital commentators, the majority of whom represent a very "small fraction" of the population indeed. Hence the question: For whom does the dubject offer its doublings and spacings of remediated selfhood?

We get a clearer sense of the dominant identity politics of the dubject by considering what I might call "discourses on dubjection": statements and speculations on the transformation of the self through media, many of which are characterized as fantasies of "uploading consciousness" from human bodies to machines. The fantasy of "uploaded consciousness" recurs among a particular class of thinkers, who represent this fantasy according to two common and conjoined rhetorical moves: first, in the name of an ostensibly universal but ideologically specific collective, "we"—the species on whose behalf the imperialist white capitalist patriarchal subject entitles himself to speak—who will have become posthuman; and second, as an act or movement of disembodiment, a separation of digital from physical, mind from body, with all the violence of gender- and class-coded subordination it suggests. Recall, for instance, in William Gibson's novel *Neuromancer* (1984), the starkly gender-coded contrast between the disembodied, cerebral transcendence of cyberspace and the "rotting darkness" of "meat" existence. As Amanda Fernbach writes of *Neuromancer* in 2000: "Like the fantasies played out in contemporary discourses about the internet and virtual reality, Gibson's cyberspace allows for the disavowal of bodily differences in a fantasy that privileges the white male body. . . . The notion

---

b "WEIRD" is Henrich et al.'s acronym for Western, Educated, Industrialized, Rich, and Democratic, which of course most of the world isn't; the WEIRD thesis challenges the global representativeness of claims for "human" psychology and society that many disciplines generalize on the basis of sampling Western, Anglophone postsecondary students.

that online personas transcend social and cultural hierarchies remains a utopian myth" (Fernbach, 2000: n.p.) Fernbach's reflections still resonate today. The "democratizing rhetoric" that Fernbach notes includes the ideological language of universal inclusivity—ideological in its arrogation of species representativeness to a tiny, privileged fraction of the citizenry—and the similarly ideological imagery of dubjectivity's remediated embodiments in terms of disembodiment, the transcendence of corporeality.

McLuhan's media theory exemplifies these rhetorical moves. In 1971, McLuhan alludes to both television and incipient computing in his statement that "what is very little understood about the electronic age is that it angelizes man, disembodies him. Turns him into software" (1996: 79). The gender category "man" here, together with the epochal imagery of the "electronic age," serves to universalize the experience of remediation. McLuhan later elaborates on this idea of disembodied remediation in a 1978 article: "when you are 'on the telephone' or 'on the air,' you do not have a physical body. In these media, the sender is sent and is instantaneously present everywhere. The disembodied user extends to all those who are recipients of electric information" (1996: 80). Derrick de Kerckhove (McLuhan's successor as the director of University of Toronto's Centre for Culture and Technology) also uses this rhetoric to express ideas of doubling and spacing the self in telecommunications and virtual reality. "In the simulation and extensions of our nervous systems," he writes, "we personally figure as nodal entities, travelling back and forth on electric current patterns" (1995: 186).[4] The author Douglas Coupland provides a sardonic version in his 2006 novel *JPod*: "Remember how, back in 1990, if you used a cellphone in public you looked like a total asshole? *We're all* assholes now" (2006: 270, emphasis added). As seen in statements like these, the universalization and disembodiment of digital identity couple in a consummation devoutly to be wished—by a very specifically gender- and class-bound tradition of thinkers. Disembodiment is the ideological fantasy that structures the estranged embodiments of the dubject; universalization is the ideological fantasy that authorizes its restriction to privileged agents of imperialist white-supremacist capitalist patriarchy.

We also see these rhetorical moves in read-write web services that invite users to generate content, and, in the process, solicit this arguable "self-commodification" —from a relatively privileged "target" demographic—as a relatively privileged and non-exploitative kind of commodification, as Andrew Feenberg discusses earlier in this volume (see also Hesmondhalgh, 2010). The commodification of the self—the transformation of subject to dubject—is a valued object of

Terms Of Service (TOS) licensing because the users who generate content constitute a conspicuously privileged demographic: "The social demographics of UGC platform visitors bespeak an average user who is highly educated, well connected and well paid ... UCG users—whether active creators or passive spectators—form an attractive demographic to advertisers" (van Dijck 2009, 47).

In this context, for all the symptomatic articulations of hegemonic, colonizer privilege in his projections of "electronic man," McLuhan, like Toronto poet Christopher Dewdney with his premillennial speculations on "transhumanism" (1998), can at least be credited with gesturing to the political economic implications of this transformation's corporate structuring. While television is his new medium of choice, McLuhan writes of new media's public-private convergence and conflict was very suggestive for the Internet, in his statement that "we have leased our central nervous systems to various corporations" (1964/2003: 100). McLuhan tended to use "corporate" in its non-business sense as a synonym for "collective," but a statement like this indicates a grasp of political economy otherwise muted in (or absent from) his work. Dewdney, for his part, pays more attention to the business contexts of the Internet. He tempers his extrapolations from virtual reality to virtually unrecognizable futures—in which "the term 'identity' may not even apply" (1998: 191)—with projections of a growing role for corporations. "If consciousness should, ultimately, prove to be uploadable," he writes, "corporations will hold patents on the software that will embrace our minds" (1998: 178). Pursuing the corporate copyright implications further, he speculates on the "possib[ility] for recipient individuals to acquire copyrighted living simulations of a portion of a gifted individual's brain, as licensed by the manufacturer"—but asks whether "becoming, even partially, a corporate cognitive product may be an identity threshold that humans will not wish to cross" (1998: 179). From McLuhan's perspective to those of social media TOS agreements, this threshold may be one that "we"—a specific, privileged class of subjects—have already crossed.

A theory of the dubject, as outlined here, might suggest that corporations already do hold such patents (and fight over them), and that the uploading of consciousness is not only what they trade on but what they actively structure, solicit, and stimulate—for profit-maximizing purposes, and also for meeting the surveillance demands of the state governments that under neoliberalism now serve more as clients and enablers of corporate interests than as stewards of public interest. If digitization is about replacing labour with capital, then what is the digitization of the self? Especially in private sites that only simulate public space? The dubject's digital redistributions of identity effectively disperse citizens across domestic and alien jurisdictions: Canadians using U.S.-based services such as Google, Facebook, Dropbox, and Twitter, for instance, store the content they upload to these services in U.S.-housed data centres, where they are vulnerable to Patriot Act search provisions. Enacting dubjection entails supplying work and product (content) for corporate and state powers; dubjecting one's self in the digital nexus, each click and keystroke generating data for unknown private interests to analyze, the user becomes a participant in his or her own oppression and exploitation—while also finding ways to leverage agency from these tools for opposition and praxis, as shown by Wikileaks and the organizing affordances of social media.

Between the back-end analytics and the front-end interface, the doubled and spaced digital self constitutes both colonizer and colonized according to how Internet services and platforms permit certain orders of discourse, produce certain kinds of subject positions. That is, the Internet *interpellates* the user, and then also dubjects the user, independently of the user's agency or awareness, as an abstracted, analytic commodity, a self made of metadata—a self made, for the most part, unconsciously. If the user doubles and spaces him- or herself across the digital nexus, he or she can do so only according to specific and sometimes subtle premises and priorities of imperialist white-supremacist capitalist patriarchy.

Social media such as Facebook and Twitter interpellate a privileged subject, the liberal humanist-turned-consumerist subject of the neoliberal capitalist system that has innovated and popularized the read-write web (Smith and Watson, 82). A growing body of scholarship critiques the social media user as commodity (van Dijck, 2009; McNeill, 2014). In a complementary analysis of the encoding of neoliberal ideology and privilege into contemporary consumer technologies, Alice Marwick argues they solicit users' participation as entrepreneurs, as marketers of the self as brand (see also Smith and Watson, 2014: 79), and in the process they entrench intersectional socioeconomic inequalities. (For instance, when's the last time you checked the "Stocks" app on your iPhone? Right . . . I never have either.)

Recent articles by Rob Cover and Aimée Morrison analyze how Facebook hails and coaxes users to post and share—that is, how it *interpellates* users. Cover analyzes the creation and maintenance of a user's profile: "the management of the profile . . . is an act of self-governance, which produces embodied selves and subjects through an interpellation that 'hails' one to choose the coordinates of identityhood" (2014: 64). Cover also notes how Facebook constrains these coordinates: "the profile-provided categories on social networking sites offer a notion of freedom to 'choose,' which is endemic to neoliberal thinking ... yet they risk for some users the violence of a normative truth-regime, which excludes alternative [ways of] doing subjectivity otherwise" (65–66). "Unrecognizable selves," as Cover observes, "demand explanation" (59). Similarly, Morrison describes the interpellations of Facebook as "coaxed affordances": "Facebook's status update feature makes use of designed affordances and constraints, as well as emerging cultural convention, in order to coax life narratives from its users" (2014: 119). Consequently, Facebook's "coaxed affordances" render "some kinds of statements impossible" (123), and thanks to more recently introduced features, they tend now to identify the user's digital profile with the user "in real life"; as Morrison observes, the recently introduced "Timeline" format "increasingly conflates ... a user's entire social media history ... with that user's entire life" (127).

Twitter lends itself to the kind of close reading Cover and Morrison give Facebook. On first visit, Twitter "welcomes" you, it invites you to "start a conversation, explore your interests, and be in the know." You are invited to sign up or sign in (and if you don't unclick "remember me?" to stay signed in). If you botch the sign-in, you get this pop-up query: "We gotta check ... are you human?" This might be interpellation's most exemplary expression: the undefined but ostensibly corporate "we" —"we" who ask on behalf of Twitter—self-deprecatingly, colloquially, innocuously ask to "check" whether the user is "human." Ironically, the "we" who asks is not human—it is a corporately directed and programmed subroutine—but this "we" still presumes, in the phrasing of its question, to coax a human response. On a user's page, the "coaxing affordance" is a text-entry field showing a greyed-out invitation to "Compose new Tweet ..." *Compose*: the exhortation is to write and to craft, to communicate economically. As I have tweeted elsewhere, the constraint of brevity imposed by the interface is a clue to Twitter's neoliberal encoding: "Twitter's textual economy normalizes for communication the neoliberal ideology that fiscal austerity is the only way to run a public service" (2009b). By this point, the implied subject of both the "we" and the "human" in Twitter's "check" should be legible as the imperialist white-supremacist capitalist patriarch of the overdeveloped world. So should the implied subjectivity of "real identity" that is increasingly demanded by digital service firms.

As Cover says, social media interpellate users doubly, according to competing demands: "the Enlightenment demand that one articulate oneself as a rational, coherent, and intelligible subject and a decentered and fragmented subjectivity, which fulfills the demand that we express identity in fleeting ways through forms of consumption" under late capitalism (2014: 61). Social media doubly interpellate users—that is, it dubs and versions them (as the sites constantly version themselves [Morrison, 2014: 120]); social media hails users to become dubjects. Morrison further observes that while social sites interpellate users as content creators, the site affordances enable not authorship but a kind of algorithmic "auto-assemblage . . . the result of ongoing selection and appropriation of content across several modes brought together into a constellation for the purpose of self-representation" (Whitlock and Poletti quoted in Morrison, 2014: 113). In this context, processes of dubjection entail the "uploading of selves" (McNeill, 2014: 160) not only as voluntary self-representations but also as involuntary sets of data and metadata, which we might call the technological id counterpart to the ego of the user-generated content.

Social media sites routinely demand "real identity" details of users to access and authenticate their accounts. This demand for "guarantors of authenticity" informs most sites' interpellation strategies, and it relates "to the ideological formations of global capitalism" (Smith and Watson, 2014: 76–77), as a naturalization of "capitalist realism" (Fisher, 2009), of "white mythology" (Derrida, 1974), and of "the legal and capitalist structures that demand the fixity of the rights bearing subject" (Puar, 2011)—as well as a legitimization of ubiquitous digital surveillance. The growing corporate insistence that the user provide one's "real" identity marks a dramatic reversal of the privacy and promise of the early open web. In the 1990s, the web garnered countless critical theorizations and popular celebrations for enabling a quintessentially postmodern playfulness and experimentation with digital identity. Mark Poster's "Cyberdemocracy" (1995) makes a representative statement: "The salient characteristic of Internet community is the diminution of prevailing hierarchies of race, class, age, status and especially gender" (1995). Contrast this utopian expression of the possibilities of postmodern digital self-creation with the effects of the present Internet's insistence on identification and verification: the horrific misogynist violence levelled against feminists like Anita Sarkeesian; the anguish and tragedy of online bullying and sexual harassment; the ugly unveiling of "upsettler" racism in reactions against #IdleNoMore; and an ever-tighter web of constant, ubiquitous surveillance, which digital security Bruce Schneier describes as a "surveillance state effective beyond Orwell's wildest imaginings"—all made possible through users' willing participation:

Everything we do now involves computers, and computers produce data as a natural by-product. Everything is now being saved and correlated, and many big-data companies make money by building up intimate profiles of our lives from a variety of sources. . . . Maintaining privacy on the Internet is nearly impossible. . . . Governments are happy to use the data corporations collect—occasionally demanding that they collect more and save it longer—to spy on us. And corporations are happy to buy data from governments. (Schneier, 2013)

Cognizant of the critiques of approaches to the Internet as a utopian space for postmodern self-fashioning—such as Nakamura's critique of "identity tourism" (2014: 45)—I still like to think that tactics of defamiliarization offer critical resources for occupying a digital milieu whose demands for "real" identification serve neoliberal capital and the surveillance state. Like social media terms of service that demand authenticity, the terms regulating intellectual property (IP)—which apply both to the user's own content and to third-party IP appropriated by the user—illustrate the tension between social media strategies of interpellation and user tactics of defamiliarization. Against these demands and terms, several feminist intellectuals, artists, and activists lead appropriations of both "realness" (Smith and Watson, 76) and IP, different practices of dubjection that may point to "new ways to conceive of identity itself" (Poletti and Rak, 2014: 17). Exemplary cases of social media use that critique and subvert hegemonic subject formations of the neoliberal digital sphere—through intertextual appropriations—include the extensive YouTube work of Anita Sarkeesian to critique gender tropes in digital culture, and the self-proclaimed "pop culture piracy" of Elisa Kreisinger, whose remix work teaches and models fair use.

To take up the IP angle, and return to the example of Twitter, some "viral" Twitter accounts like @FeministHulk, @FeministTSwift, and @BrideOnAcid illustrate possibilities for critical digital *détournement*. One commonality among all three is how they exploit Twitter's affordances for self-identification, which are much more free-form than Facebook's presentation of profiles fixed to coordinates of age, gender, relationship, and location. Another commonality is how they deploy pseudonyms and distinctively styled voices to construct uncanny identities, at once immediately recognizable yet profoundly strange. FeministHulk and FeministTSwift both appropriate the "realness" of celebrity brand names. FeministHulk gender-bends a highly profitable and hyper-masculinist comic book character, and adopts a textual style—all caps and broken English—that both mimics the original character's speech and puts refreshingly progressive words in his mouth: "HULK UNWIND FROM LONG DAY OF SMASH. SIP TEA, WATCH OLD FEMINIST FREQUENCY VIDEOS, MAYBE MAKE CURRY WITH CSA SHARE. AH! BIG GREEN SELF-CARE." FeministHulk has also propagated its own genre of Twitter parody accounts; FeministTSwift arguably counts among the FeministHulk's belligerent and numerous progeny, taking not the Hulk label but the feminist flag to construct the user as a fan of Taylor Swift who then reconstructs herself as a feminist version of Taylor Swift: "Happy. Free. Confused. Oppressed by the patriarchy. At the same time." FeministTSwift's updates are almost entirely composed of lines from Taylor Swift songs, rewritten with feminist theory: "I don't know about you / But I'm feeling 22 / cents underpaid on the dollar."

Given the relentless lobbying and punitive litigation corporate copyright holders pursue in order to protect their content monopolies, not to mention the licensing fees they charge for song lyrics, FeministTSwift's extensive use of Taylor Swift lyrics seems especially bold—it may constitute fair use, but user rights haven't stopped copyright holders from pressuring users to pay for their use, or alleging trademark infringement; the same goes for FeministHulk's use of Marvel's lucrative comic book character (see Tushnet 2007 on fair use and gender critique).

BrideOnAcid, though, works differently, more in the style of what's been called "Weird Twitter" (Schmidt, 2013). This account's particular genius is to condense a narrative plot into the user name itself, implying that the feed represents a bride who has dropped acid on her wedding day. The feed is a very funny, feminist satire on weddings as a billion-dollar business and a heteronormative institution. "got my teeth whitened for the big day. kind of a waste since they all just crumbled away." The premise of drug use provides a familiar device of alienation effects that makes everything about a wedding day powerfully strange—well, stranger than a wedding day already is. (Consider the unpredictable quality of conversations in your own activity feed by all the users you know from different circles. Ever feel like moderating comments in your feed is like moderating an open mic at a wedding reception?) BrideOnAcid appears no longer to be regularly updated, but this account's now-archival character does not disqualify it from consideration as an exemplary dubject. As Cover says, the archiving affordances of social media let users' constructions of identity continue to signify in their absence or even death, and maybe even sustain subjectivity more robustly than offline performances. An all-too-familiar example of this, in Facebook, is the automated invitation to "friend" a user whom you know to be deceased. How is it that the recording can dictate?

It is important to note that, for all the *Verfremdungseffekte* such critical and appropriative Twitter dubjects achieve at the level of content, their mode of production in occupying a corporate platform like Twitter ultimately provides free labour to feed the firm's appetite for analytics, and thus bolsters its bottom line, just as well as noncritical content does. However critical the front-end content, the back-end analytics can only create a metadata dubject that is a fully compliant and unprotesting puppet of neoliberal capital. This contradiction between critical user-generated content and unconscious metadata production illustrates capitalism's resilient and robust ability to capitalize on critical resistance to its own forms and norms. That said, to acknowledge that the effectiveness of resisting the dominant interpellations of social media is more symbolic than material is not to discount the significance of the symbolic as such. Such defamiliarizing demonstrations as the aforementioned Twitter users model, for sizeable Internet audiences, how these platforms' interpellations may be answered not straightforwardly but against the grain, not in the affirmative but in the interrogative. Such demonstrations critique the ideological foundations and presumptions of Internet user identity.

More than just an imposition on privacy, the corporate demand for users' "real" identities curtails freedom of expression, and reinforces a pernicious ideology of authenticity, of "common sense," of "bottom-line" realism that forms an ideological kernel of both white mythology and neo-imperialist capital. In social media's interpellations, philosopher Tobias van Veen reads "the cryptofascism of corporate perception"—orders of discourse structured and limited by corporate social media: "the technics of perception in which uncitizens engage with the social network aligns desire with socially networked consumerism. Desire is directed toward a ceaseless flow of objects and data (either LIKED or absented in response)" (2011). Van Veen's point is that social networks erase the nation-state and thus cripple democratic participation in it: since, in social networks, the nation-state "does not exist as such—which is to say as a metric of consumer desire," then its virtual nonexistence enables its material dismantling by neo-imperial capital.

According to a postcolonial view of the persistence and transformation of historical empires in neo-imperial global capital, a more extensive inquiry into subject theory, a close reading of discourses on dubjection, and a cursory reading of how Internet services interpellate their users, a fuller image of the dubject develops: not just colonized but colonizer, embodying and enacting the contradictions and complicities of remediated everyday life under imperialist white supremacist capitalist patriarchy. As a model of remediated and redistributed subjectivity, the dubject already occupies an uncanny dimension between authenticity and simulation, autonomy and automation, presence and haunting, public and private, user and commodity, colonizer and colonized. The theory of the dubject already posits a defamiliarization of the subject, its transmutation from corporeal performativity to the different embodiments of digital representations and occupations. Amid the demands for "real" user identification, and despite the encodings of neoliberal ideology in the affordances that interpellate the users who are also their products, Internet users remain capable of producing profound alienation effects—defamiliarizations of digital identity which remind us that subjectivity, as we knew it, was always a fiction anyway. Max Headroom lives: news reporters outsource the writing of articles to code robots, but keep their authorial bylines (Dingwall and Mattar, 2013). Facebook suggests people you may know, some of whom are deceased but maintain profiles (Walker, 2011). Data miners assemble and trade the latent *doppelgängers* of Internet users' manifest *doppelgängers* for profit, for favours, for blackmail, for tax breaks. A stellar wind needles the groove of *The Well-Tempered Clavier*, stirring Gould's fingers. The machine doesn't stop; it is steered by the dead and living hands of the privileged and the entitled; it is fed by the ghosts of the dead and the living.

ACKNOWLEDGEMENTS

I wish to thank the Athabasca University Research Committee for funding this work, the MA-IS program's former director Raphael Foshay for inviting one line of this inquiry to the 2013 Digital Nexus symposium, the Canadian Society for Digital Humanities for inviting another line of this inquiry to its 2014 conference at Congress, and my erstwhile graduate research assistant Sarah Mann, for asking the questions that prompted this work and providing feedback on its progress.

NOTES

1 In my 2012 chapter, I wrote that Voyager 2 left the solar system in 1989, but that claim is imprecise: while Voyager 2 is now twice as far from the sun as Pluto, it has yet to exit the heliosphere, the outermost "bubble" of the solar system where the sun's solar wind balances against the stellar winds of other stars (NASA 2012).

2 The augmented reality argument is also an interesting case of open review, more than peer review: the idea was no sooner blogged about than it caught on by dint of distribution power, given its authors skilled exploitation of both social and

major print media; what it needs—and what, to its credit, its proponents openly invite—is more rigorous peer review and debate.

3 As an alternative to Prensky's framework, David White and Alison Le Cornu (2011) have proposed a typology of "visitors" and "residents" that both dispenses with the racist and imperialist assumptions of "natives" and "immigrants" and also allows for a continuum of movement between these positions.

4 Not a postcolonialist scholar, de Kerckhove refers to analyses of media imperialism in the quotation I've used as an epigraph: while his claim that "the colonizers are always the first victims of the colonizing technology" is an egregious misrepresentation of colonialism to say the least, it can also be read, more generously, in the spirit of Freire (1970/2000), for whom the dialectic of oppressor and oppressed dehumanizes both, but vests agency in the latter to educate and so liberate both oppressed and oppressor alike (1970/2000, 54).

REFERENCES

Althusser, Louis. 1971. "Ideology and Ideological State Apparatuses." In *"Lenin and Philosophy" and Other Essays*. Trans. Ben Brewster, 121–76. New York: Monthly Review Press.

Annesley, James. 2001. "Netscapes: Gibson, Globalisation and the Representation of New Media." *Forum for Modern Language Studies* 37(2): 218–29.

Apter, Emily. 2008. "Technics of the Subject: The Avatar-Drive." *Postmodern Culture* 18(2): n.p. doi: 10.1353/pmc.0.0021.

Barry, Wayne. 2007. "Digital Imperialism: The Tyranny of Technology." *The Accidental Technologist*, 29 Nov. http://www.waynebarry.com/blog/?p=45.

Bayne, S. and Ross, J. 2007. "The 'Digital Native' and 'Digital Immigrant': A Dangerous Opposition." Annual Conference of the Society for Research into Higher Education. http://www.malts.ed.ac.uk/staff/sian/natives_final.pdf.

Blade Runner. 1982. Dir. Ridley Scott. Warner Brothers.

Bolter, Jay David, and Richard Grusin. 1999. *Remediation: Understanding New Media*. Cambridge, MA: MIT Press.

Bredin, Marian. 2001. "Bridging Canada's Digital Divide." *Canadian Journal of Native Studies* 21(2): 195–215. http://www2.brandonu.ca/library/CJNS/21.2/cjnsv21no2_pg191-215.pdf.

Canadian Council on Learning. 2010. "Learning to Be: Access to Broadband Internet." *Composite Learning Index*. http://www.cli-ica.ca/en/about/about-cli/indicators/be-internet.aspx.

Chiefs Assembly on Education. 2012. "A Portrait of First Nations and Education." Assembly of First Nations. 1 Oct. http://www.afn.ca/uploads/files/events/fact_sheet-ccoe-3.pdf.

Coupland, Douglas. 2006. *JPod: A Novel*. Toronto: Vintage Canada.

Cover, Rob. 2014. "Becoming and Belonging: Performativity, Subjectivity, and the Cultural Purposes of Social Networking." In *Identity Technologies: Constructing the Self Online*, eds. Anna Poletti and Julie Rak, 55–78. Madison: University of Wisconsin Press.

Davis, Erik. 2004. "Roots and Wires: Polyrhythmic Cyberspace and the Black Electronic." *Techgnosis*. http://www.techgnosis.com/cyberconf.html.

de Kerckhove, Derrick. 1995. *The Skin of Culture: Investigating the New Electronic Reality*. Toronto: Somerville House.

Delboeuf, Joseph. 1885. *Le sommeil et les rêves considérés principalement dans leurs rapports avec les théories de la certitude et de la mémoire*. Paris: Félix Alcan.

Derrida, Jacques. 1974. "White Mythology: Metaphor in the Text of Philosophy." *New Literary History* 6(1): 5–74.

Dewdney, Chris. 1998. *Last Flesh: Life in the Transhuman Era*. Toronto: HarperCollins.

Dingwall, Dawna, and Pacinthe Mattar. 2013. "What Does 'Robot Reporting' Mean for Journalism?" *The Current*. 19 March. Toronto: CBC. http://www.cbc.ca/thecurrent/episode/2013/03/19/what-does-robot-journalism-mean-for-the-industry/.

Doctorow, Cory. 2003. *Down and Out in the Magic Kingdom*. New York: Tor Books.

Eshun, Kodwo. 1998. *More Brilliant than the Sun: Adventures in Sonic Fiction*. London: Quartet.

Fernbach, Amanda. 2000. "The Fetishization of Masculinity in Science Fiction: The Cyborg and the Console Cowboy." *Science Fiction Studies* 81. N.p.

Fisher, Mark. 2009. *Capitalist Realism: Is There No Alternative?* Zero Books.

Fontaine, Phil. 2013. Keynote. *Ignite! Ideas for Post-Secondary Education*. University of Alberta. 21 Feb.

Freire, Paolo. 1970/2000. *Pedagogy of the Oppressed*. New York: Continuum.

Gibson, William. 1984. Neuromancer. New York: Ace.

Gould, Glenn. 1963/1999. "Forgery and Imitation in the Creative Process." In *The Art of Glenn Gould: Reflections of a Musical Genius*, ed. John P. L. Roberts, 204–21. Toronto: Malcolm Lester.

Haraway, Donna. 1991. "A Cyborg Manifesto: Science, Technology, and Socialist-Feminism in the Late Twentieth Century." In *Simians, Cyborgs and Women: The Reinvention of Nature*, 149–81. New York: Routledge.

Hawthorn, Jeremy. 1992. *A Concise Glossary of Contemporary Literary Theory*. London: Edward Arnold.

Hayles, N. Katherine. 1999. How We Became Posthuman: Virtual Bodies in Cybernetics, Literature, and Informatics. Chicago: University of Chicago Press.

Hedges, Chris. 2012. "Colonized by Corporations." *Truthdig*, 14 May. http://www.truthdig.com/report/item/colonized_by_corporations_20120514

Henrich, Joseph, Steven J. Heine, and Ara Norenzayan. 2009. "The Weirdest People in the World: How Representative Are Experimental Findings from American University Students? What Do We Really Know about Human Psychology?" University of British Columbia. 5 March. http://www2.psych.ubc.ca/~henrich/pdfs/Weird_People_BBS_final02.pdf

Hesmondhalgh, David. 2010. "User-Generated Content, Free Labour and the Cultural Industries." *Ephemera* 10(3-4): 267–84. http://www.ephemeraweb.org/journal/10-3/10-3hesmondhalgh.pdf

hooks, bell. 2000. *Feminism Is for Everybody: Passionate Politics*. Cambridge: South End Press.

Hopkinson, Nalo. 1996. "A Habit of Waste." *Fireweed* 53.

Jurgenson, Nathan. 2011. "Digital Dualism versus Augmented Reality." *Cyborgology* 24 Feb. http://thesocietypages.org/cyborgology/2011/02/24/digital-dualism-versus-augmented-reality/

———. 2012a. "The IRL Fetish." *The New Inquiry* 28 June. http://thenewinquiry.com/essays/the-irl-fetish/

———. 2012b. "When Atoms Meet Bits: Social Media, the Mobile Web, and Augmented Revolution." *Future Internet* 4(1): 83–91. http://www.mdpi.com/1999-5903/4/1/83

Kellogg, Paul. 2013. "The Tar Sands: A Made-in-Canada Problem." *PolEcon.net*, 4 Jan. http://www.polecon.net/2013/01/the-tar-sands-made-in-canada-problem.html

Kittler, Friedrich. 1986/1999. *Gramophone, Film, Typewriter*. Trans. Geoffrey Winthrop-Young and Michael Wutz. Stanford: Stanford University Press.

Kravets, David. 2013. "Appeals Court Curbs Border Agents' Carte Blanche Power to Search Your Gadgets." *Wired*, 8 March. http://www.wired.com/threatlevel/2013/03/gadget-border-searches/

Kreisinger, Elisa. 2010. *The Queer Carrie Project. Pop Culture Pirate*. http://www.popculturepirate.com/queercarrie.html

———. N.d. "What Is Pop Culture Pirate?" *Pop Culture Pirate*. http://www.popculturepirate.com/about/

Marwick, Alice E. 2013. *Status Update: Celebrity, Publicity, and Branding in the Social Media Age*. New Haven: Yale University Press.

Max Headroom: 20 Minutes into the Future. 1987-88. Perf. Matt Frewer. Warner Bros.

McCutcheon, Mark A. 2009a. "Downloading *Doppelgängers*: New Media Anxieties and Transnational Ironies in *Battlestar Galactica*." *Science Fiction Film and Television* 2.1: 1-24.

———. 2009b. "Twitter's textual economy . . ." Tweet. 2:06 pm, 5 Oct. https://twitter.com/sonicfiction/status/4637678320

———. 2011. "Frankenstein as a Figure of Globalization in Canada's Postcolonial Popular Culture." *Continuum* 25(5): 731–42.

———. 2012. "Towards a Theory of the Dubject: Doubling and Spacing the Self in Canadian Media Culture." In *Selves and Subjectivities: Reflections on Canadian Arts and Culture*, eds. Manijeh Mannani and Veronica Thompson, 235–64. Edmonton: Athabasca University Press.

———. 2014. "Dubjection: A Node." In *McLuhan's Global Village Today*, ed. Martin Kuester, 59–73. London: Pickering and Chatto.

McLuhan, Marshall. 1964/2003. *Understanding Media: The Extensions of Man*. Ed. Terrence Gordon. Corte Madera, CA: Ginkgo Press.

———. 1996. *Forward Through the Rearview Mirror: Reflections on and by Marshall McLuhan*. Toronto: Prentice Hall.

McNeill, Laurie. 2014. "Life Bytes: Six-Word Memoir and the Exigencies of Auto/tweetographies." In *Identity Technologies: Constructing the Self Online*, eds. Anna Poletti and Julie Rak, 144–66. Madison: University of Wisconsin Press.

Morrison, Aimée. 2014. "Facebook and Coaxed Affordances." In *Identity Technologies: Constructing the Self Online*, eds. Anna Poletti and Julie Rak, 112–31. Madison: University of Wisconsin Press.

Nakamura, Lisa. 2014. "Cyberrace." In *Identity Technologies: Constructing the Self Online*, eds. Anna Poletti and Julie Rak, 42–54. Madison: University of Wisconsin Press.

NASA. 2012. "Mission Overview." *Voyager: The Interstellar Mission*. Accessed March 15, 2012. http://voyager.jpl.nasa.gov/mission/index.html.

Opikokew, Cassandra. 2013. Panel presentation. Ignite! Ideas for Post-Secondary Education. University of Alberta. 22 Feb.

Poletti, Anna, and Julie Rak, eds. 2014. *Identity Technologies: Constructing the Self Online*. Madison: University of Wisconsin Press.

Poster, Mark. 1995. "Cyberdemocracy: Internet and the Public Sphere." University of California Irvine. http://www.hnet.uci.edu/mposter/writings/democ.html.

Pregeson, Judge Dean. 2006. "Order Granting Defendant's Motion to Suppress Evidence." *United States of America v. Michael Timothy Arnold*, 1 June. http://www.wired.com/images_blogs/threatlevel/files/CR05-00772DDP.pdf.

Puar, Jasbir. 2011. "'I would rather be a cyborg than a goddess': Intersectionality, Assemblage, and Affective Politics." European Institute for Progressive Cultural Policies. Jan. http://eipcp.net/transversal/0811/puar/en.

Rey, P. J. 2010. "Data'll show 'em: Internet Access in the US." *Cyborgology*, 17 Nov. http://thesocietypages.org/cyborgology/2010/11/17/datall-show-em-internet-access-in-the-us/.

Ronnell, Avital. 1991. *The Telephone Book: Technology, Schizophrenia, Electric Speech.* Lincoln: University of Nebraska Press.

Sarkeesian, Anita. 2012. "About Feminist Frequency," *Feminist Frequency* http://www.feministfrequency.com/about/

———. 2012. "The Mirror." TEDxWomen, reprinted in YouTube http://www.youtube.com/watch?v=GZAxwsg9J9Q

Schmidt, Alex. 2013. "10 Weird Twitter Beings Worth a Follow." *Paste Magazine,* 16 Nov. http://www.pastemagazine.com/blogs/lists/2013/11/10-weird-twitter-beings-worth-a-follow.html.

Schneier, Bruce. 2013. "The Internet Is a Surveillance State." *CNN Opinion.* 16 March. http://www.cnn.com/2013/03/16/opinion/schneier-internet-surveillance.

Siemens, George. 2013. "Identity Formation in Distributed Networks and Social Spaces." Identity, Agency, and the Digital Nexus: An International Symposium. Athabasca University, 5 April.

Smith, Sidonie, and Julia Watson. 2014. "Virtually Me: A Toolbox About Online Self-Presentation." In *Identity Technologies: Constructing the Self Online,* eds. Anna Poletti and Julie Rak, 70–98. Madison: University of Wisconsin Press.

Thomas, Angela. 2007. *Youth Online: Identity and Literacy in the Digital Age.* New York: Peter Lang.

Turkle, Sherry. 1995. *Life on the Screen: Identity in the Age of the Internet.* New York: Simon and Schuster.

———. 2012. "Connected, but alone?" Ted Talks. April. http://www.ted.com/talks/sherry_turkle_alone_together.html

Tushnet, Rebecca. 2007. "My Fair Ladies: Sex, Gender, and Fair Use in Copyright." *Journal of Gender, Social Policy, and the Law* 15(2): 273–304.

Twitter. 2012. "Terms of Service." *Twitter,* 25 June. https://twitter.com/tos.

van Dijck, José. 2009. "Users Like You? Theorizing Agency in User-Generated Content." *Media, Culture and Society* 31(1): 41–58.

van Veen, Tobias. 2011. "Technics and Decrepit Democracy." *Fugitive Philosophy.* 3 May. http://fugitive.quadrantcrossing.org/2011/05/technics-decrepit-democracy.

Videodrome. 1983. Dir. David Cronenberg. Criterion.

Walker, Rob. 2011. "Things to Do in Cyberspace When You're Dead." *New York Times Magazine,* 5 Jan. http://www.nytimes.com/2011/01/09/magazine/09Immortality-t.html?pagewanted=all

Watts, Peter. 2006. *Blindsight.* New York: Tor.

White, David and Alison Le Cornu. 2011. "Visitors and Residents: A New Typology for Online Engagement." *First Monday* 16(9). 5 Sept. http://www.uic.edu/htbin/cgiwrap/bin/ojs/index.php/fm/article/viewArticle/3171/3049

7 The Network University in Transition

Bob Hanke

In 1979, in regards to identity in relation to the scenario of computerization, informatics, and telematics, Lyotard noted, "A self does not amount to much, but no self is an island; each exists in a fabric of relations that is now more complex and mobile than ever before (1984: 15). "Data banks," he continued, "are the Encyclopedia of tomorrow. They transcend the capacity of each of their users. They are 'nature' for postmodern man" (51). It is tempting to see the last thirty-five years as a confirmation of the predictive value of his hypothesis that processes of delegitimation and the predominance of performativity sounded "the knell of the age of the Professor: a professor is no more competent than memory bank networks in transmitting established knowledge, no more competent than interdisciplinary teams in imagining new moves or new games" (53).

Following in Lyotard's footsteps, Readings (1996) described how the University of Excellence displaced the University of Culture's cultivation of citizen-subjects within the liberal nation-state. He recognized that the cash nexus of the post-historical, capitalist bureaucratic university was coming to the fore and that computerization was altering the technological context of writing, publication, and reading. Lyotard's focus was the status of scientific knowledge in a computerized society while Readings' was the detachment of the contemporary university from the "historical development, affirmation and inculcation of national culture"

(6). Taken together, we could see that the end of the age of the professor was the beginning of the age of the administrator, while the "idea of culture as the object, as both origin and goal, of the human sciences" (10) was replaced by the techno-bureaucratic notion of "excellence."

Since these two reports on knowledge and culture in the twilight of the modern university, "informational culture" and the "informational university" have converged (Terranova, 2004; Bousquet, 2008). Moreover, the history of the unmaking of the U.S. public university has been written (Newfield, 2008) and the language of corporate culture has replaced the language of education (Woodhouse, 2009). According to Angus (2009), the "emerging science-technology-communication unity is undermining the traditional basis of the university" (62). Furthering this point, he suggests that the "network university" is "an emerging form of, and role for, the university in the network society, which is based on technoscience" (Angus, 2009: 64). Revising Readings, the idea of excellence has been superseded by innovation and an ethos of entrepreneurialism.

In the fifth edition of *The Uses of the University*, Clark Kerr revisited the U.S. "multiversity" to observe the end of the "golden age" of the U.S. research university. In his 1995 commentary, he noted, "The operation of the nerve system of academic life is now more dependent on computer terminals and facsimile machines . . . and less and less on face-to-face contact" (Kerr, 2001: 146). Among the great uncertainties for the new millennium, one source was "whether or not the greatly improved hardware and software for the new electronic technology may, at last, start to penetrate teaching as it already has research and administration" and bring about the "fourth revolution" of instructional technology that the Carnegie Commission on Higher Education already expected in the early 1970s.

Kerr was of two minds: on the one hand, "experience to date suggests that each new technology adds to but does not totally supplant prior technology— oral teaching added to the apprenticeship experience, the written word added to the spoken word, printing added to handwriting, and it seems likely that the 'chip' will add but not replace all the methods that have gone before" (Kerr, 2001: 195). On the other hand, the first item of "new business" was to use information technology more widely and more effectively. In the face of uncertainty, he wished for "careful studies" of "the new information technologies—what is working and what is not?" (Kerr, 2001: 228). In 2010, the U.S. Department of Education granted Kerr's wish and issued a meta-analysis of online learning studies that compared face-to-face and online learning; hybrid teaching methods were found to be more effective than either face-to-face–only or online-only courses (Means et al. 2010). For Kerr, video and e-mail were new media in higher education; today, course management systems, podcasts and video chat forums, intelligent tutoring systems and MOOCs represent the latest means of teaching and learning.

In this chapter, I examine the network university in transition. The digital nexus of activity in general, and the relation between digital technology and techniques in particular, have been instrumental to the transmutation of the university. It has been difficult to move beyond the issues of access to information, knowledge, and expertise to other matters of concern, such as hypermangerialism and the reproducibility of teaching. To make sense of what has happened over the past two decades, this chapter will make the case that the university has become a "network enterprise" (Castells, 2010) that shapes the "internal outside" that is the "unassimilated background" of our academic professions (Moten and Harney, 2004). Innis and McLuhan's thought illustrates how Hansen's (2010) notion of "mediatic regime change" is an historical occasion for thinking about media and the university. By adding Kittler's account of university-based media history to their viewpoints, we can trace the impact of mechanization, cybernation, and binary code on the liberal humanist subject. As I hope to make clear, the current scene of scholarly communication and pedagogy is still between print and digital codes and conventions, but we need a new kind of inquiry to talk about the network digital media-based university. Information technology strategy can be understood as a mode of institutional development that fuses technological and organizational change, facilitates administrative control, and alters the relational ecology between the faculty and student body. We can describe the institutional context as a milieu of circulation. To gain a deeper understanding of academic being within the mediatized academic world, we must remain attentive to media and spacetime.

The black-boxing of campus network infrastructures (combined with the performativity criterion, presentism, and the novelty of new media) is only the first set of difficulties. Achieving clarity about the contemporary university presents further problems. In these neoliberal times, due to corporatization, commercialization, managerialism, and bureaucratization, the problem of the public university has been framed as a "crisis." Elsewhere, I have spoken about the university's triple crisis: faculty employment, global finance, and knowledge (Hanke, 2011). From a classical Marxist perspective, cost-cutting was the spearhead of neoliberal restructuring; for faculty and students the changes could be summed up as "proletarianization" and "precarity" (Callinicos, 2006). In the wake of the financial meltdown of 2007–08, Canadian universities are facing further budget cuts. This kind of shock doctrine and resultant underfunding exacerbates structural changes such as job shedding and casualization of academic labour, unfilled academic positions and bigger teaching loads, course and program closures, bigger class sizes and more e-learning to increase access and accelerate graduation. To this, we can add two qualifications. First, there is the symbolization of university finances. On the one hand, top-level administrators represent York University's "financial gap" as the result of a vicious circle (financial downturn▶expenditures exceed revenues▶annual budget cuts▶new efficiency measures and tuition fee framework) that is leading to an unsustainable future. On the other hand, there is increased spending on presidential salaries and bonuses, administrative salary increases, consultants, campus building construction and renovation projects, a new athletic stadium, artificial turf and field lighting for stadiums, security measures and equipment, as well as rebranding campaigns. Second, there is the political-economic reality outside any particular university. Economic "crisis" has ceased to be an intermission; as Žižek (2010) argues, we are in a period "where a kind of economic state of emergency is becoming permanent: turning into a constant, a way of life" (96). But rather than declaring bankruptcy and asking for a government bailout, this crisis has been used by administrators to implement neoliberal policy. As the eighty-five-day 2008–2009 strike of contract faculty and teaching and graduate assistants at York University and the recent labour dispute at Simon Fraser University reveals, growth-at-any-cost strategies are paid for by the most vulnerable workers—teaching assistants, sessionals, contingent faculty, and staff (Various Authors, 2012).

In the third place, there are the difficulties that arise from making the university an object of intellectual inquiry and critique. As Weber (2001) notes, the specific university we work in may not provide a justification for generalizing about the university. Nonetheless, in what follows I shall sometimes take my own university as emblematic of the Canadian public university. To put it on another scale, we may assume that the structuring effects of the neoliberal "global university" are more or less taking place in every local university in Canada. Consider the "internationalization" of Canadian universities. In his address to the Empire Club of Toronto, York University's president—a mechanical engineer by profession—spoke about higher education services in the "knowledge-based economy" as a value-added Canadian import (Shoukri, 2013). From this perspective, international education is an "economic advantage for the host country." The proof is in the statistics on consumer spending; between 2008 and 2010, international students' spending on tuition, accommodation, and other discretionary goods and services increased from $6.5 billion to $8 billion.

My project draws upon the materialistic theory of media and networks. When it comes to academic being-there, technics, and time, the academic form of life is a "repetitive life" (Sloterdijk, 2012). And yet, after the digital turn, our embodied engagement and practice of reading and writing in network culture is not what it used to be in a book culture. As Ian Angus (this volume) explains, "Digitization functions as both a universal medium of translation and also as a specific medium comparable to others, in that its specific network social relations prevail when re-embedding is within the digital form"(71). This generic communication depends on the production of networks and their utilities. In the mid-1990s, campus-wide networks were built with commercial hardware from the private IT systems industry. Today, as Mejias points out, privately owned "social network services exhibit dual processes that enable both the creation of new public spaces and the controlling and monitoring of these spaces through mechanisms facilitated by the architecture of the network itself" (2010: 603). He goes on to make a useful distinction between "nodocentrism"—if "something is available on the network, it is perceived as part of reality"—and the "paranodal": "if it is not available, it might not be real" (611). With these concepts in mind, we can grasp how the dual processes of the publicly assisted network university have consequences not only for knowing what is capitalist or noncapitalist about the university but also for what exists beyond the borders of a node within it or outside it that might animate the network university. Network university space, despite control of the edges, has expanded, and network university time, despite the shortage of time, is open to events.

NET WORK

Rather than joining the long line of scholars who have pursued the idea of the university, I start with the concept of networks. The first problem is a definitional one – the suitability of the term "network" itself. There have been various contenders for renaming the university—corporate, virtual, entrepreneurial, ecological, and more—but I find "network" to be a useful conceptual tool. The term "network" has five senses. In the first place, the network university reflects the birth of network society and the transition from a pillar model to a web model of university life (Standaert, 2009). A campus network is not merely a metaphor but a sociotechnical network articulated to organizational culture (Lewis, Marginson, and Snyder, 2005). In the second sense, by the early 1990s, academic culture could be defined as "the network of interrelated and explicit beliefs about academic practices of teaching, learning and research and about the social significance of those practices" (Ringer, 1992: 13). Latour (2005) has proposed dropping the polysemy of "network" in favor of worknet or action net. In the third sense, I prefer to retain the concept because "work" is embedded in "network." We do knowledge work (Liu, 2004) while our computers work to process information and manipulate data. The faculty body is connected to the same universal machine and Internet with flexible ties to epistemic networks within and across departments and organized research units at varying scales. However, information technology (IT) professionals are also actors who design, build, test, configure, secure, repair, and maintain campus networks. In actor-network theory, actors and networks constitute each other: IT professionals constitute the technical network and faculty constitute epistemic networks. Fourth, drawing on Shaviro, who follows Deleuze, the network is "political to the core" because it is a system of distributed control (2003: 21). The university displays the hybridization of physical and digital space that characterizes virtual environments (Dourish, 2001); moreover, network space is "always folding, dividing, expanding, and contracting" (Shaviro, 2003: 7). Finally, understanding networks as they unfold over time is more complicated when the "virtual" is not simply opposed to the real university. To borrow from Thacker, the "abstract-but-real is the network that is always enacted and about to enact itself" (2004, xiv).

By some earlier accounts, the late modern university has lost its unifying idea to a plurality of functions. What unifies the various functions? I take it as axiomatic that communication is the "force that binds together the sociological and the epistemological, giving shape and substance to the links between knowledge forms and knowledge communities" (Becher and Trowler, 2001: 77). After reviewing the idea of the university, Habermas realized that the multiplicity of the disciplines could no longer tie all the functions together. He went on to express his belief that it is "communicative forms of scientific and scholarly argumentation that hold university learning processes in their various functions together" (1989: 124). Even if faculty and students are working alone, they are embedded in a public communication of researchers. Because this cooperative enterprise refers back to structures of argumentation, he claims that truth, or the reputation achieved by a scholarly community, "can never become the mere steering medium of a self-regulating subsystem" (1989: 124). In his argument, which overlooks the functioning of networks, it is the norms of scientific and scholarly activity that set the university apart from society, even as it shares the communicative rationality of that society.

This normative ideal was undermined by the rise of the "promotional condition" of the university (Wernick, 1991). The university would enter into an exchange with the discourse of advertising—the symbolic system of twentieth-century late capitalism. As a species of rhetoric, it not defined by what it says but by what it does. It targets the reputation of a university, not in the eyes of scholar-professors but in the eyes of consumers. The first casualty is not, as we might assume, the truth but rather the "very meaningfulness of the language material which promotional messages mobilize" (189). Moreover, promotional rhetoric cannot be disentangled from what is promoted—promotionalism is reincorporated back into remaking of higher education. Due to under-investment, this process of promotionalization has been intensified; universities have been busy rebranding themselves and marketing campaigns are deemed to be "strategic investments." In the competition for higher education market share, media relations units pursue "strategic messaging" by pitching university stories and faculty research achievements to the media and the positive news stories generated are measured by their "PR value" and "media impressions."

Since the advent of a campus-wide distributed network and the increased use of computing for administrative support, one source of concern over academic quality and freedom is hypermanagerialism. New managerialism embraced new technology. As Reed and Deem (2002) describe it:

> The "cultural revolution" that "New Managerialism" sets in motion
> requires a technology of workplace control, which a restructured
> governance structure and management structure, in order to make it a
> viable programme of change, grounded in a set of practices and devices
> focused upon the highly complex task of re-engineering the labour
> process within and through which public sector professionals and man-
> agers do their work. (130)

Stepulevage (2009), for example, analyzes how Enterprise Resource Planning (ERP) technology in higher education institutions modeled the reality of the university as a unified, ordered, stable system, which, in turn, embodies the myth of "best practice," which may not take account of how work is actually performed. McNally (2010) goes a step further to argue that enterprise content management extends Taylorist and Fordist principles into intellectual labour. Faculty have been reskilling themselves to perform digital labour but so have system administrators; the upshot is greater managerial control over the academic labour process.

Today, hypermanagerialism encompasses audit culture, institutional research, spreadsheets, web clients, performance indicators, info capture, remote control by marketing, and more. At York University, for example, staff in the Faculty of Liberal Arts and Professional Studies were subject to a twelve-month departmental review by an HR business partner with experience in "design and implementation of process efficiencies" and "design of job-specific competencies." This partner came to York from Toys R Us Canada, Eurocopter Canada Limited, U.S. Steel, and the City of St. Catherines. In this way, the work of staff is embedded in work processes that span the private and public sector. The relative autonomy of the faculty body vis-à-vis managerialism's mandates is a fading memory. As Godard (2010) has observed, "information flows bureaucratically down from the administration's marketers as a culture of secrecy replaces a 'community of dissensus'" (30). At the same time, information that flows bureaucratically up positions the faculty as clients within a service organization. As part of the process of departmental review within the Faculty of Liberal Arts and Professional Studies at York, faculty feedback on administrative services and support, following the recommendation of chairs and directors, is taking the form of online surveys.

Meanwhile, the administration's latest "Academic and Administrative Prioritization" exercise—which has been given impetus by U.S. consultant Robert Dickeson—aims to integrate academic and financial planning by weakening the constitutional role of the faculty senate and its committees in overseeing academic programs (Heron, 2013). The administration has the right to gather information while the senate has responsibility for academic policy. Even if a senate subcommittee participates in designing the template for information, such an exercise would necessitate gathering copious amounts of data from every program to rate them and make decisions about areas of strength and weakness, (re)investment, deinvestment, and growth. This exemplifies how consultation and codification of templates with faculty-generated academic criteria would enhance the managerial gaze into departmental performance indicators rather than curb the rationalization process for making budget cuts. Even with democratic validation, departments may become more visible and professors more assessable. Deploying this managerial technique would further decrease faculty's power to act and increase the neoliberal government's financial power as a power of public evaluation (Lazzarato, 2012).

There is danger in the pursuit of the reproducibility of teaching through digital network media. The work of teaching in the age of mechanical and digital reproduction has a history that can be traced from Sidney Pressey's 1924 teaching machine (Petrina, 2004). This was a mechanical machine to lift the burden of drill and practice from teacher's shoulders. While there is new software and analytics, the desire to make teaching less labour-intensive is not new. Computer tutoring researchers are working on artificially intelligent tutoring systems for STEM courses (VanLehn, 2011) and automated essay-scoring engines are being developed to autograde student essays (Stross, 2012). Free essay-grading software has been created by EdX, the nonprofit open-source online learning platform governed by Harvard and MIT. This software, which learns the grading technique of a human instructor, represents the fulfillment of the dream of instant grades. Such artifacts are at the experimental stage, however, and may never become part of the enterprise-wide software systems and applications of most universities.

THE NETWORK UNIVERSITY

The network university has emerged out of the modern "university in ruins" (Readings, 1996) to become a node in Castell's "network society" (Pruett and Schwellenbach, 2004). As Agre notes, infrastructure and institutional change are linked; information technology strategy can be understood as a mode of development that fuses technological and organizational change (2002). To go beyond economism—the idea that the network university's form and role are embedded in an economic crisis that it responds to by connecting techno-science with techno-capital—I argue that we must make a detour through media theory and history. Hansen (2010) has proposed that new media can be regarded as "new" in a new way: media do not only store experience, they also "mediate the conditions of mediation" (81). From his viewpoint, we are in the midst of "mediatic regime change." Digital media and their networks have become necessary to the everyday functioning of the public university, circuits of knowledge, and faculties' and students' communication, thinking, and worldly engagement.

In the Canadian context, Harold A. Innis's and Marshall McLuhan's thought illustrate how "mediatic regime change" is an historical occasion for thinking about media and higher education. Picking up where Plato's critique of writing in the *Phaedrus* left off, Innis writes that, in the age of the printing press and radio, "improvements in communication," particularly in the mass production of words, "have weakened the possibility of sustained thought when it becomes more necessary" (1946: xiv). From the standpoint of the Western university's oral tradition of instruction, the textbook and the exam system represented the threat of mechanization. "Machine industry" and the media of print, radio, and film, he argued, accelerated the "dissemination of facts that would lead to the closing of student minds" (Innis, 1951 [1947]). In his view, mechanization undermined the university's two real functions: "the life of study, whether for a few years or during a whole career, and to bring together during that period, face to face in living intercourse, teacher and teacher, teacher and student, student and student" (1946: 81). Surrounded by totalitarianism during World War II, he was troubled by the disjuncture between the rise of modern science and the post–World War "rehabilitation of civilization"; the "ivory lab," as he put it, "destroys the ivory tower" (73). Due to political pressures from the state and the "judgement of business men," he believed that universities would become "one of the kept institutions of capitalism" (75). "To buy universities," he concluded, "is to destroy them and with them the civilization they stand for" (75).

In contrast to Innis, McLuhan eschewed writing any lament for the university as a crucible of Western civilization and its decline. Rather, he viewed new communication and information technology as an opportunity to experiment and create the educational future. Whereas Innis looked to the past and remained a firm believer in balancing time- and space-biased media, McLuhan advocated the arts as "dynamic feedback" on our technological environment (McLuhan, 1964: xi). In contrast to Innis, McLuhan was historically positioned to attend to the rise of television and to perceive the impact of the scientific revolution as "cybernation." He grasped that "instantaneous retrieval of information by electricity" would make possible inventories of "materials in continuous process of transformation at spatially removed sites" (1964: 300, 310). He foresaw how "automation affects not just every phase of consumption and marketing; for the consumer becomes a producer in the automation circuit" (1964: 303). Surfing the wave of first-wave cybernetics and its computer-brain analogies into expanded consciousness, McLuhan signaled the consequences of electric media and cybernation for typographic man—also known as the liberal humanist subject.

It would take another forty years for the post-human subject to be registered. In "Universities: Wet, Hard, Soft and Harder," Friedrich Kittler argues that the hardware of the lecture, the library and the mail enabled a "cumulative and recursive production of knowledge" (2004: 245). He foregrounds the relation of recurrence between the Greek alphabet and binary code and the parallels between the hardware of the early modern and late modern university. After 800 years of university-based media history, computing has spread from mathematics departments to every other department. In his account of the technological enframing of the university, "universities have finally succeeded in forming once again a complete media system" (2004: 249). The consequence of this technological convergence, he believed, was a "new uniformity of knowledges, disciplines, departments" and "ontology or the logos of Being, has materialized in computing machines" (2004: 250). When binary code replaces letters, images, and sounds, he hopes the "methodological integration of studies in language and music, film and poetry may begin" (Kittler, 2004: 250). In his post-human vision, cultural technologies, not man, will become the proper subject of the humanities (Kittler, 2004: 251).

Despite these happy consequences, Kittler was also concerned about the commercialization of chip designs, operating systems and interfaces and proprietary solutions, patents, trademarks, and copyrights. New software such as Coursera does not eliminate concerns about commercialization and "copy-far-left" has only reached the manifesto stage (Kleiner, 2010). The 2012 Copyright Modernization Act, which contained amendments to fair dealing that recognized reader's/user's rights for educational purposes, has set the stage for litigation. In April 2013, Access Copyright, the Canadian copyright licensing agency, filed a lawsuit against York University in the Federal Court of Canada over the off-campus photocopying of course packs. In response to the General Counsel's "Document Preservation Notice," which states that any "document that has a semblance of relevance" must be preserved for this legal proceeding, the York University Faculty Association filed a policy grievance based on the memo's fear-mongering and overreaching requirements.

There is more to university-based media than computerization and copyright. Because of technological convergence, the academy's lost monopoly over knowledge, and the overlap between education and business, Alan Liu (2004) has explained how knowledge work harnessed to information technology has changed not only "literary" study but scholars as well. In the post-industrial era, he writes, "Scholars are themselves knowledge workers in a complete sense: they are intellectuals but they are also middle managers responsible for an endless series of programs, committees, performance reports, and so on" (21). Following Bourdieu, he argues that information is not ideology; rather, "information

·consumed without concern for technological mediation ... is our contemporary habitus. It is the habitual information environment in which 'subjective principles of organization' (as Bourdieu puts it) are deeply in-formed by a world defined as technology-object" (41). From his perspective on production, IT is a mode of development that "generates what amounts to semiautonomous doxa—a belief in information or in technology" (40) at the same time "new corporatism" identifies "culture with technology and technique" (69). Managers work to align technology and technique for efficiency and productivity.

I now turn to three sets of considerations, beginning with philosophy and Derrida's seminal essay "Mochlos, or the Conflict of the Faculties." Kant's philosophical project was to define the university and the faculty judgment capable of deciding. Derrida contends that Kant tried to save rational discourse by separating knowledge from the publication of knowledge. Whereas Kant's philosophical demand centered on language, Derrida suggests: "This philosophical demand is best represented by an information technology that, while appearing today to escape the control of the university—in Kantian terms, of philosophy— is its product and its most faithful representative" (2004: 98).

In Derrida's reading, the contradiction within Kant's text becomes irresolvable when publication, archiving, and mediatization expand. The new journal *Amodern*, whose inaugural issue is devoted to the future of the scholarly journal, describes the shift from print to digital network media in these progressive terms:

> The scholarly knowledge system we have today originated in the seventeenth century. It sanctifies the individuality, originality, objectivity, and intellectual property of scholars working alone (or in small groups) within a knowledge system defined by the fixity, uniformity, and proprietary status of print. Now, networked IT proffers an apparatus in which information and knowledge no longer tend to be fixed and proprietary; where cultural breakthroughs occur as the result of exercises in collective intelligence, large-scale collaboration, assemblage, and continuous revision; and where authorship and authority are increasingly established communally and anonymously rather than individually. (http:// amodern.net/)

Parallel to forms of production of knowledge are forms of production of subjectivity. Here we can turn to Peter Sloterdijk's philosophical contribution. In *In the World Interior of Capital*, he describes the consequences of the use of digital media for subjectivity after the printed book and electronic media. In his philosophical view, "the postmodern 'user self', is beginning to replace the more ponderous form of subjectivity, the 'educated self' of the Modern Age" (2013: 219). Relieved of the burden of gathering experiences by using techniques for retrieving information, "reader subjectivity dissolves into user subjectivity" (2013: 219). In a culture of search engines and databases, the user collects addresses rather than experiences. For him, downloading "expresses the transition into a post-experiential age" that is accompanied by a "post-personal, post-literary, post-academic cognition regime" ahead (2013; 220). In *The Art of Philosophy,* he provides an account of the rise of the observer in a culture of rationality. Returning to Plato, he contends that the academy was an innovation in spatial creation. It is, he writes, the "architectural equivalent of what Husserl apostrophized as epoché—a building for shutting out the world and bracketing in concern, an asylum for mysterious guests that we call ideas and theorems" (2012: 33). Within this space, he describes how the humanities' mode of looking, which has its roots in the European mode of reading, was based on an analogy between the world and the book. This "classical analogy," he observes, "has completely disintegrated in the age of monitor screens and keyboards" (2012: 54).

The second set of considerations is political-economic. As Schiller (1999) has described, the Internet originated in the U.S. and was created for use by universities, government agencies, and large corporations. As a spearhead for globalization and ecommerce, the Internet accelerated the metamorphosis of education and subordinated education to the economy. Economism is the great intruder that trespasses upon the enclosed space of the public university.

Since the late 1980s, critiques of the business-like university have piled up. The information and communications technology (ICT) "revolution" brought technological change to the fore. In 1998, Langdon Winner, a critic of "runaway technology" who teaches science and technology, presented his "Automatic Professor Machine." In response to the surge of online education, this satire portrays the work of faculty in the age of automation against the will to exploit technology for the higher-learning industry.

David Noble, in *Digital Diploma Mills: The Automation of Higher Education,* launched a serious critique of commercialization, commodification, and administrative mandates to use computers for education. In his view, technology was being deployed by management primarily to discipline, deskill, and displace labour for profit. In his historical view, the danger was that academic labour would be caught within an industrial capital/labour dialectic. However, since the advent of word processing and email, faculty have been participating in a mass apprenticeship to acquire new digital skills. Moreover, from the perspective of Italian autonomous Marxism, academic work has always already been "immaterial labour," a new concept of labour that fuses informational, cultural and affective content, work and nonwork, actuality and virtuality. Even if we are composing alone, scholarly work and life is knowledge-rich, and it entails cooperation and coordination. But in both Winner's and Noble's visions of the future of higher education, technology is a Trojan horse for efficiency and commodification. They view new technology as an industrial trend that should be resisted. Even though commodification remains a concern, this risks misunderstanding the technological affordances of media and the role of design in shaping technology.

Côté and Allahar's *Ivory Tower Blues: A University System in Crisis* offers the concept of "disengagement contract" to illuminate the sociological aspects of higher education. Due to various factors, they argue that undergraduate students have become "reluctant intellectuals" and faculty "reluctant gatekeepers." In their 2011 follow-up book *Lowering Higher Education: The Rise of Corporate Universities and the Fall of Liberal Education*, they assess the question of whether new technologies will save the day. They conclude that "new technologies can facilitate learning, they do not replace teachers" (2011: 174). Second, these technologies "are best used for the fun of learning concrete, personalized material (e.g. popular culture), not for the work of developing critical thinking skills, and learning how to deal with abstractions in written and verbal forms" (2011: 174). While their first point is that professors, not the Internet, incarnate wisdom, their second point seems to hinge upon a simplistic division between cognition and affect, and to overlook the connections between thinking in any disciplines and media.

Looking backward, we are in a better position to see what higher-education future has arrived. The PC, Internet, email, WWW, electronic indexes, digital journals, ebooks, e-reserves, course-management systems, search engines, mobile phones, and tablets have altered scholarly communication and traditional on-campus classes. In the first instance, the flipside of unsubstantiated techno-optimism is top-down administrative control. The threat of virtualization is that the "will to power of university administrators which now use 'the' network for information and image control, surveillance, unidirectional communication, edicts and coercive demands on actors lower down" (McCarthy et al., 2009: 48). On the teaching side, we have seen the rise of the blended learning model. This model put an end to the late-1990s face-to-face versus online platform debate. It borrows from existing practices and assimilates new technology in search of "best practices." In general, course websites, audio podcasting, content or learning management systems, video capture, and digital media are believed to be more stimulating than any "sage on the stage."

Course management systems (cms) such as Moodle also expand the archive of a course and enable the manipulation of the time-axis of the course. Combined with video recording and distribution, they afford the possibility of "flipping a course"—reallocating in-class time that would have been spent listening to a lecture to discussion, small group work, problem solving, or hands-on or peer learning. This development fails to appreciate that the lecture is a form of talk (Goffman, 1981) and that reading with an academic purpose, active listening, and note-taking are academic skills. The flipped model of instruction is on the move from elementary and secondary to postsecondary education as universities develop "institutional learning outcomes" in parallel with provincial government's feasibility studies on assessing learning outcomes across oecd countries (see Ministry of Training, Colleges and Universities, 2012). Due to the student population explosion, the upper size limit of the lecture as face-to-face communication—even with amplification and projection—has been exceeded. There is a growing belief that networked digital media will free up time in large lecture auditoriums for more authentic learning and space for even more students.

However, connectivity means both connection and disconnection (Shaviro, 2003). Students may believe they no longer need to write down what they see and hear because they have easy access to digital content. Posting documents, however, does not guarantee they will be read just-in-time for a lecture or tutorial. Since adopting Moodle, my activity reports show that the percentage of students accessing the lecture outlines I produce and post before class declines as end of term approaches. Moodle creates a hybrid classroom space but it cannot resolve contradictions in the student's temporal economy. In this economy, paid work and accumulating debt are the biggest obstacles to students' academic performance.

Beyond the issue of disconnectivity, there is the transmission model of pedagogy to consider. In his analysis of cyberspace and student bodies, Mark Nunes points out that "any restructuring of the classroom by way of networked spaces of everyday life must therefore involve a restructuring of the student as well (2006: 131–32). Students are instituted, through their interaction with networks, into a "network subject position within a casualized community of transmission and exchange" (2006: 148). The rhetoric of "student-centered learning" masks how going online reinforces the "conduit fallacy of communication." The next step is to think about the subject who is registered for courses and addressed by the university as a "client." This is the network student subject that is flexible, mobile, and easily withdrawn from the life of study.

Notwithstanding any such analysis of the student subject, current managerial style continues to push eLearning. At York University, there are incentives for faculty to develop "best practices" of "technology-enhanced" learning that can be scaled up. At the same time, UIT are building more platforms for eLearning to suit the "mobile nature" of students. Despite warnings from Heather Kanuka (2006) of a disconnect between the belief in the effectiveness of eLearning and the results of empirical research, the York Institute for Research on Learning Technologies has called for more research and development of business cases for increasing the number of e-courses. "Technical Reports" that evaluate blended learning take their criteria from evaluation rubrics but group the questions according to criteria in the universities' eLearning business case (Owston and York, 2012–13). The first criterion is to "increase York's ability to respond to enrolment pressures." The first recommendation pertaining to students is "striving for a higher level of course satisfaction (e.g., 80 percent) and making all decisions regarding course design and delivery with this goal in mind." In such reports, we can glimpse how organizational agency works to shift teaching in a more online direction. Like earlier initiatives in web-based education, this research is "framed and fanned by the managerial transformation of universities" (Brabazon, 2007: 10). In lieu of a debate on higher educational leadership and responsibility or reflection on the conditions of academic work, "student-centered learning is an excuse for cheap learning" (Brabazon, 2007: 77).

The challenge is to conduct educational research in the public interest that is not determined by enrollment pressures and to design courses that are not influenced by sovereign student-consumers. As Kanuka (2006) also points out, vignettes and websites touting advantages have flooded out findings that eLearning has its disadvantages. In a sociological study of forty-two professors at three research-intensive U.S. universities, David Johnson found that "academics perceive instructional technologies to have limited value in enhancing education and that technology use is rarely motivated by pedagogical innovation" (2012: 126). Instructional technology is not mandated but the pressure of teaching more students at once is sufficient to induce faculty members to adopt technology in ways unrelated to improving learning. According to Norm Friesen, discussion about web-based education since the mid-1990s has centered on the differences between online and offline. The debate is hindered by a "technologized" understanding of communication, experience and education (2011: xiv). The reduction of debate to a consideration of distinctions between on- and off-line may make for more appropriate educational uses of technology that deflect our attention from technology and the politics of instruction. The more "effective" instructional technology for student-centered eLearning is perceived to be, the more we should perhaps conclude that eLearning has the potential to erode faculty choice and control. When privately owned network services are incorporated, the same door of educational opportunity also swings open to the market and commodification.

The networked space is also reflected in the faculty habitus. According to *University Affairs*, we are becoming "Prof. 2.0." Media have always been extensions of our scholarly practices. We are still working and living within academic tribes but we have become more nomadic. Due to the grammatization of scholarship, we are in between print and digital codes (Robertson, 2013).

While who we are depends on which academic generation and rank we belong to, and a method is only as good as its teachers, we have all experienced an increase in Internet working and interface time. The social media represent another technological wave: Students with smart phones have real-time access to the flow of social networking media, universities are promoting themselves on Facebook, Twitter, and You Tube, libraries are calling for participation in the growth of their social media networks, and employee intranets with dashboards to access applications, online systems, and social media platforms are being rolled out. In the public university after social media, faculty are becoming adjuncts to platformativity.

To go beyond the satisfactions and dissatisfactions of social media, we need a new kind of inquiry. Media studies is well equipped to study the university-media relation (Rowe and Brass, 2008: 2011). In addition to representation and discursive formations, we should critically examine the metaprocess of "mediatization" (Hepps, 2013). As a concept to direct research, this concept emphasizes that the network university is in formation in a particular time and culture. On this view of the media saturation of our academic life world, we are no longer talking about media in the university, or university-media relations, but the network digital media-based university. As Bernard Stiegler suggests in his multivolume work on technics and time, the programming industries unleash a synchronization that tends to be a "becoming-media of all instruments of work and socialization (including the school . . .)" which leads to a loss of psychic and collective individuation (2011, 100).

We could begin by looking at administrative practices and IT strategy, and by asking how did my university become a network university? The networking of York University is probably paradigmatic. The 1995 switch from IBM mainframe computing to Cisco Systems shared client-server networks created an IT infrastructure that was decentralized but too heterogeneous to fit the mold of a "comprehensive university." To facilitate expansion, switched Ethernet became the new topology in line with TCP/IP protocol and another technics of organization would be tried. In the late 1990s, the boundary between "administrative" and "academic" computing was breached. By the mid-2000s, a "utilities-oriented" infrastructure was combined with "service-oriented" applications. By the late 2000s, "The discussion around IT is becoming increasingly about managing the University, not just managing IT" (IT Strategy working group, 2009). During this period, IT professionals acted as technological intermediaries between IT industry vendors and their "clients"—administrators, faculty, staff, and students. University libraries have been at the forefront of digitization to create infrastructure to share ejournals, ebooks, and data sets as well as access to citation management tools. Like other universities, York University has implemented an institutional repository to store the intellectual output of the institution and provide space for programs, departments, and their collections. Another major Canadian initiative is digital journal hosting in the Open Journals System. These developments further support Kittler's (1990) proposition that all "libraries are discourse networks, but all discourse networks are not books" (369).

For IT professionals, an instrumentalist view of technology is hegemonic. In the former Faculty of Arts at York University, between 2005 and 2010, faculty were called to participate in computer technology planning in their units but they were instructed by managers to view IT as "merely a tool that would enable units to achieve their teaching, research and administrative goals." The limited role of faculty in making technological choices or decisions parallels the "decline of senates, bi-cameralism and the governance role of faculty" (Wernick, 2006: 7). One has to go back to 1997 to discover the last time that the York Faculty Association weighed in on IT issues in the collective bargaining process: the faculty's retention of copyright and the right to judge the appropriate use of technology.

The faculty's perceived affordances of email listservs seems to have changed. At York, one professor's email on the changing role of a Senate listserv is worth quoting at length:

> I was on Senate from 2001 to 2008. At that time, I found Senate-L to be a useful venue for discussion in advance of Senate meetings. It can lead to more active engagement of Senators in the business of Senate. I find that the floor of Senate is not the best place for serious discussion and reflection, or for suddenly raising new viewpoints on items that are coming for vote. I rejoined Senate in 2012. There seems to have been a change in the role of Senate-L: there appears to be less willingness to engage in discussion. Perhaps in the intervening years there has been an understanding, implicit or otherwise, that Senate-L would be used mainly for announcements, and that two-way discussion would not necessarily be encouraged (even if not actively discouraged). Or perhaps not. In any case, I am not comfortable with the extended silence on Senate-L. (Madras, 2013)

The decline of online discussion corresponds to a decreased attendance at Senate meetings. A July 2013 survey of faculty found that 80 percent cited "interest" as a reason for attending but only 56 percent felt it was their "duty" to attend. Those who attended five or fewer meetings did so because they reviewed documents and had no concerns.

For educational researchers, programmable machines and digital media are media of a pragmatic worldview. In the late 1990s, educational research on the use of the Internet decoupled class size from quality. Since then, discourse of cognitive psychology, social constructivism, and connectionism have framed the development of instructional technologies. Some educational researchers presume that an "educational divide" exists when there is a disjuncture between the academic technoculture and the student experience of new media outside the university. The onus is then on researchers to keep pace with technological innovation. Therefore, educational research tends to focus on novel technologies in order to measure achievement or effectiveness, and to bracket off digital experience from the rest of the university. Notwithstanding these analytical limits and the workshops that promote adopting new media, a recent survey of 15,000 Québec students showed they want an engaging lecture (Charbonneau, 2012). Another noteworthy finding is that only 53 percent of students had a positive perception of how ICTs were used in lectures compared to 86 percent of teachers (Charbonneau, 2013).) After the rise of social media, it is more difficult to separate educational from social uses (see Chapter 7).

Minority faculty reports on digital media in the classroom are rare yet instructive. One example is Mann's (2012) editorial-opinion "Let's Unplug the Digital Classroom." In response to the Ontario government's white paper on "Strengthening Ontario's Centres of Creativity, Innovation and Knowledge," unplugging is the most radical action that he can imagine. To avoid increasing class size even more, the government is demanding "innovation" to enhance productivity. To quote from this vision of "technology enabled education": "Rather than faculty 'transmitting' lecture data to students sitting in a hall, digital delivery of course content can free faculty in traditional institutions to engage in direct dialogue and mentorship with students" (2012: 10). In this formulation, face-to-face communication is reduced to the exchange of data while online communication is favoured for its immediacy. In addition to ignoring the corporeality of faculty and student bodies, this policy hijacks the concept of culture by linking it to "innovation," and it whitewashes how the public university has been thrown into crisis by neoliberalism.

In the network university, "culture," in the Euromodern sense, has been displaced from the center and replaced by the culture of information. To put it another way, if the network is the medium, the message is the network social relation. To be more specific, "network sociality" is what weakly ties faculty and students together (Wittel, 2001). In the wireless university without walls, the rise of new modes of connectivity parallels the decline of university sociability (Boyer, 2011). The "technical capacities of digital mediation," he notes, "can reinforce greater physical isolation as well as virtual connectivity, senses of alienation as well as emancipation, depending on their particular mode of institutionalization" (184).

Some of the cultural indicators of the network university are information glut and data deluge, scrolling (rather than reading), distraction (rather than fascination), surface attention and stupefaction (rather than discernment). As Sampson (2012) succinctly sums up: "Social subjectivity," in the age of virality and network relations, is a "hypnotic sleepwalk somewhere between unconsciousness and attentive awareness" (13). In the contemporary battle for collective intelligence, one enterprising student has developed an interactive application for professors to engage with their students using the devices they already own. Building upon the classroom technology of student response systems, this is an application to gauge student confusion in real time. Without raising their hand, students can anonymously click "confused" or "understood" and their real-time Prof 2.0 can see the percentage of students who understood. At the core of this application, "a fiendishly clever algorithm builds in a 'half life.' Each response decays and then disappears" giving Prof 2.0 "just enough time to notice it." The digital ICTs that brought us the "just-in-time" student are linked to a networked application that brings us the "just-in-time" professor. The adoption and use of this application would maintain a student's techno-bubble while robbing them of the classroom experience of the ambiguity of meaning or clash of ideas.

THE MILIEU IS THE MESSAGE

I want to go on to argue that we can describe the institutional context as an academic milieu of circulation. In his 11 January 1978 lecture, Michel Foucault says the milieu "is what is needed to account for action at a distance of one body on another. It is therefore the medium of action and the element in which it circulates" (2007: 20–21). He transports this notion from physics and biology into town planning in the sixteenth and seventeenth century. The milieu is less a space where discipline is carried out than the planned space where possible events or elements are regulated. Politically, it is also a "field of intervention in which . . . one tries to affect, precisely, a population." In the milieu, circular links are produced between causes and effects and these effects bear upon all who live in it. Like town planners and builders of bridges and quays, the York University president and the Board of Governors have regarded the university space as a site of real-estate development and IT projects. For IT managers and support groups, it is a matter of organizing the circulation of information and integrating technological developments into the academic plan and everyday functioning of the university.

In his January 25, 1978, lecture, Foucault defines "circulation in a very broad sense of movement, exchange and contract, as a form of dispersion, and also as a form of distribution, the problem being: How should things circulate or not circulate?" (2007: 64). We can also use this question to understand the network university's neoliberal outside. For example, the Ontario government's white paper charges the post-secondary system with improving productivity through "innovation" to increase student-consumer "choice" and "labour-market outcomes." People in their mid-20s are at the "peak of their mobility." The problem is that this population is more mobile than credentials and credits. What the neoliberal economy requires is more fluidity among learning, training, and the workforce. Under neoliberal rule, the economic value of credentials and credits depends upon transferability within and across systems.

Other scholars have written about how the age of digital reproduction presents new possibilities for new practices of scholarly communication (Borgman, 2007) as well as open access research and scholarship (Hall, 2008). According to Wilson (2013), over 50 percent of higher education institutions use open-source software on servers and desktops. The Moodle Virtual Learning Environment is considered a "success story" in higher education. He sees customizing open-source code as an extension of academic creativity and freedom. But as Galloway (2012) has suggested, another important question to ask is "How does open source shape systems of storage and transmission of knowledge?" (9). As for open peer review and data sharing after Web 2.0, Accord and Harley's research reveals how the adoption and use of digital technologies are conditioned by disciplinary cultures (2012).

While scholarly communication has become more open, universities have standardized and centralized their information systems, resulting in "distributed centralization" (Liu, 2004: 147). From standpoint of cognitive labour, Franco Berardi describes two relevant processes. First, there is the capture of work inside the network. Faculty have experienced the downloading of administrative work to their computers. Second, there is the dissemination of labour into autonomous departments that are formally autonomous, but substantially coordinated and dependent (2009: 88). On the one hand, the network form is nonhierarchical, reinforcing the image of academic independence where everyone is engaged in cognitive labour. On the other hand, a new dependency arises in the fluidity of the network university when data on institutional-level research performance is processed and used by upper-level administrators to manage lower-level faculty-administrators.

I shall finish with some closing observations and propositions. Vilém Flusser proposes that communication enterprises could be organized to facilitate "net-dialogue" (2002: xvii). Looking at York University's website and organization, what we see instead is an amphitheatrical communication structure superimposed onto a pyramidal modern institution. York's imagined community does not dialogue with itself. In 2013, a Better Workplace project group implemented an employee intranet called YUlink. This faculty portal enables customization of home pages and personalization of content. There is a forum for questions "related to working at York" that are answered by staff "subject matter experts," and a section for soliciting "community feedback" on draft planning documents without any inscription of dialogue. Overall, the development of centralized distributed networks affords both networked faculty performativity and hierarchical operativity. A centrifugal tendency toward opening up the university through new practices is offset by a centripetal countertendency that decenters faculty agency, imposes and contains innovation, extracts and captures surplus value from knowledge production.

What is new about the network university is the shift from rationalization to circulation (Hanke, 2009: Whitner and Nemser, 2012). The rationalization of whatever resource continues and the depressive effect on faculty morale cannot be overestimated. At the same time, driven by SSHRC and CIHR, knowledge generation has been articulated to mobilization. This function has been added to research and teaching in order to connect research and expertise to government and community agencies. York University is considered to be a leader in knowledge mobilization units that co-create knowledge products that have "research impact" on programs, policy or practice. Within these knowledge networks, research must not only be "good" but "useful." It is difficult to imagine how traditional or digital humanities scholarship could be translated into a "research snapshot format" that can be transferred to "decision makers."

What is new about the academic milieu can also be distinguished in terms of space and time. In regards to spatiality, Peters and Bulut offer this formulation: "The new spatialization of knowledge and education in the postmodern age is based on the 'soft architecture' of the network, which increasingly defines the nature of our institutions, our practices and our subjectivities" (2011: xxx).

What is at issue is the shape of this networked scholarly space as it expands and contracts. This spacing bears upon our research interests, pedagogic relationships, and what Ronald Barnett describes as the "space of being an academic" (2011: 77). He observes:

> This space is opening and becoming more fluid, as academics are invited, encouraged or even cajoled to take on wider identities. Its boundaries with the wider world are more porous. The roles of academic as entrepreneur, manager, quality assessor, mentor, facilitator and curriculum designer (and others) stretch out the ontological space of academic being. (Barnett, 2011: 77)

Following these scholars, we must develop a deeper sense of the interplay of meditatization, space, and time. The university still follows the traditional rhythm of the timetable and the calendar. At the same time, the network university is embedded in an accelerated technoculture. Multitasking is the norm, time and concentration for solving difficult problems is down, increased tutorial sizes means less time for each individual student, and more students "cramming" before exams admit to using caffeine, sugared energy drinks, and nonprescribed "study drugs" such as Ritalin, Concerta, Adderall, and Dexedrine to increase their mental focus and stamina. In academic planning, more year-round undergraduate courses are being offered, undergraduate curriculum is "streamlined" to decrease time to graduation, and graduate studies have been hastened. In academic employment, "part-time" no longer refers to temporary replacement faculty and full-time faculty compete for teaching-release time that is crucial to research time. At the institutional level of temporal economy, where time for the work of teaching and research is already a finite resource, "corporate time, which is sped up, accelerated, and compressed," turns this resource into a deprivation (Giroux, 2007: 121).

As Meyeroff, Johnson, and Braun (2011) have argued, the effect of neoliberal policy on workers not only amounts to a shortage of time, it has been felt as a "very real crisis of time." What is at risk is the academic form of life; hence, "there can be no reworking of the university without an analysis and remaking of the times that it produces" (485). If, beyond a certain threshold of speed, acceleration becomes alienation, and the network is the "empty ground" of our academic being (Liu, 2004), then we are more likely to experience alienation from the mental space and work rhythm of the university (Rosa, 2010). From a systems perspective, chronic underfunding produces constant organizational turbulence. In Ontario, policy experts have declared that the entire public university sector is unsustainable (Clark, Moran, Skolnik, and Trick, 2009). Any public university system that is deprived of new inputs will tend toward entropy. The long-term tendency of subprofessional faculty employment weakens the interconnection between energetics and intellection for some faculty more than others. Due to internal differentiation of functions and the academic division of labour, this vital connection is more sustained for tenured professors working in research areas aligned with strategic research priorities and supported by university vice-presidents of "research and innovation."

Finally, there is also an emerging biopolitical dimension when the state turns to the management of the health of the student population. In 2011, the Ontario government—in the name of "strengthening student support"—continued to support banks in the student loan business by rolling out an application that enables "busy students to get up to date information and check their loan status on their smart phone." Among indebted Canadians, student debt now ranks third behind household mortgages and car loans. Along the continuum between exam panic to money woes to mental disorder, staff are being trained "to look for signs of a change in behaviour; someone suddenly showing up late or disheveled or who no longer makes eye contact or hands assignments in late" (Brown, 2013). Rather than recognizing that student loans are immoral (Ross, 2012), Brad Duguid, the Ontario provincial government's minister of training, colleges and universities, announced in March 2012 that it will spend $27 million over three years to address campus mental health problems. This includes $6 million for a helpline that will provide support for students 24 hours a day, 365 days a year, no matter where they are. Such policies treat the symptoms rather than the causes of a public university crisis founded in expansionist policies that increase access for students "no matter where they live" without any measures for reforming the multitier faculty employment system that degrades the quality of post-secondary education.

To put it otherwise, the spacetime of the network university matters. The milieu is the message in a double sense: the milieu has been shaped by technologies and techniques enfolded within the institution and, in turn, the milieu shapes the way of being faculty and students. The network university can be viewed as a network enterprise—an open, yet bounded, digital nexus of discourses and technology, practices and processes, culture and subjectivity. Academic print and digital culture has its actors, interests, values, agency, and networks but university presidents, boards of governors, and administrators have the upper hand in modulating the milieu to adapt to and implement neoliberal government policy. While the network university is a heterogeneous, nonrepresentable assemblage, the mode of institutionalization orders the milieu for performativity and operativity, and this milieu bears upon all faculty who work within it.

REFERENCES

Accord, Sophia K., and Diane Harley. (2012). "Credit, Time and Personality: The Human Challenges to Sharing Scholarly Work Using Web 2.0." *New Media and Society* 15(3): 379–97.

Agre, Philip. 2002. "Infrastructure and Institutional Change in the Networked University." In *Digital Academe: The New Media and Institutions of Higher Education and Learning*, eds. William H. Dutton and Brian D. Loader, 152–66. London: Routledge.

Angus, Ian. 2009. *Love the Questions: University Education and Enlightenment.* Winnipeg: Arbeiter Ring Publishing.

———. 2016. "Emergent Meaning in the Information Age." In *Digital Nexus: Identity, Agency, and Political Engagement,* ed. Raphael Foshay, 49–69. Edmonton: Athabasca University Press.

Barnett, Ronald. 2011. *Being a University.* London: Routledge.

Becher, Tony, and Paul R. Trowler. 2001. *Academic Tribes and Territories: Intellectual Enquiry and the Culture of Disciplines.* 2nd ed. Philadelphia, PA: Open University Press.

Berardi, Franco. 2009. *The Soul at Work: From Alienation to Autonomy.* Los Angeles, CA: Semiotext(e).

Borgman, Christine L. 2007. *Scholarship in the Digital Age: Information, Infrastructure, and the Internet.* Cambridge, MA: MIT Press.

Bousquet, Marc. 2008. *How the University Works: Higher Education and the Low-Wage Nation.* New York: New York University Press.

Boyer, Dominic. 2011. "The Institutional Transformation of Universities in the Era of Digital Information." In *Making the University Matter,* ed. Barbie Zelizer, 177–85. Abingdon, Oxon: Routledge.

Brabazon, Tara. 2007. *The University of Google: Education in the (Post)Information Age.* Aldershot, Hampshire; Burlington, VT: Ashgate.

Brown, Louise. 2013. "Queen's Park Earmarks $27 Million to Tackle Mental Health Issues on Ontario Campuses." *Toronto Star,* 26 March.

Callinicos, Alex. 2006. *Universities in a Neoliberal World.* London: Bookmarks Publications.

Castells, Manuel. 2010. *The Rise of the Network Society.* 2nd. ed. Chichester, West Sussex: Wiley-Blackwell.

Charbonneau, Léo. 2012. "Students Prefer Good Lectures Over the Latest Technology in Class." *University Affairs,* 21 November.

———. 2013. "More on Student Preferences: Good Lectures Vs. Classroom Technology." *University Affairs,* 16 January.

Clark, Ian D., Greg Moran, Michael L. Skolnik, and David Trick. 2009. *Academic Transformation: The Forces Reshaping Higher Education in Ontario.* Kingston and Montréal: McGill-Queen's University Press.

Côté, James E., and Anton Allahar. 2007. *Ivory Tower Blues: A University System in Crisis.* Toronto: University of Toronto Press.

———. 2011. *Lowering Higher Education: The Rise of Corporate Universities and the Fall of Liberal Education.* Toronto: University of Toronto Press.

Derrida, Jacques. 2004. "Mochlos, Or the Conflict of the Faculties." In *Eyes of the University: Right to Philosophy 2*, trans. Richard Rand and Amy Wygant, 83–112. Stanford, CA: Stanford University Press.

Dourish, Paul. 2001. *Where the Action Is: The Foundations of Embodied Interaction.* Cambridge, MA: MIT Press.

Flusser, Vilém. 2002. *Writings/Vilém Flusser.* Trans. Erik Eisel, ed. Andreas Ströhl. Minneapolis: University of Minnesota Press.

Foucault, Michel. 2007. *Security, Territory, Population: Lectures at the Collège De France, 1977–78.* Trans. Graham Burchell. Ed. Michel Senellart. Basingstoke; New York: Palgrave Macmillan.

Friesen, Norm. 2011. *The Place of the Classroom and the Space of the Screen: Relational Pedagogy and Internet Technology.* New York: Peter Lang.

Galloway, Alexander R. 2012. *The Interface Effect.* Cambridge, UK: Polity Press.

Giroux, Henry A. 2007. *The University in Chains: Confronting the Military-Industrial-Academic Complex.* Boulder, CO: Paradigm Publishers.

Godard, Barbara. 2010. "The Risk of Critique: Voices Across the Generations." In *Academic Callings: The University We Have Had, Now Have, and Could Have*, eds. Janice Newson and Claire Polster, 26–34. Toronto: Canadian Scholars' Press.

Goffman, Erving. 1981. *Forms of Talk.* Philadelphia: University of Pennsylvania Press.

Habermas, Jürgen. 1989. "The Idea of the University: Learning Processes." In *The New Conservatism*, trans. Sherry Weber Nicholsen, ed. Sherry Weber Nicholsen, 100–127. Cambridge, UK: Polity Press.

Hall, Gary. 2008. *Digitize this Book! The Politics of New Media, Or Why We Need Open Access Now.* Minneapolis: University of Minnesota Press.

Hanke, Bob. 2009. "Reflections on the Academic Milieu of Media Studies." *International Journal of Communication* 3: 551–77.

———. 2011. "The Triple Crisis of the University." Conference Paper. Canadian Association of Cultural Studies, Liminal Labours: Plenary Panel on Academic Labour Conditions and Equity Issues, Montréal

Hansen, Mark B. N. 2010. "New Media." In *Critical Terms for Media Studies*, ed. W. J. T. Mitchell and Mark B. N. Hansen, 172–85. Chicago: University of Chicago Press.

Hepp, Andreas. 2012. *Cultures of Mediatization.* Trans. Keith Tribe. Cambridge, UK: Polity Press.

Heron, Craig. 2013. "Robert Dickeson: Right for Ontario?" OCUFA.

Innis, Harold A. 1946. *Political Economy in the Modern State.* Toronto: Ryerson Press.

———. 1951. "Adult Education and Universities." In *The Bias of Communication*, 203–14. Toronto: University of Toronto Press.

IT Strategy Working Group. 2009. "Meeting Challenges—Seizing Opportunity":
York University Information Technology Strategy.

Johnson, David. 2012. "Technological Change and Professional Control in the
Professoriate." *Science, Technology and Human Values* 38(1): 126–49.

Kanuka, Heather. 2006. "Has E-Learning Delivered on Its Promise?" *Academic
Matters*, 5–8.

Kerr, Clark. 2001. *The Uses of the University*. 5th ed. Cambridge, MA: Harvard
University Press.

Kittler, Friedrich A. 1990. *Discourse Networks 1800/1900*. Trans. Michael Metteer,
with Chris Cullens. Stanford: Stanford University Press.

———. 2004. "Universities: Wet, Hard, Soft and Harder." *Critical Inquiry* 31 (1): 244–
255.

Kleiner, Dmytri. 2010. *The Telekommunist Manifesto*. Amsterdam: Institute of
Network Cultures.

Latour, Bruno. 2005. *Reassembling the Social: An Introduction to Actor-Network-
Theory*. Oxford: Oxford University Press.

Lazzarato, Maurizio. 2012. *The Making of the Indebted Man: An Essay on the
Neoliberal Condition*. Trans. Joshua David Jordan. Los Angeles, CA: Semiotext(e).

Lewis, Tania, Simon Marginson, and Ilana Snyder. 2005. "The Network University?
Technology, Culture and Organisational Complexity in Contemporary Higher
Education." *Higher Education Quarterly* 59(1): 56–75.

Liu, Alan. 2004. *The Laws of Cool: Knowledge Work and the Culture of Information*.
Chicago: University of Chicago Press.

Lyotard, Jean-Francois. 1984. *The Postmodern Condition: A Report on Knowledge*.
Trans. Geoff Bennington and Brian Massumi. Minneapolis: University of
Minnesota Press.

Madras, Neil. 2013. Purpose of Senate-L.

Mann, Doug. 2012. "Let's Unplug the Digital Classroom." *Toronto Star*, 6 October.

Markoff, John. 2012. "Essay-Grading Software Offers Professors a Break." *New York
Times*, 4 April.

McCarthy, Cameron, Vivian Pitton, Kim Soochul and David Monje. 2009. "Power
in the Academy." In *Power in the Academy*, eds. Jerome Satterthwaite, Heather
Piper, and Patricia J. Sikes, 35–60. Stoke-on-Trent, UK; Sterling, US: Trentham
Books.

McLuhan, Marshall. 1964. *Understanding Media: The Extensions of Man*. New York;
Scarborough: Mentor Books, New American Library.

McNally, Michael B. 2010. "Enterprise Content Management Systems and the
Application of Taylorism and Fordism to Intellectual Labour." *Ephemera: Theory
& Politics in Organization* 10(3/4): 357–73.

Means, Barbara, Yukie Toyama, Robert Murphy, Marianne Bakia, and Karla Jones. 2010. *Evaluation of Evidence-Based Practices in Online Learning: A Meta-Analysis and Review of Online Learning Studies*. Washington, D.C.: U.S. Department of Education, Office of Planning, Evaluation, and Policy Development.

Mejias, Ulises. 2010. "The Limits of Networks as Models for Organizing the Social." *New Media and Society* 12(4): 603–17.

Meyerhoff, Eli, Elizabeth Johnson, and Bruce Braun. 2011. "Time and the University." *ACME: An International E-Journal for Critical Geographies* 10(3): 483–507.

Ministry of Training, Colleges and Universities. 2012. *Strengthening Ontario's Centres of Creativity, Innovation and Knowledge*. Toronto: Queen's Printer For Ontario.

Moten, F., and S. Harney. 2004. "The University and the Undercommons: Seven Theses." *Social Text* 22(2): 101–15.

Newfield, Christopher. 2008. *Unmaking the Public University: The Forty-Year Assault on the Middle Class*. Cambridge, MA: Harvard University Press.

Noble, David. 2002. *Digital Diploma Mills: The Automation of Higher Education*. Toronto: Between the Lines.

Nunes, Mark. 2006. *Cyberspaces of Everyday Life*. Minneapolis: University of Minnesota Press.

Owston, Ron, and Dennis York. 2012. Evaluation of Blended Learning Courses in the Faculty of Liberal Arts and Professional Studies and the Faculty of Health—Winter Session 2012: Institute for Research on Learning Technologies.

Peters, Michael, and Ergin Bulut, eds. 2011. *Cognitive Capitalism, Education, and Digital Labor*. New York: Peter Lang.

Petrina, Stephen. 2004. "Sidney Pressey and the Automation of Education, 1924–1934." *Technology and Culture* 45(2): 305–30.

Pruett, John, and Nick Schwellenbach. 2004. "The Rise of Network Universities: Higher Education in the Knowledge Economy." http://www.utwatch.org/archives/the%20rise%20of%20network%20universities.pdf.

Readings, Bill. 1996. *The University in Ruins*. Cambridge, MA: Harvard University Press.

Reed, Mike, and Rosemary Deem. 2002. "New Managerialism: The Manager-Academic and Technologies of Management in Universities—Looking Forward to Virtuality?" In *The Virtual University? Knowledge, Markets, and Management*, eds. Kevin Robins and Frank Webster, 126–47. Oxford: Oxford University Press.

Ringer, Fritz. 1992. *Fields of Knowledge: French Academic Culture in Comparative Perspective, 1890-1920*. Cambridge: Cambridge University Press.

Robertson, Benjamin. 2013. "The Grammatization of Scholarship." *Amodern* (1).

Rosa, Hartmut. 2010. *Alienation and Acceleration: Towards a Critical Theory of Late-Modern Temporality*. NSU Summertalk. Malmö: NSU Press.

Ross, Andrew. 2012. "NYU Professor: Are Student Loans Immoral?" *The Daily Beast*, 27 September.

Rowe, David, and Kylie Brass. 2008. "The Uses of Academic Knowledge: The University in the Media." *Media, Culture and Society* 30(5): 677–98.

———. 2011. "We Take Academic Freedom Seriously": How University Media Offices Manage Academic Public Communication." *International Journal of Media and Cultural Politics* 7(1): 3–20.

Sampson, Tony D. 2012. *Virality: Contagion Theory in the Age of Networks*. Minneapolis: University of Minnesota Press.

Schiller, Dan. 1999. *Digital Capitalism: Networking the Global Market System*. Cambridge, MA: MIT Press.

Shaviro, Steven. 2003. *Connected, or What It Means to Live in the Network Society*. Minneapolis: University of Minnesota Press.

Shoukri, Mamdouh. 2012. "Is Education Canada's Next Great Export? Our Role in Lifting Global Competitiveness." Address to the Empire Club, Toronto, ON, Nov 7. http://www.yorku.ca/president/communication/speeches/docs/addresstoempireclub.pdf.

Sloterdijk, Peter. 2012. *The Art of Philosophy: Wisdom as a Practice*. Trans. Karen Margolis. New York: Columbia University Press.

———. 2013. *In the World Interior of Capital: For a Philosophical Theory of Globalization*. Trans. Wieland Hoban. Cambridge, UK: Polity.

Standaert, Nicolas. 2009. "Towards a Networked University." In *Rethinking the University After Bologna: New Concepts and Practices Beyond Tradition and the Market*, 11–15. Antwerp: Universitair Centrum Sint-Ignatius Antwerpen.

Stepulevage, Linda. 2009. "ERP in Higher Education: The Reinforcement of Myths." In *The Myths of Technology: Innovation and Inequality*, ed. Judith Burnett, Peter Senker, and Kathy Walker, 83–112. New York: Peter Lang.

Stiegler, Bernard. 2011. *Technics and Time, 3: Cinematic Time and the Question of Malaise*. Trans. Stephen Barker. Stanford, CA: Stanford University Press.

Stross, Randall. 2012. "The Algorithm Didn't Like My Essay." *New York Times*, 9 June.

Terranova, Tiziana. 2004. *Network Culture: Politics for the Information Age*. London: Pluto Press.

Thacker, Eugene. 2004. "Foreword: Protocol Is as Protocol Does." In *Protocol: How Control Exists after Decentralization*, ed. A. Galloway, xi–xxii. Cambridge, MA: MIT Press.

VanLehn, Kurt. 2011. "The Relative Effectiveness of Human Tutoring, Intelligent Tutoring Systems, and Other Tutoring Systems." *Educational Psychologist* 46(4): 197–221.

Various Authors. 2012. "Open Letter from SFU Faculty in Support of Striking Workers." http://rabble.ca/blogs/bloggers/campus-notes/2012/11/open-letter-sfu-faculty-support-striking-workers.

Weber, Samuel M. 2001. *Institution and Interpretation*. Expanded ed. Stanford, CA: Stanford University Press.

Wernick, Andrew. 1991. *Promotional Culture: Advertising, Ideology, and Symbolic Expression*. London; Newbury Park: Sage Publications.

———. 2006. "University." *Theory, Culture and Society* 23(2-3): 557–63.

Whitener, Brian, and Dan Nemser. 2012. "Circulation and the New University." *TOPIA: Canadian Journal of Cultural Studies* 28: 165–70.

Wilson, Scott. 2013. "Open Source in Higher Education: How Far Have We Come?" *The Guardian Higher Education Network*. http://www.theguardian.com/higher-education-network/blog/2013/mar/28/open-source-universities-development-jisc.

Wittel, Andreas. 2001. "Towards a Network Sociality." *Theory, Culture and Society* 18(6): 51–76.

Woodhouse, Howard Robert. 2009. *Selling Out: Academic Freedom and the Corporate Market*. Kingston and Montréal: McGill-Queen's University Press.

Žižek, Slavoj. 2010. "A Permanent Economic Emergency." *New Left Review* 64: 85–95.

8 Spinning the Web

Critical Discourse Analysis and Its Online Space

Leslie Lindballe

The capacity for language is a quintessentially human one, though its ubiquity means that it is sometimes difficult to theorize. We can never move beyond language in order to study it from outside itself, but meta-linguistic study helps us uncover the ways in which the most dubious of human traits have been embedded in this, our most important adaptation. A series of theoretical building blocks, from Wittgenstein to Saussure, from Derrida to Foucault, help us look at language as it is built and as it functions in society. Pragmatically, we know that meaning is stable in some way, for we are able to use language to communicate with one another, but by conceptualizing the relational nature of language—that being the way that meaning is generated through the syntagmatic and paradigmatic relationship between signs—we can see that meaning is more elusive than grammatical arrangement suggests.

Language is an emulation of the natural world rather than a straightforward referent to it, and examining the significance of particular terms throughout history demonstrates how meaning shifts over time as certain forms of telling become (un)sanctioned. This brief exercise in deconstruction is essential to lay the foundation for critical discourse analysis (CDA). At the base of CDA, we recognize that "knowledge [and its linguistic expression] is not a matter of getting an accurate picture of reality, but of learning how to contend with the world in the pursuit of our various purposes" (Barker and Galasiński, 2001: 3). By analyzing language in use, we can see how some groups are more successful in their pursuits than others based on the ability to participate in desired social constructions. Individual utterances either contribute to or resist structures of power that are constantly being built, reproduced, and defended, even as they are dismantled, re-mixed, and attacked. CDA seeks out these sites of contention and examines the solid ground asserted when accumulated power is able to fix meaning in a constructed (and often exploitative) truth. From these temporary centers, analysts can "hope to transcend our acculturation" by finding linguistic "splits which supply toe-holds for new initiatives" (Rorty quoted in Barker and Galasiński, 2001: 20). For CDA researchers, language holds the potential to both restrict and liberate its users.

Historically CDA research has been limited by modes of publication, with texts being produced within (and sometimes in service of) the exploitative systems that CDA hopes to challenge. The advent of the World Wide Web has created an expanding corpus of living language that speaks in the voices of the corporation and the factory worker, the voice of the bureaucrat, the voice of the power broker, offering the CDA researcher more economical access to the voice of the every-person than has been available in the past. Oddly, CDA has been slow to apply itself to this collection for a variety of reasons. Following Rebecca Rogers et al.'s (2005) explication of the terms "critical" "discourse" "analysis," I problematize CDA's engagement with the digital world, and add to arguments first put forth by Gerlinde Mautner (2005) calling for consideration of digital texts. Finally, I point to contemporary developments that are ripe for input from critical discourse analysts, as the power structure of the web begins to shift from emancipation to indoctrination.

DISCOURSE

At the heart of critical discourse analysis, we have discourse. Broadly defined we can think of discourse as a "communicative event" (van Dijk, 2001: 98), that is, an interaction meant to share information or ideas. With this definition we are able to analyze "conversational interaction, written text, as well as associated gestures, facework, typographical layout, images, and any other 'semiotic' or multimedia dimension of signification" (van Dijk, 2001: 98). Any instance where one entity is using a sign or symbol to communicate with another we can claim a form of discourse is taking place. In order to create a manageable research subject, CDA researchers identify varying levels of discourse to uncover multiple layers of meaning.

One of the significant CDA scholars, James Gee, breaks discourse into two factions, what he calls "'little d' discourse and big D' Discourse" (Gee, 2004: 10). Little d discourse refers to the bits of language, signs, or symbols that make up a communicative event. It is "the syntax of sentences and formal relations between clauses or sentences in sequences: ordering, primacy, pronominal relations, active-passive voice, nominalizations and a host of other formal properties of sentences and sequences" (van Dijk, 2001: 107). Despite the name, little d discourse is a complex set of relations within the text that give keys to understanding. Little d discourse pays close attention to the detailed structure of the language and how that structure functions in the text. As this is the foundational level of language, CDA is not complete without this type of analysis.

Teun van Dijk begins an analysis of a text by focusing first on what he calls the "global meaning" (van Dijk, 2001: 102) of little d discourse. This is the semantic macrostructure of the text, that is, what the text is about. It is the aspect of the text that is easiest to recall, and can be outlined by looking at topic sentences or general impressions from specific sections of a text. From there van Dijk moves on to what he calls the "local meaning" (van Dijk, 2001: 103) of the text. This is when we begin to look at specific word choices in order to understand what is being explicitly said about the topic. A couple of important aspects to consider are pronoun use—how the text constructs "us" and "them"—and hyperboles: the degree to which bias is evident in the way both sides are described. Both of these sites reveal the extent to which there is positive presentation of the self and negative presentation of the other. Van Dijk also asks what is missing from the text. Examining cases of active/passive voice may show missing or hidden agents, lexical choices and metaphors emphasize polarization and downplay exclusions or eliminate negative aspects. Throughout the investigation of little d discourse, the researcher examines the text in its own unity—as an entity in and of itself—and seeks to uncover the secrets hidden in its linguistic structure.

Little d discourse becomes particularly problematic in the digital world, where publishing platforms and text are dynamic rather than static entities. For example, the website where a text is published determines the extent to which there are language bits that are not applicable to the text under study. Websites that feature external advertising will have ads that change not only with each visit to the site but often within a specific time frame. While this type of outside encroachment on the text may be easy to dismiss, other websites feature user-generated content, including links to previous posts, personally endorsed ads, and links to whole texts via recommended reading and blog lists. Looking more closely at the text in question, we approach the challenge of hypertext: bits of language that the author purposefully imbues with content that lies outside of the specific utterance. In some cases, the author is making familiar moves, such as citing or referencing direct quotations as well as directing the audience to relevant resources that contribute to the theoretical foundation. In this instance, the hypertext can assist in interpretation but it is not required. However, in other instances, authors will use hypertext to link to salient aspects of discourse that have been published in other locations. Without the information contained in the hypertext, the audience cannot fully understand the text at hand. This unique aspect of digital text confirms that while little d discourse is important, analysts must also examine context. This brings us to what Gee calls "big D" Discourse.

Big D Discourse situates discourse within its myriad relationships. It takes into account not only what is being said and how, but evaluates who is speaking to whom, when the discourse is taking place, and the purpose. Big D Discourse argues that any text "need[s] a historical, cultural, socio-economic, philosophical, logical, or neurological approach, depending on what one wants to know" (van Dijk, 2001: 97). Van Dijk's global and local distinction is also useful in specifying the parameters of big D Discourse.

Global contexts of big D Discourse situate the text historically, politically, socially, and culturally. When we investigate the global context of an utterance, we are identifying circumstances that both the transmitter and receiver take for granted and are not necessarily mentioned in the text. Having a context allows language users to make selections of pertinent information and to omit superfluous or inapplicable details. This does more than just situate the text within its historical, cultural, socioeconomic, and philosophical context. When we identify the global context, and begin to reveal the positions of the transmitter and receiver of the text within larger society, we can begin to make inroads into local context, where the mental models of the participants begin to play a role.

The local context considers the interactional situation. Where is this exchange taking place and in what form? Is the text itself a command, argument, request, or action (say, a piece of legislation)? Who is participating and what social role does each individual play in relation to the topic and each other? What knowledge, intention, goals, norms, and beliefs do the participants have? All of these factors contribute to the ways in which a text is constructed, delivered, and received, and so inform meaning. For example, Gee discusses the example of the sentence "the cat broke" (2004: 21) in order to demonstrate how the signifier "cat" can have multiple meanings based on the context. In this case, the specific contextual meaning is a statue of a cat.

This local level of context is the crux of critical discourse analysis, for this is where the questions of agency and hegemony arise—two of the central concerns of the term "critical." Van Dijk argues that there is no direct link between discourse and society, and so there must be a necessary detour through the mental models of the participants. These models contain markers of socially situated identity, including ways of thinking and feeling, beliefs and solidarity with particular social groups, ways of acting and interacting, and value systems that influence how the recipient will understand what is being related (van Dijk, 2001). Gee says,

> how people say (or write) things (i.e., form) helps constitute what they are doing (i.e., function). In turn, what they are saying (or writing) helps constitute who they are being at a given time and place within a given set of social practices (i.e., their socially-situated identities). Finally, who they are being at a given time and place within a given set of social practices produces and reproduces, moment by moment, our social, political, cultural and institutional worlds. (Gee, 2004: 48)

This observation is key to understanding discourse. While on the surface any language is, in its own terms, as linguistically sound as any other, over time we come to understand that vernacular choices can yield very different results. Each time we assert a certain identity through discourse we are re-enacting social norms that have provided our blueprint for the desired identity. In this way, "discourse moves back and forth between reflecting and constructing the social world [. . . and] cannot be considered neutral" (Rogers et al., 2005: 369).

In traditional texts, multiple levels of editing, including assistance from others, are used to help us make sure we are properly negotiating the language in order to achieve the desired results. Even in oral presentations we are careful to consider our audience in order to adopt the appropriate discourse, including dress and facial expressions. This care and attention will be compounded if we are being recorded. As we prepare to present ourselves in the digital world, however, we come up against the disorienting feeling of what Michael Wesch calls "context collapse" (2009: 22). Multiple layers of access mean we are not always sure who will be a part of our audience. We must choose an appropriate discourse to present ourselves to the "generalized generalized other" (24)—a discourse for all possible contexts. Further, this discourse is direct in that it is usually unmediated by editors, and the speed and ease of publication means that we are sometimes able to bypass some of our own internal editors and publicize an utterance charged by emotion or out of character. On the one hand, this question of context collapse makes it difficult for the CDA researcher to distinguish global and local context and account for the mental models that may be pertinent to understanding. On the other hand, it can provide a more intimate view of the speaker or author, a view that has been emphasized in CDA in relation to oral situations, such as research in classrooms.

We can see that CDA is not simply concerned with the grammatical structure and word choice of a text, nor is it limited to the social, cultural, and political context an utterance speaks of and from. CDA research also examines the ways in which individuals understand, appropriate, and reuse discourse in order to produce, maintain, or enact identity.

ANALYSIS

With such a broad scope, the analysis of discourse requires practitioners to account carefully for the aspects of the context, both local and global, which are pertinent to an examination of the communicative event in question. This is known as the "frame problem" (Gee, 2004: 32) and is one of the main sites of criticism in CDA. There is no explicit theory of context, and in order to counter accusations of mining data for examples supporting their arguments, CDA researchers must be explicit in both their analytical frames as well as their justifications for data choice. Another prominent scholar in the CDA field, Norman Fairclough (1995), has developed one of the more comprehensive frameworks for analysis. His method grounds analysis first in text, then in interaction or discourse practice, and finally in society or sociocultural practice (Sheyholislami, 2001).

In this method, the first level of analysis is textual; that is, we are looking at little d discourse, and from it we are gleaning linguistic evidence that helps us construct a frame of context. This linguistic evidence includes the ideas being discussed, the construction of identity of the writer and reader, and the way this relationship is constructed. These factors aid in understanding the second level, the interaction level, which is slightly more interpretive. Similar to van Dijk's discussion of mental models, Fairclough positions interaction as the dynamic space between text and society (Sheyholislami, 2001). This asks how participants receive and interpret texts and subsequently either reproduce or transform those texts. In this space we can begin to analyze traces of intertextuality, or how the text appropriates "snatches of other texts, which may be explicitly demarcated or merged in, and which the text may assimilate, contradict, ironically echo, and so forth" (Sheyholislami, 2001: 8).

Interactional elements become embedded in text, either through direct quotation or by mirroring conventions of discourse, providing linguistic attributes that point analysts toward viable frames at the social level. Finally, at the social level a multidisciplinary approach is used to explore the complex structures of power present in a particular discourse. Fairclough looks at the media type and evaluates access. In traditional media, there is often an overrepresentation of powerful groups, leaving many voices unheard. Considering the politics of the media context uncovers the relationship to the state, an elite class, a major corporation, or other vested interest. The cultural aspect analyzes social values as well as the norms of production and consumption. Finally, "the economics of an institution is an important determinant of its practices and its texts" (Fairclough quoted in Sheyholislami, 2001: 10), with content selection and bias toward economic interests being obvious consequences.

All these levels of analysis means that the CDA researcher must not only account for the choice of text, but must defend the various frames of meaning that establish the context. The frame problem is a possible reason that CDA researchers have been slow to engage with the Internet; "principled criteria for choosing what should go into the corpus need to be developed and applied" (Mautner, 2005: 815), but "there is no such thing as an explicit theory of context" (van Dijk, 2001: 108). Indeed, web-based utterances even remove markers of corpus that have been previously used in data selection. In traditional forms of media, "demarcation lines between texts are easily drawn and provide clear guidance for corpus compilation. Most hypertext, by contrast, is 'borderless,' not only with respect to beginnings and ends but also, through clickable links, at the 'sides'" (Mautner, 2005: 819). Further, as mentioned in the discussion of Big D Discourse, the issue of context collapse makes the evaluation of the interactional and even societal level of Internet discourse problematic. As Gee states, the socially situated identities of individuals are of importance to CDA researchers, and, unless we consider the web as a world of its own rather than a reflection of our analogue existence (which would require a further level of inquiry), "the given time and place" and "given set of social practices" (Gee, 2004: 48) that frame a digital discourse are not always evident.

Considering the frame problem in the digital world also hints at a deeper tension within CDA in general. As researchers must carefully account for these levels of analysis, it is recommended that web-based researchers freeze content in order to maintain a hold on their research subject. This process denies the emergent nature of knowledge and removes authorial agency, as the researcher moves the text from an unstable to a fixed form in order to use it for tests of verifiability. These analytic practices encourage researchers to exercise power over the text and the author, a position inconsistent with the overarching stance of CDA: the critical perspective.

CRITICAL PERSPECTIVE

When CDA freezes content, it is demonstrating the ways language selection produces structures of authority. Concern for structures of power and authority is what distinguishes CDA from other forms of linguistic analysis. As van Dijk notes, "unlike much other scholarship, CDA does not deny but explicitly defines and defends its own sociopolitical position. That is, CDA is biased—and proud of it" (van Dijk, 2001: 96). CDA is not interested in simply describing the linguistic aspects of the text; it seeks to explain them in terms of social relations and social structures. Further, it aligns itself with critical theory, following from the Frankfurt School, and positions analysis in the service of uncovering conditions of inequality. Critical theory is not a unified approach, as such, but a common thread is its overarching concern with power and justice. From under this umbrella, critical theory shows great diversity in approaches to critiques of power. Considering racial, neocolonial, feminist, and queer theories, among others, critical theorists seek to identify the many forms power assumes: "ideological, physical, linguistic, material, psychological, [and] cultural" (Rogers et al., 2005: 368). By deconstructing or problematizing power structures, critical theorists are able to argue that facts are not neutral and are cultivated within and in service to established hierarchies. One feature that crosses most approaches to critical theory is Antonio Gramsci's notion of internalized hegemony, or the tendency of oppressed groups to willfully adopt their subjugation through a process of coercion and consent.

Explorations of present trends in the online world beg for input from CDA scholars in order to keep the Internet "considerably less prejudiced in favour of élites" (Mautner, 2005: 816). In 2005, Mautner described one of the difficulties in doing CDA online:

in the absence of gate-keepers, who structure and vet content in the traditional media, the onus falls on the researcher to establish the nature of the data that search engines have laid before him or her, and to select those sources that will be useful in answering specific research questions. (Mautner, 2005: 817)

While the frame question became more problematic on the web, from a critical perspective, the openness and accessibility of the Internet meant that an entire host of voices that were hitherto difficult or impossible to include in discourse analysis could be accessed in a "huge repository of authentic data" (Mautner, 2005: 809). Over time, however, the Internet has lost some of its impartial flavour, as argued by Eli Pariser (2011) in his 2011 TED talk. "There's this kind of shift in how information is flowing online, and it's invisible," he says, pointing to the growing personalization of the web by large service providers such as Google, Facebook, Yahoo, *The Huffington Post*, *The New York Times* and others. Almost in conversation with Mautner, Pariser outlines how

in a broadcast society there were these gatekeepers, the editors, and they controlled the flows of information. And along came the Internet and it swept them out of the way and it allowed all of us to connect together and it was awesome. But that's not actually what's happening right now. What we're seeing is a passing of the torch from human gatekeepers to algorithmic ones [. . . and they] don't have the embedded ethics the editors did. (Pariser, 2011: n.p.)

Using data frames that could be found in a CDA paper—namely, geographic origin, time of publication, and mode of access (if you are not logged in to your search engine account), and authorship, gender, age, and detailed patterns of consumption (if you are logged in to your search engine account)—search engines now produce customized results to any query. It is "very hard for people to watch or consume something that has not, in some sense, been tailored for them" (Eric Schmidt of Google quoted in Pariser, 2011: n.p.). Of course the first question that a critical analyst asks is, "Tailored by whom?" With the search filter Pariser describes, individuals "don't actually see what gets edited out" (Pariser, 2011: n.p.) of their searches. This allows for systems of power to determine access to web-based discourses based on algorithms that are not publicly scrutinized. The potential for continued patterns of exploitation are ripe if the "Internet is showing us what *it thinks* we want to see" (Pariser, 2011: n.p., my emphasis).

Pariser's sentiments have led me to question my own experience using the search page Blackle, a low-energy alternative powered by Google. While I have a Google account, I am not usually signed in, limiting the personal information Google can access to flesh out issues of relevance. Using the most basic search page, I still find curious manipulations of text that produce spurious search results. Van Dijk outlines useful rhetorical devices to recognize and consider overt manipulative tactics promoting particular mental models in the audience (van Dijk, 2006). I will employ his model as I consider power discrepancies promoted by Google's search queries.

At the level of text, I have noticed while searching my own digital and musical identity, onepercentyellow (one word), that Blackle will automatically "correct" my search criteria, modifying my search to one percent yellow (three words). This yields dramatically different results, as my unique web presence is subordinated to the grammatical markers of spaces and separate words. Below the search box a question appears: "Did you mean onepercentyellow?" In addition, the page titles and snippets generated for a search result may also be manipulated. According to Google's Webmaster Central Blog, sometimes "a single title might not be the best one to show for all queries, and so [Google has] algorithms that generate alternative titles to make it easier for . . . users to recognize relevant pages" (Far, 2012: n.p.). Between tailoring of results and manipulation of user and content text, Google may be presenting a search result that is "incomplete or lack[s] relevant knowledge—so that no counter arguments can be formulated against false, incomplete, or biased assertions" (van Dijk, 2006: 375).

At the level of interaction, personalized results can mean that past constructions of the self determine the world that will be reflected back to the user. This means that rather than exploring the varying horizons of existence, we are interacting with ourselves more and more, increasing a sense of comfort in a world that is as we would predict. It is difficult to comprehend the multiple ways that Google gathers information that could be used to generate personalized results, and many are unaware that this is occurring at all. This covert manipulation of access to information means that "fundamental norms, values and ideologies" that go into the algorithms tailoring results "cannot be denied or ignored" by users (van Dijk, 2006: 375).

At a social level, access to search tailoring is restricted to Google itself (or whatever site you are considering); questions of economic and political affiliation are valid concerns. The longstanding existence of the most popular search engines, along with the highly specialized knowledge required to understand

the process, "induce[s] people into tending to accept the discourses and arguments of elite persons and organizations" (van Dijk, 2006: 375). These elite persons control access to the largest repository of knowledge in human history.

Addressing van Dijk's final aspect of manipulative rhetoric, focusing on the
eliciting of emotional response, I was struck by what I will call Google's performance rating on each result. What is the purpose of telling me that my search
delivered 2.5 million results in .22 seconds? By demonstrating the vastness of the
Web at every search, "emotions . . . that make people vulnerable" (van Dijk, 2006:
375) are drawn into each encounter with the digital world. If my search alone has
generated more than a million results, how could I negotiate the vastness of the
entire web without the assistance of Google or another search engine?

POSITIVITY

Of course there are many aspects of the web that contribute significantly to CDA.
While CDA researchers acknowledge the inequity in access to technology, the
advent of Web 2.0 or the Social Web has reduced the technical skills required to
participate in digital discourse. This "access is egalitarian [. . . and] Web content
is not subject to the ordering and standardizing influence of institutions and
the professionals active within them" (Mautner, 2005: 817). Take, for example,
Sheryl Prentice's (2010) examination of Scottish independence. By combining
historical discourse, corpus linguistic technique, and CDA, Prentice conducted a
keyness comparison between British newspapers and a pro-independence website in order to determine correlations and divergences between the language
of popular Scottish opinion and sanctioned British voices. Before the spread of
web-based textual discussion forums, a study of this kind, which boasts access
to over three million words from the every-person, could have never taken place
without extensive and costly interviews or questionnaires.

The "size of the Web creates an *embarras de richesses*" (Mautner, 2005: 815),
but extraction, tagging, and computer-assisted analysis software has become
user-friendly, addressing the technical requirements that made the first versions "beyond the majority of CDA researchers" (Mautner, 2005: 816). Prentice
used automated semantic tagging software in place of by-hand tagging done
by the researcher, making the analysis of the corpus possible. Prentice argues,
"automated semantic tagging can be used to lend reliability to the tagging process, which in turn lends reliability to one's findings" (Prentice, 2010: 431). As

reliability and verifiability have been disputed in CDA, research in the field is bolstered by appeal to a more quantitative gathering and tagging of data.

In contrast with traditional print media, the web allows a current glimpse into any research subject. As "the medium is so dynamic and flexible, it reacts with unprecedented speed and precision to social change" (Mautner, 2005: 821), allowing for web-based CDA to examine minute shifts in social power relations that may be omitted from other media. In another study, Nelya Koteyko found the Web to be a "useful resource of words and phrases that are too rare to appear in any standard purposefully-built corpora" (2010: 655). In this study, more than 80,000 RSS feeds were examined in order to conduct a concordance examination of compounds involving "carbon." Not only did this provide a diverse list of word compounds, the "variety of data representing different social domains" (Koteyko, 2010: 658) points to the web as a space to gather a more representative sample than could be created under analog circumstances.

CONCLUSION

CDA puts under a microscope the most important of all human innovations: language. It aspires to do this in the explicit service of uncovering and combating systems of exploitation that are present in our linguistic structures and reflective of larger social and global power systems. CDA examines how discourse moves from a local, personal communicative event into constituting social and global structures of power. The link is not direct, and instead occurs first through cognition—the individual gets it (from somewhere) and then interaction—the individual spreads it to someone else. If we are to understand the dimensions of control and authority in the present time, we are remiss if we fail to look to the Internet as a crucial space for CDA engagement. From the use of the web as a repository of authentic data to the examination of the structures emerging on the web, CDA has a major role to play in this developing medium. Further, the ephemeral quality of the web makes it a site on which we can revise our understanding of knowledge. If we can see that "knowing is a matter of being able to participate centrally in practice and learning is a matter of changing patterns of participation (with concomitant changes in identity)" (Rogers, 2004: 12), we may be able to use CDA's understanding of authority to address the continued development of exploitative power structures in the digital world.

REFERENCES

Barker, Chris, and Dariusz Galasiński. 2001. *Cultural Studies and Discourse Analysis: A Dialogue on Discourse and Identity*. London: Sage Publications.

Fairclough, Norman. 1995. *Media Discourse*. London: Edward Arnold.

Far, Pierre. 2012. "Better Page Titles in Search Results." *Google Webmaster Central Blog*. Accessed January 2012. http://googlewebmastercentral.blogspot. ca/2012/01/better-page-titles-in-search-results.html.

Gee, James. 2004. *Discourse Analysis: What Makes It Critical? An Introduction to Critical Discourse Analysis in Education*. Mahwah, New Jersey: Lawrence Erlbaum Associates.

Koteyko, Nelya. 2010. "Mining the Internet for Linguistic and Social Data: An Analysis of 'Carbon Compounds' in Web Feeds." *Discourse Society* 21: 655–74.

Mautner, Gerlinde. 2005. "Time To Get Wired: Using Web-Based Corpora in Critical Discourse Analysis." *Discourse Society* 16: 809–28.

Pariser, Eli. 2011. "Beware Online 'Filter Bubbles'." Filmed March 2011. TED video, 9:05. Posted March 2011. http://www.ted.com/talks/eli_pariser_beware_online_ filter_ bubbles.html.

Prentice, Sheryl. 2010. "Using Automated Semantic Tagging in Critical Discourse Analysis: A Case Study on Scottish Independence from a Scottish Nationalist Perspective." *Discourse Society* 21: 405–37.

Rogers, Rebecca, Elizabeth Malancharuvil-Berkes, Melissa Mosley, Diane Hui, and Glynis O'Garro Joseph. 2005. "Critical Discourse Analysis in Education: A Review of the Literature." *Review of Educational Research* 70: 365–416.

Rogers, Rebecca. 2004. *An Introduction to Critical Discourse Analysis in Education*. Mahwah, New Jersey: Lawrence Erlbaum Associates.

Sheyholislami, Jaffer. "Critical Discourse Analysis." MA Thesis, Carleton University, 2001. http-server.carleton.ca/~jsheyhol/articles/what%20is%20CDA.pdf.

van Dijk, Teun A. 2001. "Multidisciplinary CDA: A Plea for Diversity." In *Methods of Critical Discourse Analysis*, eds. Ruth Wodak and Michael Meyer. 95–121. London: Sage.

———. 2006. "Discourse and Manipulation." *Discourse and Society* 17(2): 359–83.

Wesch, Michael. 2009. "YouTube and You: Experiences of Self-Awareness in the Context Collapse of the Recording Webcam." *EME* 8(2): 19–34.

9 Paramortals, or Dancing with the Interactive Digital Dead

Roman Onufrijchuk

Zombies are everywhere. They appear to embody deep-seated fears of contagion, paranoia, a military-industrial complex R&D run amok, and the dead—if not the dead, then perhaps their memory—the sins of the past, secret guilty pleasures? And what a weird dead they are! Inhabited not by a Haitian god or sorcerer but by malevolence for the living: mindless, shambling, intent on violation. No elegant, seductive vampires, nor noble savagery of the Lycan clan; these are proles, maddened nobodies, *ressentiment*-filled and infected neighbours, waiters, clerks, former beer buddies, bus drivers, nurses, housewives, middle executives, sheriffs, an obligatory preacher or two, and the homeless. We see them on the TV screen, on the cinematic screen, on the computer gaming screen. And they're fun to kill, right (providing there's some effective way to kill what's already dead)? You can't even refer to Plato's *organon empsykhon* (*Phaedrus* 276a) since there's really no ventriloquist throwing a voice or puppeteer pulling the strings. No, these are ferociously, individualistically mindless, things. And yet, the dead, in all their mythic and horrific packaging, continue to fascinate.

WHAT'S WITH ALL THESE ZOMBIES?

John Durham Peters, in his *Talking into the Air*, presents the reader with an arresting, disturbing, if self-evidently true, observation: "All new media bring back the dead" (Peters, 1997). He's not talking about zombies, and since they've had nothing to say other than to growl inchoately, there's not much to say about them. Lycans aren't dead, and the undead are a different matter altogether (although under some circumstances they can emerge from the same sorts of terror-engendering zombies, but are to be differentiated from the latter by their seductiveness, intelligence, and grooming). No, Peters is on about the apparent immortality new media forms can accord to our late twentieth and early twenty-first century gods—the celebrities and stars of the entertainment media; and not just these—you and your family too. Like the funerary cults of the ancient Egyptians, our recording and web practices extend a "life everlasting" up and down the social ladder.

Think of all the photos, video or 16mm footage, audio recordings, letters, and mementos, along with all the e-mails, web entries and postings, memos and digital a/v collections we leave behind us like a wake. All of us born after 1900 have in one way or another left a data wake of thousands of moments and situations recorded. Family photo albums, video collections, documents, and all the institutional information kept on us since our birth: birth certificates, child-hood drawings and paintings, school report cards, driver's licenses, passports, medical records. As the twentieth century unfolded, these life records grew. Increasingly, we could restore much more vivid representations of ourselves, the generations whence we came, the dreams we dreamt for ourselves and others, our achievements and failures. And then came the process of gradual digitiza-tion. Worried we'd lose our growing biographical *mementos vitae*, we began to transfer our slides and photographs, audio recordings, films and videos into the digital element and store them in our desktops, laptops, smart phones, tablets, hard drives, and clouds.

This, along with the opportunities afforded by new digital and networked media and information mining and processing, sets up an environment where "bringing back the dead" can take on a very different dimension and mean-ing from what's offered in the zombie "folklore of industrial *man*," to poach from Marshall McLuhan (1951). When considering the "insistent technolo-gies" Robert Zingrone describes—technologies we've dreamt about or dreamt of having since human origins—it seems we're catching up to our dreams in nearly every domain except one: death (1991). We're no less mortal than Enkidu of the Gilgamesh epic, nor any more immortal than Hector. We still mourn like Gilgamesh, Hecuba, and Priam. Killing death may well become a growth industry with an ever-growing sophistication in the not too distant future. What was once a promise of nearly all religions will be taken over by the geeks, and in time, death will die.

The effect will be neither zombies nor vampires nor anything we'd expect to see in situations of a rambunctious or malevolent paranormal. No, this will all be very normal, as normal as a smart phone to which you can talk, and which, on your behalf, will then order restaurant reservations, buy airline tickets, or show you the way to the washroom in some city you've never been to before. Why should any if this come as a surprise for us who play computer games or even engage in separate lives through avatars, for us who carry audiovisual and data records of ourselves in our companion technologies, who generate ever wider and deeper wakes of ourselves every time we interact with each other—ourselves, or our technologies—in our networked Internet-powered lifeworlds.

Let's concentrate for a moment on that wake, the one we all produce, a wake of relatively permanent data. That data—some of it in our companion technologies, some of it in the cloud—is considered a treasure trove of important information by the corporate and government sectors. Data miners sort through the wakes we leave to learn more about us, to better "see us" and understand us, so that the marketing apparatuses can provide us with something we've always wanted but never known we've wanted, as Ralph Caplan put it when describing successful new product design (1982).

Once this skill was a matter of intuition; then it became a matter of systematic study though focus groups and surveys; and now it's become a "science" of information analytics. And the important point is that the purpose is clearly predictive, in aid of prescience and mostly for profit. Time will tell whether all the scientific analytics can displace the creative surge and intuition of old, but for now it is evident that much about future behaviour can be learned from past and present actions, communications, preferences in entertainment and consumer goods and services, purchases and memberships, postal codes. And where, in the past, such data was episodic, appearing only in fragmentary forms, today it is truly biographical, almost in real time, a day-by-day record of interactions, transactions, comings and goings, people and places, mobile device records, all chronological, much of it saved chronologically, infinitely sortable and mashable, manipulable, and, providing the current keeps flowing, permanent.

Remember, this is conjecture; had I the imagination for it, it'd have been science fiction. But having no gift for inventing tales, I'm stuck with conjectures based in the world I live in at this moment, not some extravagantly imagined world. This is more pedestrian stuff, based on current developments in IT, robotics, information science, the Internet, cloud computing, artificial intelligence, and what the traditional media content of new media affords.

That said, consider the following scenario: As you get closer to life's departure gate, you, like an ancient Egyptian, start taking a scroll of information very seriously, but for slightly different reasons and an entirely different application. The ancient Egyptian, usually through a considerable financial investment, when getting on in life, sought out *The Book of the Dead*. At first, this guide to dying and "a happy-ever-aftering" was available only to the Pharaoh and his immediate kin. With time, a crack at the good life post-exit off the mortal coil was extended to wider reaches of elites, and then offered to what we'd read as the middle classes—scribes, doctors, court officials, tax collectors, priests and merchants (cats and crocodiles too, but they got to them later).

The Book of the Dead, usually illuminated with images, contained a step-by-step guide to what happened once the embalmed dead were entombed; once they entered into the land of the dead (Faulkner, 1997). Readers were given the correct answers to give, ways to behave, persons to hang with, where to dally and what to avoid—an extended algorithm, code, or crib sheet to life eternal, once all the incantations, stages, ordeals were done. The difference between the two scrolls, yours and the ancient Egyptian's, is that she or he went to meet Osiris in a mythical realm; you, on the other hand, will continue to "be here" long after you've gone. In a way both scrolls ensure immortality, but yours will have moving bits, bits moving between the newly resurrected digital you and the living, or even others just like you. The ancient's scroll was done in ink and pigment on papyrus; yours will be done in algorithms and databases, perhaps in the slightly more distant future with the abilities of Siri on steroids (that is, an intelligent software assistant and knowledge navigator functioning as a interlocutor application using databases drawn from, or incorporating, your data wake).

Another major difference is that the ancient Egyptian needed his or her scroll to ensure that, when gently judged by Ma'at, the consequence didn't put their soul in Ammit's jaws and belly but rather gained entrance for it into the light of everlasting life. This was promised by the scroll's title, not (as we now call it) the *Book of the Dead*, but rather *Emerging into the Light, or Emerging into the Day*, presumably, of forever. For you, there'll be no land of Osiris, no Anubis or Thoth, neither a Ma'at nor her scales, where your heart will be weighed against a feather. So far as we know, there'll be nothing at all, but a you will be available to interact with those who wish to interact with that you.

LIVING [WITH] PARAMORTALS

Is this something to look forward to? It was rehearsed back in 1982 in *Dead Men Don't Wear Plaid*. In this comedy pastiche of the *noir* genre, Steve Martin interacts with a cast of the mostly dead (most were by the 1980s, and those who weren't sure didn't look in the 1980s the way they had in their prime of life in the 1940s): Edward Arnold, Ingrid Bergman, Humphrey Bogart, Wally Brown, James Cagney, William Conrad, Jeff Corey, Joan Crawford, Bette Davis, Brian Donlevy, Kirk Douglas, Ava Gardner, Cary Grant, Alan Ladd, Veronica Lake, Burt Lancaster, Charles Laughton, Charles McGraw, Fred MacMurray, John Miljan, Ray Milland, Edmund O'Brien, Vincent Price, Barbara Stanwyck, Lana Turner, and Norma Varden. Of course this was done by selective cannibalism of 1940s footage very effectively integrated into the look, feel, dialogue, and action of the movie. Throughout, Martin often called Marlowe/Bogart on the phone for advice. Marlowe/Bogart, thanks to the script and positioning of cannibalized footage, oozed attitude, was both relevant and helpful, and very dead. While *Dead Men* was pastiche and dark comedy, it foreshadowed things to come for both the living and the dead.

Elsewhere I have inquired into the effect of the digital environment on material culture, conjecturing the emergence of a new animated form of stuff, a lively stuff, the *animates* (Onufrijchuk, 1997). I saw the emergent elements for the animates in the development of new materials, increasing sophistication of sensors and actuators as applied to and emerging out of MEMS (micro-electro-mechanical systems), and gradual convergences between the biomechanical and information sciences. Animates would benefit from advances in neurology, expansion of the Internet and always-on personal digital companion devices, social and technological demographics, as well as advances in robotics applications, performativity, and technology. At that point the press was reporting "smart" this and that: "smart paint, "smart dust," "smart floors," "smart houses," "smart diagnostic toilet plumbing," "smart cars." The "smart phone" was around the corner and the tablet just down the street. Not only did this conjecture incorporate a convergence between IT and the furnishings and functions of daily life and stuff, it also included semiautonomous robotic companions, caregiving, instructional, and military devices. In this conjecture, we'd inhabit a lifeworld where things interact through natural language, monitor our health and wellbeing, carry out varied tasks, and survey aspects of our reality for us, as deputized lieutenants such as those described in Bruno Latour's actor/network theory (Johnson/Latour, 1995). At that point I'd not yet conjectured domestic and companion semi-autonomous robotic devices into which one might also be able to load an OS driven by an inferential personality drawn from databases, a paramortal operating system as animator of an animate thing. Such a paramortal would reproduce an inferential personality based on and incorporating the data wake of the deceased, and produce a personality based in interactions with interlocutors, cohabitants, and, of course, other paramortals.

Should paramortals be limited to mere repetition of a few lines twistable by appropriate questions to answer anything intelligently, pure Platonic *mimēsis*, they'd become a version of "talking tombstones," not much better than an a/v digitized record/album embedded in a rock or your phone: mnemonic in depth perhaps, but hardly interactive. Even as this is written some enterprising morticians offer the soon-to-be deceased and their offspring a produced AV webpresence in perpetuity (with reasonably high production values). I suppose, in our mechanized interoperant world, one could always put a reminder in one's automated calendar to hit the memorial URL on a set date. But that's a machine talking to a machine, not a paramortal personality with which one can commiserate, confide, debate, negotiate, celebrate, converse, or consult. It's exactly all this, and probably more depending on the psychology of the living and the inferential psychology of the dead, that a paramortal offers. And it poses a question beyond information analytics and data—the aesthetics of presence.

And what a can of worms that opens, this aesthetics of presence! Where will a paramortal live: In a vessel the size of a breadbox? A computer? A smartphone? It seems appropriate that such a being would be found in a cemetery in a headstone, a place of pilgrimage, expiation of festering guilt, and consultation with the almost-dead. We could conjecture that the development of robotics will lead to domestic technologies that could become homes for paramortals: say, a carebot that possesses granny's paramortal remains as the OS. What better way to cheer a mortal granny than the paramortal of a grandchild whose paramortal's development has been stopped at about age five? Why not as a chip embedded in the brain, thereby reversing the process conjectured by Julian Jaynes, reopening the doors of the bicameral mind, so granny can talk directly to us in our heads? Spooky it may be, and also just down the road, if not right around the corner. The point is we've not begun to imagine how a paramortal would appear; we as yet have no idea of the sensuousness neither of its presence, nor indeed of the consequences and conditions of living with one. What level of autonomy could they be given: for instance, the ability to make appearances through whatever medium they choose? Would their access to other paramortals and worlds for gaining experience and personality be controlled? To what degree would the programs running them be controlled by their "owners"? If we agree that ownership of another human being is a crime against humanity, then can we "own" a "paramortal," which would be, in effect, a human-based consciousness of a sort?

A reasonable conjecture: paramortal existence will first come as a push, and then it will develop both a pull and a normative character. So long as the current flows, stored digital data is, in effect, immortal; it's just octets of zeros and ones and can survive happily in a drive or in the cloud. If it's been posted on the Internet, it might get cached, remaining available in all its digital manipulability through search engines a century from now. So it's not too far to conjecture that paramortals will become the post-living norm for the next digital generation. Perhaps this will take the form of a lifelong preoccupation, to gain as much of the available data as possible and edit one's own paramortal, so that the light of posterity will not shine too brightly nor revealingly on the life as it was lived. A media form of this kind, combining knowledge navigators and machine learning along with natural language interactivity and data and information wakes, all creating an inferred and evolving personality, is an artist's dream come true. It is like making a living entity. Why confine it to the dead? Why not remake one's childhood with the grisly details omitted, the ones that lead one into adult neurosis or psychosis? Create someone exactly like you, but without the traumas you've lived through? Or, if trauma is what one is after, why not the paramortal of a past lover now gone behind a slammed door? One could go over the same ground over and over, trying to understand what led to the relationship's ending. One could commission or construct a "perfect" other personality, tailor-made to be a confidant and only true friend. . . .

Regardless, this is all safe conjecture. Forget the zombies, the vampires, ghosts and the whole range of the paranormal; something far more materialistic and real is potentially coming our way. The paramortal essence of friends and relatives past with which we can communicate could well be equipped with smart-agent knowledge navigator software and a real-language interface. And, if we load them into a game of some sort, a virtual world populated by others like them, and enable them, when not interacting with the living, to go on adventures, interact with one another, and learn, develop, and share that growth, then will we not have in some sense killed death? Does this imagining take us to some great archive, storing millions who interact with one another in a great illusory world, not unlike *The Matrix* series? There is one crucial distinction between the virtual world inhabited by the film characters of *The Matrix* and the reality of a great virtual world filled with the lively paramortal remains of the real-dead: there will be no other reality, nor any bodies to return to. Will our species have finally killed death?

Ah, meat! Maybe overcoming the death of others, without having eradicated the shadow following each of us individually as we move toward a blinding light . . .

REFERENCES

Caplan, Ralph. 1982. *By Design: Why There Are No Locks on the Bathroom Doors in the Hotel Louis XIV, and Other Object Lessons*. New York: St. Martin's Press.

Dead Men Don't Wear Plaid. 1982. Dir. Carl Reiner. Aspen Film Society, Universal Pictures.

Faulkner, Raymond. 1994. *Egyptian Book of the Dead*. Chronicle Books.

Jaynes, Julian. 1976. *The Origin of Consciousness in the Breakdown of the Bicameral Mind*. Boston: Houghton Mifflin.

Johnson, Jim (a.k.a. Bruno Latour). 1995. "Mixing Humans and Non-Humans Together: The Sociology of a Door-Closer." In *Ecologies of Knowledge: Work and Politics in Science and Technology*, ed. Susan Leigh Star, 257–77: New York: SUNY Press.

The Matrix. 1999. Dir. Andy Wachowski and Lana Wachowski. Warner Bros., Village Roadshow Pictures.

McLuhan, Marshall. 1951. *The Mechanical Bride: Folklore of Industrial Man*. New York: Vanguard Press.

Peters, John Durham. 1999. *Speaking into the Air: A History of the Idea of Communication*. Chicago: University of Chicago Press.

Zingrone, Frank. 1991. "Laws of Media: The Pentad and Technical Syncretism." *McLuhan Studies: Explorations in Culture and Communication* 1(1): 109–15.

Part Three

Digital

Politics

10 The Rise of the National Surveillance State in Comparative Perspective

Peter J. Smith

In late spring and summer of 2013 the *Guardian* newspaper (U.K.) published a series of stories detailing massive and previously unknown surveillance by the United States National Security Agency (NSA). The stories were triggered by leaks from former NSA contract employee and whistleblower Edward Snowden, who himself became the target of a worldwide U.S. manhunt. These revelations triggered a cascade of other stories about the extent of secret NSA surveillance programs that went beyond the authority of the Foreign Intelligence Surveillance Act (FISA). What was stunning for many observers was that massive amounts of electronic data were being collected indiscriminately and without a warrant on most Americans and millions of persons living in countries overseas. Chronicling the activities of NSA is beyond the scope of this chapter, but suffice it to say it clearly went well beyond its mandate, and demonstrated that national security risks were not limited to select targets but were becoming globalized to include entire populations or very large subsections of them.

While the revelations about the scope of NSA surveillance surprised many, for others they were consistent with longer term trends. For years, Balkin and

Levinson claim, the U.S. government has been busy constructing the "National Surveillance State":

> This National Surveillance State is characterized by a significant increase in government investments in technology and government bureaucracies devoted to promoting domestic security and (as its name implies) gathering intelligence and surveillance using all of the devices that the digital revolution allows. (2006: 131)

The National Surveillance State (NSS) is, I argue, the logical culmination of what Giorgio Agamben (2007) describes as the "state of exception" (or emergency) that governments employ during times of crisis. Here digital technologies appear not as technologies of freedom but as technologies of control. In this chapter I discuss the rise of the NSS and the threat it poses to the Internet, democracy, freedom, privacy, and human rights, comparing its development in the United States, United Kingdom, Australia, and Canada. The NSS is not particular to Anglo-American liberal democracies; it has become globalized, with states networked and working together on common standards of data gathering, surveillance, and information exchange. Increasingly, however, the NSS is being viewed with alarm and is now facing resistance that is intensifying, globalizing, and meeting with a degree of success.

Agamben's work provides insight into the National Surveillance State's establishment and operation in the U.S. context. While surveillance is omnipresent in society, the dominant actor in surveillance, in both scale and sophistication, is the state. Moreover, with the NSS, it is the executive that dominates all other parts of the government apparatus. Legislatures are continuing to wane in their importance, while at the same time providing a veneer of legitimacy to state surveillance. The latest developments of the NSS in the United Kingdom, Australia, and Canada provide a comparative context for the U.S. version. Here it is important to understand that while each state is attempting to territorialize the Internet they do so under the auspices of international agreements such as the Budapest Convention on Cybercrime (2001) and the European Union Data Retention Directive (2006). As state surveillance becomes more invasive, however, resistance is spreading as well. In the midst of this mounting confrontation, the following questions arise. Is the National Surveillance State a given? Can we only hope to make it more benign? What are the implications for democracy? Freedom? Privacy? Human rights?

According to Balking and Levinson, the National Surveillance State (NSS) began emerging in the aftermath of 9/11, which created a global moral panic leading to countries around the world passing new surveillance legislation. Lyon observes that these laws "tend to relax the limitations on previously stricter laws, such as those to do with wiretapping or indeed any message interception" (2004: 143). In an environment of perceived threats the state responds by "taking action in the online environment to secure national interests in a global network" (Birnhack and Elkin-Koren, 2003: 16). Accordingly the state "implements its ancient duty of securing individual safety and national security. In this context the digital environment is perceived as threatening national security" (Birnhack and Elkin-Koren, 2003: 16).

While the focus of Balkin and Levinson is on the NSS as a contemporary phenomenon, it has both ancient and modern antecedents, explored in Agamben's work on the "state of exception" (emergency). The state of emergency has its roots in Roman law and has become part of the constitutional fabric of most modern states. In an act of self-preservation the sovereign (state) can declare a state of emergency whereby the "normal law" of the state is not abolished but suspended in terms of application. The law, however, technically "remains in force" (Agamben, 2007: 31). The state of emergency, in brief, represents a space without law: a "threshold of indeterminacy between democracy and absolutism" characterized by sweeping grants of power by the legislature to the executive (2007: 3).

The state of emergency has historically been imposed in wartime and suspended thereafter. In the twentieth century, the state of emergency has expanded to include economic or labour crises, and today, the unending "War on Terror." According to Agamben, "the state of emergency tends more and more to present itself as the dominant paradigm of government in contemporary politics" with deep roots in the political and legal fabric of the state (2006). A report commissioned by Congressional Research Services acknowledged the extent to which national emergency law had become "rooted in statutory law" (Relyea, 2007: 21). According to the report:

> Under the powers delegated by . . . Congressional statutes, the President
> may seize property, organize and control the means of production,
> seize commodities, assign military forces abroad, institute martial law,
> seize and control all transportation and communication, regulate the

> operation of private enterprise, restrict travel, and, in a variety of ways, control the lives of United States citizens. (Relyea, 2007: 4)

In controlling the lives of citizens, the report is alluding to the biopolitical power of the state to target and isolate certain subsections of the population, for example, foreigners, by means of detention (for instance, Japanese Americans during WWII) or surveillance. Today, in the aftermath of 9/11 the state of emergency is becoming prolonged. Furthermore, Agamben claims "history teaches us how practices first reserved for foreigners find themselves applied later to the rest of the citizenry" (2004a). These practices include digital means of surveillance, which have now "reached previously unimaginable levels" (2004a). As the state of exception becomes normalized the population of the state itself comes under suspicion and surveillance. Indeed, as this chapter will show, targeting entire populations is becoming increasingly common. As the state of exception becomes total and normalized, it thus radically changes the relationship between state and citizens to one of state and suspect.

It is the United States that took the lead in governing the hostile environment of the post 9/11 world. Congress passed a variety of pieces of legislation giving the executive sweeping powers to identify, detain, and conduct surveillance on foreigners. These include the Patriot Act in 2001 and the Foreign Intelligence Surveillance Act in 1978 (FISA), amended in 2007 and 2008, along with other pieces of legislation. By the latter part of the twentieth century the U.S. had at its disposal a wide range of new means of surveillance that it was employing against a host of perceived threats stemming from the Internet. While the "War on Terror," the basis for the ongoing "state of exception," is the primary factor in the creation of the NSS, the availability of these technologies made it almost inevitable that they would be more widely used on the population as a whole.

While the U.S. has a host of agencies such as the NSA that conduct surveillance on its population, they rely upon the private sector for much of their data. Today, thanks to the leaks by Edward Snowden, much more is known about how widespread this illegal practice is. One NSA program, PRISM, permits top-secret direct access to servers of Facebook, Google, Apple, and Skype, among others, allowing "officials to collect material, including search history, the content of emails, file transfers, and live chats" (Greenwald: 2013a). PRISM, however, was just the tip of the iceberg in terms of the massive surveillance and widespread violation of the law by the NSA.[1]

Surveillance increases the power of governments. As Lyon notes, "whatever the purpose of surveillance . . . power is generated and expressed by surveillance" (2009: 453). This, in turn, encourages the state to invest more in the means of surveillance, thus potentially amplifying the power of the state. The result, Ogura argues, is that the surveillance state is leading to the decline of the rule of law. "Law," he argues, "is directed at the regulation of human behavior, but it cannot control computers" (2006: 286). What controls computers are code and protocol and these can be used to mask human agency and avoid the rule of law. Furthermore, Ogura asks, "is it rational to suppose that e-government [i.e., the surveillance state] will use ICT lawfully, when it has unlawful capabilities?" (286). The result, now clearly evident in the U.S., is that the rule of law and legislative bodies have a decreasing ability to act as a check on the executive branch.

The legislative branch faces decline, but the NSS still requires the legislative branch to legitimate and bless its expansion. Presciently, Balkin and Levinson argue that the NSS was the product of bipartisanship between the Democrats and Republicans, and that any president replacing Bush would continue the same policies. Indeed, as we shall see in the next section, the same is true of the United Kingdom, Australia, and Canada. One reason for this path dependency is that the magnitude of the decisions make them very difficult to undo. Second, discretion and absence of accountability are simply too tempting to ignore. Third, the state of exception has become normalized with the creation of a totalizing means of surveillance.

Indeed, this is precisely the case. In terms of surveillance and its disregard for the formalities of the rule of law and the Constitution, the Obama administration has continued in the same path as the Bush administration, and indeed has exceeded it. In continuing the same surveillance policies, including detention and counter-terrorism activities such as the illegal use of drones to assassinate enemies, American and foreign, Obama is draining these practices of any sense of partisanship. In the fall of 2012 news reports surfaced that the Obama administration had made moves to make the War on Terror permanent (Greenwald, 2012). This not only included the codification of policies on the use of drones for assassination purposes, but also efforts to further entrench the surveillance state.

The National Surveillance State is, then, a long-term project begun under a Republican president, continued and strengthened by a Democratic president, and likely to continue for the foreseeable future unless strong public resistance succeeds in rolling it back. This regime has grave consequences for democracy, civil liberties, the rule of law, and privacy. In terms of the latter, a study by Privacy

International in 2007 put the United States in its black category, keeping company with countries such as China and Russia. The United Kingdom is the other liberal democracy receiving the black label indicative of an endemic surveillance society.

Critical to understand is that the National Surveillance State is a networked state of mutual assistance and learning, with a diffusion of common standards coming from an international treaty and a European Union directive. The primary concern is that these standards impose intrusive surveillance powers, with insufficient legal protections or judicial oversight. The first of these measures is the Convention on Cybercrime drafted by the Council of Europe (COE), with the support of the United Kingdom, Canada, Japan, South Africa, and the United States, and adopted in 2001 (Vatis, 2010). As of October 2010 thirty states had signed, ratified, and acceded to the convention, which permits and encourages any country to ratify it. These did not include Canada, the U.K., or Australia, who only in 2011 and 2012 had begun the process of ratification. The United States ratified the convention in 2006.

The convention has a number of provisions that concern advocates of privacy. They include such provisions for the purposes of law enforcement as:

- Retention of specified computer data of subscribers by Internet service providers
- Requiring ISPs and telecommunications providers to produce subscriber metadata [Article 18(3)]
- The collection of content data by ISPs in real time in certain circumstances.

The convention also requires states to cooperate and render mutual assistance to another state, including employing means of surveillance to enforce cybercrimes of another country, even if that act is not illegal in its own territory or the state does not adhere to democratic norms.

The Convention on Cybercrime has proven to be controversial. Equally controversial has been the European Union Data Retention Directive adopted in 2006 and strongly supported by the U.S. and the U.K. (EFF, 2011). The Directive requires all ISPs and telecommunications providers to keep all metadata for a period of six months to two years, depending on the member state (Bignani, 2007). The Directive is facing constitutional challenges in a number of European countries, but its principle of data retention has been proposed in the U.K. and Australia, with Canada conforming more to the Convention.

THE UNITED KINGDOM AND THE NATIONAL SURVEILLANCE STATE:
THERE OR ON THE WAY?

This section, and the ones to come on Australia and Canada, profiles each country in terms of growing emphasis on state surveillance, focusing on legislation
proposed or introduced in 2012 that indicates the intent to place the entire
population of each state under suspicion and surveillance. Prior to the analysis of these latest developments some background and context is provided on
surveillance and the War on Terror for each country. These developments have
not come without resistance in each country, a phenomenon examined as well.

Background: United Kingdom
The 9/11 attack also created a moral panic in the United Kingdom. Many of the
legislative changes that resulted, Wong argues, provide "an interesting parallel to the changes to U.S. law and policy." Wong claims that overall the U.K.
"trend appears to parallel that in the U.S., i.e. to consolidate and enhance government surveillance powers, at least where national security and other fundamental public interests are at stake" (Wong, 2006: 216, 223). Fenwick and
Phillipson characterize these powers as "draconian" and "authoritarian" (2007:
457, 458). There are some critical differences, however. Unlike the U.S., which
took a largely military approach to combatting terrorism, the U.K. government
approach is police-based (Fenwick and Phillipson). In certain areas the U.K. has
gone further than the United States. Although closed circuit television cameras
(CCTV) have been in place in the U.K. since the 1980s, there has been an explosion of their presence in the past decade. The result is that there are over 4.2
million surveillance cameras in the U.K., one for every 14.2 people, with the possibility that a person may be recorded over 300 times a day (Wood and Ball,
2006: 6, 7). Their presence is becoming ubiquitous in all locations of the state,
including secondary schools and academies (Big Brother Watch, 2012a).

In 2006 the U.K. Parliament introduced a mandatory national ID card with
fifty categories of information on each person. The cards provided government
agencies vast amounts of information unrelated to fighting crime, terrorism,
and the delivery of public services, including what hotels a person stayed at in
the U.K. Initially national ID cards were strongly supported by all parties (and
the national press), but at the time of passage Labour had to rely on its majority
to pass the bill due to growing public resistance. This resistance eventually led

the newly elected Conservative Liberal-Democratic coalition to repeal the act in 2011, although it was retained for foreign nationals outside the U.K.

By the middle of the decade the growth of a surveillance state, and equally so a surveillance society, was meeting with mounting criticism. A 2006 report stated "we are already living in a surveillance society" (with a heavy state presence), which had been growing at an alarming pace since 9/11 (Wood and Ball, 2006). In 2009 a House of Lords committee report noted: "There has been a profound and continuous expansion in the surveillance apparatus of both the state and the private sector." Moreover, "successive U.K. governments have gradually constructed one of the most extensive and technologically advanced surveillance systems in the world." The report claimed that the widespread expansion of surveillance by the state was posing "a significant threat to personal privacy and individual freedom" (2009: 5, 26). Concern was expressed that widespread surveillance was changing the relationship between citizen and the state to one of mutual distrust. One witness to a parliamentary committee warned:

> Mass surveillance promotes the view . . . that everybody is untrustworthy. If we are gathering data on people all the time on the basis that they may do something wrong, this is promoting a view that as citizens we cannot be trusted. (Norris, quoted in report, 27)

According to Ogura this perspective by the state (and the private sector) is consistent with a "modern/postmodern surveillance-oriented society rooted in a deep skepticism of humans . . . and assumes . . . that being human lies at the root of uncertainty" (2006: 277).

ON TO TOTAL SURVEILLANCE?

The foregoing, as well as the work of Agamben (2004a; 2004b; 2005), suggests that state surveillance would not be limited to target populations, but rather that the entire population would be seen as a source of risk. Indeed, this is the thrust of two proposed changes in legislation, first under Labour in 2008, and later under the Conservative/Liberal-Democratic coalition in 2012. In 2008 the Labour government announced plans to introduce the expected Communications Data Bill, which would create a massive national centralized database that would retain data gathered from Communications Service Providers (CSP). The metadata would include every phone number a person dialed, every website visited, addresses of e-mails sent, and all social media contacts. Use of the data would not be limited to terrorism or organized crime but would be expanded to include all law enforcement (Open Rights Group, 2012a).

The bill was being proposed to conform to the EU Data Retention Directive, of which the U.K. had been a prime proponent, an interesting circular logic. The Labour government's proposed legislation would retain communications data for a period of one year. Labour dropped the program after negative responses by the public and service providers. Notably, the opposition also condemned it. The Conservatives opposed the government's plans, and in a report promised to take a very different approach to surveillance, stating:

> Labour has excessively relied on mammoth databases and wide powers
> of data-sharing, on the pretext that it will make government more
> effective and the citizen more secure. Its track record demonstrates
> the opposite, with intrusive and expensive databases gathering masses
> of our personal information—but handled so recklessly that we are
> exposed to greater risk. . . . We believe that your personal information
> belongs to you, not the state. (2009: 1)

These promises soon proved to be hollow, for not long after their election in 2010, the Cameron-led Conservative-Liberal Democratic coalition government began to backpedal on their promises. In 2012 the government introduced draft legislation for discussion, paralleling what Labour had been planning, with one notable difference: that service providers would be required to collect and store the data, not the state. Again, data retention was at the heart of the proposed legislation, the Draft Communications Data Bill. In brief, the government was introducing a nationwide surveillance regime that would log nearly everything the British did online for a period of up to one year. The legislation was needed, the government claimed, to fight terrorists and criminals and protect children from pedophiles.

Even before the legislation was introduced it was criticized both at home and abroad. The conservative *Telegraph* published several articles sharply criticising the government's plans (Whitehead 2012). In response to criticism the draft bill underwent prelegislative consultations by a joint committee of the British House of Commons and Lords in the summer of 2012. Oral evidence and written submissions were extensive, but the most extensive commentary and criticism came from a network of privacy organizations.

The hub of this network is the Open Rights Group. It was joined by such groups as Privacy International, Big Brother Watch, NO2ID, and the Global Network Initiative (GNI), among others, in appearing before the joint parliamentary committee. Of particular concern was that surveillance would no longer be targeted but expanded to include the entire population. Big Brother Watch expressed their concern to the joint committee as follows:

> This Bill ends the presumption of innocence as we know it. It represents a shift of targeted surveillance of those under suspicion . . . to surveillance of the entire populous just-in-case some of them eventually commit crimes. (Written Evidence, 2012b: 63)

Here Privacy International concurred, warning that the vast expansion of surveillance "would create a situation in which everyone communicating in the U.K. would effectively be treated as a potential criminal suspect" (Written Evidence: 482). The Open Rights Group also expressed concern that the Bill would "result in a generalized surveillance of the population" (2012b, Written Evidence: 448).

The concern about privacy was a recurring refrain in the oral testimony and written submissions to the joint committee. Some privacy critics asserted that the dichotomy claimed by the government between contact (the source of meta-data) and content was a false one. It was argued that profiles could be created on individuals and that mass data collection would mean that "the data could identify a protester who posts to a radical politics site, and their location at any given time" (Open Rights Group, 2012b; Written Evidence: 456). The result could be a chilling panoptic effect on the behaviour of anyone using digitized means of communication.

Finally, concern was expressed about the assertion of surveillance requirements for foreign service providers. Requiring foreign service providers to identify all their U.K. users and collect data on them, providing it to U.K. authorities as requested, could have unintended consequences, set a bad precedent, and have grave implications for freedom of speech and privacy rights (Global Network, Written Evidence: 203).

The joint committee appeared to have received the message that the provisions of the bill were excessive, stating the Draft Bill must be "significantly amended to deliver only necessary data that law enforcement needs" (Report, December 2012). Lord Blencathra, chair of the joint committee, stated: "We are very concerned at how wide the scope of the Bill is in its current form" (Report, December 2012). Whether this will translate into significant changes by the government is another question. Certainly, while the public had severe misgivings (Ashford, 2012), the PM remained committed to giving police and security services new powers to monitor Internet activity, despite criticism of current plans (Public Service.Co.UK, 13). However, coalition partner and Liberal-Democratic Deputy Prime Minister Nick Clegg insisted that the Communications Data Bill was dead, stating: "What people dub the snooper's charter, that is not going to happen—certainly with Lib Dems in government" (Clegg, 2013). The result, for now, would appear to be a stalemate.

AUSTRALIA: FOLLOWING IN THE FOOTSTEPS OF BIG BROTHER, THE U.K.?

Again, like other parts of the world, 9/11 led Australia to pass an onslaught of new laws establishing as primary responsibilities of the federal government national security and the combatting of threats of terrorism. Overall, there was an avalanche of antiterror legislation between 2001 and 2011, fifty-four pieces in all, an extraordinary amount of legislation (Institute of Public Affairs, 2012: 3). The comparison with Canada in this regard is striking. For example, by 2007 Canada had "only enacted two major pieces of anti-terrorism legislation since 11 September, 2001 ... while Australia ... enacted close to 40 pieces of such legislation" (Roach, 2007: 53). Australia's response put the country in a league of its own, exceeding the United Kingdom, the U.S., and Canada. Moreover, "these laws attracted bi-partisan agreement and were enacted with the support of the Labor opposition" (Williams, 2011: 1145). Most of the legislation was passed under the (conservative) Liberal-National coalition government led by John Howard. The Howard government, in fact, passed a new antiterror statute every 6.7 weeks after 9/11, compared to six pieces of legislation during the Rudd and Gillard governments from 2007 to September 2011, which refined, but did not wind back, the Howard government legislation (Williams, 2011).

The passage of such a high volume of legislation that permitted access by law enforcement agencies to the content of email, SMS, and voice mail messages stored by a service provider (but only under warrant) was often done in rushed circumstances. However, unlike during World Wars I and II, when national security legislation was passed and ceased to operate on the cessation of hostilities, the Australian government has consistently stated that "the threat of terrorism to Australia is real and enduring," that is, the state of exception is permanent (quoted in Williams, 2001: 1138). According to Williams, "It is now clear that the greater body of this law will remain on the Australian statute book for the foreseeable future" (2011: 1171). One outcome of the legislation is that it has shifted the balance of power to the executive. The result may be that Australia's democratic freedoms and the rule of law are in danger (Williams, 2011).

Current Developments

Australia's antiterror legislation has been influenced by external forces and precedents (Roach, 2007). Indeed, there is a convergence between Australia's recent proposal to create a massive national surveillance system, and what was discussed earlier in the U.K. However, the U.K. is not the only source of inspiration. Australia intended its proposed legislation to be a means of both ratifying the Convention on Cybercrime discussed previously (Rodriguez, 2011), and conforming to the EU Data Retention Directive (DRD) (Bowe, 2012).

The DRD was particularly influential in shaping Australia's national surveillance policy. In June 2010, the Labour-led coalition government admitted that it had "been looking at the European directive on data retention, to consider whether such a regime is appropriate with Australia's law enforcement and security context" (Grubb, 2010). Almost immediately a Senate Standing Committee began investigating the issue of data retention, recommending in 2011 that the government consult with stakeholders and only retain data necessary for law enforcement. In July 2012 the Attorney-General's Department released a discussion paper, "Equipping Australia against Emerging and Evolving Threats," and soon after a Parliamentary Joint Committee on Intelligence and Security began public consultations.

The discussion paper's focus was clear, stating: "The common thread of national security runs through the proposals, which seek to respond to threats from international state and non-state based actors, terrorism, serious and organized crime and cyber crime" ("Equipping Australia," 2012: 4). The discussion paper is an extensive document with eighteen primary proposals and forty-one individual reforms. Criticism, however, has primarily focused on the issue of data retention, with the discussion paper proposing "tailored data retention periods for up to 2 years" (11). Of significance as well was the proposal to "enable the disruption of a computer" (11) which would permit "law enforcement to add, delete, or modify any software or data on a computer system in order to execute a computer access warrant," possibly including the planting of Trojan horse software, keystroke logging, malware or other privacy invasive software on a targeted computer (Pirate Party Submission, 2012a). All this would be done in a new system of warrant control providing greater ministerial discretion over warrants ("Equipping Australia," 2012). This would bring Australian legislation in line with what the U.K. had proposed.

In particular, it is the data retention proposal that has been the lightning rod for public criticism. Critics such as Green Senator Scott Ludlam stated data retention was "premised on the unjustified paranoia that all Australians are potential criminal suspects" (Ludlam, 2012). The Pirate Party maintained that the proposals would "make suspects of us all, destroying once and for all the concept of being innocent until proven guilty by placing everybody under surveillance, regardless of suspicion or need" (Pirate Party Submission, 2012a). The Privacy Foundation claimed the government's current proposals would, if enacted, "very substantially shift the balance away from privacy, and in favour of a significantly expanded 'surveillance state'" (Australian Privacy Foundation, 2012:8). As in the U.K., communications service providers would become "agents of government" (7). Critics warned the result of a surveillance state would mean the end of privacy.

The Privacy Foundation warned that the proposals would end the "balance, in a free and democratic society, between law enforcement capabilities and privacy and civil liberties" (2012). The Pirate Party warned that "people under constant surveillance stop behaving like free people; to the detriment of society" (Submission, 2012a: 6).

The government tried to persuade the public that its proposals were not as invasive as thought, echoing a similar distinction made by the U.K. government and the EU Data Retention Directive between contact and content (Roxon, 2012). Critics responded that there was a false dichotomy between contact and content and that contact information could be used to create a profile of every user. Furthermore, the plan to monitor every website visited by every Australian would be like having a government "agent seeing every news story you read, every TV show you watch and every issue you research" (Pirate Party, 2012 b, Supplementary Submission, 7).

The committee hearings concluded in September 2012. At present the proposals are in a legislative limbo, in part because of the controversy they have created. In June 2013 the committee released its final report and punted responsibility back to the government, stating: "If the Government is persuaded that a mandatory data retention regime should proceed, the Committee recommends that the Government publish an exposure draft of any legislation and refer it to the Parliamentary Joint Committee on Intelligence and Security for examination" (Australia Joint Parliamentary Committee, xxxiii). The Attoney-General in the Labor government, Mark Dreyfus—a government dependent on the Green

Party for support—stated in response that it "will not pursue a mandatory data retention regime at this time" (Taylor, 2013). The 2013 election brought the Tony Abbott–led Liberal/National coalition to power. So far, the new government has not signaled its intent on introducing new surveillance legislation.

CANADA AND THE NATIONAL SURVEILLANCE STATE

Delayed, if not buried, are the key words for the efforts of the Conservative government in Canada to pass legislation, Bill C-30, in 2012 that would have permitted the government to ratify the Convention on Cybercrime and put Canada on the road to a surveillance state. Bill C-30, in fact, represents only one of several attempts by Canadian governments, Liberal and Conservative, to enact sweeping national surveillance legislation beginning with the Liberals in 2005, a process that may be difficult to permanently derail.

Legislative changes to fight the war on terror have been modest in Canada when compared to the United States, the U.K., and Australia. The Canadian Anti-Terrorism Act (2001) gave the government new surveillance powers for the purposes of combatting terror and the gathering of foreign intelligence, permitting, for example, "warrantless interception of foreign communications" (Lawson, 2012: 74). Beyond that, the Canadian state has relied upon the Personal Information Protection and Electronic Documents Act (PIPEDA), passed in 2000. While PIPEDA is intended to protect the privacy of Canadians in certain circumstances, Internet service providers can voluntarily provide law enforcement agencies subscriber information if it relates to an offence or to national security.

However, for over a decade the Canadian government has been under pressure to enact more extensive surveillance legislation, both internally from Canadian law enforcement agencies (LEA) and externally from the U.S. and the U.K. (Lawson and Valiquet, 2006). In response, in 2005 the Liberal government introduced Bill C-74, the Modernization of Investigative Techniques Act, which had two primary objectives:

- To require ISPs to install interception capabilities that could retain subscribers' personal information, target specific subscribers, and remove any encryption on data.
- To provide LEA access to subscriber information on request without a warrant or court order.

This information could include metadata that could be used to create profiles of Canadian citizens accessing the Internet. The legislation was strongly criticized by Jennifer Stoddart, the government's privacy commissioner, and by civil society groups (Valiquet 2006). The bill died when the minority Liberal government was forced to call an election.

In June 2009 the minority Conservatives introduced their own version of Bill C-74, Bill C-47, the Technical Assistance for Law Enforcement in the 21st Century Act, which died on the Order Paper when Parliament was prorogued at the end of the year. In the next session of Parliament the same legislation reappeared but as three separate pieces of legislation. Again, Canada's privacy commissioners were sharply critical of the proposed legislation (Letter, 2011). These pieces of legislation never made it past first reading when another election was called.

These legislative proposals, Liberal and Conservative, had a number of features in common, including giving LEA greater powers to access "subscriber information" without warrant, requiring ISPs to preserve this information even without prior judicial authorization, and expanding scope to track GPS data by any mobile means. Thus Canada would have joined other countries, such as the United States and the U.K., where "new laws have contributed to an explosion of state surveillance" (Lawson, 2012: 6).

BILL C-30: A LESSON LEARNED OR MERELY ANOTHER ATTEMPT?

With the foregoing as a prelude, one can see that Bill C-30, "An Act to Enact the Investigating and Preventing Criminal Electronic Communications Act," (otherwise known as the "Protecting Children from Internet Predators Act"), introduced in February 2012, was but the latest effort by Canadian governments, Liberal and Conservative, to move in the direction of a surveillance state. While it was eventually withdrawn and left to die, international pressure on Canada to find a means of acceding to the Convention on Cybercrime has continued. For this reason, it is important to see what the Conservative Government was attempting with Bill C-30.

Bill C-30 was a product of pressure from Law Enforcement Agencies (LEA) (primarily the RCMP and municipal police forces) across Canada and the government's desire to ratify the Convention on Cybercrime, though the latter was never mentioned in the press. In the only parliamentary discussion on the bill, Kerry-Lynne D. Findlay, Parliamentary Secretary to the Minister of Justice, stated that Bill C-30:

> would allow Canada to ratify the Council of Europe convention on cybercrime. In order for Canada to ratify international treaties, it must first bring its law into conformity with the requirements of the instrument. (28 February 2012)

The bill would have made ISPs part of the state's surveillance apparatus by forcing them to install equipment that could log the Internet activity of their users and turn over subscriber information to LEA without a warrant. ISPs would also be required to provide back-door access to LEA, permitting remote access in real time to the activities of subscribers. The government could also require that ISPs install any equipment necessary to perform its surveillance functions, thus emulating features of the NSA PRISM surveillance program. In addition, Section 487.0195 permitted ISPs to voluntarily provide to LEA the content of emails and the browsing habits of subscribers. In brief, the distinction between contact and content was dispensed with. This was particularly evident in section 33 of the bill, which would, in Orwellian terms, have allowed the minister to appoint an "inspector" who could access any ISP and take any information that the inspector (Ottawa) desired. As one journalist remarked, "we might as well just put a webcam in our homes and give the minister a link to the live feed" (Kline, 2012). Finally, the legislation provided for preservation of data on ISPs, twenty-one days for domestic violations of the law and ninety days in cases of the violation of a law of a foreign state, substantially less than the countries discussed previously, but given the capacity of the government to access and copy information at any time, the preservation (data retention) requirements may have been redundant.

Criticism had been building in anticipation of the bill with civil society organizations and privacy experts objecting to massive online surveillance (Letter, August 2011), as well as the Information and Privacy Commissioner of Ontario (Cavoukian, October 2011). The maladroit Public Safety Minister Vic Toews, the minister responsible for the legislation, stoked strong criticism when he told an opposition MP that he could "either stand with us or with the child pornographers." The Internet and mass media lit up with criticism (Harrison and Rodriguez, 2012). Thousands of Canadians signed an online petition and two Conservative Members of Parliament publicly criticized the bill. What probably doomed the legislation were the results of a public opinion poll indicating that most Canadians were opposed to the legislation, with the strongest opposition coming from Alberta, the Tories' bastion of support (Grenier, 2012). The legislation never made it past first reading. In February 2013 Justice Minister Rob Nicholson pulled the plug on the legislation, saying the government "had listened to the concerns of Canadians on this" (Payton, 2013). This, seemingly, was the end of the matter. However, in late 2013 important aspects of Bill C-30 reappeared attached to new legislation to fight cyberbullying and protect children: Bill C-13. These aspects include requiring Internet service providers to release metadata in their possession to the federal government, as well as a grant of immunity to ISP and telecom companies for disclosing personal data of Canadians in their possession. As of this writing the bill was proving to be highly controversial and had not yet passed Parliament.

CONCLUSION

This essay has focused on only four countries, but clearly what is occurring is a global trend. In a yearly review of state surveillance the Electronic Frontier Foundation made the following observation:

> States around the world are demanding private data in ever-greater volumes—and getting it. . . . Several laws and proposals now afford many states warrantless snooping powers and nearly limitless data collection capabilities. (Rodriguez, 2012)

In sum, states are expanding their capabilities to surveil their populations in targeted and wholesale ways.

In the United States Balkin and Levinson are pessimistic, arguing "there is no serious possibility of completely forestalling" the shift to a National Surveillance State (2006: 526). Rather, they argue, the questions are: What type of surveillance state will it be? Can the risks to individual privacy and civil liberties be mitigated? Can measures of accountability and transparency prevent the dangers attendant upon increased powers in the executive branch of government?

One can make a case that the state needs to gather information in a world where dangers and threats may actually exist. Moreover, the state needs to act in concert with others to combat these dangers and threats. Surveillance, per se, is not necessarily bad. According to Wood and Ball, "Surveillance is not a malign plot hatched by evil powers. Much surveillance has good or at least neutral intentions behind it: desires for safety, welfare, health, efficiency, speed and co-ordination." The danger thus comes when more and more everyday activities are perceived in terms of risk, and thus "what was previously exceptional security becomes normal" (Wood and Ball, 2006, 4). With normalization of surveillance comes a shift from targeting certain persons as risks to perceiving the entire society as a source of risk.

Agamben himself foresaw the potential of the move from "targeted" or select surveillance of certain persons to "untargeted" surveillance of the entire population. In explaining his refusal to go to the United States in 2004 to speak because it meant he would have to give up his biometric information, Agamben (2005) argued that in his case it would have been analogous to the Nazi use of photos in "occupied countries to locate and record the Jews, thus facilitating their deportation," an example of targeting a sector of the population. The question Agamben then asks is, "What will happen when a despotic power makes use of the biometric records of an entire population?" He then points out that European countries are, in fact, preparing to move from select biometric supervision of immigrants to imposing it "on all of their citizens." If this happens the "normal relationship of the State" to its citizens will be one of "generalized suspicion" (Agamben, 2005). In all instances it is the state that has the power to ultimately decide what is "valid" surveillance and what is not.

It is this leap to viewing the entire population as a potential threat and the desire to gather and store data on it that is becoming more evident in state policy and action. Clearly, this is the case in the U.S., although the governments of the U.K., Australia, and Canada have expressed similar intent. One hopeful sign is that, as 9/11 recedes into the background and citizens become more aware of the scope of what governments are doing or trying to do, it becomes more difficult for states to consolidate a perpetual state of emergency based on terror, so useful in controlling their populations. One can see signs of pushback. In July 2013 the first serious U.S. legislative challenge to the administration's domestic spying infrastructure, a measure to defund covert collection of American's telephone records, was defeated by a narrow vote of 217 to 205. Previously, such a measure would never have made it to the floor for a vote. Elsewhere, the national ID card proved too unpopular for the U.K. government to maintain, and was scrapped. Later, when it did introduce much the same legislation as the Blair government, the Conservative-led coalition met with a cool, if not hostile, audience. Here minority governments are important as they can stall the progress of invasive surveillance measures. In Canada, for example, a series of minority governments delayed the advance of surveillance legislation. By the time the Conservatives had a majority the threats and risks of terror and crime no longer had such a purchase on public opinion, and even the spectre of child pornography could not persuade them that the risks to privacy and civil liberties were worth it.

Canada also had developed by this time a history of organizing and using the Internet as a means of resistance. The protracted struggle over new copyright legislation demonstrated that Canadians were concerned about digital issues, the Internet, and privacy. And speak out they did. With most Canadians opposed, and in particular their more libertarian, anti–big government base in Alberta, the Conservatives had to retreat.

However, it is too early to assume that the Conservatives in Canada or in the UK and Labor in Australia have given up on pressing ahead with expanding state surveillance. This is clearly not the case in Canada if Bill C-13 is any indication. If Agamben is right—that the state of exception has become normalized—then this is what should be expected. The power of surveillance technologies may be too tempting to leave alone, international pressure too strong to resist. Another moral panic over security may provide the opportunity to pass once unthinkable legislation consolidating the surveillance state. Even if this is not the case, states have demonstrated an increasing willingness to sidestep the law when it comes to surveillance. Legislatively, rather than wholesale measures, governments may try to proceed by administrative regulation, by dividing legislation into separate pieces, with a long end in view, or by massive omnibus legislation, where surveillance measures become lost among other controversial measures. Clearly, for those who cherish privacy, civil liberties, and democracy, vigilance will be the byword.

NOTES

1 For example, the existence of another NSA programme, X-Keyscore, a complement to PRISM, permits officials, without authorization, to search metadata and the content of just about everything a typical user does on the web, including examining the content of all the websites he or she visits, emails sent and received, and browser searches. Searches can be conducted in real time. NSA also gathers large amounts of metadata on the telephone calls, emails, cell phone text messages and chat transcripts on millions of Germans (Poitras et al., 2013a), tapping indiscriminately into and storing the email of millions of Brazilians (Greenwald, 2013b), and conducts electronic surveillance on European institutions and diplomats (Poitras et al., 2013b). "Metadata" is "the 'envelope' of a phone call or Internet communications. For a phone call this could include the

duration of a phone call, the numbers it was between, and when it happened. For an email it would include the sender, recipient, time, but not the subject or content. In both cases it could include location information" (Greenwald 2013c).

REFERENCES

Agamben, Giorgio. 2004a. "No to Bio-Political Tattooing." *Le Monde.* 10 Jan. http://www.ratical.org/ratville/CAH/totalControl.html

———. 2004b. "The State of Emergency." Extract from a lecture given at the Centre Roland-Barthes (Université Paris VII, Denis-Diderot). http://www.generation-online.org/p/fpagambenschmitt.htm.

———. 2005. "No to Biometrics." *Le Monde,* 5 Dec. http://www.notbored.org/agamben-on-biometrics.html.

———. 2007. *State of Exception.* Trans. Kevin Attell. Chicago: University of Chicago Press.

Ashford, Warwick. 2012. "Most UK Citizens Do Not Support Draft Data Communications Bill, Survey Shows." *ComputerWeekly.* http://www.computerweekly.com/news/2240169761/Most-UK-citizens-do-not-support-draft-Data-Communications-Bill-survey-shows.

Attorney-General of Australia. 2011. "Communiqué—Quintet of Attorneys General." 11 July.

———. 2012. "Equipping Australia Against Emerging and Evolving Threats." Australia Joint Parliamentary Committee on Intelligence and Security. Report of the Inquiry into Potential Reforms of Australia's National Security Legislation. http://www.aph.gov.au/Parliamentary_Business/Committees/House_of_Representatives_Committees?url=pjcis%2Fnsl2012%2Freport.htm

Australia Privacy Foundation. 2012. "Inquiry into Potential Reforms of National Security Legislation."

Balkin, Jack M., and Sanford Levinson. 2006."The Processes of Constitutional Change: From Partisan Entrenchment to the National Surveillance State." Faculty Scholarship Series. Paper 231. Yale Law School.

Big Brother Watch. 2012a. "The Class of 1984." http://www.bigbrotherwatch.org.uk/home/2012/09/the-class-of-1984.html.

———. 2012b. Privacy International, Open Rights Group, Internet Service Providers Association. Written Testimony, Draft Communications Data Bill. House of Lords, House of Commons Joint Committee on Draft Communications Data Bill Session, 2012–13.

Bignami, Francesca. 2007. "Privacy and Law Enforcement in the European Union: The Data Retention Directive." *Chicago Journal of International Law* 8(1): 233–56

Birnhack, Michael D., and Niva Elkin-Koren. 2003. "The Invisible Handshake: The Reemergence of the State in the Digital Environment." *Virginia Journal of Law and Technology* 6: 1–48

Bowe, Rebecca. 2012. "Why Data Retention? Australian Government Hasn't Backed Up Its Argument." 7 November. https://www.eff.org/deeplinks/2012/11/why-data-retention-australian-government-hasnt-backed-its-argument.

Cavoukian, Ann. 2011. Information and Privacy Commissioner of Ontario. Letter, October. http://www.ipc.on.ca/images/WhatsNew/2011-10-31-Letter-to-Ministers-Toews-and-Nicholson-Lawful-Access.pdf.

Clegg, Nick. 2013. "Nick Clegg: No 'web snooping' bill while Lib Dems in government." April 25, BBC. http://www.bbc.co.uk/news/uk-politics-22292474.

Conservatives UK. 2009. "Reversing the Rise of the Surveillance State." http://www.conservatives.com/News/News_stories/2009/09/~/media/Files/Policy%20Documents/Surveillance%20State.ashx.

Dorling, Phillip. 2012. "Roxon Puts Web Surveillance Plans on Ice." *Sydney Morning Herald.* 10 August 2012. http://www.smh.com.au/technology/technology-news/roxon-puts-web-surveillance-plans-on-ice-20120809-23x9l.html.

Electronic Frontiers Australia. 2004. "Surveillance Devices Bill 2004." https://www.efa.org.au/Publish/efasubm-slclc-sdbill2004.html.

———. 2011. "Europe." https://www.eff.org/issues/mandatory-data-retention/eu.

———. 2013. "NSA Spying on Americans." https://www.eff.org/nsa-spying.

Fenwick, Helen, and Gavin Phillipson, 2005. "Legislative Over-Breadth, Democratic Failure and the Judicial Response: Fundamental Rights and the UK's Anti-Terrorist Legal Policy." In *Global Anti-Terrorism*, eds. Victor V. Ramraj, Michael Hor, and Kent Roach. Cambridge, UK: Cambridge University Press.

Findlay, Kerry-Lynne D., Parliamentary Secretary to the Minister of Justice. 2012. "Opposition Motion—Charter of Rights and Freedoms." House of Commons Debates. Official Report (Hansard), 28 February.

Global Network Initiative. 2012. Written Evidence Communications Data Bill. House of Lords, House of Commons Joint Committee on Draft Communications Data Bill Session 2012–13.

Greenwald, Glenn. 2012. "Obama Moves to Make the War on Terror Permanent." *The Guardian.* 24 October. http://www.guardian.co.uk/commentisfree/2012/oct/24/obama-terrorism-kill-list.

———. 2013a. "NSA PRISM Program Taps in to User Data of Apple, Google and Others." *The Guardian.* 6 June. http://www.theguardian.com/world/2013/jun/06/us-tech-giants-nsa-data.

———. 2013b. "The NSA's mass and indiscriminate spying on Brazilians." *The Guardian*. 7 July. http://www.theguardian.com/commentisfree/2013/jul/07/nsa-brazilians-globo-spying.

———. 2013c. "XKeyscore: NSA Tool Collects 'nearly everything a user does on the internet." *The Guardian*. 31 July. http://www.theguardian.com/world/2013/jul/31/nsa-top-secret-program-online-data.

Grenier, Eric. 2012. "Lawful Access: Poll Finds Majority Of Canadians Think Tories' Online Surveillance Bill Shouldn't Become Law." *Huffington Post Canada*. http://www.huffingtonpost.ca/2012/02/28/lawful-access-poll-bill-c30-online-surveillance_n_1306256.html.

Grubb, Ben. 2010. "Inside Australia's data retention proposal." *ZDNet*. 16 June. http://www.zdnet.com/inside-australias-data-retention-proposal-1339303862/

Harrison, Annie, and Katitza Rodrigues. 2012. "Keep the Pressure On: Canadian Online Surveillance Bill on Pause, But the Fight Continues." 29 February. Electronic Frontier Foundation. https://www.eff.org/deeplinks/2012/02/keep-pressure-canadian-online-surveillance-bill-pause-fight-continues.

House of Lords. Select Committee on the Constitution. 2009. "Surveillance, Citizens and the State."

House of Lords. House of Commons Joint Committee on Draft Communications Data Bill. 2012. Report. 11 December. http://www.parliament.uk/business/committees/committees-a-z/joint-select/draft-communications-bill/news/full-publication-of-report/.

Institute of Public Affairs. 2012. "Submission to Parliamentary Joint Committee on Intelligence and Security on 'Equipping Australia against Emerging and Evolving Threats.'" https://www.academia.edu/6590064/Submission_to_Parliamentary_Joint_Committee_on_Intelligence_and_Security_on_Equipping_Australia_against_Emerging_and_Evolving_Threats_.

Internet Industry Association (Australia). 2012. "Submission to Parliamentary Joint Committee on Security and Intelligence." http://www.aph.gov.au/Parliamentary_Business/Committees/Joint/Intelligence_and_Security/National_Security_Amendment_Bill_2014/Submissions.

Kline, Jesse. 2012. "Full Comment." *National Post*. 6 March. http://fullcomment.nationalpost.com/2012/03/06/jesse-kline-on-current-threats-to-internet-freedom-the-statists-strike-back/.

Lawson, Phillipa. 2012. "Moving Toward a Surveillance Society." BC Civil Liberties Association. https://bccla.org/wp-content/uploads/2012/03/2012-BCCLA-REPORT-Moving-toward-a-surveillance-society1.pdf.

Letter. 2011. "Letter to Public Safety Canada from Canada's Privacy Commissioners and Ombudspersons on the current Lawful Access proposals," 9 March. Multiple signatories. http://www.priv.gc.ca/media/nr-c/2011/let_110309_e.cfm.

Ludlam, Scott. 2012. "Government Lunges for Unjustified Online Surveillance Powers." 4 May. http://scott-ludlam.greensmps.org.au/content/media-releases/government-lunges-unjustified-online-surveillance-powers.

Lyon, David. 2009. "Surveillance, Power and Everyday Life." In *Oxford Handbook of Information and Communication Technologies*, ed. Chrisanthi Avgerou, Robin Mansell, Danny Quah, and Roger Silverstone, 449–73. New York: Oxford University Press. http://it.mesce.ac.in/downloads/CriticalPerspectives/Reading%20Material%20CPT-S7/oxford_handbook.pdf.

———. 2004. "Globalizing Surveillance: Comparative and Sociological Perspectives." *International Sociology* 19(2): 135–49.

Lyon, David, and David Murakami Wood. 2012. "Security, Surveillance, and Sociological Analysis." *Canadian Review of Sociology* 49(4): 317–28.

Norris, Clive. 2009. Oral Testimony. In *Surveillance: Citizens and the State, Volume I: Report*. House of Lords, Select Committee on the Constitution. London: The Stationery Office Limited.

Ogura, Toshimaru. 2006. "Electronic Government and Surveillance-Oriented Society." In *Theorizing Surveillance: The Panopticon and Beyond*, ed. David Lyon, 270–96. London: Routledge.

Open Rights Group. 2012a. "Communications Capabilities Development Programme." http://wiki.openrightsgroup.org/wiki/Intercept_Modernisation.

———. 2012b. "About ORG." http://www.openrightsgroup.org/about/.

Payton, Laura. 2012. "Government Killing Online Surveillance Bill." *CBC*. 11 February. http://www.cbc.ca/news/politics/story/2013/02/11/pol-rob-nicholson-criminal-code-changes.html

Pirate Party of Australia. 2012a. "Submission to the Parliamentary Joint Committee on Intelligence and Security Inquiry into Potential Reforms of National Security Legislation." August.

———. 2012b. "National Security Inquiry Supplemental Submission." Parliamentary Joint Committee on Intelligence and Security.

Poitras, Laura, Marcel Rosenbach, and Holger Stark. 2013a. "Partner and Target: NSA Snoops on 500 Million German Data Connections." Spiegel Online. 30 June. http://www.spiegel.de/international/germany/nsa-spies-on-500-million-german-data-connections-a-908648.html.

———. 2013b. "Attacks from America: NSA Spied on European Union Offices." Spiegel Online. http://www.spiegel.de/international/europe/nsa-spied-on-european-union-offices-a-908590.html.

Privacy International. 2007. "Report: Surveillance Monitor 2007—International Country Rankings." https://www.privacyinternational.org/reports/surveillance-monitor-2007-international-country-rankings/i-summary-of-key-findings.

Public Service Co. UK. 2013. "New Communications Data Bill to Arrive 'In Due Course.'" 16 July. http://www.publicservice.co.uk/news_story.asp?id=23461.

Roach, Kent. 2007. "A Comparison of Australian and Canadian Anti-Terrorism Law." *University of New South Wales Law Journal* 30: 53–85.

Rodriguez, K. 2011. "Dangerous Cybercrime Treaty Pushes Surveillance and Secrecy Worldwide." 25 August. https://www.eff.org/deeplinks/2011/08/cybercrime-treaty-pushes-surveillance-secrecy-worldwide.

———. 2012. "2012 in Review: State Surveillance Around the Globe." 31 December. Electronic Frontier Foundation. https://www.eff.org/deeplinks/2012/12/2012-in-review-state-surveillance-around-globe.

Roxon, Nicola, Minister for Emergency Management. 2012. "Letter to Anthony Byrne MP." September.

Relyea, Harold C. 2007. "National Emergency Powers." Congressional Research Service Report for Congress. http://www.fas.org/sgp/crs/natsec/98-505.pdf.

Shaw, Erin, and Dominique Valiquet. 2012. "An Act to Enact the Investigating and Preventing Criminal Electronic Communications Act and to Amend the Criminal Code and other Acts." Parliamentary and Research Service.

Taylor, Josh. 2013. "Australian Government Shelves Data Retention Plans." 24 June. http://www.zdnet.com/au/australian-government-shelves-data-retention-plans-7000017183/.

Valiquet, David. 2006. "Telecommunications and Lawful Access: I. The Situation in Canada." Parliamentary and Research Service.

Vatis, Michael A. 2010. "The Council of Europe Convention on Cybercrime." http://cs.brown.edu/courses/csci1950-p/sources/lec16/Vatis.pdf.

Whitehead, Tom. 2012. "Email Monitoring: New Powers to Record Every Phone Call and Email 'Echoes China'." *The Telegraph.* 1 April. http://www.telegraph.co.uk/news/uknews/law-and-order/9179117/Email-monitoring-New-powers-to-record-every-phone-call-and-email-echoes-China.html.

Williams, George. 2011. "A Decade of Australian Anti-Terror Laws." *Melbourne University Law Review* 35: 1137–75.

Wong, Mary. 2005. "Terrorism and Technology: Policy Challenges and Current Responses." In *Global Anti-Terrorism*, eds. Victor V. Ramraj, Michael Hor, and Kent Roach, 200–225. Cambridge, U.K.: Cambridge University Press.

Wood, David Murakami, and Kirstie Ball, eds. 2009. *A Report on the Surveillance Society.* For the Information Commissioner UK, by the Surveillance Studies Network.

11 Democracy and Identity in the Digital Age

Lorna Stefanick and Karen Wall

The pace of social, economic, and political change in the last two decades is nothing short of stunning. The neat divisions between the East and West political blocs came crashing down with the dismantling of the Berlin Wall, and global integration and the rise of the BRIC (Brazil, Russia, India and China) is reconfiguring global economic relations. These dramatic changes, however, pale in comparison to the impact information communication technologies (ICTs) are having on every aspect of our lives. In particular, ICTs have changed dramatically both the nature of commerce and its relationship to the state. Specifically, ICTs infuse our consumer identities into the market machine and the security state through the digital footprints that we leave as we go about our daily lives. Meanwhile, citizens are increasingly unable to configure their political identities within states that are market- and security-oriented.

This chapter examines the contraction of the public sphere in which political identity is contested and created through negotiations within a geographically defined community. At the same time that our identities are being commodified for commercial transactions using ICT techniques, neoliberal discourse stifles our identity as citizens. Its emphasis on the primacy of the market elevates the role of the individual economically while downplaying the importance of the connection between the individual as citizen to the state. Security measures taken in response to the events of September 11, 2001, have further constrained the ability of citizens to question this new citizen identity: draconian surveillance policies and technologies have flowed outward from the United States to other nations, leading to a dramatic reconfiguration of the institutions and purpose of the state. The state's most important function for its citizenry now appears to be to provide security, and personal information-sharing among public and private institutions means that anonymity is practically impossible. Moreover, the distinction between public and private in individual, organizational, and sectoral terms is blurring to such an extent that it is difficult to distinguish between them. Ironically then, as citizens become atomized into individual consumers, they are simultaneously losing the autonomy that comes with having a private space into which they can retreat. Consumer profiling done by corporate entities for the purpose of selling products, combined with a political discourse that emphasizes security over freedom, makes for a toxic mix that systematically corrodes not only personal autonomy but agency as well.

What is lost to individual civic agency in the articulation of our collective identity through market activities is the expression of a larger common good that is not market- or security-related. As autonomous individuals with tenuous connections to each other in political community, we are increasingly vulnerable to the vagaries of unfettered market forces. As communal bonds weaken, citizen identity is replaced by consumer identity in the global and virtual marketplace. The intersection of these individual shifts in identity with new technologies and security interests contributes to the decline of a citizenry that understands that it has both rights and responsibilities, both of which are contested in the public sphere. This decline will have serious consequences for the health of democratic systems.

Let us look first at understanding how public and private (or personal) spaces have been conceptualized before the advent of the ICT revolution. The next question to take up is how the neoliberal reconstruction of the public sphere and the impact of the U.S. Patriot Act on individual autonomy are shaping notions of public and private space in the digital age. These reconfigurations are reshaping not only public discourse, but our conception of ourselves as citizens of a political community. This chapter uses Canadian examples to support its assertions, but this is a global phenomenon that, thanks to the Internet, has facilitated both hegemonic and reactive discourses that do not respect territorial boundaries.

In the essay "The Virtual Sphere" Zizi Papacharissi makes a distinction between public sphere and public space. While the difference between public and private is easy to grasp, the difference between a public space and the public sphere is more subtle. Referring to thinkers such as Dewey (1927) and Tocqueville (1990), Papacharissi notes, "the term 'public' connotes ideas of citizenship, commonality, and things not private, but accessible and observable by all." She remarks, "participation in public affairs contribute[s] significantly to an individual's sense of existence and self-respect" (2002: 10). It is not simply free universal access to information gathered in a public space that is crucial to the public sphere, but active participation, its creation as a site of social activity, and rational discourse constituting a collective public will. As Papacharissi observes: "A virtual space enhances discussion; a virtual sphere enhances democracy" (11). Goldberg (2011) concurs: he cautions that the nature of cyberspace as a zone of democratic discussion does not constitute the direct transfer of an ideal public sphere, if one still exists, to online contexts. Papacharissi concludes that the privatizing forces of capitalism today create a mass commercial culture that stands in place of a public sphere; the Internet in this context constitutes what can only be considered a public space.

The ideal configuration of the public sphere has long been an object of interest to those concerned with politics and democracy. Robert Putnam (1995) argues that communal bonds that come from a variety of associational networks are critical to fostering social cohesion that supports participation in public affairs. These networks comprise the dense thicket of relationships that together form civil society. As the size and activities of government contract, the importance of civil society grows with respect to both service provision and social cohesion, as groups within it step into the void left by the state. The role of ICTs in facilitating new identities within civil society has attracted much scholarly attention; the most salient point for this analysis is that identity creation is happening in a public space as opposed to the public sphere. What is missing from Papacharissi's analysis is consideration of how cyberspace is fundamentally changing individuals' ability to draw a line between their private and public personae. Privacy is the tool that is used to delineate the line between the personal and the public, both in its social and its disciplinary/regulatory forms.

The notion that group deliberation produces the best public policy has been advocated by writers as diverse as Dewey (1927), Habermas (1989), and Etzioni

(1999). While a public "space" provides another forum for discussion, it should not be conflated with the public "sphere"—an arena that should be inclusive, include a diversity of opinion, and should produce policy that reflects a plurality of viewpoints. If certain groups are systematically excluded, the public sphere fails to live up to the democratic ideal. So, for example, Fraser (1992) notes that those who have been excluded from or marginalized within the dominant public sphere will create a counter sphere. Clearly, the Internet and social media provide powerful new tools for alternative messaging. However, as Papacharissi points out:

> When individuals address random topics, in random order without a commonly shared understanding of the social importance of a particular issue, then conversation becomes more fragmented and its impact is mitigated. The ability to discuss any political subject at random, drifting in and out of discussions and topics on whim can be very liberating, but it does not create a common starting point for political discussion. Ultimately, there is a danger that these technologies may overemphasize our differences and downplay or even restrict our commonalities. (2002: 20)

Papacharissi's analysis is particularly useful for this discussion of public spaces and spheres because she recognizes that cyberspace is both public and private space. "Cyberspace provides new terrain for the playing out of the age-old friction between personal and collective identity; the individual and community" (2002: 20). Internet communities allow individuals to connect with other like-minded individuals in online communities of interest. These communities in turn help shape individual identity. Hannah Arendt argues that these communities of interest are increasingly becoming the new public sphere: "The polis is not the city-state in its physical location; it is the organization of the people as it arises out of acting and speaking together . . . no matter where they happen to be" (2005: 198). What differentiates traditional communities of interest from those mediated by technology is scale. ICTs can broaden the discourse by rendering geographic boundaries meaningless, while simultaneously fragmenting the discourse among participants who share fewer identity bonds. Moreover, self-selection in or out of communities of interest means that, by Papacharissi's definition, these fora are public *spaces* as opposed to *spheres*. Without mediation by the state that gives voice to the marginalized, the public space is limited in its utility in creating collective identity for a territorially defined political community.

What is missing from Papacharissi's analysis is a consideration of how cyber-space is fundamentally changing individuals' ability to draw a line between their private and public personae. Privacy is the tool that is used to delineate the line between the personal and the public, both in its social and in its disciplinary/regulatory forms. In the information era, this is best defined as "information privacy." Privacy rights proponents cite the 1890 article by Samuel Warren and Louis Brandeis, "The Right to Privacy," as the first articulation of "the right to be let alone." Warren and Brandeis were motivated to write this article because of the advent of photography, which allowed print media to engage in "sensa-tionalist" journalism by circulating candid images of individuals without their consent. What was previously private could now be "shouted from the rooftops" by a journalist equipped with a camera. Clearly, Warren and Brandeis could not begin to conceive of the technologies that, a hundred years later, would allow shouts on the rooftop to be heard instantly all around the globe by anyone who has a cellphone with a WiFi connection. While the Warren and Brandeis article signals the beginning of modern concern for digital privacy, it should be noted that privacy concerns date back to ancient and early modern societies such as the Greeks, Hebrews, and English Puritans. Privacy in its most basic physical form is generally seen as a place of solitude to which one can retreat for quiet reflection and contemplation (Stefanick 2011: 34).

Yet privacy has a dark side as well. The feminist call to arms—"the personal is the political"—was one of the earliest attempts to expose "privacy" as a tool for the domination of individuals; in this case, men rely on privacy to oppress women within the confines of the home. Feminists identify the traditional line that distinguishes the private realm of the "family" from the public sphere of the community as a tool that reproduces the societal suppression of women's rights in their most intimate relationships. What happened behind closed doors was not subject to discussion in the public sphere, even if it involved violence or sexual assault. According to Catherine MacKinnon, the "right of privacy is a right of men 'to be let alone' to oppress women one at a time" (MacKinnon, 1989). While this is particularly true with respect to intimate relationships, declaring that transparency is impossible because personal privacy must be protected is increasingly used as a shield behind which those in positions of authority can hide, enabling them to engage in activities that oppress individuals, free from public scrutiny.

Is radical transparency the answer then? According to Foucault the disciplin-ary power of transparency is far more effective in enforcing social conformity than is physical punishment (1977: 195–228). Using Bentham's concept of the panopticon prison where inmates are constrained by the possibility of being watched, Foucault argues that the norms of society and its subsequent expectations serve to constrain personal autonomy. In short, their actions are constrained by reflexive consciousness. Formerly, Foucault and others focused attention on the state as the site where social norms were defined, contested, and enforced. But the power of the monopoly state has given way to the distributed power of the networked state. This suggests the emergence of a synopticon state, as articulated by Thomas Mathieson (1997): rather than the single agent that watches multiple people, the many watch the few. This can result in citizens watching those in power, thus forcing accountability on those in positions of power. The networked state, however, suggests that sites of power are distributed, thus disrupting the potential power of the synopticon society. An example of this is the introduction of "Internet Eyes" in the United Kingdom. This CCTV monitoring company streams video live to subscribing viewers, who report suspicious activity to police in exchange for points toward an online game. Thus the synopticon state also suggests that the many watch not only state officials but also each other. Crowd-sourcing crime prevention suggests a scenario that is less useful from a democratic perspective; the mob watching the individual, exerting "justice" on those who deviate from social norms.

What becomes apparent from this brief overview of the conceptualization of public and private space/sphere is that, while they help to construct an analytical framework, the divisions are contested. Moreover, it is evident that Internet technology has the potential to shift the ground under our feet. The spread of neoliberalism adds additional complexity by fundamentally transforming public institutions and the roles they play in society.

NEOLIBERALISM AND THE RECONSTRUCTION OF THE PUBLIC SPHERE

One of the biggest contributors to the shrinking of the public sphere as a place where citizenship is defined is the infusion of neoliberal thinking into all aspects of government. With its focus on maximizing individual autonomy through enhanced rights to private property and the ability to engage in market-based activities, this approach advocates mimicking the private sector in almost all aspects of social, political, and economic life. With respect to the organization of state institutions, neoliberalism dictates the adoption of private-sector management practices, dramatically reducing or contracting out services to the private and not-for-profit sectors, and decentralizing authority by transferring functions to regional authorities or community boards. It effectively hollows out and de-centres the state by removing it from its pedestal of social control. The newly reconfigured state has the capacity to "steer" the direction of society but its success is dictated by its responsiveness to the market-based currents in which it is embedded. The notion of "governance" as opposed to "government" reflects this important shift in emphasis. Governance recognizes the plurality of rules and actors that influence society; societal "steering" thus becomes a networked process of negotiations among societal units whose position in the power structure is not fixed. Actors exchange information and negotiate rules and processes for managing common affairs. The rise of ITCs facilitates the information flows among actors; when this happens the flow breaks down institutional distinctions.

These developments are part of a larger reconfiguration that sees states focusing on new priorities and assuming new roles. Joachim Hirsch argues that the post-WWII welfare state is transforming into the "national competitive state." He notes that "this type of state concentrates on the mobilization of all productive forces for the purpose of international competition, setting aside the former politics of materially based social and political integration" (1997: 45).

In other words, politics are being taken out of government in order to focus on "efficiency" defined in economic terms. In the twentieth century, public service was organized around core public administration values. In contrast, the twenty-first century's public service model comprises the "networked" organization that embodies neoliberal values. As Chakrabarty and Bhattacharya (2005) observe: "Globalization has led to a 'marriage' between corporate discipline and entrepreneurial spirit, with the government discarding its traditional image of 'a doer.' Seeking to accommodate 'the market impulse,' the government has become 'an enabler.'" Indeed, Sorenson describes the state in even weaker terms: "the state has become a differentiated, fragmented, and multi-centered institutional complex that is held together by more or less formalized networks" (Sorensen, 2006: 100). A major shortcoming of this new conception of the complex networked state is that it hinders transparency. Particular interests may have an advantage that is not easily seen, let alone acknowledged.

The change in the form and function of the state is the result of a larger ideological change wherein the proper role of government is restricted to apolitical or technical activities. This necessarily downplays the role of the state in facilitating social construction that promotes inclusion, equity, and equality.

Instantaneous communication; the transnational character of most economic and political functions; and the emphasis on a smaller, leaner bureaucratic state combine to produce a new approach to public administration, referred to as "the New Public Management" (NPM).

NPM is premised on the notion that small government is good government, and that management practices from the private sector should be applied to the public sector. Productivity through competition is achieved by contracting out service provision to the private sector or to nonprofit organizations. It also involves the use of private sector managerial perspectives, geared toward "customer" satisfaction and the use of risk management techniques to minimize exposure to disruptive forces. In the world of information management, analyzing customer preferences and shopping habits against their demographic information provides critical marketing information. Every time a consumer uses a loyalty card to receive "members benefits," a breadcrumb is left on the data trail that comprises digital identity. This data provides crucial information to a retailer concerned about product placement, and also to those who buy and sell personal information. Such bodies of data are also critical to governments in the development of public policy.

Habermas (1987) refers to this infiltration of the public sphere by the private as the "colonization of the lifeworld." He argues that it is this intrusion of instrumental logic from the private, commercial sphere into the public, cultural sphere that is responsible for the crisis of legitimacy that currently experienced by established democracies. Low participation rates in voting testify to this; neoliberal governments use citizen loss of faith in their state institutions to claim that they have no option but to allow the private sector to devour the public. But perhaps the hollowing out of the state is precipitating the legitimation crisis?

The hollowing out of the state means several things. First, as the money citizens contribute to the state lessens through decreased taxation rates, citizens care less about the state. Specifically, as consumers, we tend to be most concerned about things that we pay for, especially those things with a high price tag. In addition, the contraction of global services in favour of targeted services means that the state becomes increasingly irrelevant to those who pay the most taxes (but now receive the least benefit). Second, many of the public goods delivered by the state are not "products" but are ephemeral contributions to community health and wellness, such as the support of recreation, festivals, and art and culture. Taxpayers who identify as customers of state services will have difficulty locating the product they are paying for. The decrease in "public goods," as well as the significance of these tangible and intangible goods to community well-being, make citizens more susceptible to the argument that we are consumers first and citizens second, in a digital world where the primary value of identity is to commercial interests who can use the information to target their particular product.

Corporations devote enormous resources to data mining: the art of finding patterns in data sets, using computational processes. Indeed, a 2013 *Globe and Mail* article in the Careers section had the title: "Hot Jobs, Crunch the Numbers: Data Analytics Specialists Mine Market Demand" (Galt, 2013: B1). Not only is this commercial information valuable for product marketing, it is valuable in and of itself to data-brokers, who frequently resell it to government. Information sharing between these two sectors is illustrated by the relationship of private airline companies to the federal government. The government sets the regulations, which force the companies to collect particular types of information before a passenger is allowed to get on an airplane. Airlines then pass on information to the government. Corporations are not the only ones mining data, however. Political parties use public data they receive from Elections Canada as a base from which to build a profile of voters from data attained from commercial sources. As such, the collection, retention and exchange of information do not occur on a one-way street; data flows in both directions through permeable institutional boundaries.

The market orientation of private-sector media systems controlling one particular form and flow of information further breaks down the distinctions between nation-states and private-sector entities, as well as distinctions among nation-states. As Thussu (2007) notes:

> Nationality scarcely matters in this market-oriented media ecology, as producers view the audience principally as consumers and not as citizens. This shift from a state-centric and national view of media to one defined by consumer interest and transnational markets has been a key factor in the expansion and acceleration of media flows: from North to South, from East to West, and from South to South, though their volume varies according to the size and value of the market. (12)

Media information that is decoupled from national identities in favour of a global consumer identity serves to reinforce the propensity of individuals to self-identify as a consumer as opposed to a citizen.

Once we start thinking of ourselves primarily in consumer terms (which brands do I want to identify with? Which ones will enhance my status? Do I post my location as "Fernie Alpine Resort" when I take a picture of myself skiing and post it on Facebook, or do I reject corporate branding on principle?), we have fewer expectations that the state will promote our interests as citizens. In turn, low expectations reinforce the tendency to think of ourselves as individuals as opposed to members of a collectivity. The state in the past has been the primary site for the definition of a political identity; the state, however, is in a very weakened position as ICTs have also facilitated the movement of global capital, which means that the state has to create favourable conditions for capital retention. In the end, combined with hollowing out, there is a vacuum. Who expresses our collective identity and for what purpose?

IDENTITY IN THE AGE OF INSECURITY

The preceding discussion might suggest that the power of the state is receding to the point that it has little influence on our collective lives. While the state has relinquished its role with respect to promoting the collective wellbeing of citizens through active engagement in activities that promote some degree of equality in social, economic, and political manners, it has embraced its role as protector of citizens. The scope of this role is greatly enhanced by ICTs that provide powerful new tools for surveillance. The emphasis on security can be conceived as one more example of the blurring of the public- and private-sector roles—"security" stripped down is a modified version of the private-sector compulsion to manage risks. In the public sector, however, risk management has resulted in an assault on civil liberties, particularly with respect to data management.

The passage of the U.S. Patriot Act is a milestone with respect to curtailing individual information privacy rights. Passed only six weeks after the events of 9/11, this Act gave the U.S. government sweeping powers with respect to gaining access to information. It contains provisions that allow the government to force companies to surrender information to the FBI; companies are prohibited from revealing that the privacy of the information in their control has been compromised. Once in the hands of government officials, there are no provisions in the Act that prohibit the dissemination of this information, or the use of the information for purposes other than for which it is collected. It was passed in great haste and is not subject to the usual checks that protect civil liberties.

The U.S. Patriot Act has caused great concern in other countries, as its effects bleed over national borders in the same manner as information flows. For example, any information collected by the City of Edmonton from candidates applying for jobs with the municipality are subject to provisions of the Patriot Act, as the information management company that handles employment screening (and thus candidate information) is based in the U.S. This type of information-sharing caused an uproar in B.C. a decade ago, when citizens there realized that the management of their medical information was to be outsourced to an American company (Stefanick, 2007). At a time when being HIV positive was a reason to be denied entry to the U.S., British Columbians demanded that their information be held in Canada because they worried that they would have no idea where it would end up. Would their medical information find its way to U.S. customs?

One thing 9/11 demonstrated to us is that fear can cause us to do things we might not otherwise agree to. Fairfield (2005) describes how Americans and their politicians succumbed to such fear when they abrogated civil liberties in order to give the state extraordinary powers. He notes "when politicians in the heat of the moment, resort to draconian measures, it falls to social critics and theorists to call such actions by their name rather than allow themselves to be swept up in hysteria" (45). Canada followed suit with its own antiterrorism legislation. It was not as draconian but still produced heated debate. In 2011, however, a significant change was made with little fanfare to PIPEDA, Canada's privacy act covering private-sector entities. This provision replicates the U.S. Patriot Act in allowing companies to hand over personal information to authorities without a warrant. As in the U.S., Canadian companies can be forbidden to alert individuals that the privacy of their information has been breached (Tencer, 2011).

Since 2001, the blurring of private and public sectors is most evident in private security companies, and other companies whose products can be used for security. So, for example, Google is regularly asked by governments to provide user data, and as both the legal framework and the standards are evolving in this area, the guidelines determining what is properly private data and what should be shared with government are contested—contested not in the public sphere but in the backrooms where lawyers and lawsuits reign supreme. In the U.S., it was revealed that AT&T allowed the U.S. National Security Agency to monitor its customers. Lawsuits against the company ensued, and the U.S. government moved quickly to amend FISA to protect companies from liability in the course of complying with security agencies. More important, cloud computing is now included. This is particularly problematic for nongovernmental organizations and some public sector institutions, many of which use commercial software and computing services in a bid to save money. Data monitoring by the U.S. government violates basic organizational autonomy, and in particular the autonomy of individuals within those organizations who might be deemed a security threat.

What is interesting about fear as a tool that enforces complacency at the loss of civil liberties is that it is not restricted to the governmental level, but has seeped into our personal lives. As a result, the first surveillance-complacent generation is growing up; they understand personal tracking as a given. Parents bemoan their wired youth who disappear into a virtual space of gaming and chat rooms where predators lurk. In an effort to exert their influence on their dependents, parents embrace security measures such as installing home surveillance systems (including nanny cams to watch their children or pets), monitoring their children's social activity through social media, tracking their scholastic activity through software such as SchoolZone, and monitoring their physical movements through GPS-enabled cell phones. Children (and other social media users) inadvertently contribute to their own surveillance whenever they post to social media. There is little wonder that young adults currently have a difficult time growing up and out from under "helicopter" parents. And more important, given that all the information posted on social media sites is used to categorize people for marketing purposes, the implications for personal autonomy are substantial for a generation taught that giving over personal data for corporate use is nothing to fear, and, moreover, that surveillance is a small price to pay for protection from predators. The danger with individuals trading autonomy for security is the blurring of the public and private spheres. At the same time, we, as collections of individuals, are also inadvertently trading freedom of expression for security. History has taught us that suppression of civil liberties has dire democratic consequences; the next section explores this theme with respect to those who are best equipped to critique the current trajectory of government policy-making.

SOCIAL SCIENCE, POLITICAL DISCOURSE, AND THE PUBLIC INTEREST

Surveillance provides an important example of the blurring of the boundaries between public and private space, and between the consumer-citizen and corporate-government entities. With respect to legislatively sanctioned state surveillance, there is an absence of the voices of social scientists whom Fairfield calls upon to speak up against the incursion of the state into private space. In Canada, under the Harper government, the voices of reflective reasoning that advocate for evidence-based policy making were stifled. At the federal level, there was a concentrated effort to prevent the dissemination of research results, both in the "soft" and "hard" sciences. At an international conference of scientists in 2012, scientists and journalists convened a panel entitled "Unmuzzling Government Scientists: How to Re-open the Discourse." Journalists lamented that it has become just about impossible to get information from government scientists in a timely fashion because now they must go through many layers of bureaucratic approvals before they can speak with the media. As O'Hara observes: "If we're talking about policy that's informed by fact, if we're asking people to be critical thinkers, if we're asking people to engage in democratic process and to engage in democracy, it's incumbent on all of that we make sure the process is transparent" (CBC News, 2012).

O'Hara's concern is not limited to Canadian scientists. In 2013, foreign researchers participating in a decades-old collaboration with federal government scientists claimed that a new confidentiality agreement they were required to sign was unacceptable. In the words of a physical oceanographer at the University of Delaware: "I believe this is a disturbing political climate change . . . I feel that it threatens my academic freedom and potentially muzzles my ability to publish data and interpretation and talk [in a] timely [way] on science issues of potential public interest without government interference" (CBC News, 2013). This concern for the suppression of scientific knowledge has been raised by others who have felt the impact of new government policies: for instance, the cancellation of an important statistical tool (the long-form census), and classifying librarians and archivists making presentations to school classes and conferences as engaging in "high risk" activities (Munro, 2013).

At the provincial level, the government of Alberta provides a clear example of the globalized neoliberal "reform" of education that is achieved through slashing post-secondary funding (Barkawi, 2013). Done in the name of fiscal exigency, these dramatic and deep cuts to the postsecondary education sector in 2012 and 2013 were less about money and more about promoting research that lends itself to commercialization. The emphasis on economically profitable research inevitably stifles academic freedom and the curiosity-driven research that produces critical analysis of government policy. Shortly after the 2013 budget was announced, the government of Alberta sent all postsecondary institutions "mandate letters" that sought to eliminate duplications and inefficiencies within the postsecondary system by encouraging institutions to cooperate. Ironically, this neoliberal government that supports competition in the economic sector is trying to create monopolies with respect to the production of ideas. What is more troubling, however, is the focus on those academic activities that promote the commercialization of research. Coupled with crippling cuts, Budget 2013 made postsecondary institutions more reliant on industry funding. Rather than producing citizens with critical thinking skills, this trajectory serves the short-term interests of business and the economy at the cost of an informed and critically educated populace.

These trends in education and knowledge dissemination are part of a larger reconstruction of the public sphere, both with respect to institutional structure and information flow. Structural change, new management practices, and information flows combine with heightened concerns for personal and national security to produce a profound reconfiguration of the state. This new, networked form is actually harder for an attentive public to scrutinize, particularly because of the fuzzy distinctions between public- and private-sector boundaries. The net result is the contraction of a public sphere in which ideas are contested in the course of debating the nature of a collective, political identity.

THE SECURITY STATE AND THE CITIZEN-CONSUMER

The contraction of the public sphere where political identity is contested is the result of three interrelated forces: the dramatic reconfiguration of the institutions and purpose of the state, the commodification of identity through digitization, and the subsequent blurring of the distinctions between the public and private sectors. These forces are fuelled by the ascendance of neoliberal discourse that puts a high premium on market-based activities and freedoms. Individuals are losing their identities as citizens of a geographically defined political community through their redefinition as individual consumers who identify with, and are identified by, commercial entities. This emphasis on the individual, and in particular the individual as consumer, is producing an increasingly truncated public debate in the ever-contracting sphere in which this debate can happen. A limited debate and a limited public sphere have grave implications for democracy; the expression of collective identity has shifted from public institutions to an atomistic aggregation of participation in market activities.

Yet while the rights and responsibilities of individuals as citizens are decreasing, so too are their rights as customers. The citizen-consumer produces a mountain of data in the course of everyday life. This information is collected, retained, and exchanged between and among organizations. Individual identity is being commodified, providing an important fuel for the production process and helping companies to position themselves within the marketplace. But such an atomized identity is also fed back into the machinery of the state, to be used in its role as the guardian of collective security.

The terrible events of September 11, 2001 caused many Americans to willingly sacrifice control of their personal data in exchange for security, via the passage of the U.S. Patriot Act. Citizens of other states followed suit by supporting their own states' legislative responses to the crisis. Because of the fluid nature of digital communications, the consequences of this draconian American legislation flow across national borders. Insecurity over personal safety has tumbled over into many other areas of life, feeding the propensity to use new surveillance technologies, from nanny cams to GPS tracking, in day-to-day life. As institutions increasingly scrutinize individual action, personal agency is constrained, particularly when deviance is seen as a threat to personal security. As Foucault has observed, the watched begin to identify with the watcher (1977: 202–3).

The rise of the security state is happening at the same time as the demise of the welfare state. The notion that the state gives expression to national citizenship through the provision of universal services and a social safety net has been discounted. Neoliberal ideology is systematically dismantling the form and function of the administrative state through downsizing activities and outsourcing services to the private and not-for-profit sectors. As a result of the blurring of sectors, the expression of collective identity is shifting from our public institutions to the aggregation of our participation in market activities as autonomous individuals. These market transactions are increasingly mediated through digital media that allow commercial entities to track and monitor our activities. Our commodified identities feed the market machine of the private sector, which in turn feeds the securitization machine in the public sector. The quest to manage security risks often entails that individuals give up important rights as citizens. Combined with the contraction of the public sphere, where important political issues such as relinquishing citizen rights are debated, the prospects for individual autonomy are chilling. The question arises as to who is watching the watchers.

REFERENCES

Arendt, Hannah. 2005. *The Human Condition*. Chicago: University of Chicago Press.

Barkawai, Tarak. 2013. "The Neoliberal Assault on Academia." *Al Jazeera*, 25 April. Accessed April 25, 2013. http://www.aljazeera.com/indepth/ opinion/2013/04/20134238284530760.html.

CBC News. 2012. "Muzzling of Federal Scientists Targeted by Campaign." 17 February. Accessed April 1, 2013. http://www.cbc.ca/news/technology/ story/2012/02/17/science-federal-muzzling-scientists.html.

———. 2013. "Canadian Federal Research Deal 'Potentially Muzzles' U.S. Scientists." 15 February. Accessed April 1, 2013. http://www.cbc.ca/news/technology/ story/2013/02/15/science-audio-munchow-scientist-muzzling.html

Dewey, John. 1927. *The Public and Its Problems*. New York: Holt.

Etzioni, Amitai. 1999. *The Limits of Privacy*. New York: Basic Books.

Fairfield, Paul. 2005. *Public/Private*. Toronto: Rowman and Littlefield.

Foucault, Michel. 1977. "Panopticism." In *Discipline and Punish: The Birth of the Prison*, trans. Alan Sheridan, 195–228. New York: Vintage Books.

Fraser, Nancy. 1992. "Rethinking the Public Sphere: A Contribution to the Critique of Actually Existing Democracy." In *Habermas and the Public Sphere*, ed. Craig Calhoun, 109–42. Cambridge, MA: MIT Press.

Galt, Virginia. 2013. "Hot Jobs, Crunch the Numbers: Data Analytics Specialists Mine Market Demand." *Globe and Mail*, 29 March, section B1.

Goldberg, Greg. 2011. "Rethinking the Public/Virtual Sphere: The Problem with Participation." *New Media and Society* 13(5): 739–54

Habermas, Jürgen. 1987. *The Theory of Communicative Action*, vol. 2, *Lifeworld and System*. Trans. Thomas A. McCarthy. Boston: Beacon Press.

———. 1989 [1962]. *The Structural Transformation of the Public Sphere: An Inquiry into a Category of a Bourgeois Society*. Trans. T. Burger and F. Lawrence. Cambridge, MA: MIT Press.

Hirsch, Joachim. 1997. "Globalization of Capital, Nation-States and Democracy." *Studies in Political Economy* 54: 39–58.

MacKinnon, Catherine. 1989. *Toward a Feminist Theory of the State*. Cambridge, MA: Harvard University Press.

Mathieson, Thomas. 1997. "The Viewer Society: Michel Foucault's 'Panopticon' Revisited." *Theoretical Criminology* 1(2): 215–34.

Munro, Margaret. 2013. "Federal Librarians Fear Being 'Muzzled' under New Code of Conduct that Stresses 'Duty of Loyalty to the Government." *National Post*, Postmedia news, 15 March. Accessed April 1, 2013. http://news.nationalpost. com/2013/03/15/library-and-archives-canada/.

Papacharissi, Zizi. 2002. "The Virtual Sphere: The Internet as a Public Sphere." *New Media and Society* 4(1): 9–27.

Putnam, Robert. 1995. "Bowling Alone: America's Declining Social Capital." *Journal of Democracy* 6(1): 65–78.

Sorensen, Olav, Lee Fleming, and Jan W. Rivkin. 2006. "Complexity, Networks and Knowledge Flow." *Research Policy* 35: 994–1017.

Stefanick, Lorna. 2007. "Outsourcing and Transborder Data Flows: The Challenge of Protecting Personal Information Under the Shadow of the USA Patriot Act." *International Review of Administrative Sciences* 73(4): 531–48.

———. 2011. Controlling Knowledge: Freedom of Information and Privacy Protection in a Networked World. Edmonton: Athabasca University Press.

Tencer, Daniel. 2011. "Canada Privacy Law: Amendment Mimics USA Patriot Act, Critics Charge." Accessed April 1, 2013. http://www.huffingtonpost.ca/2011/09/30/canada-privacy-law-patriot-act_n_989027.html.

Thussu, Daya Kishan. 2007. "Mapping Global Media Flow and Contra-Flow." In *Media on the Move: Global Flow and Contra-Flow*, ed. Daya Kishan Thussu. London: Routledge.

de Tocqueville, A. 1990 [1835]. *Democracy in America*, vol. 1. New York: Vintage Classics.

12 The Digital Democratic Deficit

Analysis of Digital Voting in a Canadian Party Leadership Race

Josipa G. Petrunić

In the spring of 2011, the Alberta Liberal Party (ALP) introduced a "registered supporter" system in conjunction with novel electronic (online and telephonic) voting mechanisms for its upcoming leadership race. Supporters of these systems viewed them as innovations that would revive the party ahead of a looming general election. This chapter explores the nature of the ALP's e-voting system as it was agreed upon, institutionalized, and operated within the context of a partisan leadership race in which non-fee-paying "registered supporters" and fee-paying ALP members constituted the voter pool. The "registered supporter" and e-voting mechanisms introduced to the ALP in 2011 were promoted by a small cohort of party insiders whose explicit intention it was to attract a broad base of support throughout the province. The electoral failures of the ALP a year later in the general election—which witnessed the party lose seats, popular support, and status as the province's Official Opposition—put both new systems into question. This chapter reviews the highly contingent circumstances surrounding the ALP's leadership race and reflects upon potential (general) problems that arise when digital democracy tools, such e-voting, are integrated with broad-based policies, such as "registered supporter" systems, with the explicit aim of increasing voter participation. Using a combination of interview and document data (significant portions of which stem from the archives and detailed minutes I kept as co-chairperson for the ALP leadership race throughout the summer of 2011), this chapter also analyzes Canadian cultural voting expectations with regards to the one-person-one-vote principle, the equality of voters in decentralized voting conditions, and the integrity of the voting process itself, as these variables were shaped by the combined "registered supporter" and e-voting mechanisms manifest in the ALP case study.

WINDS OF CHANGE IN ALBERTA POLITICS

On Tuesday, 1 February 2011, the leader of the Alberta Liberal Party (ALP), David Swann, met with his Liberal caucus to discuss the party's future. The meeting came after *Global News Calgary* had reported Swann was thinking about resigning. Having served one and a half terms as Member of the Legislative Assembly (MLA) for the constituency of Calgary-Mountain View, Swann observed the Liberal party shrink from nine elected MLAs to eight (in a legislature with eighty-three MLAs) following the departure of Dave Taylor, who moved to the nascent Alberta Party after publicly criticising Swann's leadership style. Swann also presided over the divisive quasi-campaigns of two other MLAs, Darshan Kang (Calgary-McCall) and Kent Hehr (Calgary-Buffalo), who had publicly declared their interest in making a similar move (Wingrove, 2011). *Global News* had reported popular support for the ALP had dipped under the Liberals' colloquial benchmark of 25 to 30 percent support across the province—a benchmark the party had reached throughout the 1990s and 2000s. An hour and a half after consulting his legislative team, Swann appeared at a news conference announcing his plans to resign as party leader. In his resignation speech, Swann stated: "It is the right time for a new leader and a new generation of Albertans to take our party into the future. . . . My decision to step down represents an opportunity to renew our party" (Kleiss, 2011b).

Swann had taken over leadership of the ALP in 2008 after defeating contenders Dave Taylor and Mo Elsalhy in a mail-in leadership vote in which members were issued paper ballots via Canada Post and asked to mail in their marked ballots for vote counting. While innovative in having offered access to decentralized voting to fee-paying party members, the 2008 ALP leadership race had not sought to expand the party base in any radical way; it had not sought to introduce digital media technologies or social media campaigns to ALP members; it had not aimed to revivify the party's base by appealing to a youthful generation of potential new voters.

By contrast, a few days after Swann's resignation, newly elected Alberta Liberal Party President Erick Ambtman claimed, "It's the right time for a new leader and a new generation of Albertans to take our party into the future" (Wingrove, 2011). Ambtman noted his own appointment as a thirty-two-year-old party president, along with the appointment of then twenty-nine-year-old executive director, Corey Hogan, "shows a lot of fearlessness on the part of our party, a willingness to take some risks, to put out people and ideas that challenge the status quo" (Wingrove, 2011). Ambtman's statements emerged within a sociological context in which Calgarian voters had recently opted for an energetic underdog candidate, thirty-eight-year-old Naheed Nenshi, to serve as their mayor in the city's October 2010 municipal election.

The Nenshi campaign had left its indelible mark on partisan staffers and journalists alike. On 2 February 2011, the day following Swann's resignation, *Edmonton Journal* reporter Karen Kleiss quoted Mount Royal University political scientist David Taras saying Alberta's "Nenshi moment" would extend to the provincial election (Kleiss, 2011b). "After 40 years, there is this sense that there needs to be change," Taras stated, adding: "There is a new generation, it's a different Alberta, it's younger, more cosmopolitan, more multicultural. . . . There is this new climate of change, and the parties have to reform in the face of this new Alberta. . . . We are going to go through these convulsions. . . . I think it is healthy" (Kleiss, 2011b). Less sanguinely, Taras also warned that a youth-led political revolution was not going to be easy: "This isn't going to happen overnight. . . . We may have a stalemate in Alberta politics for quite some time. [The provincial election] could be a coalition. All bets are off." But in the same news article, University of Lethbridge political scientist Peter McCormick was quoted as stating, "Once every generation, the Alberta political system resets itself in a very dramatic way, and this could be it." McCormick linked his proto-prophesy to the futures of both Conservative and Liberal parties in the province: "We hear talk about apathy among the younger generation, about lack of voter turnout. Well, you don't play the same song louder for them, you've got to change the tune. . . . It's a whole style of politics and a whole set of assumptions about how to do things. . . . I predict this is going to be the youth movement for both the Conservatives and the Liberals" (Kleiss, 2011b)

McCormick's speculation about a fundamental shift in Alberta politics led by a cohort of "youth" who would "change the tune" of provincial politics by changing its "style" and its assumptions about "how to do things" was echoed in the editorial pages of local and national newspapers. By the start of the federal Canadian general election on 28 March 2011 (barely two months after Swann's resignation), *Calgary Herald* reporter Richard Cuthbertson claimed: "As Calgarians prepare to vote for the ninth time in just seven years—including federal, provincial and municipal elections—politicians and their parties are looking for new ways to combat voter apathy. Many are casting their eyes to last fall's municipal campaign in Calgary, a watermark for local public interest that saw the strongest vote turnout in at least 40 years" (Cuthbertson 2011). Despite Nenshi's own warnings that political culture in Alberta had not changed fundamentally—a view he defended based on his campaign's difficulties in attempting to overcome "bitter partisanship and ridiculous caricature" (Cuthbertson 2011)—reporters continued to focus attention on the possibility of a provincial political transformation at the hands of revitalized youth voters by drawing analogies to the Nenshi case study.

In the first week of the federal general election of 2011, reporter Laura Stone produced an account of Nenshi's youth factor in a story first published via the Postmedia newswire in the *Calgary Herald* on 3 April 2011. She wrote: "Engaged young voters can energize a campaign and help lift a candidate to victory, if effectively harnessed through measures such as social media. If successful, as seen in Calgary's trail-blazing mayoral race . . . which elected 39-year-old Naheed Nenshi, it could reshape the political landscape in Canada" (Stone, 2011d). Slightly revised versions of the same story and the same quotation appeared on 4 April 2011 in Postmedia syndicated newspapers across the country, including the *Vancouver Sun*, the *Ottawa Citizen*, and the Regina *Leader Post* (Stone, 2011b, a, c).[1]

The ensuing and disastrous electoral results for the federal Liberal Party on 2 May 2011, which witnessed the denigration of Liberals to non-Opposition status in the House of Commons as a distant third party, further spurred provincial Alberta Liberals to revive motifs of "youth" and "renewal" with fervent gusto. In the weeks prior to the ALP Special General Meeting in Calgary, where new rules for the party's looming leadership race were to be finalized, a small cohort of ALP staffers and volunteers began to sow the seeds of "renewal" discourse, fertilizing the political landscape with promises of a democratic panacea for the Liberal brand in a province that hadn't been a Liberal stronghold for nearly a century. The combination of a broad-based "registered supporter" outreach system and ease-of-access digital voting mechanisms, it was argued, would ensure a Nenshi-styled surge of support across the province.

The working assumption among this emerging cohort of renewal actors within the ALP was that digital technologies could bring in new supporters (and ultimately voters) by virtue of its simple decentralized nature. A "new generation" of Liberals, it was believed, would turn out to vote in the 2012 provincial election, bringing energy and electoral success to the struggling provincial party. These assumptions glossed over numerous nuances associated with Nenshi's interactive Web 2.0–styled campaign (discussed below), and ignored significant obstacles shaping voter engagement via digital voting systems.

It was also within this this context that Michael Cormican, a former federal Liberal candidate in Lethbridge, and I, a former federal Liberal candidate in Calgary East, were recruited by Ambtman to serve as co-chairs for the ALP leadership race in 2011. Both Cormican and I agreed to serve as official chairs for the leadership race at the Special General Meeting. Our joint appointment was supported by the two sitting Liberal MLAs seeking leadership at the time—namely, Laurie Blakeman (Edmonton Centre) and Hugh MacDonald (Edmonton-Gold Bar).[2]

THE SHIFT TO DIGITAL MECHANISMS FOR PARTISAN ENGAGEMENT

In the opinion of *Calgary Herald* columnist Don Braid, Nenshi's nimble use of cheap, youth-driven social media had propelled his campaign ahead of better-established competitors, including the well-known local journalist Barb Higgins and the established city councilor associated with the provincial Conservative Party, Ric McIver.[3] Braid wrote:

> Whatever happens Oct. 18, Nenshi's campaign is already becoming a
> model of how to launch political popularity using Facebook, Twitter,
> Podcasts, You-Tube, blogs and even the iPhone. Other candidates are
> on the Internet, too, of course. McIver and Higgins both have effective
> websites. They all use Twitter and Facebook (or somebody does it
> for them.) Yet Nenshi clearly generates far more online interest and
> enthusiasm than any other candidate. Late last week, he had 3,440
> Facebook friends, compared to 942 for Higgins and 2,105 for McIver.
> Nearly 2,000 people follow him on Twitter, while McIver and Higgins
> are both in the 1,100 range. His video is ahead by about 4,000 views on
> YouTube. (Braid, 2010)

While Braid believed Nenshi's early online popularity did not guarantee an electoral win (Braid cited an estimate that held only 10,000 Calgarians at the time used Twitter at all), the reporter also believed Nenshi *could* win if the third-ranking candidate could convert his start-up online campaign into a full-blown traditional ground campaign built upon policy documents, phone calls, door knocking, lawn signs, public forums, and leaflet drops—a set of tasks it appears Nenshi's campaign team had already started to perform. As Braid concluded:

> Nenshi offered seven of his "better ideas" long before the official campaign even began. Many of his policies are accompanied by detailed background papers. The result, to judge by reams of online comment, is that people pulled in by social media saw a real campaign behind the virtual one. The online buzz then drew in more people to look. Now that the official campaign has started, Nenshi has jumped into more traditional politicking, attending as many debates and public events as he can. (Braid, 2010)

Braid's speculations about the need for a traditional campaign behind the virtual and digital aesthetics of Nenshi's early strategies were explored further in subsequent journalistic analyses following the end of the electoral period in October 2011. In her review of Nenshi's campaign tactics, journalist Kelly Cryderman traced the mechanisms by which cheap social media outlets, which served as the original foundation for the Nenshi campaign, were steadily integrated into an effective and more traditional campaign strategy by September 2010, thereby solidifying the candidate's growing appeal and ultimate win (Cryderman, 2010). The campaign had effectively integrated policy experts and volunteers early on in an effort to design ideas that would appeal to a broad base of potential municipal voters; the campaign then used social media in an interactive Web 2.0 fashion to disseminate those ideas and also to collect critical and positive responses from community members and potential voters. The campaign then integrated those ideas into its statements, policy utterances, and marketing material.

In using social media as an integrative channel for commentary, feedback, and policy development, and by recruiting community members on the other end of the digital interface to join the campaign in person, Nenshi's strategy created a sense of ownership among the online participants active in the campaign's digital discourse. These "hyper-engaged" volunteers soon constituted the core of what came to be Nenshi's growing network of campaign outreach agents. They proselytized Nenshi's message online and in person, serving as human brand carriers who travelled seamlessly between digital discussion rooms to coffee meet-and-greets back to Facebook forums.

In sum, the Nenshi campaign strategy relied on social media as a conduit for interactively sharing and refining the candidate's policies, thereby creating a sense of ownership over the campaign itself and motivating a constant transference of personnel from what might have been a temporally connected digital community to dedicated in-person volunteers, networkers, and voters. This strategic campaign approach mimicked the decentralized campaign structure first developed by Barack Obama's presidential campaign in 2008, which gave birth to the notion of recruiting online voters via a seamless web of online and in-person interaction and co-commitment. It was important that this networked strategy also unfolded at a time when Nenshi's opponents failed to grow their own bases of support, or even to view Nenshi as a growing threat and thus a worthy target for attack or counter-campaigning (Cryderman 2010).

In the offices of the Alberta Liberal Party, Nenshi's electoral success spurred staffers to focus on the youth aspect of new campaign strategies, leading to the development of the party's first-ever Twitter feed. In October 2010, the ALP announced www.twitter.com/albertaliberals—a harbinger, the party said, of its digitally facilitated "renewal." Communications staffer Jody MacPherson declared:

> With the growing influence of social media as a tool to galvanize supporters, it's time for Alberta Liberals to join the conversation. During the recent municipal election, there were weekly reports with updates on each of the Calgary mayoralty candidates' successes on Twitter, Facebook and other social media sites. Those weekly stats showed Naheed Nenshi's growing support, but many discounted social media saying that the people on Twitter and Facebook would not get out and vote. This theory is now under question with Mayor Nenshi's victory on October 18. (MacPherson 2010)

Within weeks, a handful of ALP youth (mostly under the age of thirty) created a stream of Alberta Liberal Party blogs and online commentary postings; they filled Facebook and Twitter pages with political hashtags meant to advertise the party's coming of age in the digital era.

Yet the cultural transformation MacPherson alluded to did not arise within the ALP over the course of the following nine months, that is, in the lead up to the party's leadership race, nor did it arise over the course of the following year and a half in the lead up to the province's general election. In part, this is because no thoroughgoing communications or digital infrastructure strategy was created to innovate policy-making by introducing interactive engagement with community members or individual Albertans on pressing matters of social, economic, or political importance. Neither at the party level nor at the constituency association level did the ALP launch any kind of coordinated communications strategy aimed at integrating the views of Albertans into the party's ongoing affairs. Thus, apart from introducing a Twitter feed, which remained mostly a one-way stream of communication from ALP staffers and caucus members to digital listeners tuned into the party's hashtags, the ALP ignored and failed to incorporate the most galvanizing aspects of Nenshi's Web 2.0–inspired campaign tactics—including, especially, the recruitment of interactive online actors as in-person volunteers, donors, and voters.

Thus, by the formal start date of the ALP leadership race six months later, the nuances of the Nenshi campaign—the combination of interactive online channels, the incorporation of policy views emanating from outside the party into internal platform concepts, and the translation of temporal digital engagement into material in-person participation—remained elusive. By contrast, the ALP "renewal" strategies, as presented at the party's May 2011 Special General Meeting in Calgary, focused primarily on ease of access to voting (interpreted as a no-fee structure for party "membership" or "supporter" status), and decentralized voting mechanisms (interpreted as digital and telephonic voting mechanisms). While innovative, these "renewal" mechanisms did not engender networked growth strategies for the ALP; they did, however, come packed with ambiguities and operational hiccups that led to significant growth difficulties for a small opposition party already struggling to finance itself in a provincial political landscape dominated by a well-funded and organizationally powerful provincial Conservative Party.

At the Special General Meeting in Calgary, ALP staffers did offer party members one bylaw amendment to the constitution that attempted to incorporate a policy feedback mechanism to encourage more grassroots engagement. Known as Resolution B, the proposed amendment included a series of steps by which party members could develop and put forward new policy ideas (addressing any topic in economics, health, education, environment) for consideration and approval via a membership vote at annual general meetings of the ALP. At the Special General Meeting, ALP members voted in favour of Resolution B, which thereafter stipulated (as a bylaw) that the results of votes on policy matters at ALP annual or general meetings would be used to "prioritize the Policy" of the ALP, such that those policies receiving most votes among the membership would be ranked higher and therefore most likely to be incorporated into campaign/ electoral platforms in the future (ALP, 2011: Section 27). The bylaw also noted policies obtaining the three highest scores among voters would be considered "Priority Resolutions" for the ALP and party elite would be obligated in the future to "include in its Election Platform a minimum of two out of the three Priority Resolutions from the most recent General Meeting" (ALP, 2011: Section 28). In sum, the bylaws embodied in Resolution B ensured member-produced policy passed by agreement at annual party conventions could, *in principle*, find its way into the party's electoral platform.

However, Resolution B entrenched only a once-a-year feedback mechanism by which members and party participants could voice policy ideas with the hope of obtaining enough votes to become a "top priority." The resolution did not inject a dynamic, interactive feedback mechanism by which ALP participants could frequently engage, reassess, reform, or alter core party policies through regularized interaction with party elites. In addition, while the bylaw existed on paper following the May Special General Meeting, its practical effect was not felt among party rank and file at any point in the lead up to the 2012 provincial election. At the 2011 Annual Convention held in Red Deer following the end of the leadership race (but before the general election), ALP staff and caucus did not seek policy proposals from the floor and no new policy proposals were put forward from by members of the party. Meanwhile, the "new" communications tools embodied in the party's Twitter and Facebook postings remained limited to a narrow core of participant actors composed primarily of ALP legislative staffers, ALP party office staffers, and ALP (leadership) campaign volunteers.

ATTRACTING AND INTEGRATING NEW POLITICAL ACTORS

The lack of an interactive Web 2.0 communications and volunteer recruitment strategy did not necessarily mean, however, that Liberal elites were not *trying* to alter the party's structure. Following Swann's resignation in February 2011, a cluster of executives and staffers in the party formed a tightly knit group that spearheaded efforts to redefine the 2011 leadership "rules" to ensure greater interactivity with Albertans and to initiate a "renewal" agenda. The party's new executive director, Corey Hogan, its operations officer, Corina Ganton, its president, Erick Ambtman, and its vice-president of communications, Matt Grant, led the group. Those four, all aged between twenty-five and thirty-three years old, constituted a core organizational unit of elite partisans (they were either on the ALP payroll or occupied executive party positions) dedicated to altering the structure of the ALP to attract more voters, more donors, and ultimately greater electoral success for Liberals in Alberta.

The cultural production of a new engagement equation—one that equated digital systems, social media, and youth voters to party renewal—emerged prominently in the lead up to the Special General Meeting in May 2011. Here I quote a small selection of postings made at the time by Ganton, whose enthusiasm demonstrates a seemingly unquestioned belief in the renewal virtues of youth, social media, and digital technologies. On 7 May 2011, Ganton posted on YouTube a link to a three-minute video, entitled the "Gen Why Media Project," discussing issues that might motivate young people to get involved in politics (Ganton, 2011c). Ganton followed the same day with a tweet about being a "youth" at an ALP Board of Directors meeting where leadership rules—including entry fees for candidates and vote dates—were being preliminarily discussed: "At the #ALP board meeting. Love t/ debates. It's so great to b able to b a young person around this table. Many younger faces here" (2011b). A message the same day indicated the council had agreed to baseline rules for the leadership convention. Enthusiastically, Ganton tweeted: "The latest @albertaliberals news ... #ablib #ableg LEADERSHIP RULES SET! WERE OFF TO THE RACES!" (2011d). A day later, Ganton retweeted a message by another Twitter user stating: "C'mon young Liberals - lets redefine, revamp and reenergize our federal party. Now is the time and it's up to us. #lpc #oyl #ovyl #uoyl #ylc." On 10 May, Ganton tweeted (presumably as an analogy to the provincial case study), "The next generation is the Liberals' salvation," citing a *Globe and Mail* column by Lawrence Martin, who argued politics in Canada is a "one man" show and the federal Liberal's "salvation" would come in finally choosing a "young" person (2011e).

Ganton was not alone in constructing a culture within the ALP that was meant to inspire youth-oriented political engagement via social media and digital portals. In the days preceding the ALP's Special General Meeting, Ganton tweeted: "New Liberal Post of the Day: Kick starting Renewal." The tweet linked to an online blog posting by ALP executive director, Corey Hogan, as posted on Hogan's lobby website, *New Liberal Initiative*—a site promoting the establishment of an independent organization intended to engage young voters to serve as the ALP's next generation of policy decision-makers. The *New Liberal Initiative* posted blogs supporting the incorporation of a "registered supporter" system and new e-voting mechanisms into the ALP's constitutional and operational structure.

Despite serving as the ALP's presumably neutral executive director, Hogan used his online blog to argue in favour of allowing a "registered supporter" system in which all resident Albertans could vote in both constituency nomination races and party leadership races. Rather than restricting the party to its previous practice of allowing votes by only card-carrying, fee-paying members, Hogan prophesied the "registered supporter" system would achieve significant renewal goals by virtue of being able to

> draw in new supporters who would not be willing to join the Party. Create larger lists of people to solicit donations, signs, and volunteer hours from. Choose standard bearers who are best able to connect with the voters who will be making the ultimate decision. Send a powerful signal that we are an open Party. (Hogan, 2011a)

At the time, Hogan had already authored various proposed constitutional amendments which, he predicted, would reshape the ALP's governing constitution in favour of attracting new, hitherto nonvoting Albertans into the party's fold.

Hogan's explicit inspiration for doing so came from the concept of an "open primary" system, as used in presidential nominations in select American states. An open primary system exists in those American states that allow any eligible voter within the state's jurisdiction to vote in the selection of presidential candidates for either Republican or Democratic parties. This contrasts with the "closed primary" system operating in other American states in which citizens must be card-carrying members of the given party to vote in that party's respective presidential nomination race. It also contrasts with the typically closed nomination and closed voting systems at play in Canadian political parties, where only card-carrying (and usually fee-paying) members vote for the next leader of a given party in an internal race.

To advance the adoption of an "open primary" styled leadership race, Hogan issued a document entitled *A New Liberal's Guide to Change*. The document declared the need to move ahead with major changes to the party's internal structure at breakneck speed, explicitly rejecting the need to consider unintended consequences (Ganton, 2011a; Hogan, 2011b). Hogan wrote:

> There's a school of thought in liberal circles right now about the need to think long and hard about what kind of movement liberalism is going to be before we rush forward with any dramatic overhaul of our Party. But

when it comes to organizational politics *you don't need to figure out what
needs to change before you start changing it.* [italics are Hogan's]

Complementarily, Ambtman announced the party would be using new digital
mechanisms—that is, telephone and Internet voting—in the upcoming leadership race. His announcement was made three weeks prior to the Special General
Meeting where members gathered to discuss and vote on significant alterations
to the party's operational and constitutional structure. Ambtman declared,
"[Digital voting] will allow a lot more people to have access to the contest,"
adding that the rules governing the leadership race (and its voting mechanisms) had already been unanimously approved by the ALP Board of Directors
(Massinon, 2011).

Ambtman was referring here to a meeting of the Board of Directors held that
month which included, in theory, the party president, vice presidents, regional
chairs, constituency association presidents, and the past party president. At the
meeting, board members apparently agreed to the use of digital voting mechanisms. In interviews conducted with ALP constituency executives and MLAS a year
later, however (for the purposes of the current study), interview participants
indicated a number of key positions on the board of directors were either vacant
or held in duplicate at the time of that board meeting. In other words, there
was unlikely to have been quorum at the meeting, since posts were vacant or
one person held more than one post, thereby decreasing the overall number of
votes required to pass a directive among ALP executives. No minutes exist of the
board meeting in question, but interview data suggests both the "registered supporter" and "digital voting" systems were proposed only as preliminarily ideas
and not formally approved by board members before being publicly announced
by Ambtman.

In addition, because the new e-voting mechanisms "agreed upon" changed
the rules governing nearly all components of the ALP's internal voting processes,
including who could vote, when they could vote, how they would be registered to vote, and by what mechanism they could vote, Ambtman's declaration ignored the fact e-voting affected the party's codified commitments to its
membership, and thus required membership support in the form of a majority
vote at a party convention to instantiate. Instead, the proposed e-voting mechanisms were introduced by the ALP's executive and staff as though they were
neutral administrative tools that would not affect the fundamental principles
of fairness, transparency, or other constitutional obligations the party had to

its fee-paying membership base. Unabashedly and unreservedly, the close-knit renewal team of Hogan, Ganton, Ambtman, and Grant promoted the theme of "Politics Re-Imagined" at the Special General Meeting held in Calgary between 28 and 29 May 2011, where digital voting was presumed unproblematic, outside the scope of constitutional consideration, and not subjected to a membership-based vote.

RENEWAL IN AN AGE OF DIGITAL DEMOCRATIC OUTREACH

On 28 May 2011, the day preceding the Special General Meeting, approximately 100 Liberal members (of more than 2,200 party members across the province at the time) arrived to a Calgary hotel conference room, where they were faced with the odd predicament that their executive director, Corey Hogan, whose role it was to facilitate the meeting neutrally, was handing out lobbyist booklets published by his and party president Erick Ambtman's *New Liberal Initiative*. The booklets aimed to convince members at the meeting to vote in favour of the "registered supporter" system. Entitled *YES!*, the document argued that proposed constitutional amendments would create a new category of casual party affiliate—the "Registered Supporter"—who could register support without being bogged down by long-term party identity or membership fees. Hogan's document stated the party would collect the personal details of these new supporters to allow for future communication. The lack of a membership fee would enable thousands of Albertans who would not have otherwise joined the party, due to the burden of a $5.00 annual membership fee, to do so.

The *YES!* document also stated that registered supporters would eventually encourage two-way community interaction on policy issues, because the new category of affiliate would encourage party members to "build networks in the community" and "encourage community outreach" to obtain more names and contact details in ways members had never done before:

> The nature of politics in Canada is changing. We can deny this, we can
> fight against it, or we can be the first Party [sic] in Canada to accept that
> people look at political involvement differently today. In the process we
> will be positioning our Party as the most inclusive, grassroots political
> organization in Canada. Doing so will bring in a new generation and
> create a base for this Party for years to come. *Say Yes to Change. Vote Yes*
> *on Resolutions C, D, E* [emphases Hogan's]. (Hogan, 2011c: 11)

With Hogan's strongly affirmative lobbying document in hand, and no anti-resolution document circulating, ALP members in the room the following day proceeded to vote in favour of a series of constitutional bylaws that institutionalized the "registered supporter" concept, although the mechanism by which supporters would be registered—whether by paper signature (where a person would manually complete a registration form and have her or his data uploaded to a general database by an individual campaigner or ALP office staffer), by online registration (where a person would enter personal contact details online and tick a box declaring adherence to the party's principles, or otherwise provide a digital signature to link the registration to their personhood), or by mere recommendation or inclusion arbitrarily (where campaign teams could submit names and addresses for registration based on people's names and addresses as listed in a phone book or on the province's elector's list, whom the campaign believed would support a given candidate despite having made no personal or online contact with the campaign team)—was left an open question. What was assumed, however, was that these mechanisms—however they unfolded in the months ahead—would necessarily support the party's growth and its two-way communication with communities and voters across Alberta.

On 1 June 2011, therefore, the ALP became the first political entity in Canada defined by adherence to a "registered supporter" system: a casual party affiliation not dependent upon membership fees and tied to no set of rules determining how supporters could actually be registered. With positive media coverage and internal euphoria among the vanguard group of "renewal" agents over the success of amendments enshrining the "registered supporter" system, however, few questions were raised on these points.

OPERATIONAL OBSTACLES IN NEW SUPPORTER REGISTRATION AND E-VOTING MANAGEMENT

At the operational level, the party's three-person staff (including Hogan, Ganton, and a part-time university intern) took on the task of managing, directing, and institutionalizing all aspects of the new registered supporter and digitized voting systems. By mid-August, that system had come to include nearly 20,000 names, addresses, and phone numbers. Almost by necessity (because of the small staff and many tasks the ballooning registered supporter list required), ALP voter "policies" as they related to the voter privacy and vote integrity (including the issuance of double PINS to persons with name variations, and the issuance of

PINs to the homes of people who had passed away, or who had been mistakenly or unwantedly added to the ALP "supporter" list, including pets and prank names), as well as cyber-security concerns over data ownership, data security, data theft, and the possibility of data manipulation, were developed *ad hoc* starting immediately after the 29 May Special General Meeting. A post-mortem analysis of internal party documents (including emails, all-candidates meeting minutes, and decision letters issued by Cormican and myself between May and September 2011) demonstrates that under-staffing and complex system concerns related to "registered" voters and digital voting mechanisms manifested themselves in a series of significant operational, technical, and philosophical problems for the ALP.

Formal complaints submitted to Cormican and myself, as chairpersons for the race, included Hugh MacDonald's concern that non-Albertans, dead people, and cats were appearing on the list of "registered supporters," and that there were no transparent means of stopping the issuance of PINs to those people or entities. The MacDonald campaign also complained that fee-paying members who had signed up to support his campaign were not appearing on the digitized voting list issued to all campaign teams. Raj Sherman's campaign formally complained about the publication of "registered supporter" names ahead of schedule, and the requirements for a paper trail or material signature trail to link supporter names to existent individuals, which the team felt was an unnecessary requirement. The Bill Harvey campaign formally complained there was no vetting process in place to ensure "registered supporters"—who were supposed to be at least eighteen years old, with names appearing on Alberta's voter list or as residents of Alberta, and whose intention was to vote in the Liberal race—met any or all of those requirements. The Laurie Blakeman campaign complained there had been an agreed-upon convention to use a paper-based system to sign up new "registered supporters" at the outset of the race, but that the paper-based system had been abandoned *ad hoc* and without justification, to the detriment of those teams that had spent time and money collecting paper signatures to demonstrate a paper trail to voters. Finally, as the leadership race neared its end in September 2011, the MacDonald campaign complained that returned-to-sender PINs, which were returned to the ALP office in the last few weeks of the campaign, were not properly disposed of—or that there was no known protocol for the secure disposal of those PINs, which could be misused for double or triple voters if released to pernicious actors. Indeed, minutes of the weekly all-candidates meetings held by telephone throughout the summer of 2011 (which

Cormican and I moderated in conjunction or solo) demonstrate that all five campaign teams complained at some point about one or more issues related to the lack of material (versus digital) traceability to "registered supporters" and the problem of cyber-security with relation to online registrations, online PIN usage, and online vote tabulation and auditing.

As executive director and thus *de facto* manager of the "registered supporter" and e-voting systems, Hogan's response to these concerns included the following: with regard to misuse of PINs, Hogan contended it is illegal to open someone else's mail, so household members would refrain from opening or using a child's, senior's, or partner's PIN to vote twice (or thrice) on this legal basis; that while a paper trail leading to the existent digital voter is ideal in ideal circumstances, the ALP could not guarantee such a paper trail nor would it enforce the requirement to have a material paper trail to digital voters, as it did not have the resources to do so; that returned-to-sender PINs would be disposed of by office staff (Hogan, Ganton, and the university intern, though Hogan did not explain how disposal would occur); and that the third-party provider could be trusted to save and store digital votes securely (though repeated requests for details of the ALP's contract with the third-party provider went unanswered by Hogan).

In the fortnight preceding the final leadership vote date (8 September), Cormican and I requested a formal statistical audit of "registered supporters" to ensure that a significant percentage of the names appearing on the (by then) 25,000-plus names and addresses did, in fact, belong to residents of Alberta who were eighteen years or older (or fee-paying ALP members, who could be as young as fourteen) and that each such resident had been issued with one PIN, and one PIN only (with any additional PINs issued due to name variations being deactivated in advance). Hogan responded to indicate the ALP did not have the budget (and had not budgeted for) any form of statistical review or external auditing of the registered supporter list of potential voters prior to the vote, and that the party was relying primarily on a the "honour system" among Albertans, expecting them not to misuse PINs by double or triple voting.

PHILOSOPHICAL LIMITATIONS TO DIGITAL OUTREACH AND VOTER ENGAGEMENT

Given these circumstances, the remainder of this chapter analyzes the voting principles that emerge as sites of contention and contestation within the ALP experiment. Within this discussion, two Canadian voting principles arise as worthy of detailed consideration: Integrity of the one-person-one-vote principle and the equality of voters; and integrity (and anonymity) of the voting process.

Integrity of the One-Person-One-Vote Principle and the Equality of Voters
Between 6 September and 10 September, more than 8,000 personal identification numbers (PINs) were used to log into the ALP's voting system by telephone or online, using a specially dedicated website. The vote tabulations and preferences of those voters (including their preferential listing of candidates by telephone key pad entry or online numbered selections in order of preference) were collected, stored, and hosted by the third-party private provider. In theory, each PIN issued was associated with one individual person, thereby assuring the protection of the ALP's one-person-one-vote policy.

Telephone and online voting mechanisms were meant to facilitate voting among members and supporters who were not able or who did not want to travel to physical polling stations, where they would have been issued a pencil and paper ballot to vote behind a private screen. A key assumption underpinning the ALP's e-voting mechanisms was that users of these digital technologies would not experience any significant differences in the voting experience or practice of ballot casting when compared to material, in-person voting by paper ballot. This assumption ought to be opened to critical inquiry, however, because digital voting brings with it a different space, a different set of relationships within that space, different power dynamics, and differing outcomes based on the context within which it occurs, as compared to paper-ballot voting behind a private screen monitored by neutral voting clerks.

First, let us consider the domestic space of digital voting. Online and telephone voting takes place within a context defined by particular parameters. In an egalitarian household, where each member of the household is assumed to hold his or her own political opinion and each member of the household (where the telephone or Internet connection is housed) is allowed to cast his or her own vote, such an assumption may be manifest in reality. But many households in Alberta cannot be described as egalitarian. The assumption that all Albertan households, or at least all the households participating in the ALP vote, demonstrate an equality among potential voters in political opinion and personal rights to vote unimpeded is an indefensible one. Access to the Internet or telephone, or personal privacy when using those services, might not be guaranteed. The ability to use one's own PIN may not be guaranteed. The ability to make up one's own mind when at the point of keying in a voting preference might not be guaranteed.

In sum, the belief that digital voting by telephone or Internet is the virtual equivalent of private voting booths and paper ballots breaks down quickly when the power dynamics within private households are analyzed. Domestic power dynamics determine and shape decentralized e-voting processes. When they are taken into account, electronic voting leaves much to be desired from the perspective of the one-person-one-vote principle and the presumption of a fundamental equality between voters, where no one vote gets more of a say, a louder "voice," or more ballots than any other voter.

Given the unbalanced and often unequal nature of household power dynamics (between spouses, between parents and youths, and between adults and their seniors, between able-bodied and disabled persons, or between the cognitively capable and the cognitively disabled, and so on), we must ask whether the one-person-one-vote principle in domestic digital voting scenarios can be guaranteed—is it equal in this respect to private voting booths? The question here is primarily one of power—within households, within workplaces, between people in domestic environments, and between actors (that is, voters) in any decentralized location where private, unimpeded Internet or telephone access to the voting process is a prerequisite.

Second, let us consider the psychological aspect of voting in equal or unequal circumstances. Let us assume that each person in a given household receives a PIN, which they can use to log in to an online ballot or to call in to a telephone ballot. The access to digital ballots in situ (in a person's home, where the PIN arrives by post) presupposes that all individuals in the household are respected, enjoy individual liberty and the freedom of thought, and the equal ability to practice their voting rights. The overarching assumption at play is that members of a household, regardless of sex, gender, economic status, physical status, cognitive status, or other forms of status, are equally unhindered in their voting actions by other voters or nonvoters in the household (or decentralized place of voting). A basic feminist analysis raises warning flags around these assumptions. The integrity of a one-person-one-vote principle is entirely undone in a patriarchal or matriarchal household—a household containing domineering or oppressive relations between its members, in which the recipient of a PIN does not have the necessary psychological or physical ability to vote when obligated to do so with no protective screen in place.

Not only might the PIN be expropriated and used by another recipient who has already voted, or who is not eligible to vote, or who does not want the dominated person to vote at all, but the psychological domination of some members of a household over others (including in cases of mental illness, senility, cognitive impairment, or youth naiveté) allows powerful authorities in households to control voting outcomes. When placed within the context of domestic environments, e-voting may provide no protective measures against the possibility of psychological domination and vote control.

It might be argued that voters are never fully equal in any case (domineering people might not allow subjugated members of a household to visit a voting site in person), but on-site voting does avoid the problems of domestically decentralized e-voting systems in which domineering authority figures can control the final act of voting. Those voters living in subjugated relationships who *do* manage to get to a voting site in person ultimately benefit from the last resort of a voting screen behind which they can mark a ballot in privacy without the immediate influence of the domineering agent.

In sum, power dynamics within households and other decentralized voting locations (such as the workplace) shape voting outcomes. Insofar as digital voting removes the private screen behind which a woman, a man, a disabled person, an elderly person, or a youth can express their personal political views, it fails to ensure "one-person, one-vote," potentially exacerbating inequality between voters. E-voting displaces the act of voting from a monitored site where paper, pencil, and individuated screen ensure egalitarian protections, to an unregulated, unmonitored, and potentially unbalanced site vulnerable to manipulation and domineering power dynamics.

Integrity and Anonymity of the Voting Process
Picture digital voting as it would have taken place in the case of the 2011 ALP leadership race. A person (let us say an ALP member, or a newly "registered supporter") would have received a PIN in the post with an envelope addressed to her- or himself. Inside the envelope there would have been a letter from the ALP, stating the person could use the randomly assigned PIN to log into an online ballot or telephone system to cast their preferential vote.

In the case of online voting, the person would have typed the URL for the online voting website into a web browser's address bar. She would have logged into the ballot using her PIN. She would have seen a ballot appear on the screen in which the names of the five leadership candidates appeared in randomized order from top to bottom (with each voter receiving what was claimed to be a randomly allocated lineup of candidate names, so that no one candidate's name consistently appeared at the top of the list). The voter would then have used her mouse to scroll over the names of the candidates and preferentially rate the candidates from one to five (or any number between one and five, as voters were not required to use all five preferential votes). A similar audio procedure would have occurred via telephone, but rather than using a mouse to scroll over names and type in numbers from 1 to 5, the voter would have used her keypad to select 1 to 5 for particular candidates as they were listed. The member would have then confirmed her selection, and her ballot would have been registered as cast.

But what happened in the ALP case after the member clicked "Confirm" or pressed the star key to confirm a telephone selection? The member's PIN would have been attached digitally to her voting preferences—her ranking of candidates from 1 to 5. That digital information would be entered automatically into a database that was also logging all other preferential votes submitted, each submission being attached to a particular PIN and possibly (or potentially) to a computer IP address. Telephone data would have been recorded in a digital database similarly linked to the member's PIN and (potentially) telephone number.

A number of questions emerge here. Since—in theory—PINs can be linked to names as well as IP addresses or telephone numbers, the member's name *could* be linked, indirectly, to her voting preference. To give credit to third-party service providers of e-voting systems, modern voting mechanisms and anonymity tools do allow for the disassociation in practice between PINs and voter identities to ensure anonymity in the process. However, the anonymity of a digital vote (whether cast online or telephonically) is always dependent, in principle, on those tools of disassociation being provided as a service to the client, in this case the ALP. The philosophical assurance of voting anonymity is thus dependent upon the operational assurance that the vote collector, vote storage agent, and vote counter have disassociation (or scrambling) tools available, that these tools function effectively, that the contract between the service provider and the client (the ALP) includes the purchase of these services, and that the third-party provider offers provisions assuring the use of these disassociation tools in all instances with a transparent mechanism for auditing the procedure.

In the case of the ALP, these operational assurances were nowhere to be found. If they did exist in contractual or internal form, the Liberal caucus was unaware, its Executive Board was unaware, its constituency presidents were unaware, its leadership candidates (and their campaign teams) were unaware, and leadership co-chairs (such as Cormican and myself) were unaware. Indeed, requests to obtain copies of the service provision contract with the third-party provider came to nothing, as no contractual documents were ever shared with anyone outside the ALP staff of Hogan, Ganton, and (potentially) the part-time intern. In addition, staffers hired *after* the 2012 general election to replace Hogan and Ganton, along with a newly elected party president, Todd van Vliet, were also unable to locate contractual documents upon request for this study. In sum, while third-party providers of e-voting systems may possess the aforementioned technical capacities, the ALP case study demonstrates no evidence of such technical capacity being agreed upon, paid for, or utilized in principle or in detail in this particular voting scenario, leading to questions as to whether assumptions of technical capacity always translate into practice.

A final issue in this respect relates to the ownership of the datasets produced by e-voting systems. Paper ballots can be stored in boxes for years, where their longevity is dependent upon their materiality. The disposal of material paper ballots effectively destroys the memory of votes cast. In digitized voting, by contrast, a table of votes cast (collected and tabulated) exists in digital form; the destruction of one copy of the database hardly implies the destruction of the data. Voting databases can be easily copied and shared—reproduced with relative ease. The philosophical assurance of the long-term anonymity of voters and their voting preferences is dependent upon the operational ownership of digital voting sets as well as the effective and operational destruction of all copies of voting datasets.

In the case of the ALP, lacking a transparent contract for services, it is impossible to know whether such assurances were in place. ALP staffers and executives who participated in this study between June 2012 and August 2013 report not being able to locate any information, contract, or paper trail detailing who (or what entity) ultimately owned the ALP leadership vote data, how it was managed, how it was shared, and how it was (if it was) destroyed. To this date, it is unknown whether the service provider contracted by the ALP created a database that recorded PINs, IP addresses, telephone numbers, and votes cast, or whether it scrambled and rendered anonymous data using accepted techniques for aggregating votes into indiscernible groups. It is also unknown whether the final tally and database of voting preferences was ever viewed by anyone outside of the third party provider (by any party executives or staffers). Last, it is unknown whether that database still exists or whether it has been destroyed. In the words of one long-time Liberal, "I assume someone out there knows how I voted, and that someone has a database that tells them how everyone voted." Whether this is true simply cannot be determined in the current case study, but it certainly does raise questions as to the level of detail required for digitized voting systems to ensure long-term and permanent anonymity of votes cast in such e-voting systems in the future.

In sum, the operational malfunctioning of the ALP leads to serious questions about the philosophical integrity of the e-voting process, and it highlights how serious provisions could be missed or overlooked by an entity overwhelmed by the financial and personnel resources required to ensure a free, fair, transparent, electronic voting process.

A COMPARISON BASED ON FEDERAL VOTING CULTURE

To highlight the philosophical effect of operational gaps evident in the ALP e-voting case study, it is useful to compare the example with some of the more prominent concerns set out by Elections Canada in its 1998 report, *Technology and the Voting Process*. That report explores digital voting processes and the realities manifest in potential e-voting structures at the turn of the century. In this section we review three of the most relevant standards of voting practice as described by Elections Canada with regard to formal federal voting procedures deemed "democratic" in the context of Canadian politics. The goal is to highlight key features of voting culture in Canada to understand what a typical Albertan voter would have been used to doing, and what a typical Albertan would have been justified in reasonably expecting, when casting a political vote (whether in a general or partisan election) as based on their voting experiences in Canadian (federal) elections.

According to Elections Canada, digital voting mechanisms are highly problematic; they are open to fraudulent manipulation due to a lack of cyber-security mechanisms that ensure votes cast in elections remain private, anonymous, and destroyable (Elections Canada,1998). The Elections Canada review of digital voting highlights seven areas of concern: registration confirmation; the ballot; casting a decision; ballot verification and anonymity of the elector; submission of the ballot; vote tabulation; retention and storage. Below, we explore the ALP case study to analyze the specific principles of registration confirmation, the ballot, and casting a decision.

Voter Registration Confirmation

Elections Canada reports the "the issue of effectively identifying eligible voters (e.g., PIN numbers, fingerprints, voice prints, retina scans)" as a significant hurdle for e-voting technologies (Elections Canada, 1998).

In the ALP case study, the party relied upon two databases for voter identification: the ALP membership list and the 2008 Alberta Electors List. In the first instance, members of the Alberta Liberal Party included anyone aged fourteen and over who paid a $5 fee to be a member of the party. "Members" did not have to be Canadian citizens, but they did have to be residents of Alberta. "Supporters" included anyone who appeared as an eligible voter on the 2008 Alberta Electors List. This meant supporters had to be at least eighteen years old, of Canadian citizenship, and resident in Alberta. If a "supporter" claimed eligibility to vote but her or his name did not appear on the Electors List, the ALP's vetting system was supposed to determine whether the person was a) a Canadian citizen b) lived in Alberta and c) over the age of eighteen. However, based on minutes of all-candidates meetings chaired by myself and Cormican, with ALP staff members and leadership team volunteers present, it is evident the ALP lacked sufficient personnel and financial resources to check individual names and qualifications manually. The party was unable to telephone the hundreds (and then thousands) of households appearing on the potential voters list which had been earmarked by leadership teams as potentially problematic.

By August 2011, as the list of "supporters" had grown to over 15,000 people, ALP staff members and leadership campaign teams further revealed the majority of those names had been added to the "registered supporters" list with no paper trail or individual digital trail; that is, supposed "supporters" had completed a "registered supporter" card neither manually nor digitally. The allowance of any kind of "registered supporter" became an *ad hoc* policy developed by ALP staff members as Hogan indicated a lack of institutional capacity to stop the phenomenon from happening or to check whether those individuals had expressed intentions to be listed on the ALP's potential list of voters (and thus be mailed PINs for voting).

Given the lack of paper or individual digital trails linking "registered supporters" to actual people, Hogan informed Cormican and myself of the ALP's developing protocol for voter identification: "registered supporters" who appeared on the list of voters (that is, those people whose names and addresses had been submitted to the party office as "registered supporters" by a given campaign team) were first cross-checked with Alberta's 2008 Electors List. According to notes from a telephone conversation between Hogan and myself (subsequently reported to Cormican), the ALP's proposed "cross-checking" and "scrubbing" processes involved use of at least two data points to verify a person's name against the 2008 Electors List. Either a name and address or a name and a telephone number or an address and a telephone number had to appear in combination on the "registered supporter" list to confirm the identity of the supporter. If the names, addresses and telephone numbers submitted by campaign teams passed this first check, the ALP automatically issued a PIN to the person's name and address regardless of whether the 2008 list matched current addresses or resident locations.

Alternatively, if a person's name *did not* appear on the 2008 Electors List, the name would be flagged but not removed from the ALP voters list unless an individual campaign team brought forward additional reasons for doing so. For example, names were sometimes flagged because of a spelling error in the name, an incorrect or incomplete address, or an incorrect or incomplete phone number. Problematically, the ALP did not have the financial or personnel resources to actually follow up in flagged cases. Instead, leadership teams were expected to investigate those flagged names (which numbered in the hundreds by the middle of August). Unless campaign teams brought forward evidence that the names or addresses did not correspond to real people, the ALP continued to issue PINs to the names and addresses it had received. Over 28,000 PINs were ultimately issued to households across Alberta by the first week of September. As justification for this low-maintenance system, party staffers presupposed PINs sent to homes where original inhabitants had moved, or to incorrect addresses, would simply be "returned to sender" rather than opened and used by other, potentially non-eligible voters.

Of the five campaign teams, only Hugh MacDonald's team had opened a fully functional campaign office with multiple full-time staff volunteers. Not surprisingly, MacDonald's team raised the most number of complaints pertaining to voter identification and the potential nonexistence of voters listed on the ALP voters list of combined supporters and members. In an instance of public outcry, MacDonald reported to news media, "I really don't think any campaign should have to use a séance to get their vote out." The "séance" reference alluded to MacDonald's belief the registered supporter list as it had been presented in its finalized form on 19 August 2011, the cutoff for adding supporters, contained dead people, nonresidents of Alberta, noncitizens, and even falsely constructed names.

MacDonald's reasoning was that because the ALP office had no means of verifying names on the list manually via telephone conversation, and because campaign teams lacked the resources to do so as well, the e-voting voters list was fundamentally open to abuse and falsification. As one reporter noted, "[Hogan] expected a precise number [of supporters] . . . after the list is scrubbed of duplicates and gag-names" (Gerson, 2011). But as that "scrubbing" process was fairly rudimentary, the ALP e-voting experiment unfolded with no clear or systematic protocol for follow-up confirmation or rejection of eligible voters. (There is no final tally as to how many PINs were ultimately sent, and no final tally on how many returned-to-sender PINs were sent back because of incomplete or incorrect addresses). As one participant in an all-candidates campaign team meeting stated, "This system means I could have just ripped a bunch of pages out of the phone book and submitted those as supporters." Despite informing Cormican and myself of a fundamental lack of staffing at the ALP office and a lack of resources to perform a systemic survey of names, Hogan nonetheless told the *Edmonton Journal*: "Nobody who has not proved their identification, either by being at the address that is on the electoral list, or by showing ID, is sent voting information" (Gerson, 2011).

According to Elections Canada, voter identification is one of the key ingredients in a free and fair election. The inability to identify "digital voters" (people who do not show up in person to vote) constitutes a major hiccup, and a preventative obstacle, to the fairness of digital voting (Elections Canada, 1998). One solution might be the introduction of additional technologies, such as "electronic signatures, voice prints, fingerprinting, retina scanning, and smart cards," all of which are costly. Elections Canada further notes each of the high-tech solutions proposed puts into question the privacy of the voter, given that an inordinate amount of personal and even biological data would need to be collected. The Elections Canada report concludes that although technological innovations might decrease the cost of digital voting mechanisms and identification procedures in the future, "issues related to privacy are more challenging and will require on-going assessment of Canadians' willingness to use such personal identification devices" (Elections Canada, 1998).

Elections Canada's assessment does not constitute a complete denial of digital voting possibilities. Critics could rightly point out that in federal and provincial elections in Canada today voter identification is neither guaranteed nor absolute. People without identification can still swear an oath in front of a deputy returning officer and poll clerk and in such (federal) cases they are often granted a ballot; this is, after all, how people with no fixed address (the homeless) can obtain a ballot to vote. In addition, in many jurisdictions in this country, voters who forget their identification cards at home can obtain a ballot by getting neighbors to vouch for the residency and identification of the voter at the polling site. Most voting mechanisms in Canada are thus open-ended, to ensure as high a voter turnout as possible and to ensure the homeless and economically disadvantaged are not prevented from voting by systemic barriers.

Digital voting, however, does seem to pose more potential sites for abuse, at least when judged by the outcomes of the ALP case study. The lack of a rigorous, systematic voter identification process warrants more attention to this issue at the partisan and general election level for policy-makers in the future.

The Ballot and Casting a Decision

The "current voting process" common across Canada is one in which voters cast their ballot "in person, at the polling station without assistance" (Elections Canada, 1998). The phrase "without assistance" is crucial. In Canadian federal and provincial elections, people with disabilities and people who require aid reading or understanding material on a ballot can use an "aide": a family member or friend who helps the person vote behind a private screen after taking an oath to abide by the person's intended desires in helping them to cast a ballot or in casting the ballot on their behalf. Those cases typically constitute a tiny minority of votes overall. The same cannot be said of digital voting.

Because there are no data currently available that demonstrate how many ALP voters, for example, were required to ask a friend, partner, child, neighbour, or fellow ALP member to "help" or "assist" with voting online or telephonically, I rely here on qualitative, lived experiences within my own network of voters as a means of narrating and describing the concern with greater detail.

In my household, two people—my mother and I—obtained ALP PINs allowing us to vote. While my mother does use the Internet, and she does possess reasonable computer skills (she can open a Word document, write a basic letter in English, save it as a PDF, and print it; she can open Skype and chat with her children overseas; she can log into Facebook and post messages to photos uploaded by family members; she can view various reward plans and the points in her reward accounts online, etc.), she still faces technical challenges in navigating new, confusing, or unfamiliar websites. My working hypothesis is that people like my mother are not exceptions even in the highly connected environment of Alberta. There are Albertans like her, of her generation (both native English speakers and English as a Second Language [ESL] speakers), for whom the Internet serves as an occasional toy but not a daily working or leisure tool. Thus, navigating new sites sometimes requires the introduction of new skills when the site exists for the performance of special or irregular tasks such as voting.

In the case of the ALP Internet ballot, the website was unfamiliar in design and purpose. To my mother (and to myself), the positioning of candidates' names on the ballot screen seemed oddly off centre, the text was too small to be read without reading glasses (or difficulty), and the process of finalizing or confirming the ballot was not immediately clear. In brief, I had to sit by her side to direct her to the appropriate URL, to indicate and explain what was appearing on the website, to help her move the mouse to the oddly placed check boxes, and to read the text explaining what the voter needed to do to enter preferential candidate selections. Finally, I had to guide her on clicking "submit" and closing the browser.

The ALP e-voting mechanism presupposed the process would be seamless and unproblematic for all members and supporters. But for people not fully integrated into contemporary digital culture, "assistance" is required for effective or successful digital voting. In the case of my mother, because my "assistance" was required, I know how she voted. If I were pernicious, I could have swayed her vote at the point of voting, or I could have simply voted for her given my access to her ballot and her trust in my digital skills. I did not have to take an oath in front of a poll director or a member of the party or even another member of my family declaring and confirming that I would not manipulate my mother's vote as I assisted her in casting her ballot, so there would have been no social opprobrium or pressure to not manipulate my mother had I wanted to. For people hard of hearing or for non-English speakers, the telephone ballot used for the ALP case study would have posed similar obstacles and required similar modes of assistance. The telephone system was operated by a digitized voice in English—factors that would have rendered the audio ballot potentially difficult to understand compared to a paper-based ballot. In sum, voting "without assistance" to ensure the privacy of one's vote is difficult and often uncertain when the voting mechanisms are digital and thus unfamiliar.

The difficulties manifest in the ALP case study warrant a much more detailed analysis of online or telephone voting in a world where not every citizen or voter is an equally skilled participant in digital culture.

CONCLUSION

The ALP's "registered supporter" system was meant to grow the party by allowing all Albertans (aged eighteen and over) to vote in the party's leadership race. On paper, this move extended the network of potential Liberal voters to more than two million eligible electors cited on Alberta's 2008 Electors List. In addition, the party's digital voting mechanism were supposed to allow for a relatively low cost voting system that would be easy to access, decentralized in nature, and open to all potential Albertans (with an Internet or telephone connection).

Of the approximate 28,000 "supporters" and members who signed up to vote by the end of the four-month leadership campaign, less than one-third (a total of 8,640 voters) actually cast ballots (Bennett, 2011; Kleiss, 2011a). The race did result in more votes cast in an ALP leadership race than ever before. But on a less sanguine note, it cost the party more money than any other leadership race had cost in the history of the party (in relative or absolute terms). Far from the presumed $30,000 price tag, the 2011 ALP leadership registered supporter and e-voting systems cost more than $100,000.

Perhaps more relevant, however, in the seven months that transpired between 10 September 2011 (the leadership vote day) and 23 April 2012 (Alberta's general election), support for the party waned rather than grew. In fact, it dropped so significantly that the party struggled to fill many constituencies with declared Liberal candidates by the time the writ was dropped by then Premier Alison Redford. The ALP scrambled to recruit and implant salaried ALP or legislative staffers to fill vacant constituency seats, including Ganton (the ALP operations officer) as the candidate for Vermilion-Lloydminster, Jonathan Huckabay (the ALP's chief of staff at the Legislative Assembly) as the candidate for Edmonton-Manning, and Amy McBain (the ALP's media liaison officer) as the candidate for Fort McMurray-Wood Buffalo. In the end, ALP leader, Raj Sherman, only managed to announce a full slate of candidates on 7 April 2012 – nearly two weeks into a four-week campaign (Wingrove, 2012).

In sum, the ALP's experiment with "registered supporters" and digital voting demonstrated a failure to generate interactive community-based support. The prophesied new generation of Albertan voter who would harbour a committed Liberal identity did not materialize. Contrarily, Election Day in April 2012 handed a damaging result to the party, cutting its elected human power in half. The ALP dropped from nine seats in 2008 to a mere five in 2012, continuing a negative trend from 2004, when it had boasted sixteen seats in the Assembly, rather than reversing the tide through voter "renewal." The ALP lost its status and funding as Official Opposition, and across the province it demonstrated significant loss in popular support, dropping from 26 percent support in 2008 to 10 percent in 2012.

While the number of supporters and members who voted in the leadership race in September 2011 had reached over 8,000, by April 2012 the ALP's own membership base had dropped back down to under 3,000 names, and it continued to pale in comparison to the Progressive Conservatives' more than 40,000 paid members. The "new generation" of Albertan Liberal that Swann, Ambtman, and Hogan had claimed would be attracted to the party by virtue of its innovative voting systems had not materialized. By contrast, democratic principles enshrined in the party's constitution in the one-person, one-vote principle and the assurance of anonymity of votes cast were weakened profoundly.

Far from being a panacea, digitally based voting in combination with broad-based voting systems reliant on digital registration systems for outreach require greater scrutiny, planning, financial investment, and neutral oversight to ensure gaps and obstacles manifested in the ALP case study do not unwittingly undo or dissuade voter engagement in Canadian elections (partisan or public) over the long term.

NOTES

1 Note the review of news sources and media rhetoric offered above is not a comprehensive one. A further review of journalistic discourse related to the perceived "youth"-driven NDP surge in Québec in the federal election is also of relevance, as those cultural constructions further supported the emergence within the ALP of a youth-oriented, digital-technologies-motivated, social-media-driven "renewal" agenda.

2 In the interest of full disclosure, I will also add that in December 2011, four months after the conclusion of the ALP leadership race that saw MLA Raj Sherman elected to lead the ALP by members and supporters, I won the nomination as the ALP candidate in Edmonton-Gold Bar, where I lost in the province's general election on 23 April 2012 to the Progressive Conservative candidate David Dorward.

3 In 2011, McIver sought and won the nomination to run as the Progressive Conservative candidate in Calgary-Hays, where he was elected to the Alberta legislature in 2012.

REFERENCES

ALP. 2011 (as amended 29 May). "Preamble." *By-Laws of the Alberta Liberal Party Association*, 1–22. Alberta Liberal Party, Edmonton.

Arnold, Nathan. 2011. "David Swann to Resign at End of Spring Session."
   Globalnews.ca, 1 February. Accessed March 24, 2013. http://globalnews.ca/
   news/6524/david-swann-to-resign-at-end-of-spring.

Bennett, Dean. 2011. "Raj Sherman Chosen New Leader of Opposition Alberta
   Liberals." *Canadian Press*, 10 September.

Braid, Don. 2010. "Nenshi Capitalizing on Social Media Buzz." *Calgary Herald*, 26
   September, A4.

Cryderman, Kelly. 2012. "Alberta Liberals Facing Make-or-Break Election; Holding
   Eight Seats Would Be a 'Major Victory'." *Calgary Herald*, 14 January, A4.

Cuthbertson, Richard. 2011. "Parties Look for New Ways to Combat Voter Apathy:
   Can Nenshi Factor Work on Federal Scene?" *Calgary Herald*, 28 March, A4.

D'Aliesio, Renata. 2010. "Alberta Liberals 'Back on Track': 2010 Year in Review."
   Calgary Herald, 23 December, A6.

Elections Alberta. 2011. Political Party Annual Financial Statement. January 1,
   2011 to December 31, 2011. Liberal Party of Alberta. Government of Alberta,
   Edmonton.

———. 2012. Candidate Summary of Results (General Elections 1905-2012).
   Government of Alberta, Edmonton. 21 December. Accessed March 28, 2013.
   http://www.electionsalberta.ab.ca/Public%20Website/746.htm#2001.

Elections Canada. 1998. *Technology and the Voting Process*. Government of Canada,
   Ottawa.

Forum Research Inc. 2012. "Conservatives Continued to Lead in the Polls; Wildrose
   up Since Last Month." News Release (18 January). Forum Research Inc., Toronto.

Ganton, Corina. 2011a. "A New Liberal's Guide to Change." Accessed March 24,
   2013. http://bit.ly/jLVMuh #lpc #ablib #cdnpoli #ableg; https://twitter.com/
   CorinaGanton.

———. 2011b. "At the #ALP board meeting. Love t/ debates. Its so great to b able to
   b a young person around this table. Many younger faces here." Accessed March
   24, 2013. https://twitter.com/CorinaGanton.

———. 2011c. "I liked a @YouTube video http://youtu.be/2vRiluWnL-I?a Gen Why
   Media Project." Accessed March 24, 2013. https://twitter.com/CorinaGanton.

———. 2011d. "The latest @albertaliberals news . . . #ablib #ableg LEADERSHIP
   RULES SET! WERE OFF TO THE RACES!" 2011. Accessed March 24, 2013.
   https://twitter.com/CorinaGanton.

———. 2011e. "The next generation is the Liberals' salvation."Accessed March 24,
   2013. https://twitter.com/CorinaGanton.

Gerson, Jen. 2011. "Liberal Hopefuls Question Growing List of Supporters." *Calgary
   Herald*, 20 August, A11.

Grant, Matt. 2011. "Politics Reimagined," Speech, ALP Convention 2011. 28 May. Calgary, Alberta. http://www.albertaliberal.com/blog/politics-reimagined/.

Hogan, Corey. 2011a. "Kickstarting Renewal." *New Liberal Initiative* 16: May. http://www.newliberal.ca/227/kickstarting-renewal/.

———. 2011b. "A New Liberal's Guide to Change." *New Liberal Initiative*, 22 May [cited 30 March 2013]. http://www.newliberal.ca/309/a-new-liberals-guide-to-change/.

———. 2011c. "YES!," *New Liberal Initiative*. Erick Ambtman and Corey Hogan, Edmonton.

Kleiss, Karen. 2011a. "Sherman Sweeps to Liberal Leadership; Former Tory takes 54 Percent of Vote for First-Ballot Win." *Edmonton Journal*, 11 September, A1.

———. 2011b. "Swann Gone as Liberal Chief: Move Paves Way for Renewal Within Fractured Opposition, Analysts Say." *Edmonton Journal*, 2 February, A1.

MacPherson, Jody. 2010. "Twitter and the ALP." www.albertaliberal.com, 28 October. http://www.albertaliberal.com/blog/twitter-and-the-alp-2/.

Massinon, Stephane. 2011. "Alberta Liberals Kick Off Leader's Contest." *Calgary Herald*, 8 May, A4.

McLean, Archie. 2010a. "Liberal MLA Kent Hehr Enters Crowded Field for Mayor of Calgary." *Edmonton Journal*, 6 May, B8.

———. 2010b. "MLA Quits Grits, Slams Swann; Dave Taylor Blames Liberal Leader for Party's Fortunes." *Edmonton Journal*, 13 April, A1.

Stone, Laura. 2011a. "Attracting Young Voters a Challenge." Leader Post, 4 April, A8.

———. 2011b. "Mobilizing Elusive Youth Vote a Challenge for Parties." *Ottawa Citizen*, 4 April, A3.

———. 2011c. "Parties Struggle to Attract Youth; Young Voters Care About the Issues, They Just Don't Like the Political 'Circus.'" *Vancouver Sun*, 4 April, B1.

———. 2011d. "Trying to Woo Canada's Toughest Voters—Youth; Students Passionate, Aware and Turned Off." *Calgary Herald*, 3 April, A7.

Thomson, Graham, and Karen Kleiss. 2011. "Swann Expected to Quit; Alberta Liberal Leader Plans to Discuss Decision with Caucus First, Party Sources Say." *Edmonton Journal*, 1 February, A1.

Wingrove, Josh. 2011. "A Swann Song for Alberta Liberals." *The Globe and Mail*, 2 February, A6.

———. 2013. "Alberta's Liberals Fill Their Slate of Candidates." *Globe Media*, 8 April [cited 31 March 2013]. http://www.theglobeandmail.com/news/politics/albertas-liberals-fill-their-slate-of-candidates/article4098649/.

13 Navigating the Mediapolis

Digital Media and Emerging Practices of Democratic Participation

Maria Bakardjieva

The relationship between the Internet and democracy has spawned an impressive body of literature stretching from the early years of the Internet to the present. Most of the discussion animating this literature revolves around the assessment of the "impact" of the Internet on democracy. This impact is described as either positive (enhancing, invigorating democracy through access to information and debate and low-cost participation) or negative (slacktivism, clicktivism, echo-chambers, incivility). More specific questions concerning the ways in which particular civic and political organizations have employed Internet-based media to advance their goals and participate in the democratic process have also been posed and answered. This chapter contributes to a more recent trend in the literature: it attempts to take the discussion beyond the straitjacket of "impact" thinking and to examine the relationship between the Internet (along with the numerous new communication media spawned by it) and democracy in particular instances, taking into consideration the complex social and political environment in which it takes shape. The question concerning the role the Internet and new media take on in contemporary democratic systems becomes a question of identifying more complex and contingent interactions, in which the technologies and communication formats associated with the Internet represent only one element among many. How critical is that element in particular democratic developments? What are the lasting consequences (if any) of its use by social actors pursuing their democratic interests and rights?

Here I will introduce, or rather reinvent, an anchoring concept intended to capture the web of interactions and mutual dependencies among citizenship, politics, and the media—that of the mediapolis (Silverstone, 2007). The mediapolis is constituted not only by media technologies, organizations, and content. It also comprises political bodies and civic formations, and importantly, individual people and groups living their daily lives. The mediapolis is indeed the nexus (although not always digital) where the trajectories of all these constitutive entities and forms of life meet and mesh.

The mediapolis as originally introduced is an apt metaphor for the interweaving of social and political life with communication networks and media discourses. At the same time, it poses a significant challenge: these intersections and interdependencies must be analytically disentangled in order to understand them in more concrete theoretical and practical terms. This is the project of this chapter. The question of whether the Internet and digital media have any positive or negative effects on democracy is not its concern; instead the focus is on discerning particular patterns in *how* these media are implicated in democratic processes. It will try to elucidate the inner makeup and workings of the mediapolis with the hope to put flesh and nuance in the place of the sweeping generalizations whose time has come and gone.

I have been a fascinated observer of the incorporation of digital media into civic initiatives and interventions for a number of years across different geographic locations. My project "New Media and Citizens' Voices in the European Public Sphere: The Case of Bulgaria" focused on a variety of instances of civic mobilization in my native Bulgaria, a former communist country and a newcomer to both democracy and the Internet. The project consisted in a series of qualitative case studies that relied on data collected from online publications and discussions, individual interviews with key participants, news media texts and shows, and official documents related to the events under consideration. The following analysis is informed by this dataset. I will present the individual cases only in a nutshell, omitting the details, and will aim at isolating the common threads and the specific lessons each case teaches students of the interplay between new media and democratic participation.

The quest for discovering the impact of the Internet on democracy has taken various turns, but one of its early and most popular tropes has been to ask whether the Internet has the potential to recreate the ideal-typical "public sphere," which according to Habermas (1989) was lost under the dual pressure of the market and the state. The concept of the public sphere has been a touchstone in the debates concerning the relationship between forms of communication, mediated or not, and democracy. It was only natural for academics to pick up that concept from their toolshed when trying to determine the value and promise of the newly emergent communication forms that computer networks have engendered. From early computer-conferencing systems through newsgroups, online discussion forums, Facebook, and Twitter, the question whether the public sphere is being enhanced and invigorated by the communicative practices evolving on these platforms has occupied researchers of democracy.

As much as optimism has run high, the use of the Habermasian public sphere as a benchmark when observing and assessing the deliberative quality of actual online interactions has produced disenchanting results. Already in early computer conferencing systems and mailing lists, researchers found the domination of some participants over others along with new sources of inequality, and most discouragingly, group polarization instead of consensus building (Kiesler and Sproull, 1992; Herring, 2003). As Internet discussion spaces became more widely available, and the number and diversity of people participating in them grew, behaviours such as flaming, incivility, and putting down opponents spread like wildfire. It became more difficult to find in these online fora the kind of rational-critical debate oriented toward consensus that defined the early bourgeois *Offentlichkeit* (Janssen and Kies, 2005). The tumultuous multivocality of the online discussion space defied the expectation that cool, self-disciplined, and disinterested exchanges in the name of the greater good had a chance to flourish. At best, the existing public sphere-like spaces on the Internet where issues of common concern have been discussed in the spirit of true public-mindedness have been homogenous in their ideological makeup and fragmented across fault lines of conflicting convictions and interests (Dahlberg, 2001). And all that was happening even before the market had reared its powerful head.

Once media corporations moved their business onto the digital networks, the online space quickly started transforming into a gigantic shopping mall and entertainment arcade (Dahlberg, 2005; Feenberg and Bakardjieva, 2006). The traditional corporate mass media and the failed public sphere of Habermasian theory herded public attention into the familiar pastures of mass consumption and light-hearted distraction, this time through a digital fix. This is not to say that the venerable tradition of democratic deliberation in the public sphere did not gain anything or was diminished. On the contrary, in small but significant ways the dynamics of the digital fora brought new and broader attention to the theory of the public sphere and helped illuminate some of its deficiencies. These fora gave numerous people the opportunity to enter public sphere-like situations and through trial and error to figure out what works and what doesn't in these spaces, what they are good for and what their limitations are. The notion that it is possible and indeed feasible to engage with others in a discussion of issues of common concern, even when these discussions did not produce glorious outcomes, steadily gained traction and became an element of the common sense of a wired and later wirelessly connected populace (Bakardjieva, 2008; Kaposi, 2006; Papacharissi, 2004).

A more practically oriented line of research on the democratic affordances of the Internet and digital media emerged from studies of organizational communication that sought to register the uptake and establish the relevance of digital communication media for civic organizations and movements (Bimber et al., 2005; Bennett, 2003; Bennett and Segerberg, 2011; Della Porta, 2011). To the extent that such organizations are seen as the main stakeholders and actors of civil society, it has been important to determine if and how their mandate is supported and expanded by digital communication networks. The research findings in this area paint a more optimistic picture in the sense that voluntary organizations have been shown to take advantage of digital media to construct a solid and effective communication infrastructure to support their internal interactions, both horizontally among members and vertically, from leadership to members. Organizations have been also proven to deploy digital media in connecting globally with partners and supporters and to build solidarity and undertake action across national borders. Their own structures have flattened and become more inclusive; they have made successful use of digital media as tools of mobilization and logistics in the course of larger and smaller initiatives.

A key aspect of digital media's role vis-à-vis civil society, however, remains unexplored in this framework, which equates civic involvement with formal organizing and explicit activism. That is the critical question of whether attention to and participation in civic issues and initiatives has gained a new chance to be wider and more inclusive beyond the very small cohort of those carrying formal organizational membership and those identifying themselves as activists. What about the rest of the citizens who are perhaps lured by the commercial pastures mentioned above, or simply bogged down in their daily concerns of breadwinning, child-rearing, mortgage-paying, and the rest? Does the digital communication environment make joining the organizations of civil society more attractive? Receding numbers of NGO members worldwide seem to indicate that this is not the case. And yet massive global initiatives as well as more and more frequently occurring civic actions, protesting, demanding, or charting political and social change at the national and transnational level, have been erupting around the world (CIVICUS, 2013). Technological determinism and cyber furor aside, in the complex mix of factors responsible for these initiatives, conspicuously and indispensably, analysts have found the smaller or bigger traces of digital media.

So then who are the citizens who join such initiatives? Where are they coming from if not from the organized entities of civil society? What do we know about their relationship with the public sphere and the political world? Papacharissi (2010) has offered an intriguing hypothesis concerning this question. She has argued that in the digital age citizenship gets individualized and privatized. Ironically, its locus becomes the private sphere, from where networked individuals express their personal views and selectively form thin and volatile alliances with others across the network in pursuit of privately meaningful goals. Publicly oriented activities, she notes, are increasingly enabled within a "digitally equipped private sphere," in which the individual has the opportunity to practice his or her new "civic habits with more autonomy, flexibility and potential for expression" (21). Papacharissi believes that in the private sphere individuals feel more in control of their civic fate, their civic autonomy, and individual identity. That is why it is the private sphere where contemporary citizenship withdraws and fortifies itself. The paradox of this privatized and isolated citizenship is only understandable when digital media are taken into consideration.

In an earlier study, I described the phenomenon of "subactivism" (Bakardjieva, 2009), a label that is also intended to capture the relationship between private life (or sphere) and public engagement. Based on in-depth interviews with Internet users conducted in Canada, I demonstrated that there are a variety of practices (or in Papacharissi's terms, "habits") by which people engage with public and political issues without leaving the realm of private life. To me, these are practices that remain largely subjective and submerged. They have to do with what

Giddens (1991) has called "politics of the self." These practices constitute the individual's efforts to make social and political choices in their daily life congruent with their personal values, or in more general terms, to be the person they want to be. They involve the exposure of individuals to public discourses and their responses to the positions offered in these discourses. I believe subactivism is the necessary precondition for any overt civic and political participation that manifests itself in the public realm, but, importantly, it is not all there is to citizenship.

Digital media indeed enable the individual to socialize his or her private thoughts and responses in an expressive mode. They do support a condition of "networked individualism" (Wellman et al., 2003) in which persons connect to others to the extent that their individual interests and choices coincide. But digital media by themselves do not guarantee an audience, a following and, most significantly, they do not guarantee *solidarity*. While expression can be anchored in an isolated private individual and select audience and attention can be given or traded among networked individuals, solidarity is the hallmark of the emergence of a collective—the moment where individuals recognize themselves in each other and articulate a shared goal and responsibility for developments going beyond their private lives. Solidarity can be experienced in a deeply personal way, but it goes decisively beyond the individual's private sphere and individualistic preferences. It involves other people beyond the immediate private circle, in negotiation with whom an issue, a principle, or a demand is attributed public significance and is defined as a shared object of engagement or action. Solidarity culminates in collective identity and collective action that attempts to make a difference in the public world. My argument, in contrast with Papacharissi (2010), is that the role of new media is not simply to allow citizenship to be drawn into and anchored in the private sphere, which they do, but to create a bridge between these privately meaningful civic sentiments and impulses and the larger field in which other people, organizations and institutions operate. This larger field can usefully be termed the *mediapolis*.

The mediapolis is a concept coined by Roger Silverstone (2007), in which he blends together the classical definition of the *polis* (following Hannah Arendt) and the idea that our contemporary relations with other people, be they private, public, civic or political, are fundamentally embedded in a media environment. In Silverstone's words the mediapolis is the mediated space of appearance where the world appears and in which the world is constituted in its worldliness, and through which we learn about those who are and who are not like us. It is through communication conducted through the mediapolis . . . that public and political life increasingly comes to emerge at all levels of the body politic (or not). (Silverstone, 2007: 31)

Unlike the private sphere, the mediapolis is, according to Silverstone, pluralistic and multivocal. Communication in it is multiple in form and inflection. It harbours conflicting and competing discourses, stories and images. Compared to the Habermasian public sphere, the mediapolis is uneven, fractured by power and difference. And yet it is inclusive in its own way because it is constituted in the practices of those who produce sounds, images, and narratives and of those who receive them. For my purposes, the most important feature of the mediapolis is that it mediates between the present and immediate realities of everyday life and the world that is spatially and temporally beyond immediate reach. The concept of the mediapolis captures the insight that the media have become a "second-order paramount reality" (Silverstone, 2007: 31), intertwined with the directly experienced world. Thus my choice is to look for the democratic affordances of digital media, not in the ways in which they, by themselves, make access and participation in the public sphere easy to achieve, or in the ways that they make citizenship an item of the private world of networked individuals. I choose to consider the effects of new media on civic participation by placing them within the complex tangle of the mediapolis where communication via traditional and new media formats intertwines with, and partly constitutes, the daily life of individuals in their capacity as spectators and participants. The mediapolis is the terrain where people form relationships with distant others in various forms and constellations. As such, it brings to everyday life new ethical and political dimensions.

From this perspective, then, the mediapolis is not only a public sphere because it is uneven, multivocal, and conflictual. It is not only a private sphere because it involves interaction, recognition, sociability, care, and solidarity with distant others. It is not only an organizational infrastructure because it reaches deeply into the daily lives of private individuals and becomes a conduit of the elementary agitation, engagement, and mobilization that precede any form of organizational life. At the same time, the mediapolis contains the essential elements of all these previous constructs. It emerges as a triple helix in which the strands of traditional media production and reception practices, new media use practices and organized collective action are tightly entwined. Democratic participation crucially depends on all these strands and necessitates their successful navigation. Consuming traditional media content could increase awareness of public issues and generate private discussions on these issues, but it remains enclosed in the shell of private existence, or, as I have argued with regard to subactivism, it remains subjective and submerged. Using new media formats could generate streams of free and creative interpersonal exchange outside of the immediate personal world, but it cannot exceed the limits of purely expressive efficacy. Organized collective action is citizens' best chance to impress the institutions and to bring about actual social and political change, but disconnected from the other two strands it is typically small-scale, isolated, and thus negligible. Therefore, in what follows my aim will be to identify strategies and forms of navigating the mediapolis that have succeeded in articulating the elements of the strands described above to achieve an effective civic intervention into the public and political world. With this task in mind I turn to my case studies.

BLOGS AND BLOCKADES: THE SAVE STRANDJA CAMPAIGN

The case of Strandja, a mountain in the southeast of Bulgaria that had its status of protected natural territory cancelled and then reinstated under pressure from citizen protests, captured my attention in 2007. This was a prominent example of consciousness-raising, mobilization, and action that spanned the full breadth of the mediapolis. At the core of the controversy captured by this case is a set of legal procedures initiated by interested corporations and municipalities challenging the natural reserve status of the mountain. Initially, the efforts to protect that status (and the mountain) from uncontrolled commercial development involved nongovernmental organizations, rich in legal and environmental expertise, but poor in influence and following. These organizations appealed to the political institutions and tried to intervene as a side in the legal hearings. Their claim was that the elimination of the protective mechanisms (sought on the basis of an administrative formality) would open the mountain for unbridled construction with devastating consequences for its natural habitat. These complaints and warnings, however, fell on deaf ears until the point at which the country's Supreme Administrative Court passed a decision in favour of stripping Strandja of its legal protection.

As this news surfaced in some traditional and web-based media outlets, environmentally conscious bloggers picked it up and started discussing it, vigorously amplifying its traction and significance. The Bulgarian blogosphere went on fire, spinning numerous interpretations of the court decision and making connections with endemic problems plaguing Bulgarian society, such as bandit privatization of public resources, judicial corruption, and political subservience to corporate interests. These thoughts and opinions originating from networked individuals travelled along the threads of interpersonal connections. They were eagerly reposted, commented on, and reframed via blog comments, online fora, e-mail, and SMS (social networking sites were still to gain popularity in this particular country at that time). The sites of the NGOs that had struggled against the decision started attracting traffic, and their positions and arguments were embraced by the online public. The online media, as one of my informants told me, threw the citizens' masses behind the otherwise isolated civic organizations. Excited and aware as the digital media users may have become, all the discussion was nothing more than chatter that could be easily ignored by the state institutions and allowed to subside and die out, especially in a country with less than 30 percent Internet users.

The events, however, took a different course, because on the critical day of the publication of the court decision somewhere in the space between the networked individuals with their private views, blogged as they may have been, and the structures of the civic organizations, a group of citizens marginally related to the latter created an improvised site calling for a street protest against the court decision, to be held at a specific time and place in the centre of the Bulgarian capital. Attracting a small but spirited crowd of protesters, this call made the issue fully erupt into the space of public visibility in Bulgarian society. The protesters, equipped with homemade posters, blocked a central street intersection, understandably attracting police and, subsequently, traditional media attention. Once the street protest made its way into the pages of the newspapers and the screens of the television programs, it elevated the long-neglected issue into a prime concern for the wide Bulgarian public. After a series of protest actions and escalation of media debates, this eventually led to a major shift in public opinion in support of the mountain's status as a natural reserve. At the time, the coalition government felt insecure, so the parties represented in the parliament swiftly agreed to overturn the court's decision and leave Strandja under legal protection.

Cutting through the details and country specificities, the case is indicative of the necessary connection between diverse actors in the mediapolis: formal civic organizations, private citizens and groups willing to engage and publicize their opinions on the issue, and traditional media journalists and organizations. The civic organizations contributed expertise and acted as watchdogs of the decision-making processes taking place in state institutions. Bloggers and forum participants translated the specialized terms and concerns into everyday language and spread the word across numerous intersecting circles of Internet users. They were also the ones that helped materialize the protest into real bodies and collective action. Finally, journalists and media organizations brought the turmoil into the living rooms of the majority of Bulgarians. Diverse spaces of mediated visibility—the online blogs and forums, the central squares of the city, and the pages and screens of traditional media—were also tightly intertwined in putting the issue on the agenda of the political institutions and compelling them to act on it.

While no clear-cut recipe can be extracted from the Strandja case, its analysis reveals the consciously or intuitively drawn trajectories through which civic engagement was able to break out of the confines of the private sphere and passive spectatorship and transform first into collectively targeted and conducted set of activities, and second into effective intervention into the public world and political decision-making. The various strands of the mediapolis were effectively connected through the work of key translators such as bloggers, online forum participants, and civic-minded journalists ready to break the story into the spaces of visibility provided by traditional media. The case threw into sharp relief the specific and indispensable roles of the various actors involved in the events—civic organizations, new media authors and users, traditional media, and the wider public, along with the functional links among them.

COOKING UP RESISTANCE: BG-MAMMA AGAINST GMO

A Bulgarian case revolving around adamant public resistance to the liberalization of the regulations on genetically modified organisms (GMO) offers a valuable opportunity to trace the fine mechanisms through which individual and small-group concerns shared through online media consolidated and transformed into an audible public voice and source of political pressure. A group of Bulgarian mothers frequenting a popular forum for discussing mothering, bg-mamma.com, formed a powerful alliance driving a wide public campaign against proposed legislative changes concerning GMOs. The collective action that originated from the forum discussions was the main reason the issue acquired wide public visibility and was eventually resolved by the political institutions in a way that satisfied the citizens' demands. That is why in the analysis of that case the main question posed is (to use Melucci's now-classic formulation): "How is collective action formed and how do individuals become involved in it? Through what processes do individuals recognize that they share certain orientations in common and on that basis decide to act together?" (1989: 30). The important new element that my study adds to this query is the interest in how digital media are involved in the construction of collective action. How do they help individuals bridge the conceptual and physical distances that separate their private spheres and come to understand themselves as a collective with shared identity and goals?

A careful look into the origins of the campaign leads to a thread of 700 posts that occurred in one of bg-mamma's forums, The Gossip Shop, which allows a wide variety of topics to be brought up for discussion. The in-depth analysis of the content and relationships constituted through this sequence of posts reveals the various dimensions of the issue, and the process through which individual views gradually blended into solidarity and the determination to act together, in order to bring about actual policy changes. The thread was initiated when a longtime member of bg-mamma called on fellow-participants to sign the petition started by the Coalition "For the Nature" (a coalition of environmental NGOs) regarding the proposed amendments to the Law on Genetically Modified Organisms that would allow growing GMOs in the protected (natural) territories. The Parliamentary Committee for the Environment was supposed to meet to discuss this amendment two days later and thus the author of the post insisted that an urgent response was needed.

Once again, as in the previous case, the initial formulation of the issue and its importance came from organized civil society, from the NGOs working in the area and concentrating significant scientific and legal expertise. They were the ones keeping an eye on the dealings of the parliament and blowing the whistle regarding the risks and potential detrimental consequences of the otherwise obscure legal amendment. Missis Emilia Spirolonova, the nickname of the bg-mamma user who made the initial post, acted as a go-between connecting the initiative of the NGOs with the interlocking social networks created in the process of longtime group discussion of privately significant motherly interests. Because of her status as a respected participant in the online community of mothers, her words were taken seriously and put up for consideration by forum members. Her call for urgent support of the petition was by no means blindly or obediently followed. After all, the site bg-mamma was little more than a space where networked individuals established casual relationships with one another, led by their particular motives and interests in specific topics. No agreement regarding the issue in question existed or could be easily reached, despite the interpersonal familiarity and previous exchanges among forum members. Thus, the issue was subjected to thorough critical deliberation in all its aspects: scientific, practical, economic, legal, political, and ethical.

The scientific debate asked what genetically modified organisms were and whether and how they could do harm to individual health and to naturally grown organisms that enter the traditional foods served at Bulgarian tables. Participating mothers took nothing for granted and went out to consult an impressive variety of sources, both strictly scientific and popular. The practical dimension of the issue was formulated around the role and responsibilities of mothers having to feed their families on a daily basis and thus to make decisions regarding the health risks of the foods they buy. The mothers involved in the discussion also considered the economic implications of GMO liberalization and what those could mean for traditional Bulgarian agricultural products and practices. The legislative and policy aspects of the issue had to do with Bulgaria's membership in the European Union, the legal obligations stemming from it, and the procedures through which legislative changes were implemented. The various possible economic and political interests implicated in the lawmaking were also debated at length.

Over the course of approximately two weeks and 700 posts, a small group of about twenty-five lay women and men traversed a steep learning curve to arrive at an informed decision as to which side they were on vis-à-vis the GMO debate. Their exchanges were not always levelheaded and cool, considerate and polite. There was heat, emotion, and animosity in many of the posts. And yet, the overall process contained all the elements of careful weighing of the positives and negatives based on evidence, reason, and deeply felt commitment to personal and public welfare. The meeting and clash of diverse personal views slowly led to the formation of several camps of opinion, to we-they differentiation, and thus to a set of political positions on the issue. Participants eventually identified with one of these positions and made further efforts to help their position win out in the debate. The consensus achieved by the group at the end of the day was imperfect. Those participants who did not share the opinion of the majority were not won over or integrated. They simply left. Those who stayed, for their part, were highly energized by the heated exchange. By working hard to convince others, they had reached a high degree of conviction of the merit of their cause and a feeling of responsibility for the future developments concerning GMO. They could not remain passive spectators any longer. They felt the need to do something to influence the course of events.

The next stage of the online discussion was marked by a search for the most effective ways for the group to intervene in the legislative process by making their position known to parliament and to the wider Bulgarian public. It was clear to them at this point that piling up arguments online would not make any difference. They came to the realization that the next logical step toward their now clearly set goal of stopping the proposed legislative changes would be to attract attention to the issue and to convince the Bulgarian public that lifting the tight control over GMO proliferation involved serious risks and poorly understood consequences. Once determined to act, the group had to come up with a series of steps that would take their voices and positions out of the online enclave in which they were initially formulated. Interestingly enough, as their first move to "materialize" their digital dissent, they collectively wrote an open letter to be delivered to the respective institutions and the mass (traditional) media.

After eight different drafts, crafted collectively through the online forum, the letter was finally completed and approved by the majority of the discussants. With the appearance of this text representing the collective will and position of online participants, a curious transformation from individual to collective identity and from virtual to actual involvement was set in motion. First of all, the open letter had to be signed, and so it became imperative to decide who "we," the co-signers, were. This led to the group's choosing to label itself as "an initiating committee of parents and citizens registered in the site bg-mamma." Then, the letter had to be printed out and distributed in a hard copy down formal channels, such as to governmental offices and the headquarters of media organizations. This required real people to knock on real doors and demand formal receipts confirming the delivery of their document. The online forum served as a management system distributing tasks and monitoring their realization. It helped individual actions to be collectively targeted and collective action to be implemented by individuals.

The progressive embodiment of the collective action that started with the delivery of the open letter went through several stages, including rallies in front of the parliament and in central places in the city. Drawing on its own social networks and with the help of supporters, the group issued information leaflets, organized a poster exhibition in a central place in the city, and produced an open-air concert, all aimed at attracting public attention to the issue. Once their digital voices materialized in the physical spaces of the mediapolis, the traditional media, up to this point reluctant to dedicate much coverage to the GMO debate, were compelled to step in. Although the coverage by television stations and newspapers was not always supportive of the protests, the work of some like-minded reporters gave the views critical of GMO sufficient public exposure. The mothers from bg-mamma, in the meantime, went on to build a wide coalition of civil-society organizations, including not only environmental NGOs but also agricultural producer associations and even the association of Bulgarian chefs. The position of this strategically composed united front could not be ignored by those in power.

The further stages of embodiment of the dissent involved the appearance of mothers with small children in the offices of the government and at the sittings of the parliamentary committee responsible for the legislative changes. The mothers recruited scientists and legal experts to provide evidence and justification for stricter control of GMO proliferation at this committee's meetings. After several months of struggle to influence public opinion via different initiatives by all interested parties, the parliamentary committee rejected the amendments and retained the more conservative regime of GMO regulation. Despite numerous legal imperfections in the existing legislation and control mechanisms, the wide opening of the door to the growth of GMO in Bulgaria was averted for the time being.

In the bg-mamma vs. GMO case one can clearly distinguish the already familiar strands of the mediapolis intersecting and enhancing one another, similar to what was observed in the Saving-Strandja events. Digitally mediated interpersonal and group discussions created the momentum that triggered street protests, generated traditional media coverage, and led to a shift in public opinion and eventually in institutional response. The intertwining of spaces and practices found to be central to the Strandja campaign, with some modifications, proved critical to the growth and success of the anti-GMO movement as well. Here, it was not individual blogs and sites, but an online community of interest that served as the cauldron in which the voices of individual citizens found resonance and grew in authority. The path to the pages and screens of traditional media once again passed through the streets and squares of the city, although not so much with acts of disobedience (blocking traffic), but in various creative and expressive forms.

Representatives of the mass media won over to the side of the civic action similarly played important bridging parts. The initiation of the anti-GMO campaign by a digitally constituted collective body offered a perspective on the fine transformation of private into collective meanings, interpretations, and positions, and the fluid conversion between individual and collective, virtual and embodied actions. The complex web of the mediapolis spanned and interlaced the everyday lives and private concerns of individual mothers, their publicly private online discussion, their initially modest and progressively louder and more visible pronouncements into the public spaces of the city and the mass media, their strategic interactions with civil society organizations. It brought their concerns into high public visibility and provided a platform for their dialogue with the political institutions. It was not the digital media alone, but the thoughtful navigation of the different strands of the mediapolis by the mothers that broke open the otherwise exclusive chambers of political decision-makers and allowed for wider participation in the regulation of GMO.

FENDING FOR THE FOREST: FACEBOOK FACEOFF

The third case that I turn to in my effort to cast light on the workings of the mediapolis is framed around a series of civic actions set in motion by a small group of young professionals in 2012. These actions targeted the proposed changes in the law regulating the use of Bulgarian forests. Convinced that the amendments were detrimental to the preservation of and public access to popular mountain destinations, and that they catered to the interests of a small number of commercial players, the group set out to "activate" a wide circle of citizens with a view to blocking the reform. The key members of the group described themselves as skiers and nature-lovers who felt they had a stake in the rules that regulated forest utilization. For years they had been worried by the fact that with the assistance of politicians and governments an effective monopoly—a small number of companies—was being established in the tourist and skiing industry in Bulgaria. Iconic skiing destinations were being taken over by powerful business monopolies that subsequently undertook unjustifiable and damaging construction projects in the mountains. The newly proposed amendments were going to free the hand of these companies to carry such projects even further and to consolidate their private control over these valuable public resources. "But could an ordinary person save a whole forest? Could such a person stop Tseko Minev [an influential banker with business interests in the ski areas under consideration]?"

These were the questions that one of the young skiers asked himself when he decided to start a blog looking at the developments concerning forest regulation and utilization practices in the country. He was a lawyer, and he combined knowledge, passion, and tenacity in his analytical commentary on the legislative measures and business developments concerning the forests. With time, his blog and his position became "recognizable," as he himself put it, among the main players and helped him make acquaintanceships with activists of eco-organizations. This contributed to the gradual process of his own "activation," as he described it. The notion of "activation" is central to this case. It captures the dynamic through which a private individual concerned about a public issue that is personally important to him/her steps out of the subjective and submerged "subactivist" (Bakardjieva, 2009) mode of operation and emerges into the spaces of appearance of the mediapolis, even if marginally at the beginning.

Other disenchanted skiers and snowboarders like the lawyer-blogger looked for their own ways to express their objection to the dominance of one particular company and its preferential treatment by the political powers. They organized an initiative labeled "Ride 4 Vitosha" where young people rode their skis and snowboards on Vitosha, a mountain close to the Bulgarian capital, to show that they were determined to stand up against backroom dealings that gave a select company a monopoly over the exploitation of the mountain. A short video narrating the issue and picturing the event was published on vimeo.com (http://vimeo.com/34606144) and gained over 4,000 views in a couple of days. Some media covered the action. More important, "Ride 4 Vitosha" became a Facebook profile that brought together people interested in the cause. Notably, at the time this case was unfolding, Facebook was already a prominent platform favoured by many Bulgarians, especially the young. It proved to be a key addition to the structure of the mediapolis, as it represented a space where private interactions among social networks of friends and family shared territory with public-minded issues and campaigns appearing in the form of Facebook groups and pages. Thus, it became a matter of a few clicks to pull the civic issues one supports or champions into the private horizon of people one personally knew, and vice versa, to find personal connections to the previously unknown others who supported civic campaigns.

In the experience of the group at the heart of this case, face-to-face meetings in cafes and clubs, gathering places of winter sport lovers, were also an important point of passage. These meetings could be then digitally written and thus perpetuated in platforms such as Facebook and in web pages. The diverse fabric of the mediapolis was thus thickened and strengthened around these particular actors and the issue they were championing. A closed Facebook group and a series of google.doc documents allowed them to discuss and organize internally. Subsequently, a carefully designed Facebook page became their communication platform and alternative medium from which they disseminated information and rallied supporters.

The real challenge to the group, however, was to complete what I referred to as "the triple helix of the mediapolis" by weaving in the strand comprising the traditional mass media, which provide the only straight avenue into the attention field of the public at large. Taking their message out into the mainstream media was not an easy task in this case because of intersecting business interests between the corporate players the group was critical of and media organizations. The young people had to be very creative in elaborating a strategy containing a whole range of forms intended to engage the mainstream. Their efforts could be seen as taking three main directions. Enunciating and sourcing is the practice exemplified by the blog of the young lawyer that spelled out the social and legal significance of the issue. It was further extended through the Facebook page collecting and interpreting information concerning the forests, their preservation and regulation.

Through skillful performance on such platforms, the group, now named "For Vitosha," managed to place itself as what Couldry (2010) has called a "source actor," that is, an actor who serves as a source for journalists and officials, and as such is able to exert conceptual influence on the framing of an issue. Beyond that, the online publications of the group, as members pointed out, served to translate the legal problematic into "human language," making it accessible and relevant to wider circles of people. A second distinguishable strategy is that of chiming and pestering. The group tirelessly instigated well-planned actions that attracted attention to the issue in artistic and playful ways: celebration of the end of a ski season that had never started due to the obstructions caused by the monopoly under attack; sending postcards to governmental and municipal representatives; decorating a central street bearing the same name as the mountain, Vitosha, with SOLD signs, and many others. Third, they became one of the main drivers of a substantive street protest that attracted several thousand people and blocked a central city intersection on the day the controversial amendments were voted in by parliament. This decisive takeover of a central space of appearance and the disruption of the normal course of city life, like in the cases previously discussed, led police and, along with them, the mass media to become engaged.

A populist government, which at that time was sweating under the critical scrutiny of the European Commission for failures and irregularities in its judicial and legal reforms, was finally compelled to directly address the issue. The prime minister invited representatives of the protesters to a series of discussions, and eventually, under public pressure, the changes in the law concerning the forests were vetoed by the president.

CONCLUSION

Although the cases recounted here offer solid ground for optimism, the farthest thing from my mind is to present them as recipes for civic success and, by extension, as an assurance that new media enhance democracy. On the contrary, the lesson I believe these cases teach us is that the new media are only one among many elements of the complex field of opportunities and constraints in which civic actors operate. In order for these media to become a vehicle of effective democratic participation, they need to be taken up in a way that transcends the established models, that goes beyond the rulebooks of the public sphere, but also beyond the secure and comfortable practices of individualized and privatized digital citizenship. The opportunities offered by the new media lie in their affordances for bridging, traversing, and interweaving these distinct realms and modes of operation into the fabric of the mediapolis. In the digitized mediapolis, visibility is never guaranteed to citizens, but it can be creatively accomplished through smart and open-minded navigation across isolated social and organizational realms. In terms of content and forms of discourse, the new media provide different levels of translation between social languages and cognitive frameworks. The writing of bloggers and Facebook group participants articulates complex legal, economic, and political issues in the everyday vernacular of ordinary citizens. Websites and forum discussions successively generate and elaborate on the signs and slogans carried in street protest. All these media taken together reframe the arguments put forward in newspaper articles and television shows.

Furthermore, beyond a focus on the struggle for visibility (Silverstone, 2007) and the importance of voice (Couldry, 2010b), a comprehensive concept of the mediapolis needs to include the question of audibility. Civic action in the media-polis would amount to no more than a social happening, performance, and feel-good self-indulgence, if it never achieves anything. Efficacy can have numerous dimensions and respective measures, but central among them are capturing the attention of the wider public and forcing the political and administrative institutions to respond to the demands of citizens. A series of questions along these lines arise from the case studies presented above. Who are the citizens and groups who marshal the new media technologies and expressive forms competently enough to attract attention and response? What (and whose) are the issues for the tackling of which new media prove to be appropriate and effective means? From the evidence produced by the three cases it appears that the success of the civic initiatives could be attributed to the combination of digital media affordances and the education and cultural capital (not just technological proficiency) of the middle and upper-middle class urban professionals who put them to work. This observation confirms a suspicion that has already arisen in the literature: namely, that the gift of content generation and creative expression through digital platforms and genres is far from equally distributed and gives advantage to certain classes of users and citizens over others (Hargittai and Walejko, 2008; Brake, 2014). The digital divides may be subsiding, but the visibility divides persist, even though their configuration changes.

The political and administrative institutions, for their part, face the dilemma of remaining deaf and rigid in the face of citizen demands, or on the contrary, of succumbing to knee-jerk reactivity without sufficient consideration as to how broadly shared and representative the vocal and visible concerns propagated by the digital media actually are. Yet another challenge is the need to discriminate between genuine and manipulated civic initiatives, because in the age of digital-ized production of visibility the race is on among powerful players to engineer their own "citizens' voices" and appearances.

In sum, when the full dynamics of the mediapolis are brought to light, the democratizing quality of digital media, only one of its components, can be neither neglected nor blithely celebrated. Democratic participation, it seems, remains as contested as ever. Access to it is contingent upon the coming together of new technologies of mediation and newly equipped civic agents who may be smarter and more numerous than the political and civic elites of the past, but who face their own challenges in a transformed field of opportunities and con-straints. The rules and figures of this novel quest for inclusion and audibility in a digitally enhanced mediapolis have only begun to emerge.

Bakardjieva, Maria. 2008. "Bulgarian Online Forums as Carnival: Popular Political Forms and New Media." In *Cultural Attitudes Towards Technology and Communication, Conference Proceedings*, ed. Fay Sudweeks, Herbert Hrachovec, and Charles Ess, 286–300. Perth, Australia: Murdoch University.

———. 2009. "Subactivism: Lifeworld and Politics in the Age of the Internet." *The Information Society* 25(2): 91–104.

Bennett, Lance, W. "New Media Power: The Internet and Global Activism." In *Contesting Media Power: Alternative Media in a Networked World*, ed. Nick Couldry and James Curran. Lanham, MD: Rowman and Littlefield.

Bennett, Lance W., and Alexandra Segerberg. 2011. "Digital Media and the Personalization of Collective Action, Social Technology and the Organization of Protests Against the Global Economic Crisis." *Information, Communication & Society* 14(6): 770–99.

Bimber, Bruce, Andrew Flanagin, and Cynthia Stohl. 2005. "Reconceptualizing Collective Action in the Contemporary Media Environment." *Communication Theory* 15(3): 389–413.

Brake, David. 2014 "Are we all Online Content Creators Now? Web 2.0 and Digital Divides." *Journal of Computer-Mediated Communication* 19(3): 591–609.

CIVICUS. 2013. *State of Civil Society 2013: Creating an Enabling Environment.* Johannesburg, South Africa, CIVICUS House. http://socs.civicus.org/wp-content/uploads/2013/04/2013StateofCivilSocietyReport_full.pdf.

Couldry, Nick. 2010a. "New Online News Sources and Writer-Gatherers." In *New Media, Old News: Journalism and Democracy in the Digital Age*, ed. Natalie Fenton, 138–52. Los Angeles, CA: Sage.

———. 2010b. *Why Voice Matters: Culture and Politics after Neoliberalism.* London: Sage.

Dahlberg, Lincoln. 2001. "The Internet and Democratic Discourse: Exploring the Prospects of Online Deliberative Forums Extending the Public Sphere." *Information, Communication and Society* 4(4): 615–33.

———. 2005. "The Corporate Colonization of Online Attention and the Marginalization of Critical Communication." *Journal of Communication Inquiry* 29(2): 160–80.

Della Porta, Donatella. 2011. "Communication in Movement: Social Movements as Agents of Participatory Democracy." *Information, Communication and Society* 14(6): 800–819.

Feenberg, Andrew, and Maria Bakardjieva, "Consumers or Citizens? The Online Community Debate." In *Community in the Digital Age*, ed. Andrew Feenberg and Darin Barney, 1–27. Lanham: Rowman and Littlefield.

Giddens, Anthony. 1991. *Modernity and Self-Identity: Self and Society in the Late Modern Age*. Stanford, CA: Stanford University Press.

Hargittai, Eszter, and Gina Walejko. 2008. "The Participation Divide: Content Creation and Sharing in the Digital Age." *Information, Communication and Society* 11(2): 239–56.

Habermas, Jürgen. 1989. *The Structural Transformation of the Public Sphere: An Inquiry into a Category of Bourgeois Society*. Cambridge: Polity.

Herring, Susan. C. 2003. "Gender and Power in Online Communication." In *The Handbook of Language and Gender*, ed. Janet Holmes and Miriam Meyerhoff, 202–28. Oxford: Blackwell Publishers.

Janssen, Davy, and Raphael Kies. 2005. "Online Forums and Deliberative Democracy." *Acta Politica* 40: 317–35.

Kaposi, Ildiko. 2006. *Virtual Deliberation: An Ethnography of Online Political Discussion in Hungary*. Ph.D. dissertation, Central European University, Budapest.

Kiesler, Sara, and Lee Sproull. 1992. "Group Decision Making and Communication Technology." *Organizational Behavior & Human Decision Processes* 52: 96–123.

Melucci, Alberto. 1989. *Nomads of the Present: Social Movements and Individual Needs in Contemporary Society*. Philadelphia: Temple University Press.

Papacharissi, Zizi. 2004. "Democracy Online: Civility, Politeness, and the Democratic Potential of Online Political Discussion Groups." *New Media and Society* 69(2): 259–83.

———. 2010. *A Private Sphere: Democracy in a Digital Age*. Cambridge: Polity.

Silverstone, Roger. 2007. *Media and Morality: On the Rise of the Mediapolis*. Cambridge: Polity.

Wellman, Barry, Anabel Quan-Haase, Jeffrey Boase, Wenhong Chen, Keith Hampton, Isabel Díaz, and Kakuko Miyata. 2003. "The Social Affordances of the Internet for Networked Individualism." *Journal of Computer-Mediated Communication* 8(3). http://jcmc.indiana.edu/vol8/issue3/wellman.html.

14 The Construction of Collective Action Frames in Facebook Groups

Sharone Daniel

In his book *Talking Politics* (1992), William A. Gamson argues that the construction of the three collective action frames of injustice, identity, and agency are fundamental to building a social movement, as movement members use the frames to identify an unjust situation, develop a sense of collective identity, find an appropriate target, and take action—though not necessarily in that order. In this chapter, I use the theory of collective action frames to partially explain the success of one Facebook group in mobilizing its members to take continuous, targeted, collective action and the failure of another group to do the same. Kullena Khaled Said, the Egyptian group that eventually sparked off the Egyptian revolution, managed to mobilize members to organize and carry out political actions against Hosni Mubarak's regime; Justice for Damini, a page started in protest of the brutal rape of a twenty-three-year-old woman in New Delhi in 2012, amassed 70,000 members in the space of a few weeks and then faded out in the next few weeks, ostensibly failing to make a lasting impact (though the larger movement that it was a part of did so). Although the concept of leadership is not a focal point of this essay, I hope that the reader will take note of the many ways in which this element differentiated Kullena Khaled Said from Justice for Damini.

Data used in the analysis of Justice for Damini was taken principally from the text and hyperlinks of the Facebook page itself, whose content was written in both English and Hindi, in both of which I am conversant. Data used in the analysis of Kullena Khaled Said is based in large part on the book *Revolution 2.0: The Power of the People is Greater than the People in Power—A Memoir* (2012), written by Wael Ghonim, the creator and administrator of the Egyptian group, as well as on news clippings of the event. Unfortunately, all of the content in Kullena Khaled Said is in Arabic, a language I cannot read. All of content from Kullen Khaled Said mentioned in this essay is thus taken from Ghonim's book, which contains a large number of translated posts and comments. This biases the study somewhat, as it means that the analysis is based upon the posts and responses that Ghonim considered important or relevant enough to translate in presenting his story.

Unfortunately, only five members of Justice for Damini and two members of Kullena Khaled Said agreed to and went through with an interview or sent me back a questionnaire, despite repeated requests. My efforts to contact Kullena Khaled Said members in particular were severely hampered by the fact that the group's administrators blocked both themselves and all the members of the page from posting any kind of content on it just as I began contacting people. I have thus chosen not to make any inferences from this data or to include it in my analysis. I have mentioned the responses I received at several points in the essay, however, for what they contribute in suggesting possible hypotheses for further study and verification. All names have been changed for the sake of anonymity.

APPLICATION OF COLLECTIVE ACTION FRAME THEORY IN A DIGITAL CONTEXT

Gamson's framework is easily applied to an online context, especially one in which the principal form of communication is publicly available (and understood by the author). This is because it is possible to track the development of each of the collective action frames through the neat, chronological, time- and date-stamped posts and conversations that occurred online. The danger is in the fact that there may be significant incoherence between what was written and expressed and what was felt, thought, and acted upon. However, the average member is privy to the same data as the researcher, thus making what is available online paramount. Access to private conversations, digital or otherwise, may bring out different information, pointing perhaps to a nucleus of actors with different or stronger collective action frames, but this does not take away from whatever is discovered about the larger group. Nonetheless, the possibility of a gap remains, all the more so when dealing with offline actions. While communication among members before, during, and after the event is still available for the researcher to analyze, not everything that took place when disconnected will make it to the Internet. Personal interviews help to fill in both of these gaps in knowledge. Obstacles to personal contact in groups of this size can be overcome by travelling to the region where the movement took place.

BACKGROUND

At the beginning of June 2010, pictures of the deceased twenty-eight-year-old Khaled Said's brutally disfigured face were posted online and went viral. Said had been tortured and killed by Egyptian police officers. After he saw the pictures of Said's face, Wael Ghonim, the head of marketing for Google Middle East and North Africa and an Egyptian living in Dubai, started a Facebook group called Kullena Khaled Said (We are all Khaled Said). A total of 36,000 young Egyptians joined the group on the first day, and it continued to grow at a phenomenal rate over the next few weeks. During the first couple of months of its existence, the page organized both online and offline political actions and then went quiet for a period. Following the downfall of Tunisia's dictatorship over six months later, Kullena Khaled Said decided to call for an Egyptian revolution. Ghonim created a Facebook event inviting Egyptians to begin the revolution on 25 January 2011, ten days later. Within two days, 27,000 people had RSVP'ed their participation. Many other movements, opposition parties, and activists worked together to promote, coordinate, and plan the event, which succeeded in ending Hosni Mubarak's thirty-year dictatorship within eighteen days. Though there were two administrators for Kullena Khaled Said, this essay focuses on Ghonim's actions as he reports them.

The Delhi Rape Case involved the brutal gang rape of a twenty-three-year-old Indian woman who was given the pseudonym "Damini" by the Indian media. Damini was gang-raped repeatedly by six men in a moving bus on 16 December 2012. The nature of the crime was so violent that Damini had to have most of her intestines removed and would never have been able to eat or drink again had she survived. She passed away thirteen days after the incident, on 29 December. Over the course of these thirteen days and following her death, India held mass protests calling for the death of the accused and for better security for women, among a series of other demands. During this time, various Facebook groups in support of Damini were created, the largest of which was and is Justice for Damini with over 70,000 members.

RATIONALE FOR COMPARISON

I chose Kullena Khaled Said because it was clearly a Facebook group that stood apart in terms of its mobilizing and acting power. I chose to compare it to Justice for Damini because, like Kullena Khaled Said, it was composed largely of young people and emerged in response to a crisis due to a situation of extreme injustice committed against another young urban educated person. Both groups increased extremely rapidly in membership and had anonymous administrators during the period studied in this essay. Both groups were also Facebook "pages." This means that only the group's administrator(s) could post content onto the "wall" or interface that is immediately visible upon accessing the page, giving the administrator significant control over the page's immediately visible content. Furthermore, given Kullena Khaled Said members' explicit desire not to associate themselves with political youth, as well as their rather negative view of the same, and Justice for Damini members' lack of critical political discourse and action, both groups were likely composed largely of unpoliticized youth.

That said, the groups also had important differences. Khaled Said was attacked by employees of the state because he was perceived to be a threat against an autocratic regime, while Damini was targeted by members of civil society because she was a vulnerable female. The Egyptian group was thus responding to physical violence while living under a repressive regime and the Indian group was responding to sexual violence while living within a democracy. The degree to which Damini and Said's suffering was focused on may have been different but their suffering was nonetheless a vital factor in spurring people on to action. In addition, although the link between Said's death and systemic problems may have been far more obvious to the average citizen, Damini's death has played a significant role in a movement toward safety and equality for women in India. As such, though the groups are not exactly the same, making a comparison between them is not unreasonable.

COLLECTIVE ACTION FRAMES: INJUSTICE

The collective action frame of injustice requires two elements: moral indignation and a motivated person or entity that is at least partially to blame for the injustice. Turner and Killian argue that a social movement cannot exist without a sense of moral indignation and the belief that some "established practice or mode of thought is wrong and ought to be replaced." Moral indignation is composed of "righteous anger" or an emotionally based understanding of "inequity," as well as, but not necessarily entailing, an intellectual understanding of the same. The former component was very prominent in the creation of both Kullena Khaled Said and Justice for Damini (Gamson, 1992: 32).

Righteous Anger

In Wael Ghonim's words, after he saw the pictures of Khaled's brutally disfigured face and read what had happened to him he "felt miserable, frustrated, and outraged," and was "unable to control the tears flowing from [his] eyes." While other elements influenced Ghonim's decision to create the group and dedicate large amounts of time to administering it, such as the fact that he was an Internet junkie and believed strongly in the power of technology to spark change, it was Ghonim's emotional reaction to Khaled's pictures that initiated his desire to create the page. It was also the element that regularly reignited his desire to fight against injustice in Egypt, once the group was underway (Ghonim, 2012: 51, 89).

If one visits Justice for Damini's page on Facebook, there is a similar outpouring of emotion. The group's description asks people to like the page "to show all the criminal bastards rapists [sic] that WE ARE ALL FOR ONE AND ONE FOR ALL" (capitals in original). The second post on the page is a letter full of rage and sorrow addressed to the rapist (at this point it was not yet known that there were six men involved), that calls him a murderer, thief, terrorist, and bloody dog, among other things. The majority of comments posted on the page express similar feelings of sadness and deep anger (Justice for Damini, 2012).

The same strong sentiments spill over into the interviews and questionnaires. Priyanka, for example, said that the group is good because it helped many people "feel the pain of Damini" (response to questionnaire, 12 August 2013), while Sumaiya wrote that she joined the group because "as a human you cannot ignore [the rape] and more[over], being a woman, you can imagine what was the situation at that moment of the attack [sic]" (Response to questionnaire, 9 August 2013). Bipen, who joined Justice for Damini and then created his own group in order to better express his opinions and views, said "when I read about the news of what had happened, I cried a lot coz I felt that it was the most painful way one could die. I felt terrible about what had happened" (Response to questionnaire, 4 August 2013).

Motivated Actor

Righteous anger is not enough to construct a collective action frame of injustice, however. A group of people must also be able to identify an actor, whether it is an individual, a corporation, a tradition, or a government policy, that is at least partially to blame for the act. This actor must be neither overly abstract nor excessively concrete. If the cause of an injustice is too abstract, or "actorless," such as "the system, society, life, and human nature," it makes it difficult or impossible to understand how the situation of injustice can be changed, and can lead to people feeling powerless and/or accepting that the situation "is the way it is." At the other extreme, "in concretizing the targets of an injustice frame, there is a danger that people will miss the underlying structural conditions that produce hardship and inequality" (Gamson, 1992: 32–33).

From reading the page's posts in Justice for Damini one can easily and justifiably come to the conclusion that Justice for Damini was unable to identify a suitable motivated actor and that this left the group without an appropriate target to organize against. The administrator and commenters were, for the most part, overly specific when naming the enemy. Much of what they shared was brimming with anger, disgust, sadness, and a desire to see the rapists punished. This was not problematic in and of itself. However, once all the rapists had been apprehended, a judicial process begun against them, and a committee set up to review the country's rape laws, there was not much more that protesters could rally behind that specifically concerned these six rapists. They were, after all, six random men, unconnected to a larger organization, public or private, and acting of their own volition. But this does not mean that another motivated actor could not have been identified and targeted. Certainly, the media and street protests were offering up several possibilities. One of these was the aforementioned culture that has not yet managed to teach men that sexual violence against women is unacceptable. Another was the Delhi police themselves, who systematically and overtly contribute to victim blaming and impunity (Bhalla et al., 2012). There were a number of appropriate, motivated actors or "enemies" for the movement to target.

Those posts that did offer up an alternative target suffered from the malaise of generality. For example, two posts that brought up the concept of a culture of rape blamed the whole of society for the problem. One of them, entitled "Behind every rapist" (posted on 21 December 2012), listed everyone from the "father who treated his wife as a slave" to "a legal system which has a provision for rape victim to marry her rapist" to the very people protesting against Damini's rape as the culprits. Although it was an insightful, if not perfect, post, it was a potentially fair critique, it was so all-encompassing that it ended up making the "actor-less" entity of "society" responsible for violence against women. Predictably perhaps, the comments that followed that post focused on changing oneself, and included vague appraisals of the entire Indian culture and society. They say things like "first we should change ourselves, and then our country," "Indian culture and society sucks," "we all have to change our mentality first," and "So, all of [us] are indirectly responsible for this incident . . . from now on we must be courageous enough to raise our voice and stand together against any kind of injustice." Only one comment was more focused, but no one, including the administrator, made any attempt to encourage the person's thoughts or to guide the conversation in any way.

When posts related to root causes or taking collective action were posted, they suffered from a lack of follow-through in pursuing the topic or action. For example, on 20 January, the administrator asked members to organize events and send in the links to events. This was an excellent if unfocused initiative, but, while it is true that only a handful of the 197 posts that followed contained even a par-tially formed idea of an event, none of these were commented on or reposted by the administrator so as to encourage such thinking and/or to give the seeds of ideas greater visibility. Not even one excellent initiative of a petition asking the government to force those politicians who had been accused of rape to step down was reposted. As such, the administrator as well as other members failed to play the much-needed role of leader or coordinator within the group, and to identify the "broader structure" in which the rapists were operating (Gamson, 1992: 33). Doing so might have given followers of the page a target to organize themselves around once the rapists had been apprehended and the judicial process against them begun. But it would also have been an enormously time-consuming task. Ghonim states that he dedicated so many hours to the page that he neglected both his family and work to care for it (Ghonim, 2012: 110).

Interestingly, one interviewee, Bipen, from Justice for Damini, specifically complained that the group administrator did not identify the "actual causes of " and "main reasons" behind the rape, the latter of which he identified as the Indian system of law and order. He felt that it was the administrator's respon-sibility to do this, and his/her failure to follow through with that responsibil-ity had a negative impact on the group. He created his own group, in order to "make at least the ppl of my country aware of wat wrong is going on ..." and felt that "people's awareness about injustice that exists in society against women" was lacking (Response to questionnaire, 4 August 2013). Another interviewee,

Rohan, also felt that the group was ineffective, but blamed the medium of the Internet for this problem (Interview with author, 27 July 2013).

Wael Ghonim, on the other hand, immediately identified "the corrupt practices of the Ministry of Interior, our repressive regime's evil right hand" as a concrete but not overly specific actor. This actor, and others that emerged, were not named explicitly in Ghonim's earliest posts. Right from the beginning, however, justice for Said was framed within a larger discourse of justice and freedom for all group members. For example, the first post read, "Today they killed Khaled. If I don't act for his sake, tomorrow they will kill me." The second read, "People, we became 300 in two minutes. We want to be 100,000. We must unite against our oppressor." Soon enough, Ghonim "began to focus on the notion that what had happened to Khaled was happening on a daily basis, in different ways, to people we never heard about." It would not have been a stretch, by any means, for Justice for Damini's administrator to make the same links between, for example, rape and a rape culture. This is not to say that Kullena Khaled Said did not also focus on justice for, specifically, Khaled Said, or that their chosen motivated actor was always coherent and stable; however, as an administrator Ghonim always returned to or included a broader vision of justice (Ghonim, 2012: 59–60). Zeeshan, a follower of Kullena Khaled Said, supported this idea in my interview with him. He stated that he learned to be political through the group (Interview with author, 14 August 2013).

COLLECTIVE ACTION FRAMES: IDENTITY

Moving on to collective identity, we find a slightly more complex situation. There are numerous measures of collective identity, and the consistent lack of high correlation between these measures shows that it is not "a unidimensional construct" but a multidimensional one (Ashmore, Deaux, and McLaughlin-Volpe, 2004: 100). Therefore, it is not likely that any one group will display or report the existence of all the elements. Since the list of elements that are connected to collective identity is extensive, I have chosen to focus on six of the seven main elements that, according to Ashmore et al.'s in-depth analysis of two decades of collective identity studies, are considered basic to collective identity. Gamson's definition of collective identity and Donatella della Porta and Mario Diani's understanding of the production of identity and identification rituals also provide part of the theoretical framework in this section.

The list produced by Ashmore et al. (2004: 84–93) includes self-categorization, evaluation, importance, attachment and a sense of interdependence, social embeddedness, and behavioural involvement. Much of this is self-explanatory. *Self-categorization* refers to the action of identifying oneself as a member of a particular group. It is virtually impossible for any other form of collective identity to exist without self-categorization. *Evaluation* follows quickly on its heels and refers to the positive or negative way that one evaluates, or feels that other people evaluate, the group that one identifies oneself as being a part of. *Importance* refers to the "degree of importance, from low to high, of a particular group membership to the individual's overall self-concept." *Attachment and a sense of interdependence* refers either to "the affective involvement a person feels with a social category or the degree to which the fate of the group is perceived as overlapping with one's personal fate." *Social embeddedness* is concerned with just how important a collective identity is in terms of one's social relationships. In other words, it refers to how many friends and family members belong to the same group that one is in. *Behavioural involvement* is concerned with "the degree to which the person engages in actions that directly [implicate] the collective identity category in question." For Gamson,

> The identity component refers to the process of defining this "we," typically in opposition to some "they" who have different interests or values. . . . Collective action requires a consciousness of human agents whose policies or practices must be changed and a "we" who will help to bring the change about. (Gamson, 1992: 8)

Let us begin by tracing the emergence of this sense of "we-ness" within Kullena Khaled Said through the group's participation in collective actions. Using Donatella della Porta and Mario Diani's understanding of the production of identity and identification rituals, I argue that, when organizing and taking part in collective actions, group members adopted specific "models of behaviour" that built up and reinforced the movement's identity. These models of behaviour included objects such as an identifier, "that enable[s] supporters of a particular cause to be instantly recognizable," and a character, Khaled Said, who "played an important role . . . in the development of [the movement's] ideology." By using these "objects" in collective actions, group members were clearly differentiated from "ordinary people" and "their adversaries" (della Porta et al., 1999: 97–98).

The first action that Ghonim urged group members to participate in was a public funeral for Khaled Said, organized by another youth movement, and other groups and activists. It is impossible for me to say whether or not group members attended the funeral, which was attacked by police. However, their participation appeared to have little or no effect on collective identity within Kullena Khaled Said. Then Ghonim suggested an action that "belonged" to the group. That is to say, the administrator of Kullena Khaled Said thought of the idea and asked those who belonged to the group to participate. The idea was for members to change their profile pictures to "an anonymously designed banner of Khaled Said, featuring him against the backdrop of the Egyptian flag, with the caption "Egypt's Martyr." Ghonim reports that "thousands responded positively." It was a low-risk and easy action to participate in, which was and still is common in the world of Facebook. The action asked members of Kullena Khaled Said to somewhat publicly identify themselves with the group by changing their online "clothing"—their profile pictures. In doing so, they simultaneously asserted their difference from those who had killed "Egypt's Martyr" as well as from those who had not, or had not yet, joined the group. By using a character of the movement, Khaled Said, within the logo, those who participated in the campaign were reinforcing their identity as a movement concerned with the death of Khaled Said (Ghonim, 2012: 63, 67).

In the second action, Ghonim asked members to photograph themselves holding up a paper sign that said Kullena Khaled Said:

> Hundreds did so, and we began to publish their pictures on the page. The images created an impact many times stronger than any words posted on the page. Males and females of all backgrounds, aged between fourteen and forty, now personified the movement. (2012: 68)

Again, members adopted an identifier, the name of their group, which set them apart from their adversary and from other people, in a situation of risk, and thus strengthened their sense of "we-ness." After these two actions, the movement virtually flowed.

The third action the group organized and participated in was the Silent Stand, an offline action that was a group member's suggestion. The idea was for members to wear black t-shirts, another identifier, and stand along the coast in Alexandria for an hour, five feet apart from each other, silently expressing their "disapproval of the injustice inflicted upon Khaled Said." Preparing for the action involved a great deal of collaboration among group members and ultimately required them to demonstrate their disagreement with the regime in public. Even before the action took place, it is possible to see the group's collective identity gaining form and strength. For example, members decided that they wanted to "send out a clear message that although we were both sad and angry, we were nevertheless nonviolent" (Ghonim, 2012: 70, 72).

Ghonim takes these desires and feelings being expressed by group members and reinforces them in a post that boldly asserts who the group is and is not, even giving group members the collective identity of "the Facebook youth": "We are not an organization . . . and we are not a political party . . . we have no motive other than to express our opinion in a civilized manner. . . . I swear the whole world will marvel at the Facebook youth" (2012: 72). In my interview with Zeeshan, he proudly asserts that he as well identified himself as the Facebook youth (August 14, 2013).

When the group was attacked by the government and state-owned newspapers for organizing the Silent Stand, the group's digital identity was further strengthened, as it articulated and defended its identity in the face of those who were trying to give it another, less honorable, one:

> Do you know why the media are attacking Facebook? Because it does not receive bribes to publish false stories . . . and it does not succumb to security pressure and delete a story. . . . Facebook became our means to express our opinions, ambitions, and dreams without pressure from anyone. . . . Now our message reaches as far as their biased newspapers . . . but our message is our own. . . . We are Egyptian youth who love one another, care for one another, and have a voice. (Ghonim, 2012: 74)

After the event took place, a number of people criticized it, arguing that it had done nothing to change reality and was, furthermore, foolish. Here Ghonim's post in response to these criticisms marks a clear line between the group's members and a "them" that is not the motivated actor against whom they are collectively taking action. He wrote "many people will think, 'So what? What have you gained?' . . . these are the same people who said Egyptians were cowards and no one would show up at the Silent Stand." He goes on to state what they have gained, such as "a strong message that we are a united group of Egyptians who care for one another . . . who are not passive." The post ends with the words "thank-you, Facebook youth." Ghonim reports that after the Silent Stand "feelings of solidarity overwhelmed the participants and turned the stand into a new social environment." Three more Silent Stands were held before the group experienced an "invisible" period that is common in social movements (Ghonim, 2012: 80).

As the reader can see, Kullena Khaled Said was very successful in developing a sense of "we-ness," an identity. The reader may also have noticed the presence of some of the elements that Ashmore et al. include as indicators of collective identity. Perhaps the most obvious sign is behavioural involvement, which members showed by participating in actions organized by the group in the hundreds and thousands. When it comes to membership, 75 percent of respondents to a survey Ghonim posted on the page said that "they felt they owned the page" and that "the causes the page promoted were their own causes." Many members also had a very positive evaluation of the page. For example, a number said that Kullena Khaled Said had changed their life. Clearly, there were strong signs of collective identity present in the group (Ghonim, 2012: 108, 80).

When looking at Justice for Damini, at first no specific identity emerges from the page's posts and comments, and the strong statements that we see in Kullena Khaled Said are not present. Before interviewing group members, I concluded that the group had failed to develop any form of collective identity. Until over a month had passed, there was no indication that the group or administrator agreed upon or even suggested a model of behaviour or objectives that would have differentiated them from the thousands of others of Indians who had taken to the streets, nor did the posts and comments on the page reveal any pattern of identity. On the surface, the group looks like it failed in this respect. However, in interviews, I discovered an admittedly low but detectable level of collective identity extant. While these interviewees' answers cannot be understood to be representative of the whole group, it is interesting that such feelings are present, especially considering that none of them had actually participated in the events organized by the group.

The most basic requisite of collective identity was assumed by three of the five interviewees, as they stated that they considered themselves members of the group. Two of the members also had a generally positive evaluation of the group, a second requirement of collective identity. The third member was more mixed in his criticism but all three felt that the page raised awareness about the incident and provided important updates. One person argued that it did much more. Furthermore, a clear distinction was made between the values the group upheld and the values held by those who were not welcome in the group. This became apparent in an interview with Rohan, who said he was upset with the administrator and the "boys and girls," as he referred to them, of Justice for

Damini because they were "trying to destroy Indian culture" and were demonizing men. He did not agree with a lot of what was said on the page. He argued that women should not be "going against our culture" by going to places that are "not near" their homes and going out after dark. They should, instead, be "behaving normally."

Rohan's remarks were in stark contrast to Priyanka's, who said that she respected the administrator's views and had considerable angst over the double standards, inequality, and oppression faced by Indian women. She also expressed great annoyance with people who "make foolish questions about Damini that why she was out of home after evening? What was she doing with her friend who was a boy?" (Response to questionnaire, 12 August 2013). Given their different views, it is not surprising that Rohan did not feel as strongly and confidently a part of Justice for Damini as Priyanka did. He shifted between using "us" and "them" to refer to the group, using the first person when he was voicing his support for stopping violence against women and the third person when he was objecting to the content of the page. Clearly, despite failing to identify a clear and appropriate "enemy," the page did draw a line between those who belonged (us) and those who did not (them).

When asked how they would feel if the group disappeared overnight, several interviewees said they would feel a sense of loss or sadness, an indication of affective attachment to the group and of collective identity. Priyanka was particularly sad: "I must felt very bad/shocked because it's my companion in the fight for Damini. Even now I am feeling bad when the group is not that active as it was in beginning" (Response to questionnaire, 12 August 2013).

Priyanka even made a few friends through the group, demonstrating social embeddedness, and asserted that, though she was not able to personally attend any of the events hosted or organized by the group, she "made best efforts to encourage them by the help of Facebook" and felt that this meant she "participated from home," demonstrating a strong desire on her part to assert her behavioural involvement. Given the responses above, my hypothesis is that, if the administrator became active again and if he or she had the time, energy, and expertise required, it would be possible to remobilize the members of this page around a different target or goal, for the seeds of collective identity could very well be extant (Response to questionnaire, 12 August 2013).

The third component of collective action frames is agency: "Agency refers to the consciousness that it is possible to alter conditions or policies through collective action. Collective action frames imply some sense of collective efficacy and deny the immutability of some undesirable situation. They empower people by defining them as potential agents of their own history. They suggest not merely that something can be done but that 'we' can do something" (Gamson, 1992: 7).

The first Silent Stand was a powerful moment for Kullena Khaled Said, since those who had "met" and organized themselves on the Internet saw their work spilling over into the offline world in the form of thousands of young Egyptians standing silently in solidarity against an oppressive regime. This innovative, nonviolent, and nonconfrontational idea came from one of the group members, and not from Ghonim himself. Ghonim posted the idea sent to Kullena Khaled Said's e-mail account onto the page's wall along with the date and time of the event, and asked "for all suggestions that would help bring the idea to fruition." He recounted, "Scores of e-mails flowed in to develop the idea. The most important comment was that the effort should not turn into a typical political demonstration. . . . Following a suggestion from one of the members, participants were asked to bring along a copy of the Qur'an or Bible to read in peace."

Within an hour of the first e-mail, Ghonim created a Facebook event called "A Silent Stand of Prayer for the Martyr Khaled Said Along the Alexandria Corniche." It was Wednesday when he posted the suggestion, and the Silent Stand was to take place on Friday at 5 PM. Over the next two days the group's members collaborated to write and distribute a press release, design logos and banners, invite national and international media to cover the event, make contact with the mother of Khaled Said to ask her to participate, and even to produce a video promoting the event. Members invited so many people that the group quickly grew to over 100,000. As mentioned above, the event became so big that "state-owned newspapers began to attack Facebook by claiming it was owned by the CIA and that a lot of spies and enemies anonymously used it to brainwash Egyptian youth." All of this was accomplished by a group that had been formed just a week earlier, in a space in which the principal coordinator was anonymous, and, very likely, through the collaboration of a lot of people that had not met one another, or coordinated their actions, in person (Ghonim, 2012: 70, 74).

Ghonim writes that, while he felt the actual numbers were lower, "a Reuter's news report said that eight thousand people took part in the Silent Stand." Pictures of the stand were posted online and newspapers around the world covered the story. Members stated that the group was life-changing in its effect on them, and that they had never participated in anything like it before. In response to a poll held by Ghonim, 64 percent of participants stated that the Silent Stand had been very effective or satisfactorily effective and 72 percent said they would attend the next one. A collective action frame of agency had been built up and strengthened. Nothing captures this feeling more than one of Ghonim's posts following the Silent Stand:

> Last Friday this page was launched . . . on Tuesday Mohamed sent his suggestion and it was announced to everyone. . . . On Friday more than 100,000 members had joined the group and thousands went out in Cairo and Alexandria implementing an idea that was never done before in Egypt. . . . So can we do just about anything or what?!

While the group was never undivided or unanimous in its sense of agency, and though it went through a period in which it lacked action and focus, the same strong sense of agency is apparent in other actions that the group organized, such as the Revolution of Silence and, of course, the 25 January revolution (Ghonim, 2012: 79, 81, 84, 103).

This kind of discourse and focus is starkly different from what we find in Justice for Damini, where a heavy sense of frustration and lack of agency hangs in the air. This is because, first, as you saw above in the section on injustice frames, the administrator and group members did not develop an appropriate motivated actor to fight against. They failed to place what could be seen as a random act of sexual violence by a group of unaffiliated youth into the broader structure in which they were acting (Gamson, 1992: 33). Without the right "enemy" and goal, it is hard to feel that one can change anything or that what one is seeking to change will truly make a difference. As such, just a couple of weeks to a month after the rape, "likers" of the page constantly posted messages of frustration and anger that the rapists had not been brought to justice yet. While possible, this was largely an unrealistic expectation given the time and effort it takes to prepare such cases, particularly a case being scrutinized, analyzed, and torn apart by journalists, scholars, and citizens from all over the world. It would have been ideal to have an administrator like Ghonim present at this moment, to help turn the conversation toward the broader structures of injustice that allowed a crime like the one committed against Damini to take place and identify the ways in which the group could bring about structural and long-lasting change.

There were also unrealistic and vigilantist expectations around what punishment the rapists would and should get, one of the most popular being castration. Unfortunately, these were encouraged by the administrator. For example, he/she posted a picture of a man accused of rape being dragged through the streets of Lebanon by a hook placed under his chin with the caption "This is what the Lebanon officials publicly do with a RAPIST! What is India up to? SHARE this till it reaches Indian Government!!" Obviously, for a democratic government dealing with a highly publicized case, this kind of punishment, being extra-judicial and illegal, would be out of the question. Neither is it the norm in Lebanon. A moderate voice that allowed for both anger and rationality would have been more useful, as it would have celebrated the fact that street protests had ensured that all the rapists were immediately apprehended and charged and that rape laws were being reviewed, moved followers away from the idea that getting the rapists castrated and hanged immediately was in their hands, and pushed them toward a more appropriate outlet for their anger that involved them seeing their actions have an effect on decreasing violence against women. Unfortunately, this did not happen and the page moved from having comments like "ths time . . . there will be a change! a major change!", "I also want to join dis . . . nd do smthng for this girl . . .", and "the power of people of protest . . . should cuntinue . . . then only something will come" to apologies for having "failed" Damini and complaints and sighs of resignation of how nothing was going to change (Justice for Damini, posted on 20 December 2012, spelling errors in original).

Aside from the frustration of failing to achieve unrealistic and vigilantist goals or to celebrate that which was accomplished, the page also failed to use events to help members see the results of their online micro-activism. Earlier on in the movement, Justice for Damini promoted and created events for two protests that were initiated by other groups and individuals. People were to gather at India Gate in the days before Christmas to demand justice. But members of Justice for Damini were not asked to wear or carry anything that might identify them as belonging to the page. Since there were thousands of people at the protest it is unlikely that Justice for Damini members had an opportunity to meet and talk to fellow page members and, in doing so, see that it was possible to move off of the Internet and onto the streets to demand and get results.

When the page finally did organize a protest and ask people to wear black to identify themselves, over a month had passed since the rape, members were already feeling frustrated and unmotivated, and the page had lost much of its steam. According to Dinesh, another interviewee, only around ten people showed up for this event, out of over 250 who RSVP'ed and around 70,000 page "likers" (20 July 2013). It is possible that something came out of this; however, no update on the event was posted on Facebook and Dinesh did not mention any outcomes from the gathering.

In general, however, without any evidence of a collaborative effort to engage in collective action, or a target adversary, the group appears to have been left with neither a goal nor a means to get to it. These elements would have been a major obstacle for constructing agency.

IN ADDITION

Just before wrapping up this essay, I would like to take note of two elements that do not fit comfortably within collective action frames but which are relevant when considering micro-activism's impact. The first is the fact that, regardless of their success at mobilization and action, Justice for Damini and Kullena Khaled Said fulfilled the function of providing important updates on the case to followers of the page. Second, even though Justice for Damini failed to develop and focus in on a motivated actor that the group could mobilize against, by simply declaring from time to time that there was no excuse for Damini's rape the page was taking a stance against victim blaming and victim shaming in front of an audience of thousands and thousands of followers.

CONCLUSION

Three of the elements that set Kullena Khaled Said apart from Justice for Damini and contributed to its success in engaging in collective action were the group's ability to build the three collective action frames of injustice, agency, and identity. When it came to the frame of injustice, Kullena Khaled Said was able to direct a strong sense of moral indignation among Egyptian youth against an "enemy" that was specific enough to feel as if it could be defeated or at least attacked, and abstract enough to feel as if long-term structural changes could be made. The group also used creative collective action and certain symbolic elements to develop a sense of collective identity and built up a strong sense of agency by nurturing the feeling that their efforts were not in vain, through successfully bringing Egyptian youth together in protest. All of this was made possible with the help of an involved and purposeful leader and group administrator. Unfortunately, Justice for Damini appears to have failed in all three of these arenas, though preliminary interviews with members of the group suggest that the seeds of collective identity might have grown within the group, despite its inability to come up with an appropriate target and organize around that target.

There are many more elements that must be considered when attempting to understand why one group succeeded where another one failed. The construction of collective action frames is just one of them. However, my hope is that this essay will contribute to the ongoing process of understanding and demystifying digital activism and that it will provide digital and other activists an example of how one can make informed use of social media and online tools to promote social change.

REFERENCES

Bhalla, Abhishek, and G. Vishnu. 2012. "The Rapes Will Go On." *Tehelka*, 20 December. Accessed December 28, 2013. http://www.tehelka.com/the-rapes-will-go-on/.

Committee to Protect Journalists. 2009. "10 Worst Countries to be a Blogger." Special Reports. Accessed March 18, 2013. http://cpj.org/reports/2009/04/10-worst-countries-to-be-a-blogger.php.

The Candle Light March. "Description." (online forum message). Accessed March 20, 2013. https://www.facebook.com/events/477621478945841/.

Gamson, William A. 1992. *Talking Politics*. Cambridge: Cambridge University Press.

Ghonim, Wael. 2012. *Revolution 2.0*. Boston: Houghton Mifflin Harcourt.

Justice for Damini. 2012. "Mr. Rapist." (online forum message). 19 Dec. Accessed March 12, 2013.

———. 2012. "About." Accessed March 12, 2013.

———. 2012. "Behind every rapist." (online forum message). 20 Dec. Accessed March 13, 2013.

Porta, Donatella, and Mario Diani. 1998. *Social Movements: An Introduction*. Malden, MA: Blackwell.

Verma, Ravi, and Ajay Singh. 2011. "Evolving Men: Initial Results from the International Men and Gender Equality Survey." International Center for Research on Women and Instituto Promundo. Accessed December 29, 2011. https://www.euskadi.net/contenidos/informacion/material/es_gizonduz/adjuntos/Evolving-Men_ICRW.pdf.

Afterword

Raphael Foshay

In his introduction to a collection of essays published in 1994 entitled *The Making of Political Identities*, the political theorist Ernesto Laclau encapsulated what he sees as the political situation toward the close of the twentieth century, after the end of the Cold War, the breakdown of the Soviet Union, and the dismantling of the Berlin Wall. Laclau argues that the aftermath of the clash of political ideologies that dominated the post–World War II political landscape left a certain void in the demarcation of political identities in an emerging era of neoliberal globalizing economism. Laclau writes on the cusp of what is also the emerging era of digital media transformation and recontexualization of political, social, and personal everyday experience and practice. Twenty years later, we are deep into the decontextualization of a post–Cold War global landscape, the map of which is being redrawn around primarily economic, national, and transnational hegemonies. Laclau reflects on the issues surrounding questions of political identity in terms that accord with the configuration we noted in the Introduction to this volume in relation to Habermas's analysis of the tension between a late modern and a postmodern interpretation of modernity at the turn of the millennium. Regarding the changes to the ways in which political identities are formed in what Habermas prefers to call late rather than postmodernity, Laclau notes:

> If agents were to have an always already defined location in the social structure, the problem of their identity, considered in a radical way, would not arise—or, at most, would be seen as a matter of people discovering or recognizing their own identity, not of constructing it. Problems of social dislocation would thus be seen in terms of the

contradictory locations of the social agents, not in terms of a radical lack threatening the very identity of those agents. (2)

The "radical lack" that Laclau rightly notes as constitutive of the lifeworld at the turn of the millennium has proved fertile soil for the proliferation of digital media expressions of social identity. The fluidity and constructivism in the experience of identity formation that arise from what Laclau sees as a de-ideologized global landscape (at least in terms of the way ideologies had come be characterized in the twentieth century) has encouraged an openness and adaptability to technologically transformed communicative practices. The computational turn in communication that constitutes the digital transformation of communications facilitates the rapid formation of a plurality of virtual identities that, coupled with the potential choice of anonymity or identity-masking, need not even be coordinated or consistent with one another. From Plato and Aristotle on, the philosophical tradition has worried over the epistemological and ethical status of mimetic, intentionally virtual representations. Plato has the character of Socrates in the *Republic* cite "an ancient quarrel between poetry and philosophy," exiling the mimetic poets from the ideal republic unless they can mount a philosophical justification for the value of their rôle. Aristotle, on the other hand, argues that a human being is innately mimetic, "the most imitative creature in the world, and learns at first by imitation" (1448b, 7–8). In particular, he observes:

> And it is also natural for all to delight in works of imitation. The truth of this second point is shown by experience: though the objects themselves may be painful to see, we delight to view the most realistic representations of them in art. . . . [T]he reason of the delight in seeing the picture is that one is at the same time learning—gathering the meaning of things. (1448b, 8–11, 15–17)

The delight that we naturally experience in representations, while inherently pleasurable and potentially educative, entails puzzling and even disturbing implications in its apparent freedom from the direct consequences of physical action in the world. As conduits of representation and ever more intensified virtualization, communication media display the ambivalent tensions that we experience between the elements of pleasure and knowledge attached to all representations. Before the advent of the personal computer, the heavy preoccupation with violence in the one-way media of film and television had been accompanied by a relative proscription of nudity and sexuality. The latter, however, have found a fertile environment in the more individually controlled, interactive structure of the Internet. The ubiquity and omni-availability of virtual media connection means that a significant proportion of the time of a very high proportion of the population of developed (and, with the advent of mobile devices, the developing) nations is spent in virtualized, rather than embodied, engagements, so much so that the once apparent distinction between real and virtual, the presented and the represented, no longer pertains, and a new regime of representation and virtual action, of uncertain proportions and implications, emerges.

With the increasing virtualization, through personal and mobile devices, of both solitary time and communication with others, a shift has taken place in the balance that still pertained in the era of film and television between real and virtual experience. The passivity of media consumption that predated computerization and interconnectivity maintained a certain proportionality with reading and the clarity of overt contrast between reading and action in the world. With computer virtualization and Internet interactivity, that clarity of contrast no longer pertains. We are swiftly becoming naturalized to virtual community and communications, to the degree that the former (putative) relation between nature and culture rapidly approaches (or may be well past) a tipping point in which human beings are no longer naturalized in a biosphere that has itself become deeply unbalanced as a result of the impact of scientific and technological intervention (see, e.g., Hayles, 1999; Wolfe, 2010). How human beings understand their social and species identity and take up their agency in such a vertiginous context opens new horizons of ethical and political reflection and debate. The authors of this collection on digital culture are convinced of the necessity and value of this debate on identity and agency in and of the digital nexus.

REFERENCES

Aristotle. "Poetics." 1984. *The Complete Works of Aristotle: The Revised Oxford Translation*. Ed. Jonathan Barnes. Princeton: Princeton University Press.
Hayles, N. Katherine. 1999. *How We Became Posthuman: Virtual Bodies in Cybernetics, Literature, and Informatics*. Chicago. University of Chicago Press.
Laclau, Ernesto. 1994. "Introduction." In *The Making of Political Identities*, ed. Ernesto Laclau, 1–8. London and New York: Verso.
Plato. "Republic." 1997. *Complete Works*. Ed. John M. Cooper. Indianapolis: Hackett.
Wolfe, Cary. 2010. *What Is Posthumanism?* Minneapolis: University of Minnesota Press.

Do Machines Have Rights?

Ethics in the Age of Artificial Intelligence

David J. Gunkel, Interviewed by Paul Kellogg

Kellogg: Maybe you could start by telling us a few words about yourself, where you teach and your background.

Gunkel: My background is sort of a split/dual personality in media studies and philosophy. I really couldn't decide when I was an undergraduate so I just did both and I have advanced degrees in both media production, media critical studies and then in continental philosophy. I research and work on issues having to do with philosophy of technology and related concerns having to do with ethics and digital media and new media.

Kellogg: I had the pleasure of hearing your presentation when you were a keynote speaker at the Digital Symposium in April 2013 in Edmonton. It was a very engaging presentation that raised an issue I hadn't thought about before: the question of applying ethics to the world of machines. I've had a chance to read your book, *The Machine Question*, and it was the intriguing issues that you raised in the book and at that symposium that prompted the request for this interview.

First, would it be accurate to say that a key area of your research has to do with addressing the question: "Do machines have rights?" Second, if that's true, don't you immediately encounter skepticism or resistance from people who see rights issues as completely tied to rights for humans, and hence, there is an immediate dismissal of the notion that machines could even be considered within the realm of ethics?

Gunkel: Let me respond with a preface and then get to your questions immediately thereafter. A lot of what we think about when we think technology is from an instrumental viewpoint. That is, technology is the tool that we use and in the field of communication that's always seen as a kind of medium of human action or interaction. We're communicating right now through the computer. The computer mediates our interaction with the use of Skype in this circumstance. So for a lot of our history, dealing with technology has always been dealing with something that is seen to be neutral. Technology isn't a moral component. It is how it's used that really matters and it is the human being who decides to use it for good or ill depending on how the technology is applied or not applied in various circumstances.

What is happening right now in this new century, the twenty-first century, is that machines more and more are moving away from being intermediaries between human beings and taking up a position as an interactive subject. So the computer and other kinds of machines like the computer—robots, machines with Artificial Intelligence (AI), and algorithms—are no longer just instruments through which we act, but are becoming "the other" with whom we interact. If you look at statistics concerning web traffic, for example, right now the majority of what transpires on the web is not human-to-human interaction: it's machine-to-machine and machine-to-human interaction. So we're already being pushed out by a kind of machine invasion where machines are taking over more and more of what normally would be considered the human subject position in communicative exchange and other kinds of social interaction. This has led a lot of philosophers recently to think about the machine as a moral agent. That is, is the machine culpable for things it does or doesn't do? If the machine turns you down for credit, whose fault is that? Is it the credit agency and the person who programs that algorithm or is it the algorithm? There are all kinds of questions about agency that have recently bubbled to the surface in the last decade or so.

But you're right; my main concern is not with agency. I mean, I think agency is a very important question and I think machine moral agency is a crucial component of dealing with the new position occupied by mechanisms in our current social environment. But I want to look at the flip side, what we call moral "patiency," or what might be seen as the rights issue. If indeed we have machines now that we are considering rather seriously as being moral agents and asking whether or not they have responsibilities to us, the flip side of these questions is, what about those machines makes them moral agents? Would we have any responsibilities to those machines? Would those machines have any rights conversely in a relationship with us? So you're exactly right. My recent work and where I'm really situating a lot of my own research currently is on the question of machine rights.

Having said that, your second question is very pertinent because the immediate response is: "What are you talking about? How can machines have rights?" We normally think about rights as belonging to a conscious or at least sentient kind of creature, and machines are for all we know just dumb devices that we design to do certain things. And so the question of rights immediately butts heads with a long tradition in moral philosophy that typically only assigns rights to human beings and only recently has begun to think about the nonhuman animal as having any kind of rights. The way that I counter that, or address that comment, is to really tie it all to what is happening in animal rights philosophy. In animal rights we start to break open the humanist anthropocentric kind of ethics of our tradition and ask: "You know, what if nonhuman animals could also be moral patients?"

If you go back to the founding thinkers of the Enlightenment, in this case Descartes, he thought animals and machines were the same. He thought in this term, the *bête machine*, the animal machine, that machines and animals were ostensibly the same. If we begin to open up consideration to animals, if we follow the Enlightenment tradition, there's the flip side of that which says we should probably start thinking about the rights of machines. So I pose it as a machine question because I don't have right now the definitive answer to that particular query, but I do think it's a query that we have to engage with seriously. We have to ask about the rights of machines right now at this particular moment when machines are more and more becoming socially interactive subjects that we involve ourselves with to a greater extent than we ever have previously.

Kellogg: I'm really glad you raised the issue of animal rights. I can remember twenty, twenty-five years ago when the question of rights for animals was posed, even in casual conversation around the dinner table, and people would respond with incomprehension because there was such a long tradition of animals being seen as instruments, as objects, as things that we use for food, or for our own human needs. One of the issues that changed this view was the question of the visibility of emotions that you can see in animals, especially around the hunting of seals. There is an emotive recognition that you can see because seal pups have eyes and we can look into those eyes and it seems as if there is an emotional connection between the person and the animal. That kind of connection seems more difficult between humans and machines. So at one level there is a parallel, but then the parallel seems to me to maybe break down a bit. How does that fit in with your discussion?

Gunkel: It's a good question. From the outside it seems really difficult to connect those dots. But when you start to look at the way moral philosophy has developed and the way the logic has been argued, it is really irrefutable in terms of following that thinking through in a consistent way: you can't get a result other than the rights of machines. Let me explain why. Moral philosophy has traditionally been a sort of historic development of continually opening itself up to what had been prior exclusions. So, for example, during the early period of Western thought, who counted as a moral subject were only other people like yourself. In Athens, those who counted would have been white males, and the excluded would have been slaves, barbarians, women, and children. It was only the male figure of the family who was considered a member of the moral community and therefore all these other things were considered property. So, for example, when Odysseus returns home after his journeys, the first thing he does is hang all his slave girls, and he can do so because they are property, they are not considered human beings. What we've done over time is that we've enlarged the focus or the scope of who is considered a human being. By the Enlightenment period, who's considered a human being are mainly white European males of any age, but who's excluded are Aboriginal people, Africans, and women. That slowly evolves to include these others, so with the Civil War in the United States the inclusion of African slaves or previous slaves into the community of moral subjects takes place. Slowly with Mary Wollstonecraft and other feminists, women begin to be considered subjects of moral consideration, and then in the twentieth century you have Peter Singer and Tom Regan arguing that animals now should be included in the community of moral subjects.

Now there's an important shift that happens with the animal, and you mentioned it, which I think is really crucial. Initially, as we tried to expand the community of moral subjects, it was always about an ability—it was about whether or not these others had the power of reason or in the Greek tradition, the *zoon logon echon*, the ability to speak or use language. It was argued for a long period of time that Aboriginals didn't have reason and therefore they were not considered full participants in the human community, or women were not rationally thinking subjects like men and so could be excluded from the moral community. With animal rights we move away from an ability to a passivity. Derrida says the big move in animal rights thinking was when Jeremy Bentham asked not, can they think, or can they reason, or can they speak, but can they suffer? Suffering is not an active component; it's a passive one—the ability to passively suffer and to be affected. This, Derrida says, is the real shift in moral thinking in the twentieth century because it moves away from the possession of an active ability to a passive capability of feeling pain—or pleasure, for that matter. So this, as you've pointed out, for some people was a very difficult move because it was a real shift in the way that we focused ethical thinking, from this ability of speech, language, and *logos* to the passivity of suffering.

In the twenty-first century now as we start to look at the question of the machine as a moral patient, we are again confronted with people throwing their arms up in the air and saying: "What are you talking about? Clearly machines don't suffer. They don't have anything that matters to them." It isn't like you can hurt your iPad. It doesn't have any emotion. And that seems like a really good argument, except for the fact that engineers are designing machines with emotion. So we have an entire period now—the last two decades—in which engineers involved in robotics, AI, and other kinds of marginally sentient kinds of mechanisms are designing machines with emotional capacities. To have emotions means they can talk to us and interact with us much more effectively, since we are creatures with emotions.

For example, Rod Brooks has designed robots that are afraid of the light and feel pain from light. It's an affective response designed into the mechanism to make the machine seek out dark corners and avoid light areas. You have other individuals who are working on machines that can simulate human emotion to such an extent that it is almost indistinguishable from real human pain. There is a robotics company in Japan (Morita) that makes a pain-feeling robot that is designed to help train dental students. So when the dental students don't use the drill in the right way, the robot cries out in pain that you're hurting it and most of the students say it is beyond simulation. It's so close to what they recognize as pain that they imbue the object with pain. So what we encounter here are two things that are really important to point out. One is the "other minds" problem. How do I know that an object that gives evidence of pain, whether it be an animal, a human being, or a machine, really is in pain? I can't feel the pain of anything other than myself and so all I can do is read external signs and assume that those proceed from some kind of internal affectation. Whether my dog is suffering or not is not anything I can really know for certain. I can only make some educated guess based on the way it winces from being touched in a certain way or cries out, and so on. And so the problem we are encountering here is if we design machines that give evidence of pain it's a very difficult bar to cross to say well, that's not really pain, because I could say the same of any other creature. I could say the same of the mouse: "Well, that's not really pain." I was just in Maine recently and I was told it's okay to boil the lobster because they don't really feel pain. And my question is, really? Do we know that?

Kellogg: Have we ever been a lobster?

Gunkel: Exactly. How are we able to decide that yeah, indeed, we can boil a lobster alive because they don't really feel anything? And so people working in animal studies are saying, yeah, animals feel pain but it still results in an "other minds" problem. We don't know whether anything that appears to suffer really does suffer. It is a statistical conjecture that we make, but we would have to extend the same sort of decision-making with regard to machines that are programmed to evince various pains or pleasures in their external affectation.

The other thing—and let me mention this because it's really crucial—Dan Dennett once wrote a really nice essay called "Why You Can't Make a Computer That Feels Pain." And what he does is go through about twenty-odd pages where he tries to design, through a thought experiment, a pain-feeling robot and at the end of the essay, he says, "You know what? We really can't design a computer that feels pain." But he draws that conclusion not from the fact that we can never really make a mechanism that feels pain, but from the fact that we don't know what pain is, that this thing that is a deciding factor that we call pain is so subjective a quality that we don't even know what it would be to design a pain-feeling robot. So he says you can't design a computer that feels pain, not because we have an engineering problem but because we have a conceptual problem, we have a philosophical problem. This thing that we hang everything on, pain, is such a nebulous concept that it's difficult to define exactly what that is or what it looks like.

Kellogg: Right, so you very much see your research fitting into the classic narrative about rights and the expansion of who counts as a moral subject—expanding from white males, to people of colour, to women, to animals. You're posing an issue for inanimate objects such as machines. Now then, the discussion you just raised about artificial intelligence raises another question for me. Do we have to separate artificially intelligent machines from other machines, which don't have artificial intelligence? Or are you saying that as we expand artificial intelligence we can see more ethical issues being posed in terms of our responsibilities to these new units?

Gunkel: That's a crucial question because usually the way that we address these problems is to say: "well, yeah, of course, at some point we may have machines that are sentient enough or conscious enough to be recognized as having rights and that's the AI thing." So for example, in *2001: A Space Odyssey*, Hal is clearly a well-designed AI. Whether he's sentient or not, whether he feels pain or not, those are really deep questions in the narrative of the film and it's the thing that viewers of the film have to grapple with. You know, okay, so are we harming Hal when we shut him down? He says his mind is going. I can feel it. Okay, we might grant at that point rights are a crucial issue. But when we're looking at, I don't know, a lawn mower, or our automobile, or our cell phone, clearly there's not enough AI to consider rights being an issue. This is a very good argument because it has traction in the tradition insofar as we normally decide who has and who doesn't have rights based on some internal capability: sentience, consciousness, the ability to feel pain, whatever the case is. So the argument goes when machines cross that sentient barrier, then we can talk rights, but until that time, they're just instruments and we don't need to do anything about it. And that, as I say, is a very solid philosophical argument from a traditionalist perspective.

I would like to suggest that even before we get to the point of having Hal 9000-type AI, the rights of machines are an issue, and that's because machines are socially interactive objects, in our world, that have an effect on us and our ability to act in the world irrespective of their intelligence. And so I advocate an approach informed by the philosophy of Emmanuel Levinas—a Levinasian approach—which says, even before I know the cognitive capabilities of another, I'm confronted with another who confronts me as a moral problem. How should I respond? Levinas says before we know anything about the cognitive capabilities of the other, we have to make an ethical choice. We have to choose whether to respond to these challenges as an ethical subject or as an object. This I think pushes the question downstream. In other words, we don't have to wait for Hal 9000 before we start to answer these questions. We have to start answering them now when the machines are smart at best, maybe even dumb, but we need to begin to think about the social standing of the machine because ethics really is about us in relationship to others in a wider social capacity and not about me internally deciding how to deal with the other entities I encounter. So Mark Coeckelbergh makes the argument that the relationship is what decides ethics, not the capabilities of the object in question. I think he's right. I think a lot of this has to do with how we relate to the things we find around us; animals, the environment, other people and machines.

Kellogg: Interesting. So let me take this then to a machine in the contemporary world around which there are huge ethical issues. The machine I'm thinking of is the drone.

Now, you can raise the question of ethics and retain the drone as an instrument. Take the use of the drone in Pakistan or wherever. I can make an argument that it's unethical, that it violates human rights, or it violates international law, and so on. But the ethical responsibilities lie with the people using the drone or the people making the De / cision to use the drones. That's one way of having ethics govern or assess our actions in the world. What you're suggesting, as I understand it, is, it's the relationship between us and the other that structures the ethical question, and we have to make a decision about ethics before we know the ethical capabilities of the other. From that standpoint you would deal with the issue by saying we have a responsibility to the drone to make sure that we are not forcing it to do actions that are unethical and in violation of international law and human rights. Am I getting that wrong or are those the two different ways in which we can approach the question of ethics and drones and how would you see it?

Gunkel: Drones are interesting precisely for the reason you mention. The current configuration of the drone is that it really is a kind of tele-presence instrument, right? We have pilots who are in the western United States flying these devices in Pakistan and Somalia and elsewhere, and they are engaged in "action at a distance" in which human beings are supposedly in charge of deciding when to pull the trigger and when not to pull the trigger. But these drones are becoming more and more autonomous. We discovered that they can fly for over twenty-four hours, whereas you can't have one human pilot flying for that period of time due to the fatigue. Increasing amounts of autonomy are being built into these drones. The question is at some point are we going to have drones that are going to make decisions about target-acquisition and whether or not to launch a missile without human oversight, or with very little human oversight? If you talk to people who are following drone development, they say this is obviously the next step in creating an autonomous battle drone that will require very little human supervision, much less than we have currently. But that's a question of agency, right? I mean who then is the agent in that circumstance? From the question of patiency having to do with rights, it seems like a really odd question to ask, "Does a drone have rights?" And at this point, we would say, "Nah, the drone doesn't have any rights, it's an instrument." Maybe if it gets self-aware we'll have to talk rights, and so we can kick the can down the road and not worry about that for another fifty years or so. My response to that is no, we've already decided that drones have rights. We just don't do it in terms of an international conference or consortium of philosophers. We do it through engineering practice and we do it through battlefield practice. Actions speak louder than words in these sorts of situations and we are practically deciding rights with regards to drones, whether we know it or not.

Let me just explain how this happens. Drones as we know are not the most accurate of weapons. They can insulate American soldiers from battlefield casualties, but inevitably there are incredibly high amounts of human collateral damage, civilians who die when the drone hits the wrong target or targets the wrong automobile, and this is an outrage. But here's the really crazy thing. If indeed the human rights mattered more than the machine rights, we'd stop using these things. But the fact that we still use them means we've already tipped the scale in the direction of the drone. We've already decided there is something more valuable in the drone object than there is in the other human beings at the end of that drone's missile strike. And so even though we haven't convened a confluence of moral philosophers to decide this question, the practices of the engineering community and the military have made it so that practically we have extended a certain value of a continued right to existence to the drone which is akin to a kind of right, a right that trumps the right to life of the people who are its collateral damage.

Kellogg: So you're saying that the issue of rights is already present, it is simply unacknowledged?

Gunkel: Yes, and that I think is the biggest problem. Rights are already being decided. It's being decided in laboratories. It's being decided in assembly plants.

It's being decided on the battlefield. It's being decided in action. And our thinking about these decisions lags behind the practical necessity of having to implement these decisions to get things done.

Kellogg: Were we to say that we have a responsibility toward the drone in the same way that we have a responsibility toward another human being, or a child, or in modern discourse to a nonhuman animal, then it would be a violation of that responsibility to design algorithms that gave the drone unlimited right to kill civilians. That then would structure our decisions. In other words, if there are rights and ethics associated with the drone as an "other" that we are in a relationship with, this then has implications for the way in which we structure the algorithms that govern that drone's behaviour—or is this just my traditionalist way of trying to square the circle?

Gunkel: No, I think you're on to it. I think part of the problem is we are already making decisions concerning rights of machines without recognizing that we have made these decisions, without recognizing the consequences of these daily, seemingly mundane decisions that we make. The word "decision" is really important because it means to cut, right? Decision. And a decision is always an instance of "cut" that says: this is on this side, that is on that side: these are things that count; these are things that don't count. We are continually having to do these things whether we're an engineer, whether we're a battlefield commander or whatever, not really knowing that we are designing the moral future. But we are. And I think the real task of academics and philosophers is to bring to the surface the discussion that needs to happen regarding these things so that we're not doing them blindly, so that we're not allowing these decisions to create a future that we don't know how we got to, or that we don't know what happened. I often say to my students, there's a whole lot of good critical work to be done here because we have to start to get out in front of this question. We can't lag any more, we have to be there alongside the engineers and the military commanders and everybody else involved in robotics and AI and algorithms, and start to ask what world is this creating for us? What social obligation is this engineering for our future? What ethical, moral dilemmas are occurring because of certain decisions that have been made whether we know it or not?

Kellogg: And the instrumentalization that is so often associated with science and engineering does create a situation where you can have a suspension of ethics based upon a dismissal of the machine as a nonsentient being. We now have a long history where the creations of science and engineering proceed to perform absolutely appalling things in the world.

Gunkel: Correct.

Kellogg: What your argument is doing is bringing the ethics question back in an extremely forceful way. It's not just as a question of what will this action of mine as a human being with an instrument do down the road. It's a question about the machine with which you are interacting and what ethical responsibilities we have to it. That structures how we proceed now, not in ten years when the machine is built and it's being used. It structures it all the way down the line.

Gunkel: Correct, which means then that it's not a matter of postponing the ethical question until the time that it is used. It means the ethical question begins at the very moment when we begin designing the system.

Kellogg: And it's embedded in the entire process. It's a relationship.

I teach social movements and whenever I approach the question of rights, it's, for me, invariably deeply linked with large-scale social movements of human beings engaging in attempts to break out of old paradigms and break out of old oppressions. So it's not a coincidence that Thomas Paine is writing in the context of the American Revolution. Or it's not insignificant that the first European legislature to indicate that Africans are humans is in France when delegations from Haiti arrive in the context of the great upheaval around Toussaint L'Ouverture. The Universal Declaration of Human Rights occurs in the context of the massive decolonization movement at the end of World War II, and between World War I and World War II. Is there a parallel between this narrative of social movements with the discussion that you're engaging in, in terms of machines having rights or the ethical questions associated with robots, artificial intelligence, and machines?

Gunkel: I think there is. I think the social movement, if we were to identify it, would be post-humanism, the effort since the nineteenth century beginning with Nietzsche, and continuing with Heidegger, to think through the prejudice of humanism. In other words, as we've said before, "the human" has been a moving target. It has always been a way of excluding others, whether they were

African peoples, whether they were Aboriginal peoples, whether they're women, whether they are animals, there is a way in which the concept of the human has been a way for one group in power to disempower others. Think, for example, of the way the Nazis were able to exterminate six million Jews by defining them as nonhuman. There's a way in which the concept of the human has been an incredibly devastating tool for excluding others. Heidegger knew this when he wrote the Letter on Humanism and said, I do not align my philosophy with humanism because humanism has a whole lot of problems.

And so, there's this development in the late twentieth century and early twenty-first century, now called post-humanism, embodied by people such as Donna Haraway and then Katherine Hayles and Cary Wolfe, who are all trying to think outside the restrictions of anthropocentric privilege and human exceptionalism. Animal rights philosophy is part of this. Environmental philosophy is part of this, and I think the machine question is part and parcel involved in the same. It's about trying to dissolve the kind of human-centric view of the universe that is being broken open by what we can say is a Copernican Revolution, right? We are thinking about entities and their position in the world.

Kellogg: I think there are people in the ecology movement who would echo many of the things you just said in terms of thinking beyond a human-centric world. In terms of the rights of machines, there is a parallel discourse emerging at the moment in terms of the rights of the planet. At the big meeting that happened at Cochabamba, Bolivia, in 2010, one part of the declaration was the declaration of the rights of Mother Earth. In other words, we can't just think of the earth as an instrument or as an object that facilitates human development; it has rights as well. Would you agree that's a parallel with the type of work you're engaged in?

Gunkel: Yeah. I can say in two ways it really is, because my initial philosophical formation came with my encounter with a guy named Jim Cheney who is one of the leading thinkers in environmental ethics. Through his work and through the work of Thomas Birch and others, in that sort of postmodern environmental ethics tradition, I was exposed to a great deal of this kind of thinking early on in my career. In fact I use a great deal of these environmental philosophical positions in my own work because in them I think we find a thinking of otherness that is no longer tied to either humancentrism or biocentrism. I mean there's a way in which rights expands beyond a very limited, sort of restricted, way of looking at the other as just another organism. Now it's soils, it's waters, and it's the earth itself that become objects needing some kind of response and care.

Kellogg: Fascinating. I know for myself the encounter with ecology, talking about the rights of Mother Earth, the discussion that you raised in terms of the rights of machines, forces me to try to "think otherwise," because it runs counter to a whole lot of training that we encounter in the modern education system. In part as I understand this challenge to think otherwise, it's about social construction of the "We." Who or what is included in the "We" and who are or what is excluded? How widely do you think we should cast the circle of inclusion when it comes to the machine question? Is there a methodology that can help us decide how to draw this circle of inclusion as we attempt to think otherwise?

Gunkel: Let me just say with regard to this word "otherwise," that it really is meant to evoke two things simultaneously. "Thinking otherwise" would mean thinking differently, thinking outside the box, outside the sort of established ways of thinking that we've grown up with, the legacy systems, if you want to call it that. But "thinking otherwise" also gestures in the direction of Levinas and the issue of an exposure to the other which makes thinking possible and to which thinking should respond. So I want "other" and "otherness" to be heard in that dual sense—that it is not only different, but it also is in response to the exposure to the other.

In terms of the circle of inclusion and how widely it should be drawn, I would say that my effort is not necessarily to play by those rules. In other words, ethics is always characterized as drawing a circle that includes some and excludes others, and so Derrida says in *Paper Machine* that the big issue is the difference between the who and the what. Who is on the inside and what is on the outside? And as the circle gets drawn larger, more and more things become a who, and fewer things are a what. Luciano Floridi recently positioned himself with regard to something called information ethics, which he argues is the most universal and least exclusionary ethical theory ever developed in which everything that is in existence is inside the circle and the only thing outside is nothing.

But notice that all of these gestures inevitably have to decide between inclusion and exclusion, insiders and outsiders. And so thinking otherwise in my mind is grappling with that dialectic and saying, you know what, there's got to be a way to think outside that box. In other words, my effort has been to say, not greater inclusion, but questioning the very gestures that oppose inclusion and exclusion in the first place. This is a very Levinasian point because Levinas doesn't try to create a more inclusive ethics but rather tries to create or design a different way of thinking ethics that doesn't rely on inclusion and exclusion, that thinks beyond that sort of binary opposition.

If there is a method for doing this I would say it is Derrida's deconstruction, because deconstruction is the way in which we can oppose or intervene in binary oppositions that already program us to behave in certain ways. If our ethical programming is designed in such a way that we think about things as inclusion and exclusion, we need a deconstruction of the inclusion/exclusion conceptual opposition to develop alternatives that no longer fit within that categorization, that no longer fall into one versus the other.

I think Levinasian ethics provides us with a very good model, because, in Levinas's sense, anything can be taken on face. Anything can come to be the face of the other, but there is no prior decision about what is and what is not included. In fact, it's a moving target. And Levinas says, yeah that's fine; it doesn't have to be fully decided. At different times, something will take on face and something may not, but what is important isn't whether something has or has not face, what is important is how we respond to the evidence in front of us when that occurs. So it's a very different kind of ethics.

I would say if I'm open to any charge, it's the charge of relativism. But I think relativism is a really good thing. I think relativism allows us to have a very mobile way of doing ethics, something that isn't locked down the way that Kant locks down his ethics, where everything is prescribed ahead of time and can't respond to new and unique and novel kinds of eruptions of possibility. So I think we need to look at relativism as a very positive thing that says, you know what, we are responsible not only for behaving ethically, but for designing ethics, for deciding what is ethics and doing it again and again and again in very concrete circumstances that we encounter and not being able to rely on simple pieties, simple formulas or codes of ethics that inevitably fail us in the long run.

Kellogg: Fantastic. I think that's an excellent concluding statement and it's an excellent way to draw this discussion to a close, which poses even more questions. Especially your discussion of relativism has gotten me thinking along a whole new line of inquiry, that I think takes us into new territory.

Gunkel: Let me just say one thing that may help this. You know relativism in the human sciences is considered a bad thing, but in the hard sciences, physics in particular, relativism is actually a really good thing. For Einsteinian physics, relativism says there's no fixed point from which to observe the world and make decisions about everything. Everything is in motion and I think the moral universe is also relative in that sense, that everything is in motion and that everything is decided from positions of power, from positions of privilege, from positions occupied by a certain subject at a certain time imbued with certain subjectivity. And we have to see this as not a negative thing; we have to start to look at it as a positive opportunity.

Kellogg: And that brings to a close the interview with David Gunkel. It's been fantastic and I've really enjoyed myself. Thanks a lot, David.

REFERENCES

Birch, Thomas H. 1993. "Moral Considerability and Universal Consideration." *Environmental Ethics* 15(4): 313–32.

Brooks, Rodney. 2003. *Flesh and Machines: How Robots Will Change Us*. New York: Knopf Doubleday Publishing Group.

Cheney, Jim. 1989. "Postmodern Environmental Ethics: Ethics of Bioregional Narrative." *Environmental Ethics* 11(2): 117–34.

Coeckelbergh, Mark. 2012. *Growing Moral Relations: Critique of Moral Status Ascription*. New York: Palgrave Macmillan.

Cottingham, John. 1992. "Cartesian Dualism: Theology, Metaphysics, and Science." In *The Cambridge Companion to Descartes*, ed. John Cottingham, 236–57. New York: Cambridge University Press.

Dennett, Daniel C. 1978. "Why You Can't Make a Computer that Feels Pain." *Synthese* 38(3): 415–56.

———. 1981. *Brainstorms: Philosophical Essays on Mind and Psychology*. Cambridge, MA: MIT Press.

Derrida, Jacques. 2005. *Paper Machine*. Stanford: Stanford University Press.

———. 2008. *The Animal That Therefore I Am*. Trans. David Willis. New York: Fordham University Press.

———. 2013. "The Animal that Therefore I Am (More to Follow)." In *Signature Derrida*, ed. Jay Williams, 380–435. Chicago: University of Chicago Press.

Floridi, Luciano. 2010. *Information: A Very Short Introduction*. Oxford: Oxford University Press.

Gunkel, David J. 2012. *The Machine Question: Critical Perspectives on AI, Robots, and Ethics*. Cambridge, MA: MIT Press.

Haraway, Donna Jeanne. 2008. *When Species Meet*. Minneapolis: University of Minnesota Press.

Hayles, N. Katherine. 2008. *How We Became Posthuman: Virtual Bodies in Cybernetics, Literature, and Informatics*. Chicago: University of Chicago Press.

Heidegger, Martin. 2008. "Letter on Humanism." In *Basic Writings: From Being and Time (1927) to The Task of Thinking (1964)*, ed. David Farrell Krell, 213–66. New York: Harper Perennial Modern Thought.

James, C. L. R. 2001. *The Black Jacobins: Toussaint L'Ouverture and the San Domingo Revolution*. London: Penguin Books.

Kubrick, Stanley. 1968. *2001: A Space Odyssey*.

Levinas, Emmanuel. 1969. *Totality and Infinity: An Essay on Exteriority*. Trans. Alphonso Lingis. Pittsburgh: Duquesne University Press.

———. 1987. *Time and the Other and Additional Essays*. Trans. Richard A. Cohen. Pittsburgh: Duquesne University Press.

Morsink, Johannes. 2011. *The Universal Declaration of Human Rights: Origins, Drafting, and Intent*. Philadelphia: University of Pennsylvania Press.

Paine, Thomas. 2011. *Rights of Man*. Peterborough: Broadview Press.

Regan, Tom, and Peter Singer. 1989. *Animal Rights and Human Obligations*. 2nd ed. Englewood Cliffs: Prentice Hall.

Wolfe, Cary. 2010. *What Is Posthumanism?* Minneapolis: University of Minnesota Press.

Wollstonecraft, Mary. 1999. *A Vindication of the Rights of Men; A Vindication of the Rights of Woman; An Historical and Moral View of the French Revolution*. New York: Oxford University Press.

World People's Conference on Climate Change and the Rights of Mother Earth. 2010. "Universal Declaration of the Rights of Mother Earth." *Climate and Capitalism* (27 April). http://climateandcapitalism.com/2010/04/27/universal-declaration-of-the-rights-of-mother-earth/.

Contributors

Ian Angus is Professor of Humanities at Simon Fraser University and is the author of nine books, including *Primal Scenes of Communication* (SUNY, 2000), *(Dis)figurations: Discourse/Critique/Ethics* (Verso, 2000), and *The Undiscovered Country: Essays in Canadian Intellectual Culture* (Athabasca University Press, 2013).

Maria Bakardjieva is Professor in the Department of Communication and Culture at the University of Calgary. She is the author of *Internet Society: The Internet in Everyday Life* (Sage, 2005).

Daryl Campbell is Senior Systems Administrator of the Web Unit in the Department of Computing Services at Athabasca University. He has published in the *International Journal of Badiou Studies and White: Zeitschrift fur Gegenwartkunst*.

Sharone Daniel is a student in the MA Program in Integrated Studies at Athabasca University. Her research, funded by a Social Sciences and Humanities Research Council, Canada Research Scholarship, focuses on social media and political action.

Andrew Feenberg is Canada Research Chair in Philosophy of Technology in the School of Communication, Simon Fraser University, where he also directs the Applied Communication and Technology Lab. He is author of six books, including *Transforming Technology: A Critical Theory Revisited* (OUP, 2002) and *Between Reason and Experience: Essays in Technology and Modernity* (MIT, 2010).

Raphael Foshay is Associate Professor in the Centre for Interdisciplinary Studies at Athabasca University. He teaches literary, cultural, and interdisciplinary theory and recently edited a collection of essays on interdisciplinarity, *Valences of Interdisciplinarity: Theory, Practice, Pedagogy* (Athabasca University Press, 2012).

Carolyn Guertin is a Senior Researcher in the Augmented Reality Lab at York University in Toronto and is a faculty member in the MFA and PhD programs at Transart Institute in Berlin, Germany. She recently published *Digital Prohibition: Piracy and Authorship in New Media Art* (Continuum, 2012).

David J. Gunkel is Presidential Teaching Professor of Communication Studies at Northern Illinois University. His most recent book is *The Machine Question: Critical Perspectives on AI, Robots and Ethics* (MIT, 2012).

Bob Hanke teaches media and technocultural studies in the Departments of Communication Studies and Humanities at York University in Toronto. He has published in various journals and co-edited "Out of the Ruins: The University to Come," a special issue of *TOPIA: Canadian Journal of Cultural Studies*.

Paul Kellogg is Associate Professor in Master of Arts – Integrated Studies graduate program at Athabasca University. His publications include *Escape from the Staple Trap* (2015) and articles in various scholarly journals including *New Political Science, Journal of Canadian Studies, International Journal of Žižek Studies*, and *Research in Political Economy*.

Leslie Lindballe is a student in the MA Program in Integrated Studies at Athabasca University, where she conducts research into intersections of digital and analog identity.

Mark A. McCutcheon is Associate Professor of English and Interdisciplinary Studies at Athabasca University. His research interests encompass literary, media, and performance studies, as well as the cultural politics of copyright.

Roman Onufrijchuk, 1950–2015, was Assistant Professor of Industrial Design at the İzmir Institute of Technology. He writes in the areas of media theory and the philosophy of technology.

Josipa G. Petrunić is Executive Director and CEO of the Canadian Urban Transit Research and Innovation Consortium. She publishes principally in the area of the history of mathematics.

Peter J. Smith is Professor of Political Science at Athabasca University. He has published widely in the areas of transnational social movements, globalization, and religion and politics in relation to information technologies.

Lorna Stefanick is Professor of Political Science and Coordinator of the Governance, Law, and Management Program at Athabasca University. She recently published *Controlling Knowledge: Freedom of Information and Protection of Privacy in a Networked World* (Athabasca University Press, 2011).

Karen Wall is Associate Professor of Communication Studies at Athabasca University. Her research includes collective memory, migration, intercultural encounters, social change, and modes of transformation or hybridity. She recently published *Game Plan: A Social History of Sport in Alberta* (University of Alberta Press, 2012).

204